Gilding the Market

Gilding the Market

Luxury and Fashion in Fourteenth-Century Italy

Susan Mosher Stuard

PENN

University of Pennsylvania Press
Philadelphia

The Middle Ages Series
Ruth Mazo Karras, Series Editor
Edward Peters, Founding Editor

A complete list of books in the series is available from the publisher.

10   9   8   7   6   5   4   3   2   1

Published by
University of Pennsylvania Press
Philadelphia, Pennsylvania 19104-4112

Library of Congress Cataloging-in-Publication Data

Stuard, Susan Mosher.
  Gilding the market : luxury and fashion in fourteenth century Italy / Susan Mosher Stuard.
    p. cm. — (The Middle Ages series)
  Includes bibliographical references and index.
  ISBN-10: 0-8122-3900-8 (cloth)
  ISBN-13: 978-0-8122-3900-3
    1. Luxury goods industry—Italy—History—To 1500.   2. Luxuries—Italy—History—To
1500.   3. Clothing and dress—Italy—History—Medieval, 500–1500.   4.
Fashion—Italy—History—To 1500.   5. Consumption (Economics)—Italy—History—To 1500.
6. Italy—Economic conditions.   I. Title.   II. Series.

HD9999.L853I87   2006
381'.45687'094509023—dc22   *2005050370*

Frontispiece: Opulent costume adorning the Three Kings. Altichiero da Zavio and Jacopo Avanzi, *Adoration of the Magi,* c. 1379. Oratoria di San Giorgio, Padua. Art Resource, N.Y.

Contents

Illustrations

Altichiero da Zavio and Jacopo Avanzi, *Adoration of the Magi,*
c. 1379   *frontispiece*

Plates

Figures

Chapter 1
Introduction

If the fourteenth-century fashionable could have seen themselves! If they had, perhaps the first age of fashion would have sputtered out rather than caught fire. As chance had it, mirrors adequate for head-to-toe scrutiny came into use only toward the middle of the next century, so the constructive exercise of self-scrutiny was close to impossible. Consider what those pioneers of fashion might have seen upon inspection of their decked-out selves: robes hiked up to the calf, then the thigh, right up to the brink of indecency; padded shoulders, tight fit, parti-colored tunics and hose; tasseled hoods, floppy hats, slashed and elongated sleeves, linings as rich as robes themselves; and enough gilded silverware in accessories that the swish and rustle of fine fabrics were set off by the clink and clatter of metal ornament. Garish effects, bright colors, gilt, and military affectations ushered in the age of fashion in Italian market towns. And this refers to men's fashionable garb; the curious role of women's fashion comes into the discussion later.

For both men and women the restrained, the refined, the carefully prepared aesthetic staging of self, based on a sober discernment of the niceties of self-fashioning, had to wait for a later day. The first age of fashion was blatantly obvious and adamantly garish, which goes a long way toward explaining fashion's initial impact on manners, urban culture, customer preference, and heightened demand for material goods in the fourteenth century.

Making wise decisions about the sometimes alarmingly expensive goods that composed fashionable outfits—both purchasing and disposing of them—became a pressing concern in the fourteenth century, not just in the prosperous era before the Black Plague, land wars, bank failures, and other economic misfortunes loomed over the Italian peninsula, but even in the second half of the century when fashion found its way into the normal routine of everyday town life. A fine sensitivity to the demands of *le pompe*, that is, the public display of private wealth, spread from community to community. Display of wealth was a project for market towns where fashion flourished and men took up shopping as a diverting pastime. While the high style of court society had long been recognized by Italian merchants as a lucrative market to be cultivated and fed, courts represented relatively contained and inelastic opportunity. Newer fashion-fed urban consumption promoted a more robust, if volatile, demand for goods like fine fabrics and ready-made objects of precious metal.[1] Markets widened over the century even in the face of population retraction. More and more people became part of the fashion parade as popular fashions were interpreted in cheaper editions. Fashions leapt swiftly from place to place, encouraged by fresh ideas that were both playful and alluring. The pace of economic change quickened; where fashion led, townspeople followed.

These pages investigate the increased attention paid to consumption—that is, purchase and display of fashion goods—in northern Italian towns in the fourteenth century. In a short span of years important matters began to turn on the frivolous cut of a sleeve. This was not in any sense the dawn of a new era in the medieval economy. Outside of some mechanical clocks, there were few genuinely novel products: buttons, for example, had become popular in the late thirteenth century and merely became more important over subsequent decades. There was no major reorienting of markets, and imports of fine fabrics from the East were established well before the century began; there was no startling innovation in technology to promote the luxury trades, although it may be ventured that institutional arrangements capable of reducing market imperfections were introduced. For that matter, fashions did not transform class distinctions straightaway, although their potential threat to the social order was anticipated, criticized roundly, and sumptuary laws were enacted to foil that outcome. Luxuries affected markets by promoting and enlarging exchange activity and turning urban marketplaces into proto-emporia for consumer goods, among them, significantly, fine, ready-made goods. Luxury wares like accessories of fabricated and gilded silver were in demand. Shopping became popular, too, and people of means began to care deeply about appearances.[2]

Urban markets for fashion confirm the recombinant and adaptive forces at work in an economy increasingly wracked by war, plague, and other dislocations. Aggressive sellers adapted to *compagnie di ventura* (mercenary companies) in their neighborhoods and sold luxuries to soldiers when they were flush with their outrageously generous payoffs. In a certain sense there was a flight to quality in the northern Italian economy, but that must be qualified as well, for it is apparent that an ambitious town found ways to diversify wares produced for and sold to people of lesser means.[3] The relative wealth of towns was certainly a factor here: Giovanni Villani estimates that James II of Aragon and his brother, the king of Sicily, had combined yearly incomes lower than that of the city of Florence in the 1330s. Only Philip VI of France and the della Scala of Verona, who briefly controlled thirteen city-states in this decade, significantly surpassed Florence in yearly income.[4] And Venetian wealth probably outdid Florentine.[5]

Venice dominated the luxury trades before the fourteenth century and continued to do so when the century ended, while Florence rose to prominence in luxury production, eclipsing neighboring towns and absorbing both their expertise and some of their skilled personnel. Yet even this comes as no surprise: a few cities came out on top in a century that began amid widespread medieval prosperity in Europe and ended with wars and plague, as well as the first intimations of a bullion famine in Europe. Centers of production like Siena and Lucca were left diminished when their skilled emigrants moved elsewhere and inadvertently contributed to the prosperity of more fortunate neighbors. These two cities, early successes in the luxury trades due to industry and technical brilliance, demonstrate the danger posed by wealth acquired through superior industries, coupled with political vulnerability and, in Siena's case, a strategic geographic location on Italy's major north-south route, the Francigena. Sienese sumptuary laws, a reflection of the town's precocious wealth, began as early as 1249, and new spending brakes were applied to local consumption frequently thereafter. The prudent Sienese feared raising the envy of their powerful neighbors, but laws did not succeed in diverting those who preyed on Sienese wealth.

Lucca began writing sumptuary law in 1308 and soon matched Siena in the pace of revisions.[6] Even when some of Lucca's most successful silk workers emigrated and made the fortunes of other city-states with their handiwork, silk fabric of new design poured from local looms and, cruelly, helped inspire future raids on Lucca's renewing wealth. In a sense the two city-states of Lucca and Siena were the casualties of the first age of fashion. Artisans were raided, workshops were pillaged, products were imitated or counterfeited, and governments were bankrupted by efforts at defense or buying off mercenaries— their dilemma lay in their envied wealth and renewing pool of talent.[7] The stories of Siena and Lucca are woven into the stories of their more powerful neighbors, who attacked them but, perhaps just as disastrously, absorbed some of their finest talent as well.

The transformation to consumer culture can be told through the histories of a broad spectrum of northern Italian towns. Verona produced fine cottons that were incorporated into luxury ensembles; Cremona and Pavia produced famed fustians. Padua, a prosperous university town, attracted customers to its marketplace and built up luxury trades. Prato, a satellite to Florence, was home to the loose-knit Datini trading network that at its apogee dealt in luxuries, although it began by trading more pedestrian goods and weaponry when Francesco de Marco Datini first established his trading shops at Avignon. Many cities underwent transformation to shopping cultures that attracted travelers to their streets and markets. Among these Genoa, Milan, and Bologna are of particular significance.

Unfortunately, fourteenth-century disarray in the voluminous runs of Genoese "documents of practice" and some lacunae in civil records limit attempts to obtain proof positive of substantive changes in fourteenth-century consumption and merchandizing. Genoa introduced civic sumptuary law to Italy in 1157, rendering the lack of any updated sumptuary legislation from that decade until 1402 all the more problematical, for when Genoa gives evidence of renewed sumptuary lawmaking in the fifteenth century, civil authorities promulgated eighteen new codes in less than a century, proceeding at such a clip that two laws a year appeared on two separate occasions.[8] Throughout the fourteenth century prosperous Genoese merchants traveled the silk route to locate the finest imported textiles and, as highly respected conveyers of precious goods from across the known world, supplied European markets with fine silks, brocades, and imported gold.[9] Of course this does not prove that luxury manufactures or shops flourished in town, but even here tantalizing shreds of evidence may be found. Genoa's reputation in the gold thread business was established in the thirteenth century when noblewomen contracted with merchants for production of gold thread, which was then assembled in their own households by servants who were paid for their labor by contract.[10] This production augmented the city's reputation as a connoisseur and purveyor of opulent wares.

The Genoese enjoyed a reputation for enjoying luxuries and rich attire.[11] Giovanni Boccaccio could poke fun at Ermino Grimaldi's stinginess when he refused to spend his great fortune on fine clothing or good food and drink, "contrary to the general custom of the Genoese, who are used to dressing elegantly." Boccaccio was assured of sympathetic readers because Grimaldi's fellow citizens were sure to sniff at his miserly behavior. Grimaldi wealth was legendary and far outstripped that of better-dressed neighbors, so he might well be counseled to learn to be broad handed and spread his wealth around.[12] Abroad the Genoese advertised their ability to do business with their rich attire that recommended them without a word being spoken when they set one gorgeous foot before the other in foreign markets; in a real sense, fine clothing could be justified as a reasonable expense of doing business. Gold passed through Genoese hands in abundance, but as was true elsewhere, Genoese gold was intended for coining, for use in exchange. Closer to home, Genoa's supply of Sardinian silver was pretty well played out by the fourteenth century, and this would limit the community's future capacity to mint silver coin; as a matter of course, supplies of silver for fabrication would be restricted as well. This was emphatically the case as the fourteenth century came to a close and silver scarcities became severe. This lesser precious bullion, silver, which could be profitably worked, gilded, and sold as luxury wares, required importing from afar and placed Genoa in competition with other centers of luxury production that had far easier access to it since most new silver hailed from eastern Europe.

Some direct indication of a lively local market for luxury goods derives from Lucchese silk workers, who chose to migrate to Genoa when they fled their own town after 1314. Not only the well-known migration to Venice ensued, but the Lucchese scattered far and wide and other communities profited from Lucca's highly talented and industrious workforce as well. Cooperating groups of spinners, dyers, weavers, and *cocitori* (the delicate hands who unwound silk filament from bolls of silk worms) settled at Genoa, suggesting a Genoese reputation for enthusiastic consumption at home, abetted by exports to the north. It also suggests a strong Genoese inclination to encourage luxury manufactures through government initiative, since efforts to provide a future home for Lucchese workers relied on government initiatives.[13] As a result, rewards fell to the Genoese. By the mid-fifteenth century silk weaving was the largest artisan profession in Genoa—11.6 percent of all workers in local trades—with makers of silk thread, silk dyers, and silk merchants adding further to these numbers.[14] The silk industry, on the rise in the post-plague years, had become the largest employer in town. For the purposes of this study it is a serious lacuna that the initial fourteenth-century plunge into large-scale luxury production in silk is so poorly understood, and that the link between luxury production and merchandizing cannot be traced in as great detail as in Venice or Florence.

In the last analysis, visual evidence presents the most compelling argument for a pronounced emphasis on the consumption of luxuries in fourteenth-century Genoa. In an illustration of avarice from a Genoese treatise on the seven vices, dating from the second half of the fourteenth century, a local goldsmith's shop occupies center stage (see fig. 1). A customer and the goldsmith dicker over price using finger signals while a third figure seated at the end of the goldsmith's counter tallies up the results. Within the shop hangs a pole from which a fine sword with a hilt, ready-made silver belts, and fine purses are suspended. A chasuble and a spouted silver pot stand on the Turkish-carpeted counter along with other ready-made luxury objects like an embossed casket and some tools of the goldsmith's craft. A fourth figure fills the doorway, his arms laden with other fine wares. Ostensibly he is leaving the shop, but he might just as well be returning with precious goods to be refashioned or pawned. A crenellated wall and a loggia occupying the upper third of the illustration suggest this market activity takes place in city space; all the features of the marketing of silver and gilded silver in the new manner appear to be present.[15] The message: luxurious wares encourage avarice.

Genoa's Anonymous Poet (active from 1311 to about mid-century) also warns about the temptations of *luxuria* in poem 136, although soon thereafter, in poem 138, he is caught up in praise for the marvelous jewels, furs, *naxici* (very expensive imported cloth woven with gold thread), and pearls that represented the high end of trade goods supplied by Genoese long-distance merchants.[16] The poet believed *luxuria* was the outward expression of overweening

Figure 1. Price is determined between a goldsmith and a customer using finger signals. The dickering takes place in a goldsmith's shop where tools of the trade are displayed. Fabricated ready-made accessories are displayed to tempt customers. *Treatise on the Seven Vices*, Genoa, 1350–1400. The British Library, London, Add. 27695, fol. 7v. Courtesy of the British Library, London.

pride (*soperbia* in his lexicon, that is, *superbia*), but this had become such a commonplace for a moralist of his day that he passes over the issue without much further comment. Nevertheless, a tension between condemning local spending habits while urging display of precious goods to encourage trade to foreigners is manifest in the poet's comments, in a manner similar to other admonitory literature offered in towns. Cultivating wealthy customers while attempting to curb spending at home became a source of considerable tension in market towns.

Ready-made goods that drew on more than one craft or trade were the focus of a dispute in an unresolved lawsuit in Genoa in 1359: it involved rights of haberdashers, pursers, glovers, and makers of leather laces. Who among them had the right to sell wallets, purses, and change purses, sheathed and unsheathed knives, hats, and gloves? The problem revolved around goods produced out of a variety of luxury materials and thus out of different shops practicing traditional trades. Rights to sell at retail finished goods with provenance in various artisan trades—for example, leather wares lined with silk—lay at the heart of the dispute. This is a strong indication that ready-made luxury goods had surfaced in the market and required new arrangements for distributing profits at odds with the traditional merchandizing out of a single craftsman's *bottega* that had sufficed in the past.[17]

In this less well-understood century of Genoese development, graphically illustrated ready-made articles of precious metal tempting customers in a gold-smith's shop, luxury silk manufacture, and a dispute over jurisdiction in retailing ready-made luxury goods indicate that the Genoese joined wholeheartedly in the new more consumer-oriented culture of Italian urban life. Conditions at Genoa favored transformation to a shopping culture; indeed, its citizens' long-standing reputation as connoisseurs of rich living was itself an advertisement for a new sort of *bottega* that promoted retail sales.[18] Genoa was a significant port of call with an endless stream of potential customers passing through; in particular, pilgrims debarked and reembarked here. As the century progressed Genoa was visited by increasing numbers of mercenaries when soldiers for hire exchanged battlefields in France for those of Italy, or reversed that itinerary. Mercenaries arrived from recent tours of duty with plenty of loose cash in their purses, making embellished weaponry and fine accessories desirable goods to stock in local shops.[19] The punishing sums paid to mercenary companies by towns like Siena were only recoverable in Italy if rich goods were laid out to tempt troops before they left the region.

While a robust shopping culture at Genoa is poorly documented yet very likely, archival evidence is so meager in fourteenth-century Milan that it thwarts research efforts. Once Milan had perfected plate armor around 1350, manufacturing establishments for embellished armor, weaponry, and armor garniture appear to have flourished, but how immediately and with what results it is difficult to know. Milan's experiments in marketing most likely combined the products of numerous crafts to create a single armorial ensemble.[20] Within the copious records studied by Luciana Frangioni in the Datini archives at Prato, carefully detailed lists of products, provenance Milan, might contain helmets, pointed helmets, buckles, jointed armatures, sword buckles, rings, spurs, and other assorted fighting gear ordered in the dozens.[21] Catherine King has argued that one new component of fourteenth-century artistic production was the successful integration of a number of crafts bearing on the creation of a single artifact. Reliquaries might use the skills of jewelers, goldsmiths, embossers, weavers, wood-carvers, embroiderers, and wire makers.[22] In much the same spirit military fashions and weaponry decreed a coordinated assemblage reliant on different trades; this feature of military kit in turn influenced civilian dress and the two together encouraged reliance on integrated output from various craftsmen.[23] A pourpoint (padded jacket) must fit snugly beneath plate armor and ideally be harmonized with a cloak covering that armor. Designs on armor and helmet should complement fabrics, gorgets, belts, spurs, sallets, sheathed knives, and other weapons or dress accessories. In the thirteenth century, according to Bonvesin de la Riva, "noble cloths of wool and silk were woven in Milan," suggesting that Milan provided a complex of textile crafts that supported armorers' specialties. Galvano Fiamma reiterates de la Riva's claim of fine craftsmanship in textile manufacture a century later.[24]

Since a military look frequently set fashion for men in this age, *compagnie di ventura*, diplomatic missions, traders, and other men of consequence and means may have found it convenient to travel through Milan, which was strategically situated on north-south land routes. Their visits probably encouraged craftsmen to experiment in merchandizing as well as in production, although swift evolution in the design of Italian defensive armor may owe much to the successful arms industries at Venice and Florence as well.[25] In her well-documented study *Gli inganni delle apparenze*, Maria Giuseppina Muzzarelli relies on two primary sources for fourteenth-century Milan: a sumptuary law promulgated at the end of the century (1396); and opinions of the chronicler Fiamma, although she acknowledges that surviving evidence is wholly inadequate given Milan's rise to prominence as a center of trade and production.[26] Rosita Levi Pisetzky's excellent *Storia del costume in Italia* relies primarily on visual evidence for clothing in fourteenth-century Milan; consequently, what little is known of the city is pieced together from merchant records housed elsewhere, like those of the company of Francesco de Marco Datini or from records in towns where Milanese products sold well.[27] The chroniclers have dominated opinion on Milan with their moral message heard elsewhere: foreigners are responsible for introducing new fashions to the town and townspeople seem powerless to resist. Fiamma was particularly critical of Spanish influence. He also argued that youth and women indulged themselves in the worst excesses of fashion. Meanwhile, the Milanese sumptuary law of 1396 echoes the laws of Bologna and other northern Italian cities, explaining little about important local innovations and the tradesmen who made them. For information about Milanese tradesmen who spread the fame of Milan, such as Ambrogio, Bartolomeo Ciernella, Corrente Simone, Maffio del Moia, Martinolo, Pulce, Severo, and Verubio—their very names sold spurs, mail, swords, and other armor garniture—brief references in orders within the Datini trading network are the only traces left.[28]

Luca Mola notes that Milan, like Venice, Genoa, Bologna, Florence, and parts of Germany and France, received an influx of Lucchese silk workers in the decades prior to the Black Plague.[29] The story of silk is picked up again much later in surveys of the community's economic life, but this later evidence on the silk trades tells about an evolved industry, not about how it emerged and prospered. What the Milanese silk industry accomplished in the intervening years of the fourteenth century remains largely a matter of conjecture. Nevertheless, Milan's later fame for gold thread embroideries on silk, a fame that spread throughout Italy and further afield, likely relied on fourteenth-century foundations.[30]

Wealthy Bologna was among the first cities to create dress norms for women and to curb women's spending by recourse to sumptuary law. From the first comprehensive sumptuary code written in the second half of the thirteenth century, a remarkable consistency prevailed in restraining women's excesses. Bologna was prosperous, known for its abundance and the wealth of its citizens, and the condemnation of wealthy women's efforts to dress in fashion appears to have resonated strongly in this papal town. It is possible that the Bolognese's efforts to curb women's fashions led to imitation and adoption of its laws by neighboring communities.[31] Bologna passed new sumptuary legislation every few decades, setting a high standard for keeping up with new fashions through amending highly detailed and specific provisions.[32] Whether this effort to keep pace reflected significant industries that fed women's fashion in Bologna is a different question. Bologna's laws indicate that, above all, rows of *frixis* (embroideries or beaded bands) on women's clothes were regarded as outrageous.[33] Generally speaking, fashions, not expensive material, drew the law's censure, which in time became a fairly common feature of civic sumptuary laws elsewhere as well. *Frixis* or *frisis* were trims added to fine clothes and were not overly expensive when they were sewn on at home. Bologna's sumptuary law assumed, as did Florentine and Venetian laws, that women embroidered and retrimmed their dresses producing effects that made them conspicuous and thus eye-catching. However, sumptuary codes are not reliable indicators of local manufacture since high-prestige goods in Italy traveled from town to town, and prohibitions on offending fashions, rather than on expense, often crept into the laws.

In 1313 the widowed Donna Elena Gozzadini called to account her mother-in-law to produce an inventory of goods in the estate of Elena's son, Giacomo, and her suit required an extensive listing of personal possessions. Caskets, strongboxes, swords, foodstuffs, and domestic wares appeared but, as a whole, garments and dress accessories represent the real wealth in this inventory. It is difficult to imagine *pupillus* Giacomo (at university?) finding use for his extensive wardrobe, including a dark twill housecoat "de Florentia" (connoting, most likely, a fashion). A blue mantle (*guarnacchiam*) trimmed with enamels over gold and accessory gilded silver trims were valued at ten lira, and a silver-trimmed iron collar, a military touch for his wardrobe, was estimated at five lira. Perhaps more important, Giacomo's sleeves, hose, and gloves came in multiples, not merely pairs, suggesting attention to coordinated ensembles that harmonized his numerous robes, cloaks, and furs with accessories.[34] Inventories turn out to be much better indicators than sumptuary laws of how wealthy individuals spent their money: Giacomo lived a modish life wearing Florentine fashions and sporting military touches even though he was a young man.

So consumption, even the rising consumption that repeated sumptuary lawmaking in towns implies, does not reveal much about spending patterns or urban trades. But medieval Bologna was determined to attract artisans to the community and went to great lengths to promote local industries. In the thirteenth century trained Veronese textile workers immigrated into Bologna, which helped establish a nascent cotton industry.[35] In the fourteenth century, silk workers from Lucca arrived, and in the proper combination to establish Bologna as a center of silk production. The Bolognese remarked on the former sufferings of these workers and demonstrated every sign of welcoming this highly skilled community that would increase Bologna's prosperity.[36] Veils became a specialty of manufacture, and by the sixteenth century the Bolognese introduced inventions into silk manufacture that spread throughout Italy.[37]

The Arte della Lana (wool guild) was prosperous by the last years of the fourteenth century.[38] Cloth trades balanced old, established trades like goldsmithing. With representation in the governing structures of the town, goldsmiths and silversmiths tended to set themselves somewhat apart from the center of trade in the Strada Castiglione and occupied their own street of shops (see plate 9). The noble guilds of Notai (lawyers), Cambiatori (bankers), Drappieri (cloth-merchants), and the Arte Serica (silk merchants) followed policies favorable to local trade and manufacture, particularly in the years when they dominated politics. Bologna supported other trades devoted to paper and books, which of course were luxury wares in their own right. The university community and delegations of wealthy prelates of the church who visited the town patronized local tradesmen.[39] Bologna was geographically well situated to attract customers to its markets since the town sat at a crossroads of Tuscany and Lombardy. As a university town Bologna welcomed an endless round of new students, who were valued for the wealth they brought to the community and the cosmopolitan culture they helped create. Mercenaries passed through as wars multiplied in the second half of the century. Bologna enjoyed all the advantages of a manufacturing center that presented high-end goods to a constant stream of travelers.

Although the Genoese, Milanese, and Bolognese remain somewhat enigmatic actors in the new world of fourteenth-century fashion, their histories indicate that fashions, unlike styles, were urban phenomena of consequence here as elsewhere in northern Italy. Fashion was likely to thrive where communities actively courted foreign customers and promoted manufacture of cloth, accessories, and military gear. All three wrote sumptuary laws that expressed concern over fashions that had caught on in city streets. These laws confirm that fashion was all about appearances in public places. Fashion flourished where inspiration took hold: glimpsing some feature of dress that could be echoed, imitated, mocked, parodied, or surpassed by others fed the trend. Viewing others served as an invitation to join the parade and create an extreme length for sleeves, a new cut for gowns, a new border, or a new twist to a hood or headdress, or to adopt a military accessory like gorgets, even if those iron collars sat hard on the throat. Fashion meant reworking one's old silver wares into new accessories, retrimming garments, and striving for novel effects out of materials found in home cupboards. Fashion was a wider social phenomenon than spending on wares, although it managed to soak up discretionary income and certainly encouraged spending. Fashion deepened its hold in a community where tradesmen produced expensive luxuries in cheaper editions, or secondhand clothes dealers sold worn but still serviceable fabrics to the less prosperous, or women produced their own fashions at home. Fashion obliterated local costume, replacing it with fashions that spread like lightning from town to town. Extreme fashion could stun and awe the crowd because of its great expense. But fashion was also small novelties and was dynamic, fickle, and volatile; it flourished where townspeople could not stand to be left out of the new, riveting parade in the streets.

In response, urban sumptuary laws drew distinctions among persons by sex and age in attempts to curtail spending and establish order, an indication perhaps that inhabitants' outward show in public urban space was now highly suspect as a source of disorder. By contrast royal or ducal sumptuary codes tended to distinguish entitlement by rank and office. Laws for the southern Italian towns of Palermo and Naples tend toward this latter pattern, as do those for northern cities home to, or near, royal residences.[40] A regal model also inspired codes in Rome once the papacy was reestablished there; laws from Aragon follow this model as well. In contrast, the extant 1396 Milanese sumptuary law is similar to the laws of other market towns, a response, perhaps, to the tension caused by holding the line at home while maintaining markets open to foreign customers.[41]

The reader should know that this is a study of fashion rather than style, or more precisely it investigates an era when high style, largely a product of court society, gave way to fashion, which flourished in market towns. Generally theorists have assumed that stylishness "trickled down" from courtly circles to prosperous townspeople, but the mechanism for change in towns examined here is somewhat at odds with that interpretation. Court style was generally too lavish to be imitated. As Norbert Elias has argued, "the French king felt himself to be a nobleman, *le premier Gentilhomme*, and stated that he was shaped in his actions and thoughts by the aristocratic attitudes with which he was brought up." Elias goes on to explain that this cannot be understood unless one studies the origins and development of the French monarchy in the Middle Ages.[42] Regal style was a distinctive element of the king's premier status and by definition royalty or their surrogates set court style.

When Silk Was Gold, a title aptly chosen by the Metropolitan Museum of Art for its exhibition on Central Asian and Chinese cloth of gold imported into Europe, captures the distinction between regally set and maintained style in court society, and the new phenomenon of fashion: cloth of gold, almost beyond price, was imported expressly for kings and popes; it was simply out of reach for townspeople. Christine de Pizan noted that Charles V of France purchased cloth of gold from merchants visiting his court with little if any thought to its enormous expense; kings could afford this ultimate luxury.[43] But these fabulous textiles also passed through the hands of merchants on their journey to royal and papal courts, and as such they were examined and could inspire designs for more affordable fabrics.[44] Cloth of gold figured in an urban milieu, if only fleetingly. In religious paintings Andrea di Cione, known as Orcagna (b. 1315–20, d. 1368), Bernardo Daddi (fl. 1320–48), and Simone Martini (1284–1344) developed techniques for representing these extraordinary luxury textiles; thus paintings informed audiences about precious imports.[45] Imported fabrics also inspired design among Lucchese silk weavers, not necessarily because kings bought these imports but because, for a time at least, their exquisite designs were on view to artisans who, in admiration, copied and incorporated design elements into their own weaving. Norbert Elias might interpret this as a component of a power shift in society at large, since locally woven fine fabrics lay within the reach of townspeople. Townspeople had an opportunity for participating through buying local weaves even if royal style was beyond their means.[46]

In market towns sumptuary laws placed restraints on those with the wherewithal to imitate the consuming habits of leading citizens rather than kings; these role models were also the designers of the laws. As a result laws affected, initially, the members of the community's wealthiest households: the wives and children, and on occasion the servants, of the town's wealthy lawmakers. This reveals something important about urban markets. Since markets were open to all comers, even if luxury goods were intended to serve the needs and purposes of men of wealth and standing, local wares could be purchased by, or for, anyone who could pay the price. This was the marketing dilemma that lay at the heart of the transformation of Italy to a consumer culture. Following fashion meant access to the products that constituted modish attire; wealthy households acquired and stocked such items as fine gilded and enameled belts, buttons, chains, and purses. Within households many made use of these luxuries. Wealthy fathers tended to indulge daughters with wedding gifts of great value, and husbands gave gifts to wives befitting the dignity and standing of their lineages. Fashion goods thus had a way of spreading out to wives, youths, and children within wealthy circles in a community. In these circumstances it is not surprising that family members who followed fashion proved worrisome to lawmakers. *Le pompe* was only welcome in towns where a seemly hierarchy of display could be maintained.

A few early experiments in the Florentine laws that restrained shopkeepers from selling to local women were not very successful and were not, apparently, enforced, probably because they were deleterious to open trade.[47] In

Florence a 1396 petition was received by the commune on behalf of Genoese women asking for an exemption from local sumptuary laws. A certain Mariette of Genoa had been called into court because of (locally prohibited) pearl buttons on her mantle and the Genoese community in town was not pleased by this extension of Florentine authority to their wives.[48] The Genoese, at least, believed that Florentine laws aimed to limit Florentine women, which was probably an accurate reading, but it suggests why laws tended to target the behavior of local consumers of luxuries rather than purveyors. Towns faced the two-pronged challenge of selling fashion goods to foreign customers in open markets while maintaining order in regard to the spending and consumption behavior of local inhabitants—a tall order. These conflicting agendas were probably beyond the effective reach of any attempt to create sound law, but nonetheless lawmakers amended and rewrote their sumptuary laws in this futile exercise, as though they could find no other effective course of action.

The fuller coverage devoted to Florence, which built consumer markets over the century, and Venice, with its history of successful luxury markets prospering well before the fourteenth century, is also occasioned by these cities' more extensive records of trade and a rare density of scholarship on related economic subjects, most notably on money and banking. Retailing luxury wares to the wealthy, particularly dress accessories of precious materials, was to an extent a by-product of banking and money-changing activity. Florentines set up banks in Venice at the Rialto in partnership with Venetian bankers, rendering both Venetian and Florentine merchant bankers pioneers of a sort in retailing fashions to the wealthiest customers. In Venice goldsmiths challenged bankers' traditional privileges in retailing silver and gold by the 1330s in a quest for greater market share.

The luxury trades, wherever they flourished in Italy, floated on the full tide of medieval prosperity; they took advantage of the complex European business and financial networks that had been constructed over previous decades.[49] Silver was understood to be inherently valuable, and gilding only enhanced that value. Precious bullion and jewels possessed liquidity that appealed to bankers' most affluent customers, so on occasion bankers and money changers displayed these fine goods on their benches (*bancorum*). This, of course, further raised the cachet of precious accessories. Significantly as well, this fashion of wearing precious metal emerged before the aesthetic revolution of the fifteenth century that reformed taste, favoring painterly skill over gilding, and images, books, sculpture, and antiquities over garish dress and ornate, gilded accessories.

Fourteenth-century retail markets may have lacked the power to reverse the troublesome economic currents of the last decades of the century but luxury markets added a new dimension to the medieval economy nonetheless.

Over the century luxury trades endowed urban markets with increased cultural consequence. People paid attention to what was available on markets and learned to assess displayed wealth, current styles, and any other messages that might be conveyed through apparel and display. Markets no longer met traditional or established needs; they created new demands by raising customers' visual acuity and inspiring customers to follow fashion, possess fine goods, and appear in full public view as persons worth watching. This may well be a late-added feature to the emergence of a market economy in medieval Europe; if so, it was to have significant consequences for subsequent centuries. The work of economic behaviorists who find a motive for fashion in fear of being left out rather than envy of one's superiors addresses the issues.[50] To an extent their new ideas about the motives that promote fashion have superseded Werner Sombart's formulation, which sketched a descent from stylish court consumption to the spending preferences of townspeople.[51]

The increased spending on material goods in medieval society has been a concern of economic historians for a considerable time. Carlo M. Cipolla and Robert S. Lopez both encouraged a more thorough investigation of demand in the medieval economy a generation ago. The Venetian economic historian Frederic C. Lane called for a theory of consumption to explain demand because he believed that economic needs fueling demand may include power and esteem as well as sustenance and therefore should be understood as flexible. Of the economist Thomas Eucken's ideas about economic needs Lane noted, "But man's conception of his needs and how to satisfy them has varied [over time]. These variations deserve historical study, but cannot usefully be described by [phrases like] 'meeting needs' and 'seeking profits.'"[52] Consumption that moves beyond sustenance and acts as a stimulus that encourages demand is a complex historical matter. In these pages there is no pretense at creating a theory of medieval consumption to explain this more robust demand for fine wares that appeared in the fourteenth century, but the study does try to draw together some of the relevant historical information that should be considered. A conjuncture occurred between a market driven by experiments in retailing and new consumption preferences. Effects were felt in a number of communities rather than just a few. Beyond Italy wealthy Avignon felt the impact, and the same is certainly true for royal and ducal court cities that encouraged consumption.

Prior to the fourteenth century, Eucken's proposed "economic needs" had already revealed their time-sensitive nature; the trade in spices and other exotic goods from across the Mediterranean provides a case in point. For centuries pepper had been a highly significant long-distance import that satisfied taste without meeting a need for sustenance. Social constructions of the power and esteem nexus that Lane identified continued to evolve over the course of the fourteenth century and in turn affected the way wants and needs were perceived; those changes drew on visual acuity just as surely as pepper had raised the consequence of "taste" in earlier times. By the end of the fourteenth century wealthy people in cities had determined that their outward appearance should mirror their social status and that precious materials best conveyed that message. They could marshal a variety of arguments to justify collecting luxury wares that were less perishable than pepper and provided plenty of opportunity for ostentatious display.

While there was little that was identifiably new in the fourteenth century, there are reasons for isolating this period for close observation. Many voices were raised in criticism of a new emphasis on appearance and fashion. In Italy this began in earnest among Franciscan clergy in the last decades of the thirteenth century.[53] By the end of the fourteenth century it had become a chorus of religious and lay voices, observers of the social scene who cried out against *le pompe*, even if, as was at times the case, critics themselves figured among the new more flamboyantly attired. Except for the rare person who repudiated ostentation altogether, people in towns rushed headlong after fashion and no effort could stem it: sumptuary laws were written and rewritten, punishments like confiscation and even floggings were meted out; and stiff fines were imposed. Attempts to lay blame often missed their mark and, since traders and artisans made good livings from luxuries, economic well-being was tied to the luxury trades and urban people knew it. Deep ambivalence underlay condemnations of luxury consumption wherever they were voiced.

Costume had begun to be subject to disturbing changes. As Fernand Braudel has noted, "The history of costume is less anecdotal than would appear. It touches on every issue—raw materials, production processes, manufacturing costs, cultural stability, fashion and social hierarchy. Subject to incessant change, costume everywhere is a persistent reminder of social position."[54] He goes on to discuss the sumptuary laws that, of course, began in earnest in the fourteenth century. Italians discovered fashion and poked fun at the changes sweeping across towns and cities, where local dress was replaced by new fashions arriving from other nearby places or by new and more alien modes of dress like the turban. The silhouette changed and clothes became more formfitting as well as subject to sudden whim. The simplicity of a basic garment common to men and women and differentiated only in its details gave way to close-fitting and gendered costumes where men showed off their legs in hose and women tightened their bodices, displaying their shoulders and breasts. Embellishments further heightened difference.

Braudel chose 1400 as his point of departure for consumption-driven markets, but as was his habit he stretched back his time frame, in this case to about 1350, creating a longer continuum for fashion. He could justify this, since around 1350 the components of fashion markets and heightened demand emerged all in a heap, so to speak: "If luxury is not a good way of supporting or promoting an economy, it is a means of holding, of fascinating a society. And those strange collections of commodities, symbols, illusions, phantasms and intellectual schemas that we call civilizations must also be invoked at this point. In short, at the very deepest levels of material life, there is at work a complex order, to which the assumptions, tendencies and unconscious pressures of economies, society and civilizations all contribute."[55]

In such circumstances, fashion became a kind of language: "fashion is a search for a new language to discredit the old," and it has a way "of inventing, of pushing out obsolete languages." While Braudel acknowledged it was not the best way to promote growth in the economy, he saw fashion as the means for producing "big changes," even when wrought by frivolous acts such as rich men shortening their robes. Other men were prone to adopt the fashion, and in urban societies rapt attention was paid to new ideas like shortened robes toward the middle decades of the fourteenth century. Braudel argued that "material progress was occurring: without it nothing would have changed so quickly."[56] Although it may not have been the best way to promote growth in the economy, by 1350 it was Europe's way.

Attending to fashion as a factor determining the pace of material progress has not always characterized thinking about capitalist development; indeed, demand for luxury goods sits rather precariously in the canon of classic economic theory. In *The Wealth of Nations* Adam Smith expressed disdain for those attracted to luxury spending, preventing him from assigning luxury goods any role whatsoever in theoretical formulations about demand. For Smith, luxury markets were a political consideration rather than an economic one because consumer goods played primarily a political role in bringing about the peaceful conditions required for the promotion of interregional trade among hardworking tradesmen. Luxuries, it seems, tamed the warlike feudal nobility. He noted that the feudal nobility "[made] war according to their own discretion, almost continually upon one another, and very frequently upon the king: the open country [became] a scene of violence, rapine, and disorder." Foreign commerce (he was thinking of England) introduced a change: lords could now spend their wealth on "a pair of diamond buckles, trinkets and baubles, fitter to be the playthings of children than the serious pursuits of man." Luxuries were so attractive to lords that they would divert funds from warfare, foster cordial relations with traders, and "for the gratification of the most childish, the meanest and the most sordid of all vanities [the feudal nobility] gradually bartered their whole power and authority."[57] In Smith's opinion, the sober middle classes were too canny to follow this lead. Smith's contempt for the wellborn consumer lured into purchasing luxuries was palpable, although his dismissive phrase "trinkets and baubles" may have seriously underestimated the cost of luxury goods and their capacity to serve as repositories of value. He believed the nobility were excessive in their self-indulgence and prone to foolishness when it came to assessing value in a commercial transaction; thus he awarded the luxury trades no causal role at all in economic growth.

His contemporary Jeremy Bentham did consider demand for luxuries in his theoretical formulations and in doing so revealed himself to be heir to the long history of robust consumer markets. This is most apparent where Bentham presumes the public "always" pays close attention to consuming retail goods. He notes the public is by nature prone to consume more whenever it can, so he subsumed demand for goods into theory as a constant factor, and the interpretation built upon this invariability became his tool for analyzing choice, a tool too powerful, perhaps, to risk historicizing and holding up for reexamination. Utilitarian theory assumes an individual acts rationally in self-interest, that tastes are a given and set upon acquiring goods and services, and that it is rational to respond to a fall in prices with a readiness to buy a larger quantity of any good—and to a rise in prices by buying less—with all choices consistent with income. Amassing any good leads to a weakening of desire for further increments of that good. To place under examination the moment when demand for consumer goods first became a force to be reckoned with, and began to affect demand, meant a challenge to basic assumptions on the nature of demand itself.[58]

Braudel's original periodization—1400 to 1800 for the enhancement of material life in Europe—has led to the creation of an important literature on fashion goods and the enhancement of material life.[59] Robust demand, such as Bentham described, is more easily assumed for these centuries after 1400 because of the changes that occurred over the course of the first age of fashion that came before. Bentham never dealt with the possibility that healthy markets may exist that are not derived from robust demand among local consumers. He never imagined a time when markets did not exert much direct influence over the cultural preferences of people who lived near them and made their living on them. From the late eleventh century through the thirteenth century, as medieval Europe's Commercial Revolution evolved, markets in towns flourished in the midst of populations who remained surprisingly true to their old-fashioned dress and local consumption preferences. Exotic condiments might pass through a community only to find customers further along a trade route. Markets need not be fulcrums for change in taste or create new local preferences in order to thrive on the lengthy trade route that linked East to West. Substantivists and formalists may continue to argue about the relative importance of the market forces of supply and demand in the development of the European economy, but the phenomenon that requires explanation here is a lesser one: the sudden interest in luxury wares and fashion goods among fourteenth-century townspeople who were already familiar with long-distance markets and adept at trading on them. If any transformative processes were at work, they were modest in scale and involved a set of new market features that emerged as fashion took hold. If these processes had implications for changing the social order they largely lay ahead. There was as yet no place in fourteenth-century towns or cities for the claims that have been made for the Western economy that consumption is tantamount to modernization—indeed, encompasses the entire project of becoming modern.[60]

Recent interpreters of the advent of fashion have had to scramble to find frameworks that accommodate new consumption and spending patterns. Fernand Braudel turned to Werner Sombart's earlier *Luxury and Capitalism* for some of his cues.[61] Norbert Elias looked to the development of court society as a function of power shifts in society at large. Georg Simmel pointed to the emulation of elites. In 1977 Albert O. Hirschman produced *The Passions and the Interests,* linking taste and a broad range of human behaviors to economic motives. In 1973, in a preliminary article on consumer goods, Hirschman identified envy as a universal motive for competitive consumption.[62] Mary Douglas and Baron Isherwood argued in *The World of Goods* in 1979 that Hirschman's ideas about envy produced a weak argument. The social sciences, they countered, had identified an array of social conventions and tools for accommodating or resolving envy, which prevented it from operating as a primary human motive in the economy.[63]

More recently in *Luxury Fever,* Robert Frank has argued that social context often determines spending patterns, with wealthy spenders providing the climate for others to increase their levels of spending. People tend to spend to avoid being left out rather than from the more focused motive of envy.[64] This argument has relevance to the experience of the fourteenth century. The wealthiest men in Italian cities, that is, the leading citizenry, had achieved a success that in many ways raised them to the level of Europe's most powerful magnates. They were less likely to envy kings and magnates than to take full advantage of their newfound access to circles of power and privilege. Indeed, in Venice and Florence the highest echelons of the merchant citizenry imagined themselves princes of a sort.[65] To consort with kings meant that leading citizens thought it appropriate to dress as kings, as splendid as the Magi, as depicted in paintings that celebrated the newly popular cult of the Three Kings. The aristocratization of Italian society is recognizable in these early pretensions to dress lavishly, especially when a fashionable wardrobe had the added advantage of serving as a sound investment, one that set an example for one's wealthiest foreign customers.[66] While successful long-distance merchants and bankers entered new circles of power and influence, their spending at home provided a favorable climate for other townspeople to increase their spending levels.

The theory forwarded by Frank emphasizes the forces set in play when many people wish to join the fashion parade. If men led the charge into fashion, women followed headlong after and added their own distinct contributions. Women, youths, and even children were restrained in their consumption wherever civic sumptuary laws governed behavior. Nevertheless, they were not prohibited from consuming but only limited, generally to lesser consumption, shorter lengths of trains, or fewer buttons than men. Was this enough to create defiance among women and other restrained parties? There is some evidence that married women worked over and embellished the basic wardrobes of fine dresses they received when they wed, creating fashions that they then wore out in public. If men were more lavish and constant in spending on apparel, women contributed to fashion by making swift and playful changes in their costumes. These caught the public's eye, and since they amused, begged to be imitated.

The initial line of inquiry in this study was an investigation of what sold in markets and who bought. Sales, commissions, tradesmen's account books, financial records, and inventories of goods provided that essential information that grounded later lines of inquiry. The more difficult task of hunting down fashion goods that have survived from the fourteenth century followed. These were essential for proving that what was described in the "documents of practice" noted above actually saw the light of day. Frequently fine goods described in inventories appeared too ponderous, cumbersome, or expensive to be practicable. The elegant gilded and enameled Cleveland belt, ninety-two inches in length and fabricated in Siena, illustrates the value of examining fashion goods and assessing them against the written record (see fig. 2). Next costs of luxuries were compared to cost of living. This proved to be a valuable exercise not only because it revealed how great an investment the fashionable made in their wardrobes, but also because it allowed for comparisons of what women and men owned and wore. Armed with this knowledge it was possible to next examine genre painting for what artists observed and recorded. Taken together this information provided a context for reexamining sumptuary law and literary evidence. The tensions in sumptuary law writing became more apparent and the opinions of social critics of the day resonated against a backdrop of consumer preferences, innovations in retailing and ready-made goods, and a deepening of the market for fashion goods in towns. Evidence of confusion and fear of disorder that infected urban space took on added meaning. Diane Owen Hughes captured that confusion when she wrote that people in Italy's cities believed theirs was still a society of orders. Rich apparel and fashion indicated otherwise.[67] Finally the impact on retail trade, money and finance, and demand are analyzed.

Chapter 2
Desirable Wares

Highly desirable luxury wares had always augmented the medieval trade in staples, and long-distance merchants, even peddlers, regularly carried ready-made luxury goods in their bales and packs. By the fourteenth century city shops had begun to pay close attention to the drawing power of well-displayed luxury wares and built up trade on the premise that fine objects themselves aroused interest, even strong desires to possess. Luxury wares, and their display and presentation, pose questions requiring careful study since the newer mode of presentation to customers in city shops has not received all the attention in scholarly literature that it deserves.[1]

Since fourteenth-century people lacked mirrors that provided head-to-toe scrutiny, gaining an accurate picture of one's ensemble was close to impossible and not a reliable retailing device. Small peer glasses, generally highly polished disks of metal, and a few rare unblemished pieces of rock crystal silvered on the back were all that people possessed to reassure themselves about their looks, so directing the gaze of the customer to the effects achieved by fashion was pursued through other means.[2] Flattering buyers to render shopping an emotionally compelling activity relied more on examining desirable objects and discussing their merits than regarding the enhanced self. A century later mirrors came into widespread use as a by-product of Murano clear glass or *crystallo*, and the resulting full-length observation of costume may have encouraged people to dress with greater restraint. But in earlier days a retailer learned to cue customers to admire a hat, purse, or chain, and attempted to teach buyers how to imagine themselves decked out in current fashions like short robes, parti-colored hose, pleats, buttons, slashed sleeves, or any of the other conceits of the day. Perhaps the garish and extreme effects of fourteenth-century fashions resulted from a poor perception of the effects of donning fashionable attire. Or perhaps too uncritical acceptance of a retailer's beguiling arguments drove the trend toward extremes. The fashionable tended to dress to impress with the boldest effects they could muster, and customers purchased their luxury wares as unconnected entities, which they then combined into ensembles according to their own preferences. Goods that were arresting, bright, shiny, and intricate, ones that produced novel effects or startled viewers, drove early phases of the turn to fashion.

One direction for inquiry into shopping for goods lies in exploring "taste" from its early associations as one of the five senses to its larger and more generic meaning as a sense of what is fitting, harmonious, and beautiful, or proper and appropriate—*di buon gusto*—a matter of increasing consequence in Italian letters by the early years of the Renaissance.[3] This more elusive taste was honed in a number of ways, and high on that list stood the art of choosing goods on the open market. Selecting among displayed wares was a school of sorts for the cultivation of taste. Some pupils proved adept and others, despite their wealth, were less discerning, indicating that wealth alone was not a sufficient credential for participating in a world where appearances mattered.[4]

When taste became a matter of consequence, it affected markets, and markets in turn affected taste. Pegolotti's famous list of 288 "spices," compiled sometime between 1310 and 1340, had already moved so far beyond what appealed to the tongue that the majority of listed items were not meant for ingestion at all. These other "spices" came within the specialty of the spice trade because they were exotic in origin and expensive. It was not sight (which is certainly more relevant to fashion) but taste that took on new, expanded meanings while betraying origins in the European appetite for exotic flavors.[5] When luxury goods from fabled places were displayed in markets, customers could begin to discriminate among their various properties. Pegolotti's spices included essentials for any fashionable wardrobe: which were preferable of the thirteen available types of alum used for dying fabric to the perfect shade? Was Pegolotti's Baghdad indigo necessary or would less expensive indigo of Cyprus or the "Gulf" (Adriatic Sea) do for obtaining the proper hue? Was gold in sheet form or "gold of metà" better for embellishments?[6] For making judgments *di buon gusto*, some experience in selecting for quality, or choosing the most harmonious or beautiful, the most appropriate or most proper for the occasion, was beneficial. It was also, apparently, full of pitfalls.

Excluding pepper and spices, the chief luxury goods on markets in medieval Europe were well-crafted textiles. David Herlihy has said that most of the crowd in the streets in early thirteenth-century Pisa was still clothed in some form of animal skin. Coarse cloth might be used for some undergarments but, for outerwear, skins with fur turned inward were in widespread use. The wealthy could cover cured hides or furred skins with cloth, but the poorer town dweller was unable to afford a wardrobe of well-made cloth, despite cloth's greater versatility, comfort, and cleanliness.[7] The thirteenth-century textile market required significant deepening if it had not yet reached townspeople as urbane as the Pisans. Yet a century later the textile market was so thoroughly commodified that cloth was available for purchase by a broad spectrum of customers, from the most affluent to unskilled wage earners and servants, indeed to all but the truly impoverished. The pace of thirteenth-century market expansion in the textile trades had been remarkable.

In this context of plentiful textiles, selection became a matter of consequence, with textiles imported from Central Asia or from Mongol-ruled China superior to fabrics loomed in Italy. This is well illustrated by a rarely consulted inventory attached to a very famous name: Marco Polo's will, written January 9, 1324, shortly before his death. It included an extensive inventory of a shop's contents.[8] Unlike the will itself, which was composed in proper notarial Latin, the inventory was little more than a casual document composed in dialect that listed a remarkable 173 items, some of them receptacles like chests, or caskets, small boxes that contained wares like musk, or hooks and eyes. There were numerous *cofano*, or caskets, holding numerous pieces (*peze*) and short lengths of cloth (*drappi*). One casket, described as a great box (*a modo de chofano*), like a coffin, held three quilts with Tartar worked designs—*a lavorieri tataresci.* Two pieces of Chinese voile (*peze 2 de zendadi catai*) appeared along with another piece of Chinese voile (*zendado zalo chatai*). One fine silk textile was decorated with exotic animals (*stranii animali*). *Varnimento a oro de nasizo* (the finest imported cloth of gold) may be the same textile as the *naxici* of which the Genoese Anonymous Poet spoke; both imported fabrics may have been the *nasij* (also *nashi, nashishi*) or cloth of gold woven by Muslim artisans brought by the emperor of China from Central Asia to Zunmalin, about twenty miles west of Kalgan.[9] This cloth of gold, likely only a small piece, was valued at over 20 ducats; indeed, all these fine imported pieces of fabric boasted high value.[10] Cloth of gold appears among other fine textiles described individually, like a piece of fine linen worked with silk thread. While most fabric appeared in pieces or short lengths, there were a few bolts of cloth and some rare long silks, one measuring 222 *braccia*, another 42 *braccia*. Fine textiles were sold along with jewelry and silver belts, a good half dozen of the latter, one of them with silver filament work (*zentura 1 de fil darzento*). There were jewels, including brooches, and some gold and silver rings studded with stones in the inventory. A few finished garments appear on the list and some hats, but it is significant that most of the cloth in the inventory appeared in unworked pieces or lengths (for example, *peze 10 de drapi*), and many of the identified fabrics were of luxury quality like taffeta, silk, voile, velvet, linen, and fine woolens worked with silver and gold thread; some of these bore the added designation of a place of origin. An occasional item was noted as held in pawn (*predere de pegno*) and two sacks with *colleganza* (*collegantia*, legal instruments that were used in trade) completed the shop contents.

In all likelihood a good portion of cloth imported into Europe was destined for royal courts or the ecclesiastical market. Papal inventories collected by Anne Wardwell list numerous imported fabrics from the East decorated with exotic animals including dragons, griffons, monkeys, leopards, parrots, and lions. Ecclesiastical inventory records were so precise that they noted origin, material, design, and often the use to which cloth was put, for example, from Pope Clement V's inventories from 1311, "An altar hanging of Tartar cloth with a design of many animals, monkeys and compartments in gold."[11] This was the established, reliable market for precious fabrics and what may be interpreted as the high end of the import trade.

In Marco Polo's will personal possessions appeared as well; after all, an inventory was intended to list all of the testator's possessions. Polo's widow, Donata, would inherit three fully furnished beds by the terms of her husband's will, but this inventory's greater import is the contents of a shop. Shopping and browsing among these goods would yield rare treasures from Asia and the finest in ornaments. Marco Polo's heirs, Donata and his three daughters, were about to inherit a stock of goods of great value. Fabric from Polo's shop tended to be sold in unworked condition, which allowed customers to create garments or household items to their own taste assisted by hired tailors and seamstresses. By contrast, dress accessories and ornaments appeared ready-made, suggesting that luxury fabrics sold well accompanied by ornaments that set them off and that suggested future usage for the uncut fabric. Ready-made jewelry, hats, belts, and trims displayed beside imported cloth brought to mind imaginative ways to create fashion. Polo, at least, had caught on to the value of placing accessories near fabric to help customers judge the effect of completed ensembles. His inventory provides rare documentation of one method of enhancing sales of fine textiles.

How often shops presented ready-made accessories with fine textiles remains an open question, but given the high and constantly improving quality of Italy's own textile production, opportunities to combine these two types of wares increased over the century. At the high end of the textile market, Lucca had developed a successful silk industry over the course of the thirteenth century, one that spread to other northern Italian cities with extraordinary benefits to any community where Lucchese settled in the aftermath of the political disasters that befell their town.[12] Cotton production was well established in Italy, and by the second half of the thirteenth century Italy exported cotton cloth to northern Europe and across the Mediterranean Sea.[13] The triumph of wool as an Italian industry has been stressed in the scholarly literature so often over the past century that there is little doubt as to its consequence. Any advantage that English woolens—or for that matter any wool cloth from north of the Alps—enjoyed in fourteenth-century Italy had to be based on its superiority both in the quality of local wool fleece and in its manufacture. The excellent wool from merino sheep introduced into the Mediterranean region created a successful luxury textile industry in Italy based on merino wool imports, largely from Spain. Italian workshops applied superior skill to the finishing of wool cloth, particularly in Florence.[14] When northern wool cloth was imported to Italy it might still be subjected to finishing processes that would refine the textile into a luxury product.

If the thirteenth century saw impressive success in manufacture and distribution of textiles, where the quality of fabric improved and quantity increased steadily, then why was this earlier age largely un-remarked-upon for high consumption, a "turn" to fashion, and a shift toward ostentatious display in apparel? Certainly more and better cloth meant that more of it appeared on the streets of Italian towns over the course of the century. Dress was widely recognized by contemporaries as a marker of status but profligacy was not yet personified by *luxuria* or fashion as would be the case later on, while sins of the flesh were characterized with a broader repetoire of images than the lone motif of wanton dressing. In these earlier years, clothes had yet to capture the argument about human vanity.[15] Perhaps better availability of textiles, including more finely finished, costly, and luxurious textiles, was not the issue with critics. If not, what did raise critics' ire?

The conundrum of a sudden emergence of commentary and criticism on dress, consumption, and fashionable wares that characterized the last years of the thirteenth century and continued unabated for decades provides one key to fashion's sudden rise to prominence. Social comments and sermons frequently pinpointed specific wares, or the display of them in public places, that caused offense. It is well known that revulsion against noble excess and display accompanied the ejection of Walter of Brienne from Florence in the 1340s and led to criticism of extreme dressing and high fashion in that city, provoking further curbs on spending for Florentines. But the wider phenomenon of forbidding specific fashions and goods through sumptuary law was already well established in Florence and in many other Italian cities by 1340. This broader trend of censure and efforts at civic control of *le pompe* require a broader range of investigation into the cultural consequences of fashion.

Some historians of costume have interpreted the advent of fashion as a singular turning point in Western culture and regard tight fit as the key to the increasing consequence of modish apparel. Maria Giuseppina Muzzarelli has noted that metal buttons, which became popular in the last decades of the thirteenth century, introduced tight fit to Italy.[16] Buttons spread from city to city with remarkable speed, and they were favorite targets of sumptuary lawmakers. Buttons were often gilded after being fabricated in molds or stamped out of silver and could be gilded, embellished with precious or semi-precious stones, or enameled, creating a tight fit (although some of their appeal lay in their own decorative effect). Using buttons sometimes meant applying precious materials to clothes, but buttons could also be made of glass beads, mother-of-pearl, rock crystal, brass, or bone, which was less expensive than imported ivory. Both men and women wore buttons and both obtained a tighter fit for garments when they did so. Buttons could tease minds into new ideas for garment closures like toggles, decorated hooks and eyes, pins, and brooches, and they could suggest a daring new emphasis on the body's silhouette. Buttons were popular throughout Italy, calling to mind ways in which goldsmiths produced matching sets that were enameled, etched, or filigreed. Buttons were eye-catching without being prohibitively expensive and they could be reused; a set of buttons could be snipped off one garment and sewn onto another.

However, buttons have not been as common an explanation for the advent of fashion as have set-in sleeves. In *Fashion in the Age of the Black Prince*, Stella Mary Newton argues that a new age of fashion dawned throughout Europe around 1340 with the set-in sleeve, a theory that has been highly influential.[17] Newton found the earliest descriptions of the style in Italy, specifically in accounts from Milan by Galvano Fiamma, from Florence by Giovanni Villani, and from Rome in the pages of the chronicler known today as *Anonimo Romano*. She notes that fashion affected dress and consumption in courts and cities of the north, from England to Bohemia and Hungary, and similarly across the Alps to the wealthy courts of Naples and the Iberian Peninsula. One court influenced the consumption patterns of another. The English king coveted the French throne, and, apparently, the luxurious consumption of the French court served as a model for him and for refined consumers in England. Intermarriage magnified the connections among royal dynasties and courts, so fashions leaped from one court to the next in the train of royal entourages. Where the set-in sleeve was concerned, Newton believed courts set style.

According to Newton, in 1342 Walter of Brienne introduced ultramontane French fashions to Florence, and Catalan mercenaries resident in Sicily brought fashions to its court from the Iberian Peninsula. "[A] comparison between the altarpieces, manuscript paintings and sculpture produced all over Europe in the 1340s shows that changes of fashion followed the same sequence wherever men and women wore 'fashionable' dress." In her formulation, royal courts set the style, and townsmen followed their lead, as Werner Sombart, Georg Simmel, and other spokesmen for a trickle-down theory have argued. Specialization proceeded so that "all tended to wear fine linens from Rheims, the best silks from the Holy Land or Lucca, the best [wool?] cloth from Brussels."[18] Newton argues as well that men's and women's dress was more differentiated than in the past, and fabric was often cut to achieve a better fit, but the most salient feature of fashion was a set-in sleeve that appeared on garments for both women and men. This constituted an extravagant use of fabric because cutting fabric created waste, and, of course, what was cut to fit one individual might not fit another, making it more difficult to pass on garments, as was customary. Tight clothes could not be pulled on over the head; as a result, openings, usually in the front, required fastenings. Women lowered their waistlines; men shortened their tunics.

Newton concluded that Paris was the center of this new world of fashion, although the first penned critiques of styles were found in Italy. In Florence Giovanni Villani appears to have been particularly hostile to foreign, yet not necessarily French, influences. He remarked, in what has become a famous passage, about tight fit, short tunics, German pouches, patterns everywhere, extravagant fur as trim, showy buckles, and beards. Galvano Fiamma saw the same outlandish fashions in Milan, although he viewed the tight and short clothing that men sported as Spanish in origin. The *Anonimo Romano* recorded much the same thing for Rome.[19] It is intriguing that the condemnations of fashion Newton found—passages that also praised the simplicity of earlier days when men dressed in the sober attire of the Ancients—came largely from Italy, and then from observers in towns. For information on fashion in the courts of France, Newton relied largely on drawings in manuscripts, sculpture, and paintings, augmented by occasional descriptions of garments found in royal account books.[20]

Newton has provided valuable insight into the geographical extent of the turn to fashion in the fourteenth century. Equally valuable is her suggestion that cutting fabric in the process of creating a tight, body-hugging fit was a key to fashion. But would Italy produce the first—and, for a time, the only— critiques of this turn to fashion if it were European-wide in scope and emerged out of the French court? Were the changes associated with a new fashionable presentation largely confined to the 1340s and a response to the sudden introduction of "foreign" or courtly styles like set-in sleeves into Italy's urban centers? Rosita Levi Pisetzky, working on a much broader basis of research, albeit for a much smaller region, primarily the Italian Peninsula, suggests a different interpretation. Citing Villani's observations about Florence, she states that older men continued to wear long robes while young men adopted the new short tunics that were cut to fit in the early decades of the century. Both long and short garments might feature set-in sleeves, which could be lengthened, shortened, or cut and trimmed as fashion dictated. Buttons became popular with everyone who could afford them. For urban men, variety in silhouette and layered ensembles characterized the turn to fashion. The medium-length robe, pleated and coming to just below the knee, was a new trend for mature men, and it arrived only in the 1370s.[21] Furthermore, Levi Pisetzky did not pinpoint the 1340s as the period when trend and fashion began to influence dress in Italy; many of the components of fashion had already appeared decades earlier. In Italy, Levi Pisetzky notes, there were a number of trends at work at once, and some of them were not particularly new. Clothing figured in a varied and complex production of social meaning in the streets of towns, and opulence and fashion were not the only significant markers of status. Levi Pisetzky differentiates dress of old and young, men and women, rural and urban people, as well as clerics and laypeople. City dwellers were not easily driven into following new fashions or spending their wealth on expensive wares in any event; indeed, *luxuria* was often suspect and mistrusted by the public.

Ellen Kosmer would concur with this judgment; she has noted that *luxuria* was almost always presented in painting and fresco as a female figure, quite contemptible in her excess, thus more potent a cautionary image than the *luxuria* who figured in the Genoese Anonymous Poet's metrical rhymes.[22] The fashionably dressed *luxuria* represented both *superbia* (pride) and closely associated lust or lascivious hunger (*lascivia*) in an increasingly popular interpretive schema.[23] Well swathed and well accessorized, the clothed *lascivia* served as a temptress through dress; apparently she was regarded as more fetching than the traditional nude woman who had often represented *lascivia* in earlier times and would do so again in later centuries. City people were habitually cautioned in sermons, advice manuals, and homilies about the dangers of consumption, understood as indulgence or *luxuria* run wild. Of course Christians had been warned of the dangers of *luxuria* long before fashion's advent in the fourteenth century, but earlier connotations of vice included gluttony and avarice before luxury came to symbolize any or all of the body's appetites: meaning had narrowed so that fashionable dress encapsulated all excessive indulgence. In Italy a most poignant caution against *luxuria* survived in the celebrated legend of St. Francis of Assisi (1182–1226), whose symbolic act of stripping away his rich garments in the streets tightened its grip on the public's imagination. Giotto di Bondone (c. 1267–1337) interpreted that dramatic event almost a century later in a popular image of the naked Francis thrusting a rich robe into the unwilling arms of his aghast but well-robed father (see plate 2).[24]

A fine appreciation of correspondence between the inner and outer person in regard to sanctity represented Christian orthodoxy on the consequence of dress. Through assimilating the teachings of John Chrysostom, the early church preached that the truly devout "should be discernible by everything, by his gait, by his look, by his garb, by his voice."[25] That gait should be humble, the gaze toward heaven, the garb modest, even poor, and the voice prayerful. To appear poor could signify the highest attainment open to a Christian: a higher spirituality expressed as utter disregard for the vanities of this world. Medieval observers were attuned to the multivalent meanings of dress; any new, opulent, and fashionable attire ran the risk of diminishing a person's spiritual standing by connoting crass worldliness, precisely the opposite message from that which a devout person intended. On the other hand, appropriately rich dress might convey proper messages about obligations and calling, even among the holy. The wellborn St. Elizabeth of Hungary, Landgravine of Thuringia (1207–1231), was a rare woman in that she always seemed to "get it right." Elizabeth often distributed her state garments as alms, signifying her charity and lack of concern with personal appearance. But clothes mattered. Dyan Elliott relates, "On one occasion when her husband learned that some important magnates were arriving from her father's court, he was apprehensive that he would be shamed by his wife's mean dress. Elizabeth received divine assistance, and surprised the court by appearing in an azure, pearl-encrusted robe."[26] If visual symbols were properly displayed, apparel like St. Elizabeth's miraculous robe expressed great dignity and a fitting sense of duty. Still, those who joined in the project of becoming fashionable had to constantly question the propriety of their acts of dress. Every time they dressed for an occasion they risked creating impressions that could be misconstrued. Overestimating the niceties of one's own condition or a public occasion's moral demands and social consequence were real and present dangers.

Markers of gender and age were no less evident and closely examined by the public at large than signs of sanctity. What Newton saw as a dominant new style, Levi Pisetzky tends to interpret as merely a trend among wealthy youth, the very ones who would be singled out for special mention in fourteenth-century sumptuary laws because they dressed to excess. Women found their consuming curbed by often irate urban legislators, who carefully distinguished by both age and gender in prescribing what was appropriate dress. This left, of course, the most affluent and enthusiastic consumers, those wise, grave designers of urban sumptuary laws themselves, unrestricted in their apparel and free to adopt any new fashion that pleased them. This raises the question of whether the consumption of rich materials was ever truly the issue when sumptuary laws were designed and written.

For wealthy men of all ages, who led the trend to fashion in fourteenth-century cities, an emphasis on tighter fit for a stylish silhouette gave greater importance to fastenings of all kinds. This applies not just to the use of buttons but also to the increased importance of borrowing elements from military costume that created a snug fit. Trends may have come from France, Germany, or Spain, or from the armor-producing towns of Milan, Venice, or Florence, but in each instance it was military gear that presented new ideas for fashion to men in Italy's cities. Clothes, like armor, came to rely on metal accessories, including metal belts, metal buttons, and closures of all kinds—studs, plaques, ornamental sheaths for knives, neck pieces, spurs, and chains of gilded silver—all of which contributed to tight fit, emphasized a burly silhouette, and provided a fashionable look. There were at least two dominant styles of belts: the older a long, sinuous belt made pliant by short metal plaques attached to a flexible knitted ribbon, where the tongue hung down far beyond the buckle or wrapped more than once around the body; the other a broad linked metal belt buckled snugly on the hips, from which one could hang weapons. The former had been known for centuries in western Europe: it may be seen on the effigy figure for the tomb of Queen Berengaria (1165–1230). The broad linked belt was a military-derived style, popular in eastern Europe. It may have entered Italy from Hungary or the West Balkans (see plate 5). Another style of belt with embellished plaques that were slit to fit over a running ribbon of silk, which was even more ancient in origin, probably arrived in Europe from the Far East. This style may be found among surviving treasures of the T'ang and Sung dynasties in China; here again the style was military and ancient.[27] Fashionable influences were, of course, a two-way street in this century that produced plate armor. "Suits" of plated armor drew on civilian fashion for inspiration, just as civilian fashion drew on military dress for ideas. Masculine attire became, generally speaking, tighter, brighter, perhaps more swaggering, and likely, given all that metal, audible to passersby.

The Case for Courtly Origins for Fashion

At first glance court styles as the origin of urban fashions would appear to be supported by the adoption of long sinuous silver belts. Historians of fashion who follow that line of reasoning are in line with the early twentieth-century economist Werner Sombart. He identified court society and the "new aesthetic conception of woman" in Renaissance courts as the source of new social values, including fashion's sway in the economic life of the Western world.[28] Sombart, like Georg Simmel and, for a later century, Norbert Elias, viewed style as a social phenomenon spread by emulation, with wealthy townspeople imitating their social betters and passage of sumptuary laws an attempt to maintain old social distinctions. For Sombart, women's new social consequence introduced fashion to society, thus branding style itself as feminine, with men succumbing to its appeal only later and reluctantly. The difficulty in applying this theory lies largely in its gendered formulation. Contemporary critics identified masculine fashions as the new phenomena in urban life without reference to women and their dress; thus men's adoption of fashionable elements like silver belts, daggers, chains, buttons, spurs, and other accessories of metal tends to undermine Sombart's formulation. Apparently these particular fashions acted as wedges that opened communities to fashion's sway. Furthermore, urban men did not need to turn to northern courts for these styles. Fine armor was made in Milan, Venice, and Florence. Armies of mercenaries that descended on Italy were more than sufficient for modeling military affections to a concerned civilian audience.

Nevertheless, the royal French court—or courts, given the luxury of the Valois royal uncles' residences—has often been identified as the trendsetter for Europe in this "first age of fashion." Yet even here, models for setting styles in court society were seldom women. The expenditures of the Valois monarchy's court increased steadily over the fourteenth century so that an office of the wardrobe was created in France and possibly at other royal European courts in response. The 1342 account book of Edouard Tadelin, a Lucchese merchant at the French court, "seems to be the only French account to have survived from this [early] period," Newton has noted, wondering at this lack of early documentation.[29] But surviving and highly detailed royal inventories cover later decades of the century and provide extraordinary detail on court luxuries that have since disappeared, disintegrated, or been melted down. Of course styles that originated at court also appear in manuscript illustration, particularly in books of hours where azure blue and gilt set off extraordinary luxury objects. Account books and inventories from late in the century record rich costume and opulent artifacts fit for a splendid lifestyle.

By the reign of Charles V (1364–80) consumption began to rival other expenditures of the crown. In her *Book of the Deeds and Good Character of King Charles V the Wise*, Christine de Pizan presents the king's daily routine in order to demonstrate to the reader his well-ordered life. In his hours devoted to leisure the king might receive curious gifts, "and merchants would come bringing velvet, cloth of gold and all sorts of beautiful, exotic objects or jewels, which he had them show to the connoisseurs of such things among members of his own family."[30] And, after his afternoon rest period, the king "spent a time with his most intimate companions in pleasant diversions, perhaps looking at his jewels or other treasures."[31] Jewels enhanced royal pleasures and distinguished regal pursuits from mundane pastimes. Christine provides some trustworthy evidence on where that finest-quality imported cloth of gold might find its final resting place, and her account suggests how long-distance merchants might find an entrée for influencing royal taste while catering to royal style.

In the reign of Charles's son Charles VI (1380–1422), the royal uncles Louis, duke of Anjou, Jean, duke of Berry, and Philippe, duke of Burgundy, vied with each other in display in their household furnishings, personal attire, and the costumes of their servants and members of their court circles.[32] Could imitators, that is, a buying public of townsmen, even affluent townsmen, keep pace? Very few fourteenth-century court artifacts survive, but the description of one *nef* (Latin, *navis*)—a massive silver table ornament sometimes used to house cutlery and utensils—speaks of the exquisite workmanship and great value of the royal uncles' possessions. R. W. Lightbown's description of a gilded and enameled silver *nef* in Louis d'Anjou's inventory of 1379–80 bears quoting:

[It] was a representation of a carrick at sea, except that it ran on four wheels. The castle on the poop had four trumpeters, a captain and four servants. Four men were winding the ropes of the mainmast on pulleys: three others were pulling the ropes of the mast on the prow, while a third pair sitting at either end of the cross-bar of the foremast were tying ropes that came from the mainmast. Two more men kept watch from the crow's nest on the mainmast. Every other detail of a ship was shown besides, more sailors, a water-butt with a bucket hanging from "a little tower" above, rope ladders, a trap-door to go below deck, even a hearth with a cauldron hanging in it and the ship's cook in front of it.[33]

This was, of course, a magnificent commissioned work that consumed silver in bulk and epitomized luxury consumption. Other royal courts, at Naples, at Buda, at Prague, and in England, apparently looked to France and did their best to follow.

The French court also bought luxury fabrics woven in Italy as well as imported fabrics. Centers in northern Italy like Lucca produced fine brocades, velvets, and enamel on gilt that were transported and presented to members of the court.[34] By this era the enamel work of a city like Siena differed in design and cost from the great commissioned works produced by court enamelers. In Italian cities fabricated precious wares were market goods designed to suit a variety of customers; at the French court fine enamels on gold and other commissioned luxury wares were unique objects and a significant form of stored wealth.

Peter Spufford notes of late fourteenth-century France that after a century of accumulation, royal consumption of gold and silver had become a form of hoarding. Spufford argues that the desirability of owning a great show of plate, all cunningly designed and engraved, did not seem to be of much aesthetic value to Charles VI or his Valois uncles. In an emergency the finest masterpiece was sacrificed with little regret in order to refill royal coffers with coin. Meanwhile, spectacular increases in the amount of secular plate in the households of royalty meant that on occasion the Paris mint "came to a standstill because the money-changers refused to supply it with bullion. . . . When called upon to explain their action, one pointed out that Monseigneur de Berry needed gold to mount his collection of gems, others added that Monseigneur de Guyenne and the King of Sicily '*désiraient des calices*' [wanted precious stones] and jewelry, and so they could not respond to the wishes of the mint."[35] Monopolizing the supply of bullion in Paris so thoroughly by the turn of the century suggests that French royal preferences in consuming outran the capacity of others to follow royal models of expenditure. Luxury wares of precious metal, enamel, and gems, goods that seldom appeared in any great quantity on medieval markets under any circumstance, dwindled to such short supply that leading court figures handily absorbed those available.

Initiatives begun earlier by Charles V to make the monarchy itself the focal point of French national interest had the added effect of justifying opulence and permitting wealth to be withdrawn from treasury revenues to support outlay. In Charles's view a sound currency, the traditional use for the realm's stored gold and silver, was justifiable primarily as a form of largesse: "We ought to make good and strong gold and silver coinage, besides alloyed currency, whereby the poor can freely be given alms," he stated in his decree of 1360.[36] Apparently the interests of commerce were not at the front of his mind. French royalty captured imaginations throughout Europe with their acts of charity, largesse, and great extravagance, but royalty did not intend that their subjects imitate them. When ostentation and largesse reach a level where others cannot follow, emulation as Sombart and others have conceived it is more or less out of the question.

Courtly French dress, what is sometimes called "feudal, " or Late Gothic ultramontane style, may have set some styles that were adopted by others and, in doing so, influenced consumption patterns in Europe, but more often than not French Gothic or Late Gothic as stylistic attribution has come to mean something else. In studying *cassone* Ellen Callmann has claimed that Late Gothic (French) courtly motifs first entered Italy only a century later, in the early decades of the fifteenth century.[37] The International Style based on Late Gothic or French Netherlandish influences, redolent of court patronage and eclecticism, as the French art historian Louis Charles Jean Courajod (1841–96) first defined them, has taken on a variety of meanings and a highly flexible timetable. [38] It seems reasonable to conclude that Late Gothic and "courtly" as stylistic markers are only roughly synonymous, and while courts influenced each other in the matter of style and dress, courtly style lent itself to reinterpretation on a broader basis only when it came within the means of lesser men or could be reinterpreted in cheaper versions. Only then were courtly styles likely to contribute ideas to the spread of a fashion.

Nevertheless, skilled artists who were capable of creating splendid objects sought out French royal patronage. Princely patronage, expressed as a reliable stipend, might well appeal, appearing to artists as a perfect instrument for unleashing their creative talent, a precursor of sorts to the living wage or salary that came in time to differentiate the artist from the artisan, in Martin Warnke's well-known formulation.[39] But a royal commission was not without pitfalls; a skilled craftsman who enjoyed a stipend from a prince was also at the mercy of his patron, who might encounter a change of fortune or simply change his mind. In the later decades of the fourteenth century, Gusmin, a highly renowned goldsmith from Cologne who sculpted brilliantly and was "most gifted, learned and excellent in this art," saw the loss of his prized work at the hands of his royal patron, Louis d'Anjou. In his *Commentaries* Lorenzo Ghiberti (1378–1455) turned Gusmin's dilemma into a cautionary tale for all who presumed to be artists: "[Gusmin] saw his work, which he had made with such love and skill, destroyed in order to meet the Duke's financial needs and when he perceived the vanity of his labours he threw himself on his knees, raised his hands and eyes to heaven and said, 'O Lord, who governs the Heavens and earth and who created all things, let me not be so foolish as to serve anyone but Thee: take pity upon me' and forthwith he gave away all his possessions for love of the Creator of all things. He went up into a mountain, where was a great Hermitage, entered it, and there did penance for the rest of his days."[40]

Ghiberti related this story in the second book of his *Commentaries*, after enumerating and praising his own antecedents among the great Italian painters and sculptors who found a less arbitrary market for their works in Italy. The output of those artists stood while poor Gusmin's creations had been melted down to meet a crisis—a lesson holding little comfort for an artist contemplating a career sculpting for great and powerful men.

The story of Gusmin had come to Ghiberti secondhand and it dwelt on sudden changes of fortune for an artist dependent on the patronage of a royal benefactor. Ghiberti recognized Gusmin's talent and heaped praise on his sculpting, of which Ghiberti had seen a great many casts. Gusmin sculpted nude parts and heads marvelously; he was gifted, learned, and excellent in his art, quite perfect in all his endeavors, although perhaps his figures were a trifle too short. A medium as precious as gold may impose constraints on an artist, Ghiberti recognized, but the loss of a great artist's oeuvre was a pain almost too great to bear. For the Florentine Ghiberti, who early apprenticed himself to a goldsmith (his stepfather, Bartoluccio, that is, Bartolo di Michele) and who joined the Florentine goldsmiths' guild by 1409 where he soon numbered a gold mitre for Pope Eugenius IV among his finer works, stories about the destructive acts of fourteenth-century royal patrons were a caution.

Neither Master Gusmin nor skilled goldsmiths like Guillaume Arrode and Jean Duvivier, who also served members of the French royal family, dealt with customers other than their royal patrons and a few select members of court.[41] Often their task lay in melting down old plate and creating new objects for royal patrons; frequently these new creations were circulated as royal gifts. Indeed, the rules of a gift economy, the demands of largesse rather than exchange, governed the production of luxury wares commissioned by royal or ducal patrons. Highborn patrons set priorities and, at times, solely dictated an artist's output. In turn patronized artists—the terms artist and artisan were synonynmous and would be for some decades yet—numbered among the most brilliant craftsmen and women of the day, persons capable of creating harmonious, novel, and beautiful objects, that is, the most desirable wares. Still, the charge to them was to accommodate royal wishes in all things.

Absence of an alternative market for fine wares patronized by wealthy citizens, or of commissions from churches and charitable foundations, became on occasion a disadvantage for the court-patronized artist. Even if courtly taste succeeded in setting a style that others wished to copy, it was unlikely to accrue any advantage to the creative mind and skilled hand that thought up the new style or forged the new artifact. Lavish royal displays constantly ran the peril of outstripping the purchasing power of those who would imitate; as such they were unreliable for establishing broader trends. Kings and great courts could prevent artists from distributing to the public what they wished to monopolize, so fine wares that under other circumstances would appeal broadly and reward their creators with wealth and prestige never reached wider audiences. Courts may have raised sights to new wonders in the world of goods, but they were less reliable for transforming consumption patterns. Royal consumers distinguished themselves from their subjects by using royal treasuries to support their consumption, and royal aspirations to outshine others with displayed wealth carried the day. For this reason Sombart's "emulation" spreading outward from a Renaissance court setting does not account all that well for a shift to heightened demand from a suddenly fashion-conscious public.

Men and Fashion

In marked contrast to court culture, markets in cities provided an opportunity to introduce intermediaries between the wealthiest and more modest consumers. Rich and opulent as fourteenth-century urban fashions might be, a variety of wares and gradations of quality and cost among an array of goods placed some new trends within the reach of less affluent townspeople, and this proved to be an effective way to arouse interest in consumption. Much rested on the stimulus provided by a great variety of wares. In the streets the example of those only relatively wealthier than oneself, coupled with an accessible and reasonably flexible marketing system, allowed fashion to take hold. Certainly garish wares, exhibits of poor taste, and even at times vulgar displays proliferated where luxury markets widened and deepened, but the aesthetic of this age was seldom restrained even in court circles.

In towns and markets, the change most closely associated with new patterns of consumption was greater differentiation in costume for young and old and for men and women. In towns the chief trendsetters of the day were likely to be affluent mature men, who could best afford to buy luxury goods. Townsmen chose to wear short tunics and hose or long and stately robes; townsmen took to foreign-inspired dress. Fashionable men startled local critics into complaints, and when their fashions were, in turn, imitated by women, as they invariably were, this proved to be an even worse affront. Giovanni Villani specified what created a fashionable young man, with his German pouch and torso-hugging clothes; Galvano Fiamma condemned men's fashions at Milan and mentioned women only secondarily as imitating men insofar as they were able. Indeed both Fiamma and later the monk Henry Knighton of England defined fashion itself as a masculine pursuit. Speaking of France, Jean de Venette stated angrily that soldiers were responsible for the outrageous new fashions that men seemed to love and follow.[42] When women wore new tight-fitting outfits they did not so much become fashionable as masculine in the eyes of critics: women sacrificed their femininity and became manlike in contemporary eyes. Apparently this confused and offended critics since such acts of dress were then censured as against nature. So firm was men's grip on fashionable dress that for Fiamma female interlopers in tight-fitting garments with golden girdles were Amazons and thoroughly outlandish. Apparently any masculine fashion assimilated into women's dress aroused anger. Henry Knighton called women brazen imitators of men when he saw them parading around at tournaments with their belts set below the navel and lavishly decorated in gold and silver, while wicked little daggers, a male accessory if ever there was one, hung down even lower.[43]

If fashion is construed as a masculine pursuit, it is easier to understand why women were restricted in wearing fashionable dress. Urban sumptuary law legislated by gender and sometimes age, targeting women even while the weight of evidence suggests that men were the initiators of the most grand, expensive, and widely imitated fashions of the day.[44] For some, fashion was a male prerogative justified as a source of prestige and renown for a community, and held the added benefit of promoting local industries. Fashion could be interpreted as investment dressing among financiers and wealthy merchants whose fortunes underwrote others' livelihoods. Sumptuary law restricted women from wearing "dishonest fashions," that is, dissembling through rich apparel and accessories, but it is apparent that most laws left men's consumption unrestrained.[45] In the 1320s and 1330s, when the first great spates of civic sumptuary law were passed in Italy, almost all fashion was understood as gendered and censurable in women, which would continue for decades to come. The gendered complexion of the century's turn to fashion, and the link forged between men's dignity, that is, gravitas and the new interest in consumption, is a significant factor for driving the market.

There are two possible avenues of approach to understanding fashion as a masculine pursuit: the more difficult—the ensemble that was created out of a wide range of garments and accessories—or the simpler—the individual luxury articles that were available for men to purchase in local markets. The ensemble, that which fourteenth-century people had to construct without the aid of full-length mirrors, is of greater importance. For comparative purposes an early twelfth-century Venetian noble's ensemble helps highlight what had and had not changed in men's dress by the fourteenth-century turn to fashion.

It was fortuitous that when Gratianus Gradenigo, a Venetian, died at sea some time before 1176 his goods were gathered and brought to Pisa. The doge of Venice sent an envoy named Guido to see to the interests of Gradenigo's

heirs. Guido secured the goods, which were then inventoried by a certain Ildebrandus, and then Guido auctioned them off at Pisa that very year. He
returned with the proceeds to Venice and, presumably, distributed the money
among Gradenigo's heirs. The prices these new or used wares brought at auction, as well as a description of the goods themselves, permit an analysis of
what a wealthy Venetian merchant might wear in the late twelfth century.
(Items were often singular and their state of wear was noted, so Gradenigo's
personal possessions as well as his trade goods were inventoried and sold off
at this time.)[46] In analyzing this inventory Louise Buenger Robbert has
described two suits of clothes, one inexpensive and one expensive, from this
list. The former cost a bit more than twenty solidi, Pisan; the expensive ensemble, more than forty-eight solidi. The inexpensive suit included one shirt, one
pair of breeches, an old jacket, an old gown of dark blue, a mantle of heavy
wool, a pair of old boots, and a belt with a round pocket hanging from it. The
expensive outfit included a linen shirt, a pair of Saracen-style breeches, a gown
of silk with old fur, a cloak of hare covered with vermilion, a pair of hose, a
brimmed sun hat, and a pair of boots described as somewhat "funny looking,"
which may mean in a foreign style.[47] Within the inventory were many more
furs including two rabbit fur jackets, one covered in scarlet cloth and the other
covered in green cloth. Also on the list were two shirts with pairs of sleeves, a
torn linen shirt (*camisiam*), an old shirt, woolen breeches in numerous pairs,
five men's cloaks, four full-length robes, jackets and shoes, stockings, leggings,
belts, a knife, and a torn bag or briefcase (*saccum 1 fractum*). Linen bedding, a
featherbed, and netting also figured in the inventory; however, the containers,
business tools like weights, the many bulk textiles, baskets, record-keeping
materials, and tailor's supplies also listed tell more about the man's business
life than his personal appearance. Perhaps most curious of all were the two
separately listed Saracen-style codpieces among his garments (*toppam 1 sara-
cenicam*, repeated). These may have complemented his Saracen-style breeches
or were worn with hose laced to a shirt or doublet.

The wealthy Gratianus Gradenigo had changes of clothing in different
states of wear. His ensembles, whether simple or opulent, would consist of a
shirt, possibly with a pair of set-in sleeves, and breeches, or he could wear long
hose and boots. Over these items he might wear a gown, and over that a jacket
or a cloak or both. A hat completed his outfit. Three layers would take Gradenigo through the change of seasons in Italy and comfortably through sun and
storm at sea. But perhaps more to the point, this twelfth-century Venetian
could adopt more than one style of dress. He could wear breeches, presumably
loose ones, or tight hose and he had the codpieces to complete the ensemble.
He could wear a short fur jacket with a green or scarlet covering facing outward and he had the belt to achieve a tight fit, or he could wear a long loose
gown and a cloak over that. He had many bright and dark colors from which

to choose. He had light blue boots, green and scarlet jackets, and a vermilion cloak, as well as silk and wool and linen. One hat was specifically described as brimmed to keep out the sun (*capellum de filtro pro sole*). Beyond his Saracen-style accessories he owned one long robe in a style described as Slavic (*sclavinam*).[48] While one of his old pairs of boots was given to the poor for the good of Gradenigo's soul, most of the rest of his wardrobe was considered sufficiently valuable to auction off. If he wished, Gradenigo could appear in outfits that the more elegant fourteenth-century man would likely call fashionable, perhaps even censure for ostentation. Indeed, the introduction of the codpiece is generally assigned to the fifteenth century although without the designation Saracen; it has been widely assumed that men adopted the codpiece only when tunics became extremely short.[49]

What Gradenigo could do and did do by way of creating an ensemble are two different matters. However, the luxury of his apparel, the choices at his disposal, and his brightly colored wardrobe suggest wealth and care for a luxurious appearance. He did not possess gems, gold, or silver, at least at the time when his goods were inventoried (though the torn briefcase does give pause); he did carry seven pieces of coral. None of his clothing was described as trimmed with rich borders as might be the case for men of his station later; fur was used quite lavishly for linings but apparently for warmth rather than display. His linen shirts had several pairs of sleeves, and while the sleeves may have been separate from the shirts themselves, they may just as well have been set in or sewn in. In either case such pairs of sleeves required cutting fabric for construction as separate components from the shirt.

Gratianus Gradenigo's wardrobe is a caution against taking any claim for men's fashionable attire as a startling new phenomenon of the fourteenth century at face value. His wardrobe contained almost all the components of fourteenth-century fashion although it lacked fine accessories and dress embellishments, and even that finding is somewhat unreliable. In the city of Venice itself the mosaics on the front of St. Mark's, completed around 1200, present the doge, who is carrying relics into the basilica, wearing a purple tunic, purple stockings, and, of course, a red biretta. Nobles who accompany him wear embroidered cloaks belted at the waist. The dogaressa wears a red mantle over a blue embroidered dress and a crown on her head. Her retinue of women wears gorgeous gowns, headdresses, and fine cloaks.[50] Robert S. Lopez published an inventory from early thirteenth-century Genoa that included a comparable diversity of luxury items in masculine wardrobes: men of wealth in Genoa wore layers of garments, silver belts, medallions, furs, and rings by the early decades of the thirteenth century.[51]

In Italy's cities affluent men were exposed to a wide variety of choice for their wardrobes and they invested considerable sums of money in keeping up appearances. Pisa, Venice, and Genoa were, of course, seaports and therefore open to new influences from abroad, and exotic fashions may have arrived first in maritime towns. Long-distance merchants not only imported new wares but apparently returned home and wore them. That appears to have been the case with Gratianus Gradenigo and his Saracen and Slavic styles, so what distressed later critics in interior cities like Florence and Milan may have appeared less remarkable and censurable in port cities. Nevertheless the 1176 date of Gradenigo's inventory is a useful caution against regarding claims for a turn to fashion in the fourteenth century as incontrovertible. It is evident that lavish and bright garments were popular among men from a much earlier date. Giotto di Bondone (1280–1377), whose artistic career began in the late thirteenth century, depicted robes with deep folds and rich borders from the very outset. His magnificent *Ognissanti Madonna* (c. 1305) features a narrow worked gold border on the Virgin's drapery and gold crowns on the surrounding saints (see plate 3). Giotto used his superb mastery of drapery and his knowledge of contemporary dress to highlight the consequence of figures from the start of his career.

Perhaps no image better presents the iconographic messages that may be conveyed through fashionable dress than Giotto's *Expulsion of Joachim from the Temple* (see plate 4). On the central figure of the expeller Giotto placed a brilliant green surcoat with rich bands of trim, its prominent borders articulating the side panels of the garment and its wide set-in sleeves. The expeller's well-clad back is turned to the viewer. As Giotto's audience would immediately understand, this figure wears contemporary dress of great opulence and daring—witness the borders, set-in sleeves, and the mid-thigh length of the fine surcoat that reveals another embroidered garment beneath.[52] Through his mastery of layered fabrics and folds Giotto achieved arresting monumentality for both Joachim and the expelling priest, but Giotto's derisive message about power rests on a contrast between a simply and classically clad Joachim and the opulent stylishness of the gesturing priest. An urban audience would read overweening pride into the preemptory outflung arm and the priest's fashionable back with a set-in sleeve and bands of trim on the seams turned to the viewer. That contrast may be lost to us today, but it would have struck Giotto's contemporaries as he intended.

Giotto's artistic renown grew over the course of the fourteenth century to such heights that Giovanni Boccaccio could later base a joke on Giotto's well-known acuity in decoding the visual messages conveyed by masculine dress.[53] In the *Decameron*'s Fifth Story of the Sixth Day, Giotto and a certain Messer Forese, out traveling, protected themselves from a summer rainstorm with a peasant's borrowed and ragged fustian cloaks along with two hats "gnawed with age." The sight of so disreputable and poorly clothed a figure brought this reaction from his friend Forese: "Ha! Ha! Giotto! If a stranger who had never cast eyes on you before, were suddenly to meet you in this condition, do you suppose he would take you to be the finest painter in the world, as indeed you are?"[54] This was surefire humor for the day since Giotto was famous for depicting clothes in order to reveal character and likely a snappy dresser himself. Men had become what they appeared to be in this visually more acute society. For this reason Boccaccio's story of shabbiness that deceives occasioned hilarity, even if the humor in it is less engaging today.

Exotic foreign styles, such as those that were identified by the notary Ildebrandus inventorying Gradenigo's clothes in 1176, entered Italy at a steady pace over the medieval centuries. A twelfth-century reference to Saracen style proves to be unusual among Italian inventories of the twelfth century, but by the fourteenth century a carpet noted in the Florentine sumptuary law of 1355 was described as *saracinescho*, or Saracen, while today it might be called a Turkish carpet.[55] Later in the century a Florentine inventory described drinking cups as *sarecinescho* or *saracinescho* in style, and another carpet similarly described as Saracen appeared there as well.[56] Sienese and Venetian painters, as well as Lucchese silk weavers, were keen on Middle Eastern (Persian) and Far Eastern motifs.[57] The artist's pleasure sometimes lay in combining exotic Eastern designs with a dash of classicism, with perhaps some Gothic elements from the hunt added in. Eclecticism characterized the design aesthetic of the age.

Slavic styles entered Italy with some regularity. The bangles (*circellis sclavoneschis*) that women presumably wore on their wrists or ears in the late thirteenth and fourteenth centuries were not particularly valuable since silver—or even gold—wire could be spun out until it was very thin, but they were popular imported wares and were associated with the Balkans where new silver and a little gold were mined.[58] They could, of course, be worked in larger dimensions to create circlets or crowns to wear as headdresses (*cherchielli*). The designation of a cloak in Gradenigo's wardrobe as "Slavic" could be found with some frequency in Italy, although whether this referred to a fabric or a style like that of the ecclesiastical garment traditionally called a *dalmatica* would be hard to establish. One rather coarse cloth was identified as Slavic (*schiavine*) in Venetian records.[59]

Marco Polo's will, not surprisingly, referred to the style of *catai* or *Chatai*, that is, Cathay or China. It also included a reference to a style *al tartarescha*.[60] According to Charlotte Jirousek, Tartar or Turkish styles became important in Europe in the later Middle Ages. This was particularly true for headgear that increased in relative importance in fashionable ensembles. For the year 1380 she identified a turban adorning a Genoese male figure as Turkish in origin; the term she applied to it was *chaperon*, and it sat on the head of a Genoese money changer.[61] However, *chaperon* was a generic term applied to many different styles of hats; turbans were only one style among numerous *chaperons*. Jirousek claims that the later trend in women's very tall hats that were divided into peaks, or horns, the sort favored by Anne of Bohemia when she was queen of England (1380–96), was Turkish in origin as well. Carpets were sometimes designated as Turkish, that is, when they were not referred to as Saracen.[62] The weavers of Lucca employed Persian motifs, particularly the palmetto, which was popular in both woven brocades and paintings.[63]

Traditionally fabrics took their names from their place of origin in the East—*damaschi* (Damascus fabric) or *ormesini* (from Ormuz in Persia), for example. Place designations for different kinds of fabric could just as easily refer to different locales in Europe, as with *renso* (linen) from Rheims. In Venice one referred to certain styles as *da florenza* (Florentine) by 1325, while throughout Italy the *dogalina* traditionally meant an elite, or ducal, style of garment with sleeves fitted at the elbow, linked to the wife of the Venetian doge.[64] The *Zibaldone da Canal*, a collection of business and educational material relevant to a merchant's career in fourteenth-century Venice, lists fabrics by city of origin, and the record provides a most imposing list of cloth arriving at Venetian markets. There were 104 different textiles set out here to be memorized by a would-be merchant, as well as furs, old cloths, flax fiber, wool, ribbons, and various trimmings. A few textiles were designated by color, but town of origin dominated the *zibaldone*'s classification. There were, for example, stamfords from Arras, England, and Monza, as well as others from England bought by weight, not length, and still other narrow ones designated as from Saint Omer, Paris, Valencia, or Monza.[65]

In 1380 in Florence, a small belt (*cintoletta*) could be referred to as *franciescha* when it had raised work in gilt with enamel and featured a buckle.[66] Here *franciescha* may refer to enamel work or what has been called, sometimes generically, "Limoges." But the fourteenth century saw so many belts, with so many names attached to them, that consumers needed many different designations to keep them all straight. In commercial centers, in contrast to royal courts, the market created a mechanism wherein a number of different fashions, and fine wares from a number of locales, met to become part of new presentations; this characterized the furnishing of interiors of fourteenth-century dwellings as well.[67] Weavers, particularly those producing fine brocades, favored the eclecticism of combined Levantine and Gothic motifs.[68] Meanwhile, port cities in Italy were well positioned to combine imported and local goods in ensembles that encouraged fashion. A merchant trading on an urban market was wise to promote any new product or style that complemented his own wares. A pleasing variety could be produced from a choice of imported goods coupled with imitations of foreign goods by local artisans, which might still retain a place-name even if the product was made elsewhere, like stamfords from Monza.[69]

The fashionable ensemble for men in Italian cities in the first decades of the fourteenth century relied first of all on plentiful fabric. Where wool cloth became suppler through finishing, and fine linens, silks, and cottons, not to mention satins, velvets, and brocades, were also available, splendor was expressed with deep folds, flowing garments, and many-layered ensembles. In the matter of color, choices appear to have increased significantly over these decades. Traditional herbal dyes could produce pale or drab colors, but the highly attractive and expensive *azzurrato*—azure or ultramarine, an intense deep blue—was very dear and hard to obtain; it was forbidden to all in the 1355 sumptuary law of Florence.[70] Ultramarine became the mark of the century from the moment Giotto first introduced deep blue as his background color. Venetians further set off *azzurrato* by contrasting it with gold in mosaics and for decoration. Upon visiting Venice in 1384 Lionardo di Frescobaldi remarked on seeing "a room of gold, that is, decorated with fine gold and ultramarine blue"; he was dazzled by the sight.[71]

In retranslating Cennino Cennini's *Il libro dell'arte*, Daniel V. Thompson notes that an older translation into English had missed the changed meaning of *violante* in fourteenth-century text. By Cennini's day, about 1390, the term no longer meant a degree of force but instead a color: violet or a pale shade of purple.[72] Deep reds from imported kermes in contrast to the orange red produced from the dye called *grana* became a component of the dyer's repertoire by the end of the century.[73] Violet and a clear, intense, dark red joined the articulated palette where simple designations of primary colors no longer sufficed. *Biavo* (pale blue) was not *paonazzo* or a purple blue that required baths in both blue and red, nor was it *perso*, or dark blue, or *sbiavato*, dull blue-gray, much less *azzurrato*, the wildly popular and expensive bright and deep luminous blue so loved by Venetians. Consumers were schooled in making careful distinctions about shade, and, as a result, educated buyers became discriminating consumers in markets. This is evident in their newly expanded nomenclature for color. *Festeshin*, or nut brown, was a far different thing from less appealing shades of drab brown and thus was awarded its own descriptive name, while gray and shades of black were distinguished from each other.[74] Nothing matched the rich reds and purples in splendor or expense, however. From the folios of the Florentine Prammatica of 1343 Laurence Gérard-Marchant has prized out a remarkably rich code of color for red hues: *rubeus* or *ruber, scarlattus, scarlattinus, scarlattinus minutus* (none of these three to be confused with the fabric in different hues, which might also be identified by variants of these last three terms), *vemilius, afiamatus* (flamboyant), *sanguinus, cardinalescus, porporus, porporinus, violatus, pagonazus* (violet), *colore rossico, incarnatus, pili leonis* (tawny), *rosellinus,* and *rancius* (orange).[75] There was also *amuscato*, marked with dark spots of muscat (from the Persian gulf port?), a wine color.[76] Giovanni Conversino, who was attached to the chancery at Padua and a humanist who kept in touch with Venetian men of letters, believed that order and proportion in paintings corresponded to virtue, while color signified wealth. The association of rich color with luxury was fixed in the minds of many and would prove to be enduring and potent.[77]

Art historians of the early Renaissance continually caution that cultural objects are not restricted in their meanings; when they are borrowed and employed in a new context they may signify entirely new things. In Giovanni Boccaccio's first fiction, *Caccia di Diana*, stags were transformed into men when they plunged into water and reappeared clad in vermilion cloaks.[78] A bit of colorful Turkish carpet in an Italian painting drew resonance from the audience's knowledge of the object as desirable, luxurious, and exotic in origin; it had lost its meaning as an aid to Muslim prayer, if indeed it had ever held that connotation for Italians. When Gentile de Fabriano (1370–1442) painted vivid embroidery bordering the Virgin's robe in his *Adoration of the Magi*, there may be read the first words of the Muslim profession of faith: there is no God but God; nothing but a simple reference to the fabric's exotic origin was intended.[79] In earlier decades Simone Martini, Andrea di Cione, and Bernardo Daddi had developed special techniques for depicting imported luxury textiles.[80] Imagining the audience for the great age of painting and fresco that began in the fourteenth century as discriminating in perception of color, motif, exotic pattern, and foreign materials is to imagine them as urbane people newly schooled in provenance, in shade and intensity of color; they were men fully capable of assigning meaning to new elements of fashion and to the new descriptive color palette mentioned above that had entered into the vocabulary. Broad palettes of color were described variously in inventories, in lists of goods for sale, and in sumptuary law, and, of course, they may still be observed today in surviving paintings and frescoes. Luxury wares in vivid hues were scrutinized, handled, judged, and possessed (or not, as with forbidden ultramarine blue in Florence); their presence in markets had the capacity to change public sensibilities.

From the vantage point of trade, the first decades of the fourteenth century were consequential in establishing a more fashion-conscious consuming public because of a conjuncture of influences. As Chapter 7 argues, the marketing of precious wares was piggybacked on banking and financial networks. Florentine banks supported a diaspora of merchant bankers who presented luxury goods in courts and cities across Europe. Venice possessed highly integrated investment and bullion markets that attracted investors to the Rialto from all over Italy and beyond the Alps. Banking customers were tempted by a wide variety of luxury goods sometimes displayed on bankers' benches; they might take away earned interest in the form of luxury goods. Minting gold as the currency of long-distance trade freed available stores of newly mined silver, the basis of currency in earlier decades, for use in fabrication of luxury wares. Trade routes to sources of exotic Levantine goods were traversed. At home domestic output of fabric and the development of specialized manufacture of luxury wares made consumption goods, even ready-made goods, more widely available.

It should be noted as well that the aesthetic revolution of the fifteenth century, which would dampen the public's enthusiasm for gilt, brilliant hues, and garish effects, had yet to arrive. Michael Baxandall has argued that in time, a shift away from the gilt splendor of the fourteenth century would occur: "While precious pigments become less prominent [in the fifteenth century], a demand for pictorial skill becomes more so."[81] He restricts this claim about a more refined aesthetic, noting the shift away from garish effects was selective—the fashions of Philip the Fair of Burgundy and Alfonso of Naples remained as lush as ever—but nonetheless fashions would change for many urban people. New, more subdued fashions brought austere black to the fore and to an extent diminished interest in azure and gilt. But fourteenth-century consumers were as yet blithely unaware of the refinements in taste that lay ahead; indeed, consumers were just beginning to appreciate the opportunity to own, wear, or display their bit of gilt splendor and ultramarine blue. *Le pompe,* more widely available on markets, attracted consumers who gave every appearance of enjoying all the bright and gaudy objects they could accumulate.

On the other hand, the first decades of the fourteenth century were not remarkable for any single innovation that can account for the advent of fashion and heightened consumption. Most of the techniques in the production of luxury products had been known for decades, if not centuries, and certainly imported luxuries were not new. Murano crystal, which permitted the manufacture of gilt-backed mirrors, had yet to appear; *jaune à l'argent,* a silver stain used to modulate tones of white to yellow in stained glass, was introduced about 1300 but its influence was largely restricted to the traditional ecclesiastical market for glazing church windows. By about 1300 enamels could be made in cheaper versions and were therefore more widely available, but *basse taille* and *en ronde basse,* favored techniques of the century, came into wider use only; they were not startling new technology.[82] Goldsmiths demonstrated brilliant engineering in the pivots, buckles, and other moving parts of the consumer goods they manufactured, but for the most part they improved on old designs rather than inventing new ones. Most stylistic elements popular in the fourteenth century had been known earlier, before the turn to fashion became a major topic for social critics. Fourteenth-century markets were flooded not necessarily with new products but with more products of greater variety in design and with greater differentiation in cost to the consumer.

The decorations Giotto di Bondone had employed in his *Expulsion of Joachim from the Temple,* that is, borders on robes and set-in sleeves, appear to have been important stimuli for trade. To create trim or borders on cloth, gold or silver could be stamped onto fabric. Thin ribbons woven with gold or silver thread, or both, could be sewn on garments as trims. Fur could be added as border and another contrasting fabric could be used: for example, a heavy cut velvet border would add substantial weight and dignity when affixed to the hem of a lighter wool or silk garment. Jewels or "false" jewels could be used. Combinations of these features were possible, with a cloth border further outlined by a ribbon woven with gold and silver thread. It was possible to affix plaques of precious metals to a garment as a border; these might be studded with jewels or semi-precious stones. Borders themselves could be sewn with pearls or *veriselli e gioie false,* that is, counterfeit stones.[83] Borders could be used everywhere: on hems, on sleeves, outlining armholes, at necklines, on hoods, down the edges of front-opening garments, under rows of buttons—the possibilities seem endless. Trims and borders might add significantly to the value of a garment, and some textiles like those found in Marco Polo's shop could be purchased with trims already in place. Borders and trims bestowed dignity and flair, and sumptuary laws restricted their use among women and youth.

In the earliest surviving sumptuary law of Venice, composed in 1299, wearing *frexatura perlarum,* a border embroidered with pearls, was forbidden to women; this was no passing whim of the legislators, nor subject to one prohibition only. The fashion was probably similar to the *frixis* forbidden to the women of Bologna a few years earlier.[84] The Venetian sumptuary law of 1334 also forbade the wearing of *frexatura de perlis.* This law was highly controversial, which led to its retraction in 1339, but with provisos, one of which specified that *frexatura de perlis* were still forbidden to women, as were *drezatores perlarum* (rich ornaments with pearls) woven into the hair. Venetian wives and daughters continued to be restricted from wearing the fashion of borders, with their intimations of dignity and magnificence. This prolonged period of restriction on women's borders allowed the affectation to become a masculine prerogative at Venice, which contemporary paintings, mosaics, and frescoes confirm.[85]

With the good fortune to remain unrestrained in sumptuary law, Venetian men wore a wide variety of borders on their clothes, especially on the long and voluminous robes designed for public occasions. A heavy border that caused a garment to sway in a stately fashion as a man walked enhanced his fine, extravagantly cut garment through falling to the ground in deep, voluminous folds. Donor portraits, artistic renderings of state occasions, as well as an entire repertoire of biblical scenes depict men with borders on their clothes while, over the decades, borders on gowns and cloaks of women saints diminish and sometimes disappear altogether (see plate 13). The Virgin Mary retained her magnificent borders, but as the century progressed artists frequently omitted this opulent border trim from women's apparel (see plate 3).[86]

Along with borders, new lengths for robes became a topic of public debate. In Venice, the sumptuary law deliberations of 1334 made a special point of discussing trains, which both men and women had adopted according to the fashion of the day. Ser Thomaso Soranzo introduced a measure onto the floor of the Great Council in 1334 that all women's trains should be limited to one *bracchia* (about 68 centimeters), certainly a modest display given the long dragging trains popular at the time.[87] Women's use of trains, one of a number of fashions that could be labeled superfluous (that very term figured in the law), was restricted, and women's trains continued to be a matter of concern in subsequent exercise of sumptuary control. With restrictions on trims, trains, and borders, women's apparel was subjected to supervision by civil authorities with one unmistakable outcome: men's public apparel gained a near monopoly on certain markers of dignity and wealth. Contemporaneously the cult of the Magi endorsed long flowing trains and rich borders as masculine markers of prestige, linking power and authority to the visual drama of dragging valuable fabrics along the ground (see frontispiece).

Fastenings

Fastenings, like trims and borders on garments, underwent a comparable proliferation in the early fourteenth century, and perhaps the most acute observer of the century commented on the fashion for tight fit and precious fastenings. In the *Paradiso* of the *Divine Comedy*, Dante Alighieri (1265–1321) contrasted the peace, sobriety, and rectitude of traditional Florence in his ancestor Cacciaguidi's generation to that of the present day. He chose to make his contrast through reference to the fastenings and embellishments on garments, by which a man almost shrank to insignificance in the welter of his own finery:

Non avea catenalla, non corona,
non gonne contigiate, non cintura
che fosse a veder più che la persona.

(There was no necklace, no coronal, no embroidered gowns, no girdle that was more to be looked at than the person.)[88] Dante criticized men's garb, addressing the leaders of his beloved Florence. While modern understandings of fashion as women's domain have feminized gown, there should be no mistaking that Dante's censure of *gonne contigiate* was directed toward men. *Gonne* or *gonella* referred to distinctive long robes that men would shorten as the century progressed. With the possible exception of coronals, the fashions Dante singled out were all elements of men's wardrobes.[89] The long embroidered gown set off by a belt and an ornament for the neck was the preferred style for mature men of his day and this ensemble represented street wear. Again, there was little that was identifiably new in the buttons, buckles, pins, brooches, chains, or belts worn as components of this ensemble, but their variety, number, and value had increased. The established cloth trades, associated leather workers, *pelliparii* (furriers), and other trades experienced an increase in demand, but it could hardly match the heights of the new demand placed upon goldsmiths and jewelers. *Orafi* or *aurifici* (goldsmiths) were caught up in consumer production that began to orient them away from producing sacred objects and toward fabricating secular goods (see Chapter 6).

In Dante's discerning eye, an ensemble of fashion goods marked the turn to fashion. Embroidery on a gown, rather than the gown itself, earned his displeasure, and luxury details in belts, hats, headdresses, and neck ornaments created the startling new fashionable look he deplored. New fashions for men, whether in long trimmed robes or shorter tunics, relied on a snug fit at the waist or hips. Belts, pins, and buttons created that fit, aided by the new trend of cutting fabric and sewing to size. Sleeves were sewn in and could be fitted at the shoulder, elbow, or wrist; they were worn in easily exchangeable pairs for tunics or long gowns, sometimes incised to pull through an undergarment into a poof, but even sleeves failed to receive the emphasis lavished on the waistline in the new fashionable silhouette. Belts created definition for garments, and while the belt might be, as had been true previously, a simple knotted or buckled strip of leather, increasingly belts were made of precious materials. A silk belt with alternating gilded silver plaques, probably cast in molds because the plaques are identical, has survived in the Treasure of Colmar.[90] This cache stored away by a Jewish family, probably a family fearing persecution in a plague year, dates to sometime between the late thirteenth century and the middle of the fourteenth century. Connected by a fragment of woven silk ribbon, the gilded plaques featured alternating motifs of a woman's face and a flower; this belt is a rare surviving example of the popular fashion of the day.[91] A silver gilt belt, identified as the Baden-Baden belt, of alternating plaques of the letter A and a lion, sports a similar motif.[92] The majority of the belts described in inventories, commissions, sales, and sumptuary laws were made of precious metals. Their frequent mention and detailed descriptions in notarial records suggest that belts were the signature item of a man's—or sometimes a woman's—fashionable attire; they epitomized fourteenth-century fashion.

Inventories as Evidence

Paintings, frescoes, and literature must speak for popular fourteenth-century articles of fashion like great belts because few survive, but inventories, sales, and commissions provide their own ample evidence for belts' widespread popularity. Notarized inventories help in analysis here as well. In recording possessions, two parties or more concurred on descriptions of goods and provided a price valuation, if possible. The notary was identified in the preamble of the document, his itemization was organized, and the resulting descriptions, while formulaic, were qualified and sometimes fleshed out by notations. Notaries provide clues where they failed to complete a line in a simple omission (perhaps due to uncertainty, disagreement, or failure in descriptive powers); these are particularly revealing in some instances. Reducing private possessions to a simple orderly list was a difficult task, and, in the attempt, information distinguishing among many variants of fashion may be found.

Early inventories have come into their own as historical evidence. Drawing on inventories of 461 estates recorded from 1610 to 1680, John Michael Montias collected 1,224 inventories in which evidence on art may be found in 617.[93] They give terse descriptions at best, but when combined with charters, guild and city records, and biographical information on artists like Johannes Ver Meer (1632–75) and his various patrons, Montias was able to piece together the increasing social consequence of collecting art in seventeenth-century Delft. More recently, Dora Thornton employed inventories to understand the cultivation of Renaissance scholarly pursuits in *A Scholar in His Study*. Isabella Palumbo-Fossati used inventories to identify the furnishings of fifteenth-century Venetian palaces, and Maria Giuseppina Muzzarelli has specified the garments in late medieval wardrobes by using inventories.[94] These records help scholars calculate cost-of-living figures. The inventories of fourteenth-century Italy lack both the quantity and descriptive power of later runs, but they are a valuable and often underutilized source for studying demand and the role played by new patterns of consumption.

A bundle of charters from 1380 that provides an inventory for a gift that Madonna Margherita di Vanni degli Spini, widow of Niccola Acciaiuoli, gave to a Carthusian church makes careful distinctions among the donor's many possessions. Once distributed to the church, the largely secular, domestic, and personal articles listed in the inventory would be sold or melted down rather than worn or used.[95] Belts were carefully distinguished from each other: "Item, una cintura d'ariento isprangata, all'arma degli acciaiuoli" (Item, one banded silver belt, with the arms of the Acciaiuoli). Most likely this was a linked silver belt decorated with reiterated bands, also of silver. The arms of the family were likely affixed to the buckle, or they may have been engraved directly on the buckle if it was large. Or perhaps the arms were worked with filigree or *niello* and then studded with stones or gems.[96] "Item, una cintura conispraghe d'aruenti orata, istrema" (Item, one belt with gilded silver bands, long and narrow) followed. This was probably a long belt of the style that fell toward the floor or was wrapped around the body more than once. Gilding was probably applied as gold laminate by placing a thin sheet of gold over a sheet of silver and hammering, what Italians called *ora de metà*, and this gilt would be thin and could show tarnish from the silver beneath.[97] Other methods of gilding were more enduring but they required more gold, and gold was frugally employed in articles of wear.

Wear or tarnish would not mean that a luxury item was discarded—it maintained its value because it could be melted down and some of its value recovered. Indeed, that was the intent behind this inventoried gift: the church received an endowment in the worldly goods of a wealthy woman and the silver would be melted down and refashioned for ecclesiastical uses, if not sold. Perhaps more to the point, the notary and Brother Giovanni, listed as prior of the foundation, overseer of the inventory and recipient, had to agree on the description and differentiate the various listed items. There were, for example, over twenty belts in the gift. While individual valuations were not employed in this inventory the two belts described above were more costly than "1 cintura di chuoio con bocchola et puntale d'argiento" (one leather belt with a buckle and tongue of silver). There were also five *cintole di perle con ispranghe d'ariento orate e ismaltate* (belts of "pearls" with bands of gilded and enameled silver), a *cintoletta con nachere* (small belt with mother-of-pearl), and two other *cintole con fette verdi e fibbie d'ariento* (belts with strips of green and a fibia or pin of silver), which were made of cloth or on a cloth base, likely silk, with a silver buckle.[98] Those who drew up the inventory had to have some degree of consumer sophistication to evaluate such luxury items. In stretching their own powers of description, they reveal the complex choices that fashion brought wealthy consumers for the simple task of fastening their clothes at the waist.

The issue of the size of belts or girdles designed for men raises questions. In Ragusa/Dubrovnik, silver belts that were traded to visiting merchants or sent to Venice to be marketed could reach substantial weights. Not all traveled west; one of the grandest was commissioned for Emporer Dusan, ruler of Serbia, who ordered it along with a silver *nef* (also called a *ladica*). The two together required 13 pounds, 5 ounces of silver (there were 328 grams in the Ragusan pound).[99] A substantial *nef* weighed 5–10 pounds so the belt was a hefty one and certainly fit for a king. A belt of filament silver from 1313, one which was further decorated with raised work, weighed in at a prodigious 11 pounds according to the record, and cost over 70 ducats.[100] Some of that weight may have been in precious or semi-precious stones like coral and rock crystal; regardless, the object borders on the unimaginable. Another belt: "Unum Centrum de argent in aureate ponders libbre trigunta una et on. octa" (one belt of gilded silver weighing 31 pounds and 8 ounces) was too weighty for belief; the notary likely misstated 30 for 13.[101] Other belts of lesser size could be fabricated, but they would not compete with great, hinged belts in grandeur.[102] Even when weights were not specified but price was, two belts at 88½ ducats would be composed of a substantial amount of bulk silver.[103] When a customer did not commission the article, wares described in the records of the chancellory were likely intended for sale on the open market as ready-made goods: for example, sixteen belts ordered at one time, or twelve belts along with cups, silver necklaces, and other articles studded with stones.[104] Purchasers would have to be confident enough to wear their wealth about their waists, and they had to be men who found some advantage in doing so.

Cheap copies abounded. A copper belt with silver trim sold for a small fraction of the price of great silver belts.[105] Another belt described as "white" probably contained more lead than silver, while an order for 14 pounds of belts at 145 ducats, while a substantial investment, might yield many belts, even if they were silver gilt and featured "pearls" (in some cases glass paste or false pearls).[106] In 1324, Marco Polo's will left six fine belts to his heirs, one of silver, one of fine silver (silver of finer grade), and others of green silk *darzento,* that is, decorated with silver thread or possibly stamped with silver.[107] These represent typical gradations of value. Some orders for fabricated silver at Ragusa took the form of commissions for anticipated export, most likely to Venice, but local merchants and foreigners visiting the port of Ragusa bought their own share of precious accessories that varied in price.

Great heft characterized the belts sold in the Adriatic region, while the Sienese produced beautifully crafted silver gilt belts of fine design but lesser weight. These relied on a flexible silver thread over silk ribbon sleeve, which was then studded with gilded and enameled plaques, linked onto a metal buckle, and a fed-through belt tongue (see fig. 2). A Sienese belt over ninety inches long (238 centimeters) like the beautifully intact Cleveland belt would weigh in at considerably less than the massive linked belts of silver that came out of the Balkans (see plate 5).[108] Both versions of expensive belts flourished over the century; Ilse Fingerlin's thorough cataloguing of medieval belts crafted of precious metal suggests both styles continued in popularity for many decades—the long and sinuous (Sienese) and the short and hefty (Adriatic).

Great belts were not new to consumers. In an early inventory from Genoa dated December 1238, the two heirs of Nicoloso Nepitella received "Item cinturas duas argenti arbitratas lb. tres" (Item, two worked silver belts weighing three pounds [employing a Genoese light pound of 316.97 grams]).[109] These belts had not reached the proportions of some of the later fourteenth-century versions, but they were clearly fine embellished work from a goldsmith's shop and very precious. They stand as yet another indication that what has often been understood to be a new trend like belts of precious metal was not in fact new at all. However, the greater availability of decorated silver belts, their diversity of design and weight, and the use of other precious or semi-precious materials like gilt, enamel, jewels, or mother-of-pearl for embellishment indi-

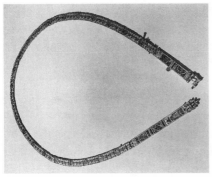

Figures 2 a, b, c. Cleveland silver gilt belt (girdle), Siena, fourteenth century, full length and two details. Brilliantly designed and executed, this belt is 90.75 inches (230.5 centimeters) in length; it has one shelf hook and two quatrefoil rings. The buckle is composed of a brace open at the top, a tang or buckle pin, and two oblong, enameled plaques. The tongue is composed of three enameled plaques (see detail). There are 27 large round enamels depicting musicians, courtly figures, and animals, spaced over the length of the belt. These are set off by 59 small enamel portraits and designs. Holes, which show wear, are set in the belt at about 36 inches along its length. After this the large enamels reorient their figures so they will appear upright as the belt tongue descends toward the ground. Courtesy of the Cleveland Museum of Art.

cate that waist fastenings increased in popularity and variety, reaching a crescendo of sorts in the fourteenth century.

And when great belts acquired their less formal designation, *zonas,* there is further indication of increased popularity. *Zonas* was the term applied to silver belts from Ragusa when they were sold on the Venetian market (on one occasion illegally, since the mandated fifth of its weight had not been turned in to the mint, in a fine recorded in 1344).[110] In Milan Galvano Fiamma condemned women wearing gold (or gilded) *zonas.*[111] *Zonas* were found in the Florentine sumptuary law of 1355, in which great belts were restricted in weight for men for the first time.[112] Henry Knighton used the term *zonas* to pinpoint the offensive fashion that masculinized English women at local tournaments.[113] The great Sienese goldsmith Giovanni di Bartolo made *zonas* for his clientele at Avignon.[114] Goldsmiths fabricated *zonas* at Bologna. *Zonas* appeared in donor portraits and in sculpture, painting, and fresco—they were subject to fines and criticism—they had become the rage. Military men favored them: from about 1360, according to Francis Kelly and Randolph Schwabe, the low-slung belt, or *cingulum militare,* which could be referred to in everyday speech as *zona,* was the most characteristic feature of military costume. This would remain true until the middle years of the following century.[115]

But why *zonas* as the everyday term for a man's belt? As François Garnier argues in *Le langage de l'image au Moyen Age, II grammaire des gestes,* belts signified a woman's virginity in a *topos* familiar to medieval audiences, and it was frequently represented in genre art by a long sinuous type of belt.[116] Ancient Romans understood the *zona* as a maiden's girdle that symbolized her virginity, but nevertheless men also wore *zonas* as money belts. While the term accumulated more generic meanings over the Classical Age, it never entirely lost its association with a maiden's purity. In fourteenth-century Tuscany the *sacra cintola* (sacred belt) figured in the iconography of the Madonna del Parto or Expectant Virgin, a clear allusion to her immaculate condition.[117] A venerated relic of the *sacra cintola* was housed at Santo Stefano in Prato and credited with many miracles that assured its fame. In the later Renaissance, a belt or girdle still retained a link with women's sexuality at marriage, although it had become both a backward-looking and a forward signifier by this time, suggesting a maiden's virginity and her future child-bearing capacities simultaneously.[118] With this heavy burden of symbolism, the simple term *cintola* would appear less fraught and preferable as a common or everyday word for men's great belts, but *zonas,* in its more generic sense, won the day.

Great belts were not worn on otherwise unadorned garments; they figured as part of a rich ensemble. With belts went purses or knives in sheaths with worked silver handles (*cuslerios*) attached by cunning small hooks to the belt itself.[119] Gems could be studded onto the hilts of knives or worked into leather sheaths; this practice was widely embraced in early fourteenth-century Italy. Henry Knighton found decorative silver daggers hanging from belts a particularly odious affect. Great linked chains of silver holding pectorals or medallions complemented great belts. As with other articles of men's apparel, great chains with or without pendants were traditional ornaments. In Genoa in 1259, a wealthy spice merchant left among his possessions a silver medallion with one red stone, four green stones, and four pearls or *margheritas* set in it.[120] The notary's care to pen a precise description of this jeweled artifact indicates its importance in the estate—and for men, chains and pendants only increased in popularity as the decades passed. Weighty chains with medallions set off the breadth of the shoulders, which were handsomely clad in padded doublets.

Jean de Venette's *Chronicle* entry for 1356 is particularly critical of the scanty but highly embellished garments he found on soldiers. He complained, "Now they began to disfigure themselves in a still more extravagant way. They wore pearls on their hoods and on their gilded and silver girdles and elaborately adorned themselves from head to foot with gems and precious stones. So assiduously did all men, from the least to the greatest, cover themselves with these luxuries that pearls and other precious stones were sold for high prices and could hardly be found at all in Paris."[121] Like gold, pearls and gem supplies could be soaked up by occupying armies. He went on to discuss the prices of gems and pearls to drive home the point.

Buttons served both as fasteners and extraneous ornaments for men. Among the jewels owned by Doge Lorenzo Celsi in 1365 were "maspillas et planetas et alios arzenteos deauratos in uno sacullo ponderis unciarum XXVII" (buttons and plaques and other gilded silver wares in a sack weighing 27 ounces).[122] It was not unusual for buttons to be ordered in sets, like the four dozen buttons ordered in 1345 for 3½ ducats at Ragusa.[123] Buttons were engraved in matched sets and worn as fasteners on the front or employed in a purely ornamental fashion on sleeves where they ran in a row from shoulder to wrist (at least for men; women could only wear buttons to the elbow in Florence). Buttons might be ordered by the dozen or in smaller sets like the four buttons adorned with silver filigree that accompanied a large order of a belt, silver cups, necklaces, knives, bracelets, and gold rings in 1327.[124]

For men, an ensemble was completed by these touches: a costume might include rich trimmed and layered outer garments, an inner robe over trousers, great belts with purses or knives, and chains with medallions. Rings, buttons, and jeweled collars might also add to the ensemble. Only hats or hoods remained to be embellished and they took on new contours as well, or were at times studded with trims like silver *lettere*. Not only were hats adorned with rich materials, but they appeared to critics to change shape with remarkable speed. Sumptuary laws often singled out women's headdresses as objects of unseemly ostentation but men's hats were also transformed into exotic fashions like turbans or wound and tasseled hoods. Rather than reflecting the distinctive style of a town or region, hats now represented trends that swept across Italy so that no man was distinguishable from any other by native dress; all, apparently, followed the latest fad.[125]

Women followed men headlong into fashion whenever they were allowed to do so. They wore borders if they could, they wore belts, they wore bangles, crowns, brooches, ornaments in their hair, and buttons, and they carried worked purses. They wanted rich fabrics, borders, trims, and trains, if they could get away with it. They were as avid for new fashions as men if the wedding gifts accompanying dowries are any indication. But what they wore did not measure up to men's consumption in weight and price despite their efforts. A small silver crown, suitable for a woman's head and worked with gold, cost a mere four ducats in 1329.[126] Crowns (*coronae*) or circlets were constructed out of as little as four ounces of silver, and a *corona alba* (white crown, probably lead in part) could be had for two ducats in 1348.[127] In running athwart sumptuary law with a new fashion, Franco Sacchetti informs us facetiously, an astute woman simply passed off her forbidden headgear as a garland (*ghirlanda*), although it might quiver with silver leaves and flowers.[128] The *Ufficiale delle donne*, charged with trying infractions of sumptuary law at Florence, knew how to spot deceptions: the popular circlet worn by Florentine women in the 1340s was labeled a crown in straightforward language (*unam cororam seu cerchiellum*) because it was made of silver gilt.[129]

In 1333, Venetians set a limit on the full complement of jewelry women might wear at thirty ducats. Sales records indicate that a man might spend thirty ducats on one great silver belt, as did the Florentine bank factor Duccio Puccii, who worked in Venice, when he bought a silver belt at Ragusa for thirty ducats. This is not to argue that women always obeyed sumptuary laws—clearly they did not—but the laws provide an indication of the range that leaders found appropriate for spending on a woman's wardrobe, and this figure may be compared with what men spent on articles for their wardrobes. While it would be misleading to assume that the availability of luxury goods on the market followed prescriptive formulae in the law, these comparisons provide useful information on emerging notions of a hierarchy for consumption. In laws the allotments for luxuries allowed to women were generous when compared to the cost of living in cities, but money spent in luxury markets suggests that men consumed significantly more in terms of precious materials (see Chapter 5).[130]

The ensemble and its parts—desirable wares all—acted as a stimulus for consumption. There were almost limitless variations a skilled craftsman might work with silver, gold, silks, gems, semi-precious stones, and glass paste shaped into pearls, not to mention the variations that clothiers, furriers, and leather workers might craft with fine imported textiles and well-woven Italian cloth. Artisans learned to accommodate customers with differing tastes and capacities to spend; cheaper versions of most fashionable articles were produced and sold in varying weights and models. Just as a "white" crown might pass for fine silver from a distance, or a decoration of filigree silver be spun out to enhance a belt and make it appear more massive than it really was, a clever artisan could invent tricks to fool the eye. Gilding was by definition an attempt to deceive viewers into an impression of higher value, and many other fashions played comparable tricks. These were ploys that deepened the market for fine wares, and it is apparent from inventory records that notaries struggled diligently to uncover the fake and distinguish the gilt from gold, *veriselli* from the genuine. Authorities in general sought standards by which to judge the real worth of precious wares—weight, perhaps, or fineness, good workmanship, the size and clarity of precious gems, or the town or shop in which it was made. But luxury goods had begun to reveal their inherent capacity to stimulate demand on the market with production of imitations. Luxury marketplaces attracted people who merely gawked and yearned, but somewhere in that market was a clever merchant or a cunning tradesman who was willing to sell "false pearls" of glass paste or leaded silver as substitutes for real gems or fine silver; these wares cost less and they allowed less wealthy customers to join the fashion parade.[131]

As the market deepened dress accessories were produced in less precious materials. Bronze could be gilded and it was a durable product. Dress accessories and domestic plate in base metals proliferated to such an extent that Europe's silted river bottoms were strewn with buckles, purses, and rings of copper, bronze, brass, and pewter that survived; silver goods were less likely to.[132] Bronze smiths and pewterers imitated fashions in luxury accessories so successfully that the varieties of fourteenth-century fashion goods most likely to be dredged up were these durable and cheaper products. Of course there is no guarantee that products of non-precious metal imitated silver and gold fashions. Pins to fasten cloaks and aglets for laces made from base metals were traditional components of medieval wardrobes, and goods of brass or pewter were just as likely to be reinterpreted in silver or gilded silver. Crosscurrents of influence and swift adoption of trade goods popularized in other media characterized production.

Preambles to sumptuary laws suggest the complexity of the new fashionable ensemble with its many desirable parts was censured since it meant confusion in the streets. An artisan's skill at making wares in cheaper versions was only one of a set of perplexing problems introduced by fashionable dress. The newly rich might dress better than men of established name and fortune; a stylish woman appeared suspiciously masculine just by her attempt to be fashionable. It was the ongoing project of fashion—displayed in church, of all places—that offended the bishop of Florence when he issued the earliest sumptuary directives written for Florence.[133] Social critics of the day offered little to explain their umbrage other than that fashionable dress disturbed decorum in the streets. We may speculate that the materials employed in a fashionable wardrobe could find better uses in other venues—but were fourteenth-century critics of fashion alert to that danger? Certainly the cloth used in long robes could clothe two or more if employed less lavishly, and silver used in belts, buttons, and medallions could be minted and circulated so that wages could be paid in a sounder currency. But fourteenth-century critics did not refer to either of those agendas: their words merely chided the well dressed for a lack of decorum, unseemliness, overspending, and impropriety, or in the case of Bishop Biliotti of Florence, gruff counsel that family wealth was better invested elsewhere.[134]

Complaints of a drain of precious metal away from civic mints due to *le pompe* were not voiced in Italy. Nevertheless, the new emphasis on fashion meant that a small urban elite had increased its proportional consumption of scarce precious bullion as well as other costly and fine materials. Henceforth some family wealth would be held in precious wares—fine cloth, silver vessels, utensils, jewels, fastenings, that is, "plate"—a generic term for precious wares. Fashion promoted demand on markets, but it was demand at the highest levels of affluence in towns and it was demand that was only beginning to deepen to include less wealthy consumers. If there was nothing entirely new in fourteenth-century fashion, the increased consequence of fashion itself was a departure, and consumption had begun to figure as a force driving demand.

Chapter 3
Gravitas and Consumption

Men in cities enjoyed being seen in their costly wardrobes, and it was their good fortune that they could indulge their preference for fine dress. In achieving man's estate a fourteenth-century citizen of an Italian town governed by sumptuary ordinances moved beyond the reach of those laws with rare exception. This chapter examines the implications for urban men who remained largely unrestrained in consumption, dress, and display while others—boys and girls, women, and, in synodal law, clergy—came under the surveillance of sumptuary laws.

In 1333 Duccio Puccii, factor of the great merchant banking house of Acciaiuoli of Florence, bought his great silver belt at Ragusa for the stiff price of thirty ducats.[1] It could have been embossed with drawn silver or decorated with gold in any number of cladding processes from beating gold into the surface, spinning out gold thread for an intricate surface design, encrusting the belt with raised designs, or mounting gold settings on it to hold precious stones. Belts of great heft spoke of wealth—who else but the most affluent could afford to carry their riches about their hips?[2] Duccio may have purchased for his employers, and since luxuries like this were saved and passed on, it is possible that this belt turns up later in Madonna Margherita Acciaiuoli's inventory of 1380, years after the purchase and the collapse of the family bank (see plate 5 for this style of great belt).[3]

Duccio Puccii—or perhaps his Acciaiuoli employers—had it both ways in their purchase of luxury wares. They became walking displays of princely apparel and as such they were worthy of emulation by other wealthy and well-born men. Moreover, silver articles were fungible assets; they did not cease to be repositories of value after they were no longer worn. Coming from the Balkans, such a belt was unlikely to possess the typical features of fine Italian trade goods. In Italy such an article would be identified by origin—a respected goldsmith or specific workshop, for example. This belt may not even have possessed identifiable hallmarks, which would be the case if it had been produced in an Italian town, so what recommended this belt was its heft, its design, and possibly the reputation of the Balkans as a source of new mined silver.[4] Neither the belt's weight or fineness was specified in the sales agreement; it could have been gilded, with or without gold trim, and with or without precious gems, enamel work, *intaglio,* coats of arms, and fancy buckles.[5] Belts were sometimes decorated with a reiterated motif like the letter A and a lion, the motif of a surviving fourteenth century example, referred to as the Baden-Baden belt.[6] Fragments of a similarly designed belt, also dating from the fourteenth century, were found among grave goods in Tuzla, in Bosnia.[7] Both the Baden-Baden and Tuzla belts were long and flexible and could be looped around twice or allowed to fall to the ground, but given its origin, Duccio's was more likely a short, wide belt of hinged segments, which would help explain its substantial price. Duccio's purchase was a lavish one for a bank factor.

Duccio Puccii gained a potent symbol of wealth when he purchased his great belt. The famed king and later emperor of Serbia, Dusan, wore his great belt as part of military-inspired regalia befitting a warrior king. Great belts may be observed in fresco on the walls of the Decani monastery in medieval Serbia. At the end of the fourteenth century a Bible of the Czech king Wenceslaus IV was illustrated with a similar great linked belt set off by a long dagger or *corda.* Belts that were buckled and composed of heavy linked segments appear to be eastern European in origin, where mineral wealth underwrote the ambitious policies of local princes. Indeed, Italians came to regard the Eastern kingdoms as treasure troves. Louis, king of Hungary, needed only to march through Italy in 1347, spending his gold coins minted in imitation of the florin, to bring the level of coining at Florence to new heights, as Louis's Hungarian florins were condemned, that is, called in, and reminted. Italians relied on the Eastern kingdoms for bullion, so they might find the impressive military fashions of the East, with their great show of precious metal, attractive and worth imitation, especially when visitors from Hungary and Serbia paraded around in their fine regalia in Italy's city streets.[8]

At the pinnacle of urban society costume was an exotic amalgam of foreign influences. Walter of Brienne, serving as Florentine *conservatore del popolo,* brought some French or ultramontane military fashions to Florence in the 1340s. Villani notes that Spanish military styles arrived in Milan and Rome at about the same time: indeed military-inspired fashions from all corners of fourteenth-century Europe influenced urban taste.[9] Muslim and Tartar military gear entered from the East, and ideas were introduced from as far away as China. Metal distributed generously around the body became an important component of Italian style, and since there were precedents in the traditional military costume of virtually all the lands neighboring Italy, the distillation of a new look out of borrowed elements was perhaps the only distinctive element of these "new" fourteenth-century fashions.[10]

As the century progressed mature men's long full robes were shortened to fall in folds to halfway between the ankle and the knee. And in the later decades of the century young men adopted very short tight-fitting tunics, laced onto long hose, sometimes covered by capes.[11] Great belts and other fastenings

Figure 3. Altichiero da Zavio, *Council of King Ramiro.* Chapel of Bonifacio Lupi, the Santo, Padua. King Ramiro is surrounded by councilors dressed in fourteenth-century fashions, with each costume and headdress carefully differentiated from the rest. Art Resource, N.Y.

remained important, and a highly dramatic display of ornamental weapons continued to be fashionable. Bonifacio Lupi, donor with his wife of a chapel in the Santo at Padua, in 1373–79, was portrayed in fresco in full military costume, befitting a man with a long career as a soldier. In contrast to his quietly dressed wife, whose sober figure is a study in unobtrusiveness, Lupi is gauntleted, booted, helmeted, and equipped with a long sword. He wears mail and a great belt on his hips as he kneels. His garments are eye-catching, as is the dress of the assembled councilors of King Ramiro drawn on the east wall of the chapel. Each councilor is robed in voluminous folds of fabric; each portrait face is set off by distinctive headgear ranging through many styles of hoods to tasseled and banded caps, or combinations of hoods and hats. These are not sedate figures, nor are they understated in their finery although their arresting portraits speak of gravity and authority (see fig. 3).[12] In Guariento di Arpo's *Angelic Orders,* figures richly dressed in God's own livery wear distinctive buckled and gilded belts, the only unique features in otherwise identical equipages, dress, and crowns (see plate 5).[13]

Gravity and authority meant color and ornamentation in masculine dress. "One tunic and a mantle of light colored twill trimmed with needle-work, pearls, voile, and other furnishings" were probably a matched set and by no means plain.[14] "Buttons and plaques and other gilded silver pieces in a sack weighing 28 ounces" belonged to the Doge Lorenzo Celsi in 1365, along with numerous jewels and a fine, varied collection of *birette* fit for all of a doge's ceremonial occasions. Jewels and other accessories brought elaborate surface decoration to the doge's fine ensembles.[15] Various shades of reds, greens, yellows, and blues appeared in men's wardrobes in brilliant displays of color. Among hats, hose, and purses, bright color and gilt were entirely accept-able, if detailed inventories are any indication.

Ostentatious display attempts to impress but may be rewarded with deri-sion. Franco Sacchetti gives one military affectation, the wearing of neck armor or gorgets, humorous treatment in his engaging Novella 178. When Gio-vanni and Piero walk out in Verona to admire, and be admired, by the local women, they are mocked for their Florentine fashion of wearing gorgets. Sac-chetti implicated all Florentines when he explained why the hapless gorget-clad Giovanni stubbed his toe on a stone: "Now we have our fashion of wear-ing these gorgets, within which our necks are held so stiffly that we cannot even look upon our feet, and we are held up to ridicule on account of them."[16] At this point in his tale Sacchetti digresses into other comments on the fash-ions of the day: problems with stiff sleeves, going without cloaks, the rise in popularity of long hair among youths, the twisting of hoods into caps, and maidens going around in collars or with strings about the neck. Florentines may be the most fashion-conscious people in the world, and they readily adopted military costume, but Sacchetti notes that in Genoa, Venice, and Cat-alonia, in fact throughout the entire Christian world, people are dressed in the same fashions, and on top of that the fashions change every day. The earlier tone of light derision, where Giovanni and Piero throw off their gorgets and catch colds while their friend Salvestro, who does not throw off his, drops his dinner of very hot beans down his neck and burns himself, ends in a brief but pointed diatribe on fashion and draws out the anticipated moral: "O vanagloria dell'umane posse, che per te si perde la vera gloria" (O vainglory of human powers, true glory is lost through you).

But Sacchetti changed his tone and his moral message in Novella 179. He begins, "In the last story I spoke of feminine vanity," which was true to a point, but the main subject of satire in Novella 178 had been gorgets, a male fashion. Next he briefly mentions women's fashions, prompting him to explain that the whole world has gone mad for fashion, recalling the conven-tion of the day that women were truly the vainglorious sex. Deflecting the reader's attention away from men's project of being fashionable. he fixes the greater blame on women's "natural" proclivity for excess. Sacchetti may poke fun at men for following fashion, but he cannot bring himself to blame men for their efforts to follow a popular trend like the new military look.

The link between men's worldly authority and fashionable dress prevailed among the powerful in cities. Local processions, ceremonies, carnivals, and saints' days inspired descriptions in chroniclers' and travelers' accounts. European princes took great care to present themselves in elegant and updated ensembles; as a result display drew on Italian models. Visual markers of authority were becoming more consequential everywhere, and if consumers at distances from Italy were willing to spend their wealth freely on Italian wares and fashions popular in Italy, then perhaps there was a basis for the Venetians' complaint that there were extraordinary luxuries and higher expenses in their own city, "more than in all other parts of the world."[17] A cynosure for all who could afford luxury and were inclined to buy—the grave, wise men of Venice knew they possessed a potent asset in their luxury markets, one that required cultivation but also careful monitoring.

Pilgrimages to the Holy Land passed through Venice, tempting one journal keeper to comment on the treasures found there before undertaking the sea voyage east. After visiting numerous relics, the pilgrim Lionardo di Niccolo Frescobaldi noted many French pilgrims who, like he, outfitted themselves with Venetian clothes for the long voyage. Frescobaldi was careful to equip himself with not only books of the Gospels but also "silver cups and other delicate things." He also procured a strong chest in which to carry these wares. While in Venice, he visited the home of Remigi Soranzi: "his house appeared a house of gold, and he had many rooms in which little was to be seen except gold and azure; the house cost him twelve thousand florins, and afterwards he had spent on it a good three thousand."[18] When accounts of this nature circulated, Venice appeared a veritable treasure house.

The urban citizen's projection of a stately, almost regal, persona through dress connoted both a sense of self as an equal to crowned heads in dignity, and a canny hunch that customers do not buy without some demonstration of how fine goods convey messages about status. Given thirty-ducat belts and exquisite fabrics in men's wardrobes, it is not difficult to imagine a wealthy urban citizen wearing one hundred ducats (or florins) of value on his back. In the interests of newly consequential luxury trades the *savii* (wise leaders) of Venice and the *buonhomini* (good leaders) of Florence graced the piazzas and street corners of Italian cities, demonstrating to the world the different ways in which a high condition might be conveyed by clothes. Great merchants were the best agents to deliver this message, because they had experience of royal courts where they donned their own best attire, a successful method for promoting sales; it was a triumph for "merchant princes" to instruct kings in the art of costume and fashion. The idea that a king should dress so that he appeared the quintessence of regality—and that this should extend beyond ceremonial robes of state as seen on coins and seals and affect all his daily routines—was best conveyed by an example of rich dressing. The export market for Italian goods rested on royal and other highborn customers' dressing to a high standard, especially when that required many changes of fine dress.

Under these circumstances it does not stretch credulity to imagine that in cities the most magnificently and prominently attired of all consumers were the wise, grave leaders. In public display they outshone the younger men of their families and their female kin; a message was encoded in their public dress that noble wares denoted a noble condition. Growing into man's estate was celebrated by donning the most luxurious fabrics and finest accessories in a display likely to impress younger men, or for that matter the public at large. Even if young men were more flamboyant in dress than mature men, reaching mature years was marked by ever more opulent wardrobes since men continued to purchase fine goods over a lifetime. Precious and exotic goods had always carried messages about worth: silver, gold, and jewels as well as relics encased in the most precious materials graced important churches and cathedrals. Scripture was bound in gem-studded silver and gold covers and as with Quedlinberg's Gospel of Samuhel, which was written in gold ink, linked precious bullion to God's very words. Magnificence was fit for kings as well. By the fourteenth century, great rulers possessed purchasing power that vied with that of traditional ecclesiastical customers, even the pope at Avignon. Given the evanescence of temporal power and the recycling of stored wealth that often accompanied shifts in power, kings might become better customers than churchmen.[19] With enthusiastic promotion of the theme of the Three Kings, Italians created an ever closer link between themselves and the most powerful and splendid princes of Europe. In encouraging the cult of the Magi, prominent leaders in cities dressed like kings, asserting that they, too, were a kind of royalty by virtue of their wealth and position at the pinnacle of urban society in sovereign states lacking monarchs.[20]

Over the course of the fourteenth century Italian artists faced a unique iconographic challenge in depicting the increasingly popular legend of the Three Kings for civic patrons.[21] From the school of Giotto's *Adoration of the Magi* in 1306, to Alticherio and Avanzi's *Adoration* from later in the century, and on to the carved ivory altarpiece of the Certosa di Pavia, with its central panel devoted to the legend of the Kings, and still further on to the middle of the fifteenth century when Antonio Vivarini and Giovanni d'Alemagna executed their crowded, and dazzling, *Epiphany* in the International Style, the theme of the Three Kings increased steadily in popularity (see frontispiece).[22] As artists presented the elaborate Kings' legend they moved beyond the traditional rendering of the Magi as three statuesque crowned figures kneeling before the Virgin and Christ Child. The legend had taken on vivid travel scenes, whose drama could be rendered picturesque by luxurious apparel and rich materials. In the altarpiece of the Certosa di Pavia, Magi on horseback, at rest, traveling, in conversation, and at prayer required an endless parade of gorgeous costumes and much gold trim. Iconographic messages about kingship represented by apparel were potent tools in a skilled artist's hands. An urban public newly aware of fine goods available on luxury markets would not find it difficult to read the artist's message. In Epiphany scenes frames became more crowded with noble retinues for the Three Kings: over time robes and accoutrements grew more and more opulent, and more extreme in cut and decoration. Artists included horses with equipages embossed with precious gems, gold, and silver—by the time of Vivarini's *Epiphany*, dogs wearing gem-studded silver collars had entered the tableau—and the masculine pursuit of the hunt had become a theme in ever popular Epiphany scenes. Perhaps artists drew on goldsmiths, with whom they had shared apprenticeships, for this new broader iconographic repertoire of evocative dress and accessories. Whatever their sources of inspiration, artists told dazzling stories about the task of bringing gifts of great value to the feet of the Christ Child, and those stories featured large casts of fashionably dressed men.

These renderings of the legend of the Magi allowed the men who commissioned them to play the coveted roles of grave and wise kings worshiping at the feet of the Virgin and Child. Donors often appeared in full splendor, and, as in the case noted below, they might even choose to present themselves as sponsored by one of the Magi. The political ideals of the early Renaissance found little conflict between a princely condition and republicanism. A firm sense of hierarchy underlay Renaissance political thought in Venice and, increasingly in the later Middle Ages in Florence and other Tuscan towns, where the idea of "an elite based on blood and social distinction" emerged by the last decades of the fourteenth century.[23] Milan was unapologetically a princely city, and increasing aristocratization marked urban life throughout Lombardy. Perhaps the greatest concession to republicanism in the urban cult of the Magi lay in the portrayal of group scenes of fashionable men, where great city-state republics possessed a crowd of princes, rather than just a few. The crowded canvases with the Magi, their brilliantly attired retinues, and their gorgeous associates afforded many of the *savii* and *buonhomini,* along with their sons, brothers, and friends, the opportunity to present themselves in regal splendor. Crowns became fashionable apparel, and men wore even this exclusive symbol of royal authority when they posed as the Kings. The regalia of monarchical power could no longer be claimed as the private preserve of a few royal families. When Italians transgressed traditional norms of austerity, they did so at the highest level of urban society where civic leaders dressed like royalty.[24]

Baldassare Ubriachi, perhaps the earliest Florentine promoter of the cult of the Three Kings, possessed a residence just outside the gates of the city later cited as the place "where the Magi are." He was also the patron of the church of Santa Maria Novella, and donor of a chapel there dedicated to the Three Kings.[25] In the carved lintel of the chapel, "King Balthazar, gift in hand, recommend[s] to the divine pair his *protégée* Baldassare degli Ubriachi."[26] Richard Trexler has argued that Ubriachi brought the cult of the Kings to Florence in the fourteenth century, that is, well before the Medici promoted the confraternity of the Magi to legitimate their authority.[27] The Ubriachi family, with their fondness for the Magi, may be claimed by Venice as well, for in this city, to which some of the family moved, they revived the family's fortunes with a workshop that imported the most precious materials obtainable through long-distance trade, and lived ostentatiously. Ubriachi negotiated the terms for the great altarpiece of the Certosa di Pavia that featured the Magi on behalf of the family workshop at Venice.[28]

Giovanni Boccaccio found regal dress appropriate for a circle of men that included not only princes and rulers but also affluent and urbane citizens. In the Ninth Story of the Tenth Day of the *Decameron*, Boccaccio's narrator, a king—certainly the proper figure to judge social pretensions—finally arrives at his moment to speak and tells a lengthy tale. The king mentions first the hospitality of his citizen hero, the crusader Torello d'Istria: in visiting Torello's home, incognito, "Saladin and his companions, in spite of their being noble lords and accustomed to splendor, could not but marvel at the lavishness, all the more astonishing when they considered Torello was no great lord but a citizen." After enjoying Torello's beautiful appointments, Saladin and his companions were given "two robes of honor for each man—one lined with silk and the other with vair [fur]. No mere town's clothes they, nor merchants' either, but fit for great lords." Adalieta, Torello's wife, presented these rich gifts, despite the fact that like her husband she mistook Saladin and his men for mere merchants. She justified her gifts with these words: "merchants are neat men, and careful of their appearance."

Saladin graciously acknowledged the honor paid him: "Madam, these are very rich gifts, not to be lightly taken. Truly, we should scarcely have dared accept them, if your prayers, which we cannot find it in ourselves to deny, had not compelled us." This display of the finest courtesy will, of course, be rewarded. On crusade, Torello d'Istria is captured and finds himself a prisoner in the palace of Saladin, who has now been restored to his accustomed high station. Saladin fails to recognize his former generous host, nor does Torello recognize Saladin, but as Boccaccio's stories often resolve their plots, in time the two men come to recognize each other, and the matter turns on rich apparel. Saladin recognizes Torello when he himself appears before the crusader dressed in his princely robes, which, fortuitously, are the very gift of clothing given him by Torello's wife. Gazing upon the richly robed assembly, the always modest Torello exclaims, "My lord, I don't know any of these garments, though I admit that those two over there look like certain robes with which I was fitted long ago, together with three merchants who happened to come to my house."

At this "Saladin can no longer contain his joy, and embracing him tenderly, 'You are Torello d'Istria,' he said, 'and I am one of those three merchants to whom your wife gave these robes. The time has come for me to show you my merchandise, as I predicted when I took leave of you.'" The unassuming Torello must be drugged into a deep sleep before rich gifts of gold and jewels may be bestowed on him, but Saladin, ever grateful, courteous, and not averse to drugging the reluctant Torello in order to press gifts on him, was up to the task. Torello leaves for his return to Pavia a rich man.

The rambling story continues to focus more and more on rich apparel, this time with a masquerade, as the plot falls into a new register of false reports and mistaken identities. Torello returns to Pavia (swiftly, by magic) in the Odyssean role of a late-returning and unrecognized husband. At his wife's wedding banquet to a new husband Torello slips a ring she will recognize into her golden cup. Adalieta recognizes first the ring and then her husband despite his beard and disguise, and joyfully clasps Torello close in her arms. The couple retires happily to their home after the ever considerate Torello has given some of his precious gems from Saladin to the disappointed bridegroom, who has shouldered the expenses of the interrupted wedding feast.[29]

Were citizen Torello's courtesy and princely gift of clothes insufficient to convince the reader, Torello's skill at falconry, the sport of kings, further identifies him as a peer to the sultan Saladin, the most courteous of great rulers. Finally a moral is drawn from the tale: "There are many who, having the means, exert themselves to generosity, but they do it with such ill-grace that they make their favors cost more than they're worth. Hence, if no honor reverts to them, it is not for them or anyone else to wonder at it." With this moral the wellborn and well-connected Boccaccio chastises those whose manners and appearance have failed to keep pace with the grandeur of their wealth and fine appearance. He holds up to citizens the challenge to not only dress as kings but conduct themselves such that it leaves the monarchs of fourteenth-century Europe in awe and envy.[30]

Other citizens may have needed to stretch to achieve Torello's fine and generous courtesy, but in matters of style and munificence the grave, wise leaders in cities could be a match for kings and princes, and this was a role worth cultivating. When the *savii* and *buonhomini* launched a new fashion it would not do to have that fashion flaunted about the streets by mere boys or by a flock of wives, daughters, daughters-in-law, aunts, and cousins; this would lead only to confusion. Gradations of entitlement exhibited through dress were much likelier to appeal to wellborn, well-placed, and well-heeled customers. Merchants cultivated their wealthy customers by giving ample thought to what values should guide choices in dress. Kings and princes were not likely to adopt new styles displayed casually and promiscuously in the streets by all passersby, when exclusivity was their right and proper due.

Writing Sumptuary Laws

There were good reasons for writing sumptuary laws, given the market for luxury goods and the role of the *savii* and *buonhomini* in promoting sales of fine Italian goods at home and abroad. The irony, of course, was that given their purchasing power and their proclivity to spend, the biggest spenders were generally beyond the reach of the sumptuary laws enacted in towns.

In the late thirteenth century when town fathers introduced sumptuary codes, Bologna and Siena set the tone for urban lawmaking in northern Italy. Earlier, in 1157, Genoa had banned the use of sable fur worth more than forty soldi, but this one prohibition was apparently dropped. Bologna and Siena, by contrast, renewed their laws, thus setting the future agenda for other towns. Their late thirteenth-century laws were comprehensive, monitored behavior at weddings and funerals, and placed limits on fashions for women and on the expense of clothing generally.[31] Women's dress was the major concern in the law of 1289 in Bologna; the same was true at Siena although a few fashions, like *fregias* (decorative elements on garments), were forbidden to both men and women, a rare curb on men's spending in these early years. Town after town followed, with Bologna providing model legislation.[32]

Florence and Venice achieved the most impressive successes in marketing luxury wares in the fourteenth century and, not by coincidence, also wrote the most frequent and most extensive revisions of sumptuary laws. In Florence, civic regulation on behavior at funerals began as early as 1281.[33] The purview of the law widened dramatically in 1290 when the first reference to the registration of women's garments may be found published in the Florentine *Consulte*.[34] By 1299 women's ornaments were restricted, and various provisions were added about specific articles of apparel over the following two decades, helping to establish *sumptus* (spending) as a reason for civic intervention into the lives of Florentine families. In a compilation of law from the years 1322 to 1325 the confusing variety of early sumptuary laws was simplified. Limits on women's ornaments and behavior at baptisms, funerals, and weddings were enacted, only to have a prohibition against head ornaments revoked the following year.[35] In 1330, a major new set of regulations on women's ornaments was ordered, and in 1333, new officials were appointed to enforce the law. Again in 1339, the sumptuary laws of Florence were compiled into a single pragmatic, and the project was carried out over two years. A unique, detailed, and lengthy description of clothes registered with the office overseeing women's finery from 1343 survives.[36]

The next spate of civic legislation began after a 1354 repeal of all civic sumptuary laws, which briefly returned authority to regulate women's dress to the church. Church law did not seem to please civil authorities any better than did the old confusing civil statutes, so a new civil law completed in 1356 was aimed primarily at regulating behavior at weddings and women's ornaments and dress. Andrea Lancia translated this law into the vernacular, ostensibly to help win compliance. Officials again oversaw enforcement of the law, but a provision of 1364 allowed women to pay a gabelle or fine in order to wear forbidden ornaments. Apparently this had been the practice at Florence all along, with husbands and fathers offering to pay gabelles so women could wear forbidden clothing. Sumptuary laws were again collected in 1373, and a schedule of the fines was included. In 1377 a plea to review whether sumptuary restrictions were too strict or too lenient was heard. The laws were gathered into another compilation, the pragmatic of 1384, and soon after further revisions began; in 1388, another vernacular translation of the laws was made. In 1396, a petition was forwarded on behalf of Genoese women living in Florence who sought to exempt themselves from local sumptuary laws. The Genoese complained they had been prosecuted for sumptuary law violations that pertained to Florentine women only. The gabelle system continued into the next century and efforts to compile and reform sumptuary laws continued.[37]

These efforts by the state to control display and consumption drew on the example of other cities and of clerical regulation. Through his efforts to regulate the behavior of the laity at religious service Bishop Latino had brought sumptuary legislation to Florence when he arrived in 1279. Later, Bishop Antonio d'Orso Biliotti published full-fledged sumptuary controls over women's dress and ornaments in his synodal constitution of 1310; women's comportment at religious services was of particular concern to him as well. The behavior and dress of children and youths were addressed, and clergy were notified that their robes should not be shortened but should reach to their ankles; this was, of course, a type of sumptuary law as well (see plate 14).[38]

This was an early skirmish in the battle to keep clergy soberly attired in the fourteenth-century turn to fashion. By the middle of the fifteenth century the rhetoric of reformers concerning clerical pomp, "which is of the devil," would reach a crescendo. Nicolas of Cusa in A General Reform of the Church complained: "There is only one college of cardinals; why are there so many types of capes? . . . [A]s if it were permissible for those who do not bind themselves to the observance of any other religious order, . . . to appear in public, now in red capes, now in golden ones, as they please?" Nicolas advocated that all should appear in capes of one color, since "[d]isparity of clothing seems a sign of levity and detracts from the gravity of so many men."[39] Still, Florentine bishops were more concerned with the excesses of the laity than the clergy in 1310, and in general fourteenth-century legislation was aimed at the excesses of the lay public.

Bishop Biliotti fixed his attention squarely on women's excesses in both conduct and dress. He forbade enamel work on women's clothing, as well as a number of carefully specified fashions; he demanded above all that women dress modestly. Where he could not prohibit, he limited. Only four florins' worth of gold for fastenings like buckles was allowed, buttons included; however, a gilded belt might be worn over outer garments to the value of five florins, in place of the ornaments mentioned above. His conviction that Florentine women were responsible for excessive expense to their families and for immodesty in public was evident throughout.

In a certain restricted sense the synodal constitution of 1310 regulated laymen as well. Goldsmiths and purveyors of ornaments were prohibited from selling forbidden wares to Florentine women under the pain of anathema, possibly in imitation of the Sienese civic law that had tried the same ploy of holding producers accountable for selling to women.[40] In the 1320s this prohibition on artisans was adopted in Florentine statute law, changing the penalty levied on producers to a fine. Apparently efforts at enforcing this clause never succeeded at Florence and the measure seems to have fallen into disuse, while Siena's attempt to control tailors' use of material in women's cloaks over the limit set in law survived.[41] The moralizing tone of the synodal sumptuary code at Florence migrated undiminished into the preambles and capitularies of the frequently revised and reedited civic sumptuary codes.

Sumptuary laws implicated laymen in another circumstance. In the civic laws of the 1320s fathers were made responsible for the compliance of their daughters, and men were included along with women in a curious prohibition of garments decorated with images of trees, flowers, animals, and birds, perhaps in imitation of the *fregias* prohibited to people of Siena and *frixis* prohibited to women in Bologna. As for jewels, only knights, judges, and physicians, that is, functionaries of the state, might wear them without restraint, and the same applied to belts with silver threads. All Florentine men could wear weapons. As market sales and commissions attest, men's finery consisted largely of ornamental weaponry, often in silver, and fastenings like belts that secured weapons to the body, so men still enjoyed wide choice in stylish dress and display in this town. A few ornaments or styles like pleats were forbidden to men and women alike, and "[a] measure in the Statute of the Podestà in 1325 forbade women to wear men's clothing and men from dressing like women."[42] Men were regulated along with women at baptisms, as celebrants at weddings, or mourners at funerals, but mature men were not singled out, as was the case with women, for the expense of their garments on these occasions.

In 1356, the new compilation of civil sumptuary law at Florence set the

Figure 4. Portrait of a youth, detail of a fresco in San Giovanni, Conca, c. 1340. (The church has been demolished.) The shortened hem, belt, purse, buttons, and other adornments suggest that this was a fashionable young man.

agenda for subsequent laws. Again, women's dress and behavior was the subject of the lawmakers' attention. A few materials and fashions were forbidden to all, and once again, both women's and men's behavior at weddings, funerals, and baptisms was regulated (only fifty men from either side of the family could attend weddings); husbands who did not pay their wives' fines were ineligible to hold communal office. However, major restrictions on men's consumption did not begin until 1377, when the law initiated three specific prohibitions on men's dress: the length of their shoes was set at one-twelfth of a *braccio* or less (a bit above five centimeters); tunics had to reach to the middle of the thigh (measured while standing, not sitting); and only two pounds of silver by weight could be used for a man's belt (see fig. 4). These were certainly generous limits, but they suggest that for the first time adult men were recognized as capable of excess in following fashion and in spending on dress. Financial strains made the collection of gabelles that secured lead seals to be affixed to garments an important feature of the law by the 1370s. Still, two of the three restrictions on men in the pragmatic of 1377 concerned specific fashions. An exemption purchased through a gabelle would then only be relevant to the weight of men's silver belts.[43]

Foreign officers charged with the laws' enforcement continued to be appointed but they were concerned with examining infringements involving women, as the name of their office, the *Ufficiale delle donne,* signified. It was rare for men to be investigated by this office at all, and they might have escaped prosecution altogether except that a number of witnesses had insisted on bringing three men up before the court on charges of wearing pleats in 1347.[44] As a matter of rule the salaried employees of the *Ufficiale delle donne* did not search out men's transgressions of the law. With the exception of the three new restrictions directed toward men's apparel in 1377, laws targeted women's consumption and display, along with that of youths and children.

In Venice, the late medieval series of civic sumptuary laws began in 1299 with regulation of behavior and expense at wedding celebrations. The major focus of the law at Venice, as in Florence, was women's dress and behavior. Men under twenty years of age received some attention, as did children under thirteen. Men were restricted along with women in terms of how many could attend weddings, and men as well as women could have only two furs. However, women's behavior and dress, particularly the bride's gifts, dress, and comportment at her wedding, took up most of the legislators' attention.[45]

The next major sumptuary law, passed in June 1334, added considerably to the extent of regulated behavior and dress at Venice. The preamble claimed that superfluity and unnecessary expense on the part of both men and women prompted this effort at legislation, but the law directed its specific clauses to women's dress and consumption and only secondarily to children; men were considered in the law in their roles as donors, as women's husbands and fathers. Males above ten years of age could not wear silk, velvet, or cloth of gold, but they could have fastenings of silver and gold. It appears that only youths were targeted in these clauses. Both men's and women's attendance and behavior at weddings and public occasions continued to be regulated. In general Venetian law favored limiting luxurious apparel rather than forbidding specific styles and materials. The exceptions were trims or borders on women's clothes and some headdresses, which had first been prohibited in 1299 and continued to be forbidden in 1334; even when the sumptuary law of 1334 was annulled in 1339, these prohibitions continued. The *frixis* of Bologna's 1289 sumptuary code prove to be an enduring concern of sumptuary legislators everywhere.[46] Sumptuary law did not run a smooth course at Venice, where complaints, repeals, and new provisions were offered in the 1340s and 1350s.[47]

In the spring of 1360 the Venetian Senate undertook a new comprehensive sumptuary law that addressed weddings, women's dresses, ornaments, and other luxurious apparel. Women were the primary focus of the law, although all children under eight and boys of twelve years of age or less came under provisions. Again, the law favored limits on expense rather than outright prohibitions. More remarkably, the law began to address men's clothes and limited belts in cost to twenty-five ducats.[48] This was a significant departure since mature men had not been singled out before as prone to excess in the expense of their apparel. Like its predecessors this long and highly detailed law did not satisfy Venetians, and more complaints and demands for revisions or repeals were heard over the following decades. In 1403, the Senate examined its process of legislating on dress and comportment and admitted "the desirability of avoiding hasty or ill-considered legislation, especially on subjects of such peculiar difficulty as sumptuary enactions." No proposition for further legislation on such matters could be put to the vote unless it had been read in the council eight days before.[49] But efforts to create effective sumptuary laws through due deliberation did not mollify either the public or lawmakers, so new legislative efforts were no more successful in 1403 than previous ones and revisions continued to be made over the following decades.

In Venice the influence of the church's sumptuary prohibitions was less apparent, but it should not be dismissed.[50] The good of the soul was invoked in justification of the civil law, and a clear sense that weddings and funerals ought to be celebrated in a holy and pious manner informed the law. The presence of the church would be felt when Venice's own Cristina Correr petitioned the pope in 1437, not the Venetian Senate, for permission to wear clothes beyond the limits set in civic law. She might well do so, since Lorenzo Guistiani, bishop of Castello, had designed the protocol against which she protested.[51] The church's disapproval of excessive display and luxury was recognized in Venice, where it justified sumptuary codes in the eyes of the public even while the authority to legislate remained in civic hands.

Still, Florence and Venice failed to pass measures that satisfied either the authorities or the people, and throughout the late medieval era sumptuary regulations continued to be matters of open dispute. Still, Florentine and Venetian lawmakers seem to have concurred that mature men should be exempted from most restrictions on their spending and display; the laws of most other northern Italian cities followed suit. Siena was the rare exception, and even Siena directed the greater number of the law's prohibitions against women. By the latter half of the fourteenth century, women, youths, and children felt the force of the law much more than men, and that trend continued into the fifteenth century.[52] Even this brief review of sumptuary lawmaking indicates that diverse and sometimes conflicting motives, numerous agendas, and many disagreements marked the entire project of legislating restraint in dress and behavior. A wider glimpse at sumptuary law in other city-states that manufactured and exported luxury goods confirms this impression.[53]

Design of the law and the legislative process by which it was enacted helps explain the increasing acceptance of government-imposed restraints on *sumptus,* even while some powerful citizens remained skeptical about the entire project of enacting such laws. Perhaps wealthy consumers in cities paid lip service to the law while circumventing specific restrictions through fair or illegal means. Despite this sumptuary law gained social acceptance over the course of the fourteenth century. Even if honored in the breach rather than practice of the law, it had become a significant feature of life in cities.

In drawing up the comprehensive pragmatic of 1356, the Florentine *signoria* went to some length to clarify the law and weed out old, confusing stipulations. To this end, the priors appointed eight men to draw up a new code, two from each quarter of the city; the chairman was Schiatta Ridolfi, a representative of the Albizzi faction. The prominent banker Piero di Gino de' Guicciardini sat on the committee as well. In July 1356 the Latin text of the reformed law was submitted to the *signoria,* where it was approved during the following month.[54]

Ronald Rainey's brief outline of the process related above cannot, of course, acquaint us with what was probably the most critical component of consensus building for the nine folios of law arranged in forty-three chapters in this new pragmatic of 1356. The *signoria* enjoyed a communal dinner on days when they met, and sumptuary law was one matter on which members of different factions might agree. Fiscal motives for collecting gabelles might enter the discussion. In 1373 the record noted, "It is well known to all that the worthy men, Benozzo di Francesco di Andrea . . . [and fifteen others] . . . have been selected to discover ways and means by which money will accrue to the commune. . . . Considering the commune's need for revenue to pay current expenses," a gabelle of fifty florins was enacted on women and girls dressed over the limit of the law.[55] Annoyance at women's and youths' disregard for economizing and propriety might be fully aired at a communal meal at which the *signoria* gathered, since wives and children were not present. Sumptuary law has all the earmarks of a popular legislative project whose beneficial effects lay in discussing and devising measures rather than in executing the law. It was hoped laws would raise revenue and act as a brake on the families of wealthy men, but airing their concerns over fashions was a popular project in and of itself.

At Venice, the process was similar. In 1334, and in the name of the doge, a commission of ten *savii* was organized into two subcommittees of five each. They were to review the law, draw up new proposals where appropriate, and report back to the Senate. The first group reporting, which included Marco Morosini, a procurator of St. Mark, was heard on June 9. They made only a few recommendations and the Senate postponed action until it heard from the other five *savii,* who reported back as part of the full commission on June 20. This group, firmed up in resolve by the second five, proved to be somewhat more assiduous in proposing measures to control spending and display, and they carried senatorial opinion on behalf of their proposals. The record carefully enumerated which commissioners pushed for stricter laws and which dragged their feet.

Eight men, not the ten commission members present, recommended most of the measures that would be enacted into the new law. On the issue of silver and gold ornaments for wedding gowns, Giovanni Sanudo proposed a further limit of twelve *solidi di grossi*, and in another recommendation he proposed that all women's gowns other than bridal wear be made without trains (*coda*). This was not the end of the matter; in discussion Thomaso Soranzo favored limiting the length of women's mantles (*doplone*) to one *bracchia* (about 68 centimeters). Discussion ensued and Soranzo won. At the other end of the spectrum Bertucci Gradenigo, one of the first group of reporting *savii*, stood outside consensus on about a third of the commission's proposals, but his dissent, while duly noted, did not carry the day. By contrast some of the more avid among the *savii*—Tomaso Soranzo, Filippo Bellegno, Marco Morosini, and Giovanni Trevisan—but not the full commission, suggested that the law be applied to all Venetians regardless of residence. Sumptuary legislation was contentious at Venice, and while reasons were not given for Gradenigo's persistent refusal to go along with the rest of the *savii*, clearly he found the project of legislating limits and prohibitions inappropriate on some grounds.[56] Sumptuary law had its enthusiasts, but it had its critics as well.

Gender Considerations

For all its troubled history, sumptuary lawmaking demonstrated little confusion about one matter—the question of an individual's social status or wealth. At Bologna, the law of 1289 paid no respect to wealth or office but governed all. Chapter 3 of the code went even further: "We order that all persons small and great neither dare nor presume to [give gifts to clergy]."[57]At Florence judges, doctors, and knights were exempt from the restriction on wearing jewels and silver thread in their belts in the 1320s, and knights and their wives enjoyed occasional exemptions, but they did so only as servants of the state. Noble standing was not the issue with knights in any event: "By 1300 in this region it was becoming common opinion that knights or *milicia* were no longer a military but a mercantile species," Philip Jones argues persuasively.[58] In Venice, both patricians and commoners felt the force of the law and were fined the same amount for violations of the law.[59] It was well-to-do patricians who were likely to feel the greater sting of the law in any case since the limits on apparel were set high. Still, non-noble Venetian families possessed fortunes and dressed accordingly. Urban sumptuary law that regulated dress, festivities, and consumption distinguished by gender and age, not class, and this was true across the board well into the fifteenth century.[60] In time, with an increasing demand for luxury goods, the continued growth of a secondhand market, as well as other opportunities for poorer townspeople to dress in the cast-offs of the wealthy, a class dimension to sumptuary restrictions would characterize the law. Urban sumptuary law's early concern with the consuming habits of members of the lawgivers' own families—their wives and children—suggests different considerations ruled the thoughts of wealthy lawmakers in the four-teenth century, even as demand began its slow move into the ranks of less wealthy persons in towns.[61]

Why gender and its accompaniment, age? Why were these the salient cat-egories in which lawgivers attempted to comprehend and control changes in consumer behavior? Two pieces of legislation mentioned above—the sumptu-ary law of 1334 in Venice and a comparable attempt at legislating restraint in 1356 in Florence—provide a glimpse into legislators' priorities.

First, it is important to note that sumptuary legislation was drawn, debated, and enacted in an atmosphere of high emotion. Gravitas may have prevailed, but it was ruffled by what lawmakers saw in the streets and in their own homes. At Venice, the amended laws on the books, based on the code enacted in 1334, satisfied few of the legislators, so the Senate deliberations of May 21, 1360, rumbled out, "And thus is noted in our city today, *more than in all other parts of the world*, more vanities and inordinate expenses among wives, and other women" (author's emphasis).[62] Could Venetians, who had gone to such great lengths to make their markets premier in the luxury trades, be so aghast at local inhabitants' response to those markets? Women's fashions brought torrents of complaint on the issue of expenses. Whether too bold or too retiring the current fashion was always wrong-headed. Immodest clothing aroused some ire but later on at Venice Ser Bartolomeo Marcello called the modest fashion of covering the head and face now favored by women "abomi-nable."[63] In Venice the law of 1334 was to be broadcast every six months in what turned out to be a vain effort to keep women and children informed—and conforming. The dour Latin of Florence's law of 1356 had been translated into the vernacular by Andrea Lancia with the intent of acquainting those only literate in the vernacular—women for the most part—about the provisions. This was evidently done to help compliant women avoid immodesty and simi-lar outrages.[64] Feelings ran high about what appeared to be superfluity (the very term was used in the Venetian law of 1334). Some voiced pique at excesses of behavior at weddings and other gatherings, and there was a strong dose of moral outrage mixed into these lengthy laws, particularly in regard to funerals and church attendance, where civic leaders saw extravagance take precedence over respect for the Holy Sacraments.

The complexity of agendas that surface when reading sumptuary law should caution any modern reader against overinterpreting the intent behind the law; preambles that express moral outrage may be particularly misleading. Because women, youths, and children were mentioned most does not mean that they possessed exclusive right to showcase the family's wealth in a manner that would become the norm in the postindustrial world. Patriarchs of families were not expected to be somberly clad producers of wealth in order to assert their probity and wisdom: men could, and did, consume with zest and display their wealth in public as befitted men who viewed spending on wardrobe as an investment.[65]

Second, sumptuary laws were catchall enactments. In 1334 in Venice when Ser Thomaso Soranzo had a sudden afterthought about the length of women's mantles, proposing to limit them to one *bracchia,* he introduced his measure onto the floor of the Senate and gained immediate and resounding approval for it.[66] This was not a provision added to the law after long deliberation but an impulse that won immediate approval from his fellow senators. Sudden notions and remembered affronts to sensibility made grab bags of these laws; they follow little system.

Third, sometimes the law fined the consumer, sometimes the producer, while enforcement fell to various offices of government in both cities, or in certain instances to the church; in particular, hapless civic notaries charged with spotting violations and granting exceptions were in the hot seat.[67] Enforcers were more likely to get it wrong than right: Venetians might wish to limit women's finery but they also wanted women of the doge's family to appear in bright colors even if they were in mourning.[68] In the latter half of the fourteenth century Florentine sumptuary law enforcers seemed to have been as interested in collecting gabelles as in eliminating "dishonest" women's fashions from the streets.

Lastly, a great *donna* could go right over the heads of local authorities. Cristina Correr did so because she wished to wear the clothes and jewels due her on grounds of her beauty and the status of her family (she specified the finery in detail).[69] Clearly, families encouraged women in their efforts to thwart the law. In fact, the *savii* and *buonhomini* often appear to have been thinking more in terms of exceptions than of the rule when it came to enforcing laws.

Lawmakers were often of two minds, as the politics surrounding the Venetian law of 1334 reveals. Passing that law required extended debate, then Ziani Baduario almost immediately proposed the repeal of the new law, which indeed did come about in 1339. However, Ser Soranzo's limit on the length of mantles remained in force in Venice after 1339, as did limits on women's wearing of two fashions: *drezatores perlarum* and *frexatura de perilis,* fashionable beaded headdresses and borders.[70] Concern for expenses at home appears to have been Soranzo's motive, but the assured measures undertaken by Venetians and Florentines to build luxury markets were not in evidence in regulating local consumers who wished to purchase attractive goods in those markets. Understanding the psychology of consumption, which these leaders did, failed to carry over into understanding the psychology of consumption at home—or did it?

It is transparently obvious today that many of the clauses of fourteenth-century sumptuary legislation were doomed to fail. This was likely understood at the time as well, because the lesson of past failures would not provide legislators with much hope for future successes. Florence could not expect to display cunningly woven Tuscan cloth shot with silver and gold, local gold-stamped leather, and imported ivory and gems without tempting its own inhabitants; local inhabitants, more than others, had been schooled to appreciate the value of native industries. Florence established itself as a center of production and trade in fine apparel, most notably beautiful fabrics, and they drew on the production and skilled personnel of neighboring Siena and Lucca as well. Fine fabrics called out to be embellished with silver or gold, embroidered with gems or "pearls," or stamped with precious metals. Where Sienese and Venetian law described gold and silver wares and gems in complex terms, Florentine law applied its most specific descriptions to fabrics, fur, and leather, and to designs of animals, trees, and flowers in fine colors.[71] Sienese laws made highly detailed provisions about the amount of silver in jewels and the designs of silver and silver gilt jewelry in a way that suggests urban legislators had a firm grasp of which locally made products tempted the citizenry.[72]

The great banks of fourteenth-century Italy attracted customers who appreciated and could afford luxury manufactures, while wealthy foreigners and newly rich mercenaries traveled throughout Italy to visit markets and buy precious wares. The psychology of foreigners' market behavior, of attraction to markets, was the business of affluent city fathers, yet traffic on these markets was also the focus of sumptuary restrictions insofar as wives and children were concerned. Keeping markets open while prohibiting local inhabitants from purchasing and wearing what was sold in the markets introduced conflicting agendas to which sumptuary law was an inadequate response.

A complication arises in regard to the various limits prescribed in the law. As Chapter 5 notes, wherever set, limits were high—not as high as the cost of the highest-priced wares available on luxury markets but nonetheless high in comparison with the cost of living in towns. Why set limits at all if they would affect only a few who could afford to consume at a high level, and why set limits primarily on youths, women, and children? To explore these conundrums, perhaps the most important finding is that legislators carefully exempted themselves from most provisions in the law. In considering this behavior some of the theoretical constructs that have been applied to sumptuary legislation in other times and places may be useful.

Legislating Restraints

Daniel Miller does not reveal why "signification between material objects and social station . . . strives to remain relatively uncomplex and controlled," but he is well aware of the consequences when this breaks down: people lower in a given hierarchy will fulfill their aspirations by changing their behavior, dress, and consumption "since it now becomes possible to mistake a poor nobleman for a wealthy trader." This is no sooner done, Miller attests, than the privileged in turn attempt to maintain differentials, since they have "access to knowledge about goods and their prestige connotation. By this process, fashion emerges as the means for continuing those forms of social discrimination previously regulated by sumptuary rulings. In other words, demand for goods may flourish in the context of ambiguity in social hierarchy."[73]

Miller is concerned with issues of class and privilege, but his analysis of the processes that can transform social hierarchies may say something about gender hierarchies. His own investigations into the early modern period found confusion of signs in regard to rank among poor noblemen and wealthy traders. This confusion broke out much earlier, in the fourteenth century to be precise, and among Italians who were citizens, both noble and common, and these men were anything but poor. They were great merchants—or at the farthest remove the kin, associates, neighbors, and former schoolmates of men who were great merchants—and they were also the men who would design and pass civic sumptuary legislation.[74] These were gentlemen who stood at the highest levels of urban society as the *buonhomini* or *savii*, a status worth protecting. And this confusion over signs emerged in the early and middle decades of the fourteenth century when fashion and trendsetting began to stimulate demand in the market economy.

These leaders' acumen for understanding and promoting their own markets gives every sign of having failed to carry over into attempts to curb their families at home, so it is possible that some answers to the perplexities of the laws they passed may lie in trying to understand what happened when civic leaders and great merchants stepped up their own consumption. Had consumption become, in Daniel Miller's phrase, "more directly constitutive of social status" and did this disturb the *savii* or *buonhomini* in economic terms, social terms, or perhaps both? The munificence of these men bordered on the legendary; indeed, it was a factor that helps explain the attraction of wealthy foreigners to the markets of Italy: foreigners often came to see and to buy, so dressing well to impress wealthy customers was an investment that could be well rewarded.[75] Was this munificence jeopardized by consumption patterns of women and children? Confusion over signs in public places and in clothing is an elusive topic, but Henry Brod speculates on the motives of men like those who enacted sumptuary law.

Brod has suggested that in understanding gender, scholars have been too ready to assume that a system of hierarchy between men and women is simply constitutive of subordinating women. He notes: "[P]atriarchy institutionalizes not just hierarchy *between* genders, but hierarchy *within* each gender as well."[76]

He believes that societies have many easier and more direct ways to differentiate women from men than the elaborate laws and tests that have been written to that ostensible purpose. Thus such tests and laws may differentiate among men as well; that is to say, there is an elaborate hierarchy of entitlement involving distinctions within masculinity as well as between masculine and feminine. This interpretation may be too labored by half in probing for ulterior motives, but it counteracts the tendency to accept the law as simply constitutive of the social realities of the day. If sumptuary law related in some way to the economic well-being of the *savii* and *buonhomini,* and to their concern over confused visual signs that might affect what foreigners sought out to purchase on their luxury markets, then there might be a plausible reason for legislating restraint on women, children, and youths.

The historiographical tradition of writing on sumptuary law has tended to take the word of the law at face value and simply assume that women were at fault for excesses because laws said they were. Certainly sumptuary legislation defined woman as "other" and at fault in uncompromising terms. In the laws a polar construct was established where women were to be limited or restrained whereas mature men were left largely unrestrained and might therefore exercise their own judgment as to proper display and attire. Children were to be regulated because their mothers tended to overdress them, and young men were restrained but it might be assumed that they would outgrow a need for control when they developed gravitas. In Venice, Fra Paolino justified such a scheme in 1314 based on his understanding of Aristotle in a popular tract on marriage and the governance of the family.[77] Close gradations in a strict hierarchy sanctioned by ancient authority provided an appealing formula for designing dress and spending codes.

It is relevant to note here that sumptuary law did not forbid consumption and display for women, youths, and children; it merely limited them and set those limits high. Youths and women were permitted finery but within specified lines; sometimes a style was absolutely forbidden, but more often limits were set on how and when apparel might be worn and by whom. These limits were set high and rose over the century while exemptions were sought continually and often gained if a citizen was willing to pay. It seems reasonable then that sumptuary laws were designed to spell out idealized hierarchies of consumption within a community based on close gradations of entitlement.

All that is missing from this picture are those at the pinnacle of society, that is, the wealthiest citizens and designers of the law themselves. They set the standard for consumption, and their priorities expressed in lawmaking reveal a possible hierarchical intent for the display labeled *le pompe.* As noted before it is not at all difficult to imagine a wealthy man walking the streets of an Italian city in apparel worth one hundred ducats, or florins, as the case may be. No restrictions disallowed a collection of finery for men; inventories suggest that ensembles of jewels, fastenings, and fine fabrics were amassed, awaiting their chance for a public airing. It appears that despite a few late-added provisions aimed at men's spending, unrestrained ostentation was largely open to men. Florentine women were permitted to sew a row of silver or gilded buttons on their sleeves reaching from shoulder to elbow and remain within the law, but adult men were portrayed in fresco and painting with the effect of a full line of buttons from shoulder to wrist (see plate 6).[78] This was unregulated display and more opulent than that allowed to women, children, or serving maids, whose buttons were regulated as well. Urban sumptuary laws were based on scales of consumption like as not, and this suggests that gradations within close hierarchies were an aim of the codes. By design the law distinguished among men according to age and authority, as well as between men and women. This was, perhaps, no less important than legislating public morality or enlisting the state's help in "holding the line" at home, that is, the stated goals of sumptuary laws.[79]

By the law of 1334 in Venice, women were permitted a rather generous allowance for finery in apparel: fifteen *solidi di grossi* for a gold ornament for the hair or neck; seven *lira di grossi* for other jewelry like necklaces. A belt or girdle could cost up to twelve *solidi di grossi* and from it a woman might append expensive items like silver knives, purses, or needle cases up to a value of ten *solidi di grossi*. Fastenings were distinguished from purely ornamental jewelry but it all adds up: at twenty *solidi* to a pound, a woman might parade around in an impressive ensemble, worth almost nine *lira di grossi* worth of silver, gold, and gems—and that does not count rich materials in mantles, robes, and head coverings, although women were forbidden to wear cloth of gold. A bride might have two dresses for celebrating her wedding and they could be costly, befitting a wardrobe that was intended to last her a lifetime.[80] A bride could be accompanied by twenty married women or widows and by ten unmarried women, all suitably decked out. These were not attempts directed at eliminating *le pompe* so much as determining the extent of display and the use of certain materials. As noted above, after the repeal of the law the length of women's mantles in Venice remained in force, and two fashions, one in headdresses and one in borders, were still forbidden.[81]

Matters were not so different in Florence after 1356. Women could not wear cloth of gold or velvet but they were free to wear silk. Trains on robes were limited to less than one *bracchia* but they were permitted. Specific fashions rather than precious materials were forbidden to women, and the law also specified that a woman could wear a girdle or belt, but it was to be of no greater value than fifteen florins.[82] This was a generous limit, in fact so generous that it might be construed as no limit at all except that there is evidence that girdles or belts of much greater size and value were traded on markets and worn by men. Furthermore, this provision of the law represented a substantial increase over the limit of five florins on women's belts in the early synodal legislation of 1310.[83] In the civic law of 1356 rich furs were forbidden to all but the wife of a *cavalieri* (knight in civic employ), and *azzurrata* or enamel work that featured the very precious shade of ultramarine blue was expressly forbidden to all.[84] A few outright prohibitions and a hierarchy of gradations continued to be features of the law.

Young men were more likely to be forbidden to congregate than to consume. They could not hold "men only" events on the day of a wedding or for fifteen days before or after in Venice. Males over the age of ten could not wear silk, velvet, or cloth of gold but they might use *peroli* or *asoleti*—buttons and fastenings of silver and gold—on their clothes.[85] In the synodal sumptuary legislation of 1310, Florentine men's dress, even that of young men, had yet to come under restrictions, and civic laws applied to only a few fashions forbidden to all. Specific prohibitions on men's fashions appeared only in 1377. Two concerned short tunics and long-toed shoes, which were youthful affectations; thus, of the three new 1377 restrictions only the one concerning the weight of great silver belts was likely to affect the consuming behavior of mature men.[86] Generational conflict fully surfaces in sumptuary law by the later years of the fourteenth century, but resolution of a sort was always at hand since young men grew into the next generation of mature adults, who in turn would write a new round of sumptuary law.

With all who could afford it pursuing fashion with zeal, it helps to remember those whom the wise, grave leaders of cities chose to include in their license to consume freely. In Venice, the *estimo* of 1379 provides clear evidence that great fortunes existed outside the patriciate. In this age when closing the ranks of the governing noble class was a pressing concern, consideration given to the pretensions of wealthy non-nobles who dared to dress luxuriously would come as no surprise, but Venetian sumptuary law was remarkably egalitarian in regard to men of substantial fortune, noble status notwithstanding. Sumptuary law licensed non-noble merchants to dress extremely well, as well as the nobility dressed. For wealthy Venetians a degree of solidarity was achieved through this permissive feature of the law, and distinctions in political status could be ameliorated through a license for all wealthy men to dress to the limit of their pocketbooks. In late medieval city-states, Philip Jones contends, the ideal of leveling up as well as down informed social values.[87] Sumptuary legislation in Italian city-states embraced that ideal. Where retail sales were important, even noble lawmakers tolerated luxurious dress for long-distance or "great" merchants, for those who cultivated wealthy customers visiting Venice, or for those who sat at the benches of banks at the Rialto or imported fine consumable wares from abroad, regardless of noble or non-noble status or, for that matter, foreign or immigrant status. If those with the statutory status of noble alone participated in political processes, they were aware that non-noble and noble alike built the trade networks on which the republic's prosperity rested. That is to say, the nobility benefited from allowing wealthy non-nobles to dress as well as they because fine dress among the wealthiest promoted solidarity and encouraged the consumption that kept them wealthy.

Frederic Chapin Lane has pointed out with regard to Venice that where governments served the interests of a cohesive circle, it was possible for men to pass with relative ease from private enterprises to public agency because the same persons dominated decision making and directed policy in either case.[88] The *savii* were the officialdom of Venice, the *buonhomini* of Florence, and the correspondence of the same men from the same families with civic officehold-ing, finance, and the pursuit of long-distance trade is well known.[89] Private need not be the antipode of public (or, in this circumstance, civic), nor would men in positions of power seek solutions to problems based on a distinction of this nature. Faction might disturb this fluid translation from private to pub-lic sphere of action, but sumptuary lawmaking does not appear to have been a factional issue in the political life of Italian city-states—with the exception of the rare dissenter like Bertucci Gradenigo of Venice noted above. Sumptuary lawmaking may have been one of the few arenas of civic concern on which legislators of different political stripes came to agree.[90] Some have detected an anti-aristocratic bias in the earliest sumptuary legislation at Florence, but men lacking noble lineage possessed extraordinary private fortunes by the four-teenth century, and the law appears as intent on curbing the extravagances of their household spending as within the old circles of status and wealth.[91] By contrast the new men who came to power in the aftermath of the Ciompi revolt appear to have been too busy with more pressing matters to concern themselves with sumptuary laws aimed at curbing consumption, and it remained for the old elites, once they were back in office after 1378, to under-take the next round of sumptuary lawmaking at Florence.

Philip Jones has argued, "Among the business classes . . . a widening divi-sion emerged between great and small merchants, though not everywhere equally: in Upper Italy, at Bologna, Milan and neighboring Lombard cities, capital and enterprise were more 'democratically' dispersed and diffused, less distinctly dominated by a merchant patriciate or *popolo grasso*, than in the Tuscan towns, Genoa or Venice."[92] Precisely here, in Genoa, Venice, Florence, and neighboring Tuscan towns, sumptuary laws provided a license for all rich men, patricians and the *popolo grasso* alike, to dress to the hilt, providing a solidarity through consumption that was lacking in other dimensions of politi-cal life.

In economic and social terms the men who thought up sumptuary legis-lation (in the case of Venice in 1334 ten *savii*, two of them highly trusted *procu-ratori di San Marco*; in the case of Florence in 1356 the named proposer

Thomaso di ser Puccio da Gobio, doctor of law and elected official of the commune of Florence, as well as Schiatta Ridolfi and his eight-man committee) stood at the pinnacle of society and were the same men, or men of the same families, who organized the principal financial markets and pursued long-distance trade. In northern Italian cities they may be characterized, according to Sir Stanley Jevons's rule, as members of an elite "calculation" community. Jevons argued that most usage of coin, that is, gold and silver, was governed by ignorance and custom but "a small class of money-changers, bullion dealers, bankers or goldsmiths make it their business to be acquainted with differences [in weight and fineness of coins] and know how to derive profit from them."[93] Overseers of the mint who set monetary policy and those who set fiscal policy may be included in this circle. Wealthy Italian men who belonged to this "calculation" community were prime promoters of luxury markets, and they also wrote sumptuary laws.[94] It is perhaps better to assume some expertise and coherent economic thinking on the part of these men than view them as prey to bouts of pique against their wives and children that resulted in unenforceable laws.

Italian financiers and merchants often made their fortunes together: in particular, Florentine banks and their factors were active on the Venetian money market because at Venice they found highly efficient financial services. Political rivalries disrupted cooperative ventures with tiresome regularity, but each time great merchants set to work to repair disrupted systems because they were the life breath of the economy. When it came down to building the alliances necessary for business, commoners and patricians collaborated, as did men of new wealth and scions of old magnate lineages. The Ubriachi workshop of Venice relied on men of old lineage from Florence who also held new grants of citizenship *de extra* at Venice.[95] Since many luxury goods relied on the bullion market, the luxury trades flourished precisely where financial markets were strongest—thus in Venice's integrated financial center at the Rialto and at Florence with its powerful merchant banking houses that sent their agents all over Europe.[96] It is quite possible that urban sumptuary law uncovers some of the more cohesive elements at work in fourteenth-century urban politics. Only the rare voice was raised in protest; most voted in favor of their pocketbooks when enacting sumptuary laws in, apparently, a shared belief that certain gradations of age and gender best suited a parade of seemly consumption for their streets.

"The dual nature of dress—the tension that can exist between what 'dresses up' reality and the reality underneath"—found a resolution of sorts in creating princes out of the wise, grave leaders of cities.[97] Was this a brash and presumptuous assertion of status? Most assuredly yes, but it was not without some solid foundation in fourteenth-century economic life. Italian bankers to kings from Sicily to the Irish Sea had private knowledge of the financial status of their royal patrons. Italian merchant bankers could compare royal wealth (and indebtedness) to their own more liquid wealth and that of their fellow townsmen, reaching conclusions that might run in townsmen's favor. Kings possessed enviable assets in land and prerogatives, but their bankers knew how often they flirted with bankruptcy for lack of liquid assets. Assertions of equal social footing with reigning monarchs, launched through setting fashions in apparel, followed easily on establishing financial markets that underwrote princely enterprises, most commonly expensive, even bankrupting, foreign wars.[98] A banker with a king as his debtor might find it appropriate to dress as well as he.

While wise, grave leaders in cities readily awarded themselves with princely trappings, they maintained a discriminating sense of just how many "princes" graced the streets of their towns and were sufficiently hierarchical in their judgment to restrict consuming behavior within their own families. Historians' discussions of sumptuary laws frequently disparage the attempt to control consumption, calling it a foolhardy project doomed to failure,[99] but this chapter suggests that fourteenth-century civic sumptuary law was more wisely directed toward a more rational, even realizable, goal: that of maintaining a seemly, even if imperfect, hierarchy of consumption. As such cities taught lessons about consumption to Italy's most valued and affluent customers: the great rulers, princes, and lords of Europe. Sumptuary legislation could be written to stimulate demand, since fine fashions became more attractive when they were regarded as prerogatives of a circle of powerful and wealthy men. Sumptuary legislation may provide one of the few windows into a long-distance merchant's thinking as he attempted to create an eager clientele out of Europe's most affluent and privileged consumers. The laws achieved a significant goal at home as well, not necessarily in dampening consumption but in setting up ideal hierarchies of consumption. Such a program instructed the rest of Europe in how dress conveys messages about wealth and status.

And hierarchy explains a great deal about the new fourteenth-century phenomenon of fashion that chroniclers, storytellers, and pundits were so fond of criticizing. Fashion may have been elusive, but it was more than the product of whim and fancy. Fashions were often based on the exotic: on military influence in masculine dress, a reference to a padded doublet (in size an approximation of armor) and form-revealing hose, sometimes called *franciescha*. It was also belts worn low on the hips in the Eastern style, ornamental knives, "tartar" hats, robes referred to as *slavonescha*, long cloaks with enameled gilt buttons, shortened garments with set-in sleeves and fine borders worked with silver and gold thread, and sometimes even outrageous pleats.[100] Fashions could at times cross over from the Muslim or the Jewish community and be accepted by Christians, like men's turbans or, in the case of Jews, women's earrings.[101] But all new elements of fashion, all exoticisms, depended on their path of adoption for authorization. Only those widely acknowledged to have sufficient dignity, that is, status worth emulating, set fashions. Daniel Miller has asserted that ambiguity in social hierarchy must be present for fashion to flourish, and in a sense that appears to be true in Italy in the fourteenth century, since poorer consumers could create ambiguity by copying in less expensive editions the consumption patterns of their wealthier neighbors.[102] However, in another sense no ambiguity existed at all: fashions were copied where they conveyed desired messages about status. Messages encoded in display linked new fashions to credentials of wealth and the privileges that wealth brought. There was a quid pro quo offered up here: if the *savii* and *buonhomini* succeeded in setting a new fashion through a clever manipulation of image, they now possessed the necessary credentials to do so, much like Boccaccio's hero Torello. This success is witness to a usurpation of social authority that had far-reaching implications for the economy of Europe, where the wealthiest, as well as the regal and wellborn, would in time come to arbitrate taste and fashion.

The project of fashion in cities was always in danger of getting out of hand. Markets were, by their nature, open to all consumers who could pay the price of goods. Fines might limit consumption, but many resolved to pay fines and consume at a higher level; such actions were even encouraged by some provisions of some sumptuary laws. Stimulated demand, a newly important late medieval component of capitalist enterprise, was difficult to control. Nonetheless, it would be a mistake to think that the *savii* and *buonhomini,* who cultivated consumption markets carefully, were simply the dupes of wives and children who flaunted the laws. These men epitomized their society in their affluence and their consumption patterns were swiftly transforming society's assumptions about masculinity and social status. Men could become what they appeared to be and visual signals of wealth and status mattered. Emulation was desirable but only if differentials, based on knowledge about goods and their prestige connotations, were respected. Fashion had emerged in Italy's cities, and it had the power to define a man.

Chapter 4
Curbing Women's Excesses

Women in Italian cities did not take well to the restrictions imposed on them in sumptuary laws. They flaunted prohibited fashions in the streets and went over the heads of local officials to gain exemptions from the law. They paid a gabelle in order to wear a forbidden ornament and did their best to interfere with the enforcement of the law. Franco Sacchetti reached new heights of satire when he addressed women's audacity in flaunting the laws.

Florence in its wisdom established a special office to oversee women's dress, the much derided *Ufficiale delle donne*. In 1384, a Messer Amerigo degli Amerighi of Pesaro served as Giudice di Ragione and answered to the *signoria* in the hapless position of a foreign judge left to execute laws in which Florentine officialdom would take no part, a cowardly dodge and one that drew Sacchetti's scorn. Sacchetti may have heard some of the incidents that he incorporated into his story since he sat on the *signoria*. For more than a generation, that is, from the years before the plague struck Florence in 1348, the *Ufficiale delle donne* operated as a separate constituency with the task of enforcing the elaborate sumptuary laws. A foreign judge like Master Amerigo recruited a notary, who was also foreign, to record and six foreign assistants to scout out infringements committed by women. Their terms lasted six months, after which the team was replaced with a new crew and the former one left town, a prudent move given their undoubted unpopularity. These men were charged with the daunting task of going about the city, lingering outside churches or on corners, to spy out and confront women who did not obey the laws. Lawbreakers were written up and indicted, and once Messer Amerigo heard a case, a fine could be imposed.[1]

Franco Sacchetti's satire found an enticing target in the absurdities of this effort at lawkeeping. In Novella 137 he related that Messer Amerigo was driven nearly wild in discharging his duty and that the *signoria* had the temerity to chastise him for lax enforcement, so Messer Amerigo vented his pent-up frustrations. His notaries, he complained, must confront women flaunting the law and they always came off badly. Women offenders argued more adroitly than they; sometimes with clever fingers they transformed a forbidden headdress before a law enforcer's own eyes, or at other times they scornfully renamed an ornament. Officials might insist, " 'You cannot wear those buttons,' to which the woman answered, 'Yes, sir, I can, because they are not buttons but beads as they lack button holes.' "[2] Women had studied the law: decorative buttons without a corresponding buttonhole had been forbidden to women in Florence by law since 1355.[3] Beads, on the other hand, could be construed as legal ornaments.

The *signoria* was not entirely unsympathetic to the plight of their hired enforcer, noting that even the mighty Romans had not prevailed against their women when it came to dress and consumption.[4] Sacchetti's empathy with Florentine scofflaws who had bested foreign law enforcers stopped just short of collusion; however, the *signoria*'s own efforts to first palm off enforcement on foreigner appointees, then take them to task, only to respond to their indignant reactions with a lax, "Well, do your best and leave the rest," found Sacchetti at his most derisive. Limiting consumption was a far different matter in practice than the gratifying exercise of debating and passing sumptuary laws.[5] Ambivalence in high places over executing these detailed law codes suggests that the grave and wise Florentines who had drawn them up knew all along that legislating restraint was a somewhat futile attempt at curbing behavior, nor would it be particularly advantageous to them if Florentines complied strictly to the endless list of specifications that had crept into the codes over time.

Florentine sumptuary law is a portal into a confusing arena of cross purposes, stated aims compromised by tolerant enforcement, and tacit permission to those restrained by the law to act as scofflaws. Less blatant but still genuine complicity with defiant lawbreakers occurred in other towns, although the Florentines appear to have been most ingenious at ducking their own law enforcement duties and shifting the burden onto the shoulders of foreigners. In the cities of northern Italy women earned exemptions and repeals of restrictions and continually flaunted the laws, which pushed limits upward on expenditures by the time the law was next amended. In one sense the project of fashion itself was encouraged by lawmaking through the predisposition of the law to set limits on consumption at high levels; many persons could consume fine wares without reaching these limits and certainly this encouraged producers to create cheaper versions of luxury goods. Laws left significant loopholes for interpretation by creating intricate distinctions: ermine but not fur was forbidden; cloth of gold but not gold and silver thread were outlawed; and only a few rich fabrics could not be worn in the streets. Gowns must fall to the ground but not drag on the ground. A woman might wear a head ornament or a jewel in her hair but not both. Beads were legal ornaments but buttons without buttonholes were not.

Nonetheless, sumptuary law has been regarded as generally deleterious to women's exercise of rights in cities, and without question women's public behavior and dress became the major focus of lawmakers' displeasure from the earliest writing of law in the late thirteenth century. Women were labeled the guilty parties overwhelmingly and identified as the vainglorious sex—Sacchetti's very words in his Novella 179; whether any individual woman was indicted and fined, the law regarded women generally as more prone to excess. In the context of vibrant luxury markets—where men were likely to be the more free-spending customers, and where men's fashions cost more than women's—women remained the primary target of the laws' censure.

In the late thirteenth century Bologna initiated legislation about the minutiae of women's costume and expenditures, and because Bologna's law was widely imitated throughout northern Italy, there was almost no town, large or small, that did not designate women the chief culprits when it came to *sumptus*.[6] Throughout the fourteenth century, the sentiments of the 1360 preamble to the Venetian sumptuary law rang out: "And thus is noted in our city today, more than in all other parts of the world, more vanities and inordinate expenses among wives and other women."[7] At Venice during the War of Chioggia (1379–81), the pre-Lenten Festival of the Twelve Maries was outlawed; one reason for the restriction was that the ostentations of women from the two competing *contrade* (districts) who staged the festival each year upset public decorum. Some lawmakers would have outlawed all *bocheta* (jeweled headdresses) to women at that time if they had had their way, but that provision failed to pass.

In Florence, Bishop Latino brought sumptuary condemnations of women's behavior to the city in 1279, and in the synodal constitution of 1310 Bishop Biliotti applied severe strictures to women's clothes on the grounds of immodesty and expense. These principles were applied to civic laws in the 1320s. The amended laws of 1356, as well as the compiled laws of 1384, were translated into the vernacular to aid in enforcement, presumably to help women, young men, and children understand their own misguided impulses and learn to obey. The Franciscan monk Salimbene, writing in the 1280s, and Giovanni Villani, writing in the 1320s, roundly condemned women's attempts to become the fashionable sex.[8] So did the *signoria*, whose enforcement agency bore the title Office Charged with Overseeing Women, that is, *Ufficiale delle donne*.

This brief review does not do justice to the constant attention paid by city fathers to women's dress. Minutes of deliberations and compilations of law record an unending undercurrent of complaint about women's costumes, as if each session brought together men freshly distraught by the outrages they had seen in the street or in their homes. This rumble of dissatisfaction erupted in a major spate of new laws every generation or so in large cities, then each new major revision was itself subjected to debate as further disagreements arose as soon as revisions were passed. Some lawmakers saw the project of legislating restraint as foolhardy and advocated repeal. Whether this was out of sympathy for Venetian women or respect for privacy, or on the grounds that sumptuary law was by nature unsound and a foolish exercise of statecraft, is not clear.[9] What is clear is that men in authority spoke and acted on the issue of women's dress without cease in cities. The problem of dress was not resolved nor could it be put to rest.

Focusing steadily on women, fourteenth-century sumptuary laws amounted to one more phase in a centuries' long program of restricting women's public rights in city-states.[10] Catherine Guimbard has suggested that sumptuary laws belong with reform of dowry practices and women's inheritance rights, with restraints on women appearing in law courts without a male *advocatus* or *mundualdus*, and with other similar initiatives that over centuries curtailed women's legal rights in Italy's cities.[11] Many of these measures, like sumptuary law itself, found precedent in Roman law. Franco Sacchetti invoked classical antecedents in Livy when comparing fourteenth-century Florentine law enforcement to Rome's repeal of the Oppian Law. Other urban lawmakers, like those of Siena, claimed that in reforming their customs—for one, dowries awarded at marriage—they now wished to live "according to Roman law."[12] Almost everywhere in Italy Roman models underlay initiatives that restricted women's personal and public rights.

Over the course of the twelfth and thirteenth centuries, wedding gifts to women were transformed from husbands' gifts to their new wives to a bride's father's gift, a Roman dowry that the bride nominally owned but did not control. Diane Owen Hughes has noted that in Genoa where this change came early, a twelfth-century annal depicted women holding up their hands in despair over the new statute that substituted Roman dowry for marriage gifts from husbands.[13] These portions from husbands were known by many names: an *antefactum*, *morgincap* or *morgingabe*, in canon law a *donatio propter nuptias*, which was strictly limited in size, or, in less formal language, as a gift called a *tercia* or *quarta* (a third or quarter of a husband's estate). Wherever they were awarded a husband's gifts belonged to a wife without restriction; she could spend, will, or alienate this gift as she wished. In Siena the last registered marriage assign from husband to wife (there called *morgincap*) was recorded in 1140 and the first Roman dowry or *dos* was documented in 1144.[14] Increasingly, husbands' gifts to wives were condemned on the grounds that they were spent on excessive and immoral dress and on wedding festivities. The church's efforts at sumptuary lawmaking, which began in the later thirteenth century, may be read as a continuation of efforts to control husbands' gifts that could be spent freely rather than preserved. But it is also clear that husbands' gifts remained so popular with brides that even when outlawed they were given informally, sometimes surreptitiously. Prosperous men often gave indulgent gifts to their brides that partially recompensed the bride's family for the major outlay of capital that a Roman dowry represented.[15]

Thirteenth-century prosperity was reflected in reciprocal gift giving, which reformers came to see as dangerous and immoral. Gifts given at weddings meant that women possessed a wardrobe of elegant dresses and cloaks to parade around town for years to come. Salimbene roundly applauded Bishop Latino's strictures on women's dragging trains and lack of veils when the bishop condemned both fashions at Florence in 1279.[16] But the church's 1310 synodal constitution more accurately targeted Florentine weddings as occasions for generous gift giving and as the underlying cause of current excesses. In that constitution Bishop Biliotti aimed to protect the patrimonies of his congregation when he noted "that the resources of the Florentines are damnably exhausted" when they are spent on women's dress; family wealth should be reinvested instead.[17] Women bore the brunt of his condemnations, but, as he knew very well, it was men's generosity that was at issue.

Venice—indeed the entire Adriatic region—was an exception to the social disruption occasioned by reorienting the direction in which marital gifts flowed, but only because Roman dowry had a long history in the region.[18] Husbands' counterdowries or gifts to wives were a long-standing feature of Venetian life, and they continued to be generous, as the sumptuary law of 1360 attested.[19] Wherever employed, a Roman dowry was hedged with restraints; by law and custom a woman owned her dowry but her husband had the management of it while he lived.[20] Although he must hold it intact in the event of his or his wife's death, he was enjoined to invest the money to increase it.[21] By the fourteenth century, a bride was entitled to only a restricted countergift from her husband but it remained hers to do with as she willed.[22] In church and sometimes civic law this gift was referred to as the *donatio propter nuptias*. From the twelfth century onward efforts were made to limit the size of this award, so what actually remained to women was likely to be an informal and customarily awarded gift of clothes and jewels that functioned as a counterdowry. When in turn sumptuary law in cities restricted the amount of this money that a woman could spend freely—indeed the sum of the finery that any bride might receive to celebrate her wedding—it chipped away at the remaining authority a married woman retained over her personal goods and wealth, which, as a result of earlier legal initiatives, now consisted largely of her personal apparel.[23]

Changes in dowry practices in cities were linked to the elaboration of canon law on marriage disputes that began to appear in decretals over the course of the twelfth and thirteenth centuries. Gratian, to whom has been attributed the resounding phrase *sine dotium non facet coniugium* (without [Roman] dowry there is no marriage), sought to distinguish between valid and invalid marriages on sound theological grounds and in clear language.[24] Gratian cited no civil law of Rome in rendering his opinions, although he likely recognized principles of Roman law when he encountered them in ancient church sources. He cited only papal opinion, church councils, theologians, and Scripture on marriage, and these provided him with the legal principles he required in resolving marriage disputes. In Canon 12 of *Questio* 5, Gratian stated, "Est ordo naturalis in hominibus, ut feminae serviant viris, et filii parentibus, qua in illis hec iusticia est, ut maiori serviant minor" (It is the natural order among mankind that women serve their husbands as children do parents; the justice in this is that the lesser serve the greater). This was followed by the biblical citation, "*vir est caput mulieris*" (man is the head and has dominion over woman). In Canon 17, Gratian spelled out the implication for women in terms of legal incapacity: "Mulierem constat subiectam dominio viri esse, et nullam auctoritatem habere; nec docere potest, nec testis esse, neque fidem dare, nec iudicare" (Woman should be subject to her husband's rule, and has no authority, either to teach, to bear witness, to give surety, or to judge).[25]

Perhaps such simple distinctions within a consistently rendered opinion made Gratian valuable to civil lawyers as well, for over the decades he became the cited authority in cities when women's rights before the law were restricted. In sum, the new laws returned women to the legal status of dependents, under what Roman law had long before labeled the *tutela*. Children were also governed by the *tutela,* but boys or young men (*iuventi*) outgrew it upon reaching their majority. Girls and women did not escape the *tutela*: the authority over them was transferred from father to husband when they married. By the fifteenth century in Florence, women were expected to employ a representative *mundualdus* if it was necessary for them to appear before a court.[26] In Venice and the Adriatic region an *advocatus* was appointed to represent a woman before the court in the later Middle Ages.[27]

Fourteenth-century sumptuary laws fall between twelfth- and thirteenth-century initiatives that placed both wives and their Roman dowries (Falcidian *quarta*, or their share thereof as *legitim* in the natal family estate) under the authority of husbands, and fifteenth-century initiatives to turn the husband's gift or *donatio propter nuptias* into a cash award, one controlled by the husband himself. The latter initiative would directly affect women's spending on apparel, while concomitantly strengthening the husband's control of all the capital given on the occasion of marriage, as Stanley Chojnacki and Jane Fair Bestor have pointed out.[28] Fourteenth-century civic sumptuary laws that followed the general principle of curbing women's spending also served as a restraining device on women's and children's control of wealth. Laws attempted to direct family spending away from personal possessions (movables) and into capital sums that could be invested. In effect civic lawmakers adopted the role of pater familias through lawmaking whenever they restricted spending in their four-century-long span of intervention into marital practices and gift giving. Civic surveillance over families provided a powerful justification for redesigning and reformulating laws; it tacitly acknowledged that heads of households needed civic laws to buttress their authority at home.[29] But whatever momentary relief heads of households may have gained with the passage of each new law, in the long run the effort to legislate restraint for all who fell under the *tutela*, women chief among them, was no more successful than had been private efforts of fathers and husbands to control spending within their own families. Heads of households, in turns strict and yielding, continued to vacillate between indulgence and restraint.

In Venice, in *The Governance of the Family* (1314), Fra Paolino had written: "Sometimes the man follows too much the will of the woman in buying her ornaments, and this gives rise to much evil, excessive expenditure, and the woman is more than ever filled with pride, and for vainglory desires still more to go out and show herself. Therefore the man should dress his wife as he thinks right, and according to the manner which prevails among his equals."[30] Without hesitation Fra Paolino grounded his disapproval of women's excesses on the premise that men made the decisions on important purchases for women. This was the case to the extent that men frequented the goldsmiths' shops, the benches of money changers that displayed jewels, gold, or silver wares, the silk shops, and the workshops of tailors (*sartori*) who created bespoke capes, mantles, robes, and gowns. Giovanni Niccolini, uncle and guardian of the bride Tommasa, bragged in 1353, "I spent when I married [off] Tommasa, for one belt, mounted in silver with a purse with silver enamel, three gold florins."[31] He was comfortably within the limit of four florins set by law on a bride's wedding belt but confident in the generosity of his gift. Husbands gave counterdowries to their brides and made important purchases for brides' wardrobes, and they often paid the gabelles for wives to wear this finery.

It is the fourteenth-century phase in this centuries-long project of state intervention into household finance that is at issue here. As Manlio Bellomo has argued, by this era the triumph of capital management over more traditional concerns for the security, comfort, and prestige of a newly married couple meant that dowry sums became a negotiation between the bride's father and her husband and as a result were strictly regulated.[32] There was little opportunity here for a family to respond to the social demands of the event itself and the promptings of affection, or demands of honor and prestige, through gift giving. The impulse to gift was folded into grants of trousseau that accompanied the *dos*, known informally as *corredi* in much of Italy. Legal opinions about ownership were offered in this contentious arena of ownership of the trousseaux. Not just regulating the capital sums in dowry but the transfer and ownership of movable goods given at marriage became matters of state; indeed, legal opinions were rendered about all of a wife's personal possessions, most notably her clothing and jewels.[33] Among wealthy families, considerable capital could be tied up in these possessions, so ownership was open to dispute. If sumptuary laws limited the ostentation of gifts given at weddings, so fourteenth-century thinking went, there would be less opportunity for disputes to arise, and, of course, family capital would be preserved.

Under these circumstances sumptuary laws served as a highly effective means for perpetuating assumptions about woman's nature that underlay the long-standing legal discourse on marital gifts. Gratian's revived polarities for defining a woman's place in the natural order of things were likely known to the designers of sumptuary law: man has dominion over woman according to a polar construct of privation. Man has capacity, thus woman as his related opposite lacks capacity.[34] No elaborate mechanism of logic worked here but a simpler and less rigorously constructed notion of opposed traits, which had the effect of defining woman as lacking *because* she was the polar opposite to man.[35] In sumptuary law this notion proved useful, with civic authority cast in the role of "head," that is, he who possesses capacity. This meant lawmakers assumed obligation for control over those who, by the polar construct of incapacity, could neither restrain nor control themselves. If, in the chronicler Giovanni Villani's words, women's clothes were dishonestly embellished (*disonesto ornamento*), that dishonesty, especially when displayed publicly, was vivid proof of women's incapacity and failure to acquiesce to necessarily imposed restraints. "[E] così il disordinato appetito delle donne vince la ragione e il senno degli uomini" (women's disorderly appetites conquer the reason and good sense of men) was a genuine concern rather than a mere verbal flourish when Villani penned it.[36]

There were serious issues at stake in composing sumptuary laws. By the fourteenth century, Aristotle's exposition of the polarity of privation was understood by any lawyer familiar with scholastic theology, even if he could not recite Aristotle's specific words: "a husband and father rules over wife and children, both free, but the rule differs, the rule over his children being royal, over his wife a constitutional rule. For although there may be exceptions to the order of nature, the male is by nature fitter for command than the female. . . . Clearly, then, moral virtue belongs to all of them; but the temperance of a man and of a woman, or the courage and justice of a man and of a woman, are not, as Socrates maintained, the same; the courage of a man is shown in commanding, of a woman in obeying."[37]

If only women would conform to their natures and obey! By choosing ornate dress women had assumed an unnatural authority; to dismiss the rhetoric that justified each new sumptuary law as mere window dressing can lead to a mistaken reading of the strength of underlying assumptions and deeply held sentiments. A gender construction of considerable power held sway here, rendered all the more persuasive because it went substantially unopposed.[38] Sumptuary laws may have been unenforceable but they were solicitous attempts to turn women away from vainglorious struggles to escape their natures and were justified by lawgivers on that account. In these laws no specific clause or restriction was ever as crucial as the law's address to a woman's underlying condition. In a well-ordered society women's public comportment was intended to mirror the truth of inherent incapacity. At least in the stately chambers of government, the leaders of cities could share a vision of a seemly order where their own natural authority remained undisputed and women happily complied as they were meant to do. Legislators in Italy's cities faced up to their duty and wrote sumptuary laws.

The asymmetry in surviving evidence—men's words and deeds balanced against women's reactions (which are seldom documented)—has led to interpreting sumptuary law as mere lighthearted scolding over frivolous trinkets and baubles—in other words, to missing the consequence of an emerging urban culture of consumption with attendant gender assumptions. Women's silence in the face of state regulations that were broadcast publicly was neither as complete as has been assumed nor a sign of acquiescence. Genoese women were recorded as holding up their hands in dismay when gifts from husbands were restricted in the twelfth century. Salimbene told of women in Romagna who protested the imposition of sumptuary law in the thirteenth century.[39] Villani's chronicle acknowledged women's great displeasure at giving up their ornaments under threat of condemnation by the new Florentine laws of 1326.[40] When a woman of bourgeois origins achieved noble and status through marriage she celebrated her escape from sumptuary regulations by acquiring rich dress and ornaments, as did the great lady Fina da Carrara, née Buzzacarini of Padua.[41]

Persistent, if imperfect, efforts at enforcing compliance with the law impede efforts today to reconstruct the emergence of heightened demand for luxury goods among women.[42] Persons of all conditions, regardless of gender or age, paid attention to markets and to the messages encoded in public apparel; this certainly included women. But it remains to be seen if secular women's acts of dress or comportment reflected their market preferences or those of their fathers and husbands.[43] In the fourteenth century a holy woman living in Italy might leave behind a substantial corpus of writing; little survives from more worldly women.[44] Women of means were sometimes literate because they were privately tutored; they might even have attended primary school in Florence, according to Villani.[45] Women administered complex households, making literacy at least in the vernacular highly desirable, while a command of currency and local market conditions were equally relevant to running households. If women did not become literate in childhood they might work diligently to learn reading and writing later on, as did Mona Margherita Datini, whose famous correspondence was recovered at Prato.[46] But written reactions to women's plight as restrained parties in sumptuary law have not survived; for spirited retorts it is necessary to look ahead to Battista Petrucci and Nicolosa Sanuti, who wrote a century later.[47] Still, the gabelles paid for women to wear fine clothes at Florence and women's appearances before the *Ufficiale delle donne* as defendants and at celebrations they enthusiastically embraced, like that of the Festival of the Twelve Maries at Venice, provide some evidence of women's reactions to the laws. It is the case here, as elsewhere, that women's acts have been filtered through men's recording of them, but women did act, and with spirit.

Festival of the Twelve Maries

"The history of the festive rites associated with Santa Maria Formosa is tortuously complex," Edward Muir has argued, "yet, in its complexity, this history best reveals the interplay between popular and elite institutions in Venetian society and, ultimately, the triumph of the government in diverting popular festivities toward a political end."[48] He also noted that during this pre-Lenten festival twelve wooden statues of Mary were embellished and paraded by gondola throughout the city, six each by two rival *contrade*. In particular this was a festival fourteenth-century Venetian women considered their own, at least until its celebration was abolished during the War of Chioggia.[49]

By 1316 this winter festival had become a matter for state intervention.[50] Special subsidies were provided for the two *contrade* that would house the wooden statues of Mary by 1341.[51] When it fell to two working-class *contrade* to host the Maries in 1347, the Great Council assigned nobles with businesses in those districts the financial obligation to pay for the festival, whether they were willing or not.[52] By 1361 a special city *estimo* was instituted to alleviate the financial burden falling on San Pantaleone and San Marco, who hosted the Maries that year.[53] State intervention and the steeply rising cost of the yearly event indicate how great its consequence had become over the course of the century.

Women of the rival *contrade* that were chosen each year by the principle of rotation accompanied the twelve wooden Maries in procession. The entire period leading up to Candlemas (February 2) was filled with formal banquets and other social affairs in both *contrade,* and women from throughout the city gathered there; in particular women attended regattas and the *ludi mariani*—the sports events in honor of Mary that capped the winter season before Lent. Privately assumed expenses could be high, particularly for the six patrician or very wealthy families who opened their homes to display one of the twelve wooden Maries. These statues were honorifically decked out in the most gorgeous jewels and fabric inhabitants of the *contrada* could gather together. Plenty of opportunity arose for women to display themselves as well. During the procession to Santa Maria Formosa, women sat together in boats for all to see (and compare, no doubt)—the more beautiful and richly attired boatload winning the greater acclaim. At gatherings in private homes and palaces the next day "[m]arried ladies and their maiden daughters entered in their finest clothes and sat quietly chatting while the men stood about, drinking wine 'in quantity.'"[54]

The reason for the 1334 sumptuary law's new allowance of two dresses for a bride's wedding day (since 1299 the law had allowed a married woman to possess four fine dresses as a lifetime wardrobe) becomes clearer in this context. Women whose families could afford fine gowns (costing about forty ducats; see Chapter 5) continued to wear their good dresses on festival occasions. The prestige of the *contrada* was at stake, and a woman tried her utmost. The best apparel of the wealthy was intended to last for decades; to do so it was, apparently, redesigned, embroidered, or retrimmed to appear new for festival occasions. No wonder borders, likely newly worked borders, had become a particular concern of sumptuary law by the 1330s. Women assumed a well-clad presence necessary for the celebration of the festival: women graced private parties, renewed old friendships, represented their *contrade*, appeared at the games, and even mixed with the general levity in the streets. Women were dressed as well as their regulated wardrobes permitted, embellished further by their needle skills and all the various trims, jewels, ribbons, plaques, and beads in their cupboards.

According to Muir, legend associated with this festival "stood the story of the rape of the Sabine women on its head." In the tenth century, an Adriatic pirate named Gaiolus, accompanied by his men, had attempted to capture Venetian maidens—nota bene, with their dowries and jewels in hand—only to be thwarted by Venetian men who reclaimed their women at the appropriately named *Porto delle Donzelle*. Women in finery recalled this legend whenever they attended festival events. While the legend may have emphasized, as Muir noted, "the protective, peaceful, inward-looking order provided by the strong, cohesive community [of Venice]," it also afforded opportunity for fourteenth-century high jinks.[55] Bejeweled women could be pursued and captured in the guise of their salvation from pirates in a replay of recalled, if mythic, events. Along with games, regatta events, and spontaneous races that interrupted the solemn procession of fleets from the two competing *contrade* toward Santa Maria Formosa, chasing well-dressed women was another occasion for unruliness and fun.

Prohibiting the popular old enactments and transforming the procession in 1379–80 amounted to a successful attempt at capturing a popular ritual for purposes of state, while the ostensible reason for curtailing the festival events was to stem the great drain on Venetian resources occasioned by war with Genoa. The festival had generally continued for days and the cost to the twelve households displaying the Maries had been so great that in its heyday the task needed to be parceled out by government order. The sumptuary dimension of the 1379 ruling reveals a similar character to other attempts to limit *le pompe* in the city. Added expenses, especially those associated with women in all their finery in processions and at games, disturbed decorum and order in the great city of Venice, it was argued. This disorderliness could be construed as scandalous when played out before the eyes of visiting foreigners. Women's behavior was understood to be in need of state intervention, although it is apparent that women sat together, not among men, in procession to Santa Maria Formosa, and sat quietly together while the men of their families drank deeply at the private parties honoring the housed statues of Mary.

So it may be assumed that in their silence women spoke eloquently, and their retrimmed, updated, and embroidered dresses did the speaking. The festival they claimed as their own came to be viewed as dangerous to public morality. By 1379 women's presence in such a public venue was equated with *luxuria*, that is, with a particular offensive female vice. Thereafter the procession to Santa Maria Formosa was transformed into a more formal and tranquil affair of state. Well-adorned, albeit largely silent, maidens and married women no longer threatened public order.[56]

Venetian sumptuary law's persistent concern with *frexatura perlarum* (an embroidered border reliant on pearls or glass beads, probably similar to the *frixis* outlawed at Bologna as early as 1289) and *drezatores perlarum* (strings of pearls or beads woven into the hair) is certainly relevant to the Festival of the Twelve Maries. By law, in 1299, only a bride could wear pearl-studded borders; these trims were forbidden to all other women. A single jewel for the hair, but not many strings of pearls or beads, was allowed to married women. By 1334 both borders and the *drezatores perlarum* were restricted for all women, and this continued after the repeal of the law in 1339, so the two prohibitions appear to have remained in effect indefinitely. In the law of 1360, specific articles of fashion were again forbidden or limited: not only belts but purses, the ubiquitous *bochete,* chains, and pearls. A failed effort to stamp out all *bochete* was mounted as part of the effort to tame the Twelve Maries festival events in 1379–80.[57] In the second half of the century the Venetian *corredi* with its many decorative components had come under a thorough review. Within that trousseau lay the necessary ingredients for refurbishing the few, if very expensive, dresses a woman was allowed by law and relied on over the course of her married life.

These trims and beads—"pearls" were likely to be the margaritas (*conteria*) of glass from Murano—had evidently become highly personal signatures of style, and married women used all sorts of trims to redesign their small but expensive wardrobes of gowns and headdresses. Glass beads, cleverly strung or sewn into patterns as trims, created eye-catching novelty at small cost, albeit considerable labor with a needle; beads were easily removed and replaced by another new trim or design, that is, if a woman had leisure and servants at her command who were skilled needlewomen. To a degree intensive labor on costume could substitute for numerous changes of gowns, renewing and transforming one of the fine dresses allowed to a married woman by law.[58]

As the fourteenth century progressed, women's fashionable presence was ever more closely associated with carnality, and when traditionally tolerant Venice joined the chorus of condemnation in 1379, this assumption was surely entrenched. Earlier when the Franciscan Salimbene and Fra Paolino Minorita had been among the few decrying women's vanities criticisms of women's dress had been at best sporadic, but as the decades progressed many outside orders had taken up the theme of inordinate vanity in women. Lay and religious criticism became a resounding chorus of condemnation.[59]

Living with the Law in Florence

In Florence, foreigners enforcing sumptuary laws kept logbooks of scouting activities to seek out dress infractions in the city streets. Ronald Rainey has located a series of entries for an assistant assigned to the notary Ser Donato, whose term in the *Ufficiale delle donne* began in January 1349. A few of Rainey's findings follow by way of illustration. The first few days of his surveillance were uneventful, but January 18 turned up two women wearing forbidden head ornaments. Gostantia, wife of Zanobio Visdomini of Florence, wore a garland decorated with enamel work and silver estimated at more than six *lira*. It was not marked with the commune's seal, which would indicate that a gabelle had already been paid.[60] Another woman of the same Christian name of Gostantia was found wearing a *cerchiellium* (a circlet for the head) worth more than five gold florins, and a third named Silvaggia wore a red and green parti-colored wool tunic contrary to the law. On February 3, Domina Lisa, wife of Giovanni di Francesco Magalotti, was noted as wearing a silver head ornament that was not registered. Domina Gemma, wife of Gerio Mallie of Montepoggio, was cited on February 16 for her silver *cerchiellium* worth more than two florins and not marked with the commune's seal. On February 25 and March 1 more illegal head ornaments were logged; in the latter case Domina Geccha, wife of Rainerio di Grifo, was caught wearing three rings, one too many according to the law.[61] An act of gallantry was recorded as well when Pepino di Antonio Albizzi intervened on Geccha's behalf, and the harassed assistant was unable to successfully write up his charge. Florentine men could not be expected to always stand by idly while a foreign law enforcer ogled their women. Finally, on March 31, Domina Laurentia, wife of Bartolomeo di Lapo Bonbieri, was found wearing a silver belt beyond the limit set in the law.[62] All the indicted were married women; at least one, Domina Lisa, was probably young because her noble husband would become an important member of the government some twenty years later. Offenders came from various parishes and in one case from the Florentine *contado*. They were wives of *populani* and wives of magnates. Ser Donato found more lawbreakers over his six-month term: in total, eight wore forbidden head ornaments; six wore sleeves longer than prescribed by the law; one case each involved a two-colored tunic, too many rings, and a silver belt; and one woman was cited for a dress decorated with mother-of-pearl. About two fines a month were collected from violators, although "Francesco Ochi, who served in the same office from July 1350 to January 1351, filled a logbook with daily entries indicating that he had gone out searching for offenses against the sumptuary laws every day during his six-month term and had found no violations at all."[63] Francesco Ochi may have been myopic but he was also a prudent man.

Over the decades other scouts sent out into the streets had greater success. Children were scrutinized as well as women, and fathers were ordered to pay fines for their offspring's violations. One little girl under five was found wearing a brown tunic with gold ribbons that sported twenty-six enameled silver buttons and another set of sixteen gilded silver buttons on the sleeves. The latter set, no doubt due to the diminutive size of the child, continued beyond the elbow, which was against the law for any woman or girl. One little boy, Gualberto Morelli, scion of a fine old family and still in his nurse's arms, wore a red and yellow *clamide* (gown) with eighteen silver buttons and gold ribbons running next to them. Another little boy wore a parti-colored cloak with gold ribbons on the lapels and a fancy hat made of wool and black silk velvet.[64] No soft pastels for these elegant children.

Other prohibited clothing that appeared in the streets of Florence was perfectly legal if an attached leaden seal (with the official lily) indicated a gabelle had been paid. In these circumstances, law enforcers would know to exempt the wearer from prosecution. Ornaments and clothes were carefully described in registers maintained by law enforcers. Diane Owen Hughes described the cloaks of the Albizzi that were registered in the Prammatica of 1343: Lady Guerriera, the wife of Jacopo di Antonio de Albizzi, and her sister-in-law Nera registered identical white mantles embroidered with vines and red grapes, while across town another member of the family, a Lady Genevra, wife of Agnolo de Giani de Albizzis, registered a white mantle embroidered with the same vines and red grapes. The garments were uniform down to the fine cloth that lined them.[65]

Florentines witnessed a riveting parade in the streets. On each corner they might speculate on what was legal in the passing scene and what was not—in terms of expense, of course, but also on the more intriguing question of which designs were appropriately displayed. Were embroidered red grapes with vines an honestly worn reflection of lineage or a counterfeit badge, an improperly assumed emblem? Could a lead seal be found that indicated the gabelle had been paid to wear those grapes and vines? The *Ufficiale*'s scouting officers turned more and more of their efforts to detecting symbols and figures.[66] Forbidden ruffles and cloth of gold, or rich ermine, or sleeves longer than the specified length were easily discernible infractions of law; distinctive designs, motifs, abstract figures, heraldic devices, and alphabet letters were more perplexing and certainly distracting, placing a new burden on law enforcement. When women wore figured devices and badges was it an inversion of a semiotic system that was men's traditional domain? Did a woman make reference to a political faction with her sewn-on designs? Was this a mockery of livery that men wore by right or tradition? Did women ever possess the right to wear insignia or a badge that proclaimed affiliation?[67]

In the world of the fourteenth century, badges, emblems, and devices of all kinds were worn as indicators of affiliation and status. The leaden fleur-de-lis attached to a Florentine garment indicating the gabelle was paid possessed its own stitching rings so it could be sewn on clothes; the same was true for badges worn by pilgrims. Among these the Veronica (likeness of Christ) grew ever more popular, and by the fourteenth century the icon was displayed at St. Peter's in Rome on Sundays, "and foreign pilgrims stood to gain 12,000 years of remission of sin for every hour that they gazed on it."[68] No wonder vernicles traveled throughout Europe as prized pilgrims' badges; wearing them was both a Christian duty and a charitable act. Rulers granted permission for devices to be stitched on clothes in some cases. In Florence, where figural elements on clothes were forbidden on the streets, it was considered appropriate that badges of civic office accompanied the deceased on his journey to burial. Any woman sporting figural devices—as badges stitched on clothes or embroidered onto fabric—ran the risk of transgressing some norm or carefully guarded privilege.

Domina Lena, wife of Maro de Pazzi, was charged in 1347 for wearing a mantle of red on which flowers had been embroidered in black and white silk thread. Her lawyer pleaded on her behalf that the robe with the flowers had been registered beforehand, and he exhibited a document of registration as proof, claiming a mistaken description in the document itself. This discrepancy—whether the flowers were yellow and white or black and white—led to debate. Her lawyer supported his case by producing a piece of red cloth with white and black flowers to which the proper leaden seal with lily had been attached. The judge suspected foul play, and no mistake on the part of the original notarial entry in the book of paid gabelles, so a fine of 75 *lira* was imposed (although half was deducted for prompt payment). Assuming with the judge that Domina Lena had two flower-embroidered *guarnacce*, one registered and one not, these dresses had been done up with very similar floral motifs with silk thread to support such a legal defense. Were these similar designs of flowers a family insignia like the Albizzi grapes? Did the lady in question have a legitimate right to this floral design in white and black flowers or, for that matter, in yellow and white ones?

In much the same way Domina Gostantia, wife of a pharmacist from the parish of S. Frediano, was charged for wearing a blue woolen dress decorated with white stars and yellow geometric designs made from silk thread; these were perhaps astrological symbols, but what message, if any, did she intend to convey by displaying them?[69] This Domina Gostantia also pleaded before the judge that the garment had registered three years earlier and had greater success than Domina Lena and her lawyer.[70] A Domina Johanna, wife of Jacopo di Silio, wore a wool dress out walking one day on which white, yellow, and red dragons of silk along with other figures in white, yellow, and green had been embroidered.[71] Might any woman properly display dragons on the streets of the city, and what did it mean if she did so?

Unlike the grapes adorning the women of the noble lineage of Albizzi, the embroidery worn by these three indicted women appears to have been highly individual, and in each case the handwork design was distinctive and personal. These cases brought before the judge did not represent costly apparel like fine furs, jewels, or cloth trimmed with gold and silver. Instead, the good wool of the matrons' wardrobes was skillfully embroidered with silk in unique designs; here cost was not at issue.[72] As the statutes of 1322–25 had stated, no person, male or female, small or great, of whatever dignity or order, could wear clothes with cut, worked, or superimposed images or likenesses of trees or flowers, animals or birds, or any other figures, under fine of 100 *lira*, and this was one of the higher imposed fines in the law.[73] Later, in 1330, a general prohibition of figured fabric (*drappi di seta rilevati*) was enacted. From the evidence of fines issued in the 1340s the prohibition on figural representation was a major concern for the *Ufficiale delle donne;* indeed, if reckoning on the number of court cases brought, as great an issue as expense.[74]

Sumptuary law could play a permissive role as well, which suggests that protecting the integrity of sanctioned signs and symbols, as well as their legitimate bearers, was an important component of legislation. Certain images like coats of arms and other emblems honestly owned were permitted when the occasion warranted. A bride might carry to her new home a treasure casket decorated with her husband's coat of arms, which would commemorate her act of transfer from paternal to spousal authority.[75] At funerals, the coat of arms on a shield or the emblem of a knight might be featured, and a symbol of a *magister*'s profession, such as a book, might be carried in procession.[76] Permissions like these related to clearly stated messages expressed in conformity with civic values. At baptism the mother of a child might receive a silver cup engraved with the coats of arms of both parents' lineages, celebrating generational renewal through an easily comprehended familial ritual of exchange.[77]

Among her inventoried goods in 1380, Madonna Margherita di Vanni degli Spini, now an Acciaiuoli widow, had a surfeit of coats of arms from the Acciaiuoli family available for ritual occasions. One coat of arms embellished an enameled gilded belt, a small basin bore the Acciaiuoli arms, and another great silver buckled belt with her husband's arms belonged to her; some curtains with her husband's arms were listed in her inventory as well, while the many pennants and flags in her possession may have featured family colors or crests as well. But Madonna Margherita also owned a footed credenza with the arms of the king, presumably of Sicily, a great seal of gilded silver with the image of the king on it, and a piece of silk with the arms of France either worked into the fabric or embroidered on it. She possessed as well a belt with green ribbon, decorated with *littere* (letters) of gilded silver, and a white bedcover worked with beasts on it (the rest of its motifs are uncertain due to the condition of the manuscript).[78] Lucca's talented weavers of brocade prided themselves on fabrics that incorporated scenes of the hunt, and weavers could have produced the figured fabric of the bedcover described here, but did these images break the law and had Madonna Margherita any right at all to the king's arms, much less other insignia of her husband's family? As for the mysterious *littere,* they possessed great cachet. *Littere* were worn by distinguished noblemen like the Marchese di Monferrato, who had a *chapillectum pro domino* adorned with 1,200 *littere* of gilded silver, a magnificent hat that must have jingled at every footstep.[79] A belt that has survived from the fourteenth century sported alternative plaques bearing a letter A (*amor* or an initial letter of a name?) and a lion.[80] A fifteenth-century French brooch featured four appended *littere* spelling out the word AMOR, a favor worthy of a courtly love poet.[81] *Littere* were very popular.

Venetians were equally cognizant of the importance of emblems and insignia.[82] In an inventory of goods from the estate of the doge Francesco Dandolo (1339), there was an overcoat of samite with the Dandolo arms worked in green, five silk banners with the family coat of arms, and two pennants of silk bearing a family insignia along with a cloth banner similarly adorned. Dandolo also left a great cloak with *capitibus* (capitals?) worked in silk, and a canopy of silk and velvet with his coat of arms. While the latter is clearly described, the embroidery of *capitibus* on Dandolo's great cloak is a mysterious design; it may have been more of the popular *littere* like those prohibited in Florentine sumptuary laws. Goldsmiths' shops were capable of turning out *littere* among their ready-made goods for market, and they seemed to have sold well in the Adriatic region.[83] Dandolo left a banner *imperiale* in his estate, creating a further mystery about whether this was a style designation or an emblem of Venetian imperial authority. If the latter, it was not to be bandied about casually by Dandolo's heirs.

According to precise phrasing within his will, the doge's property could be sold by his widow if she chose, indicating one path by which heraldic devices and symbols might fall into the hands of others.[84] As with Madonna Margherita's inventoried gift, a widow had been left in charge of the proper disposition of a man's goods including articles bearing honorific markings. In her 1380 gift to the church Madonna Margherita gave away numerous editions of the Acciaiouli arms, as well as a king's insignia. Dandola's widow had charge of the proper disposal of banners, canopies, and cloaks laden with symbols of the doge's exalted family and office.

Francesco da Barberino assigned this lament to the widows of such highly placed men:

Ond' averanno gli amici e parenti
La grande aiuto, soccorso e consilglio
Che ricevièn dattè, dolcie singniore?

(From where will friends and family have the solid hand, succor, and counsel they received from you, sweet lord?)[85] According to Barberino, a woman encountered an unplanned-for crisis in her widowhood by being made to serve as her own authority over serious matters like the disposal of honorific markings. Decisions, which had fallen to her husband as her head, no longer lay within their "natural" domain of male authority; thus a widow was incapacitated even while the need for decisions like disposal of estates persisted. Barberino struggled to advise women left in these unnatural circumstances. Even if a husband's stated intentions and the law conspired to leave a widow in authority (as, for example, prescribed in Francesco Dandolo's will), Barberino admonished a widow to find new male counselors. The allegorical figure of *Costanza* (endurance) should provide the example for widows as they entered a phase of life for which neither nature nor experience had prepared them. Barberino believed a widow's loss was much greater than mere separation from a beloved lifetime companion; a widow suddenly found herself bereft of necessary governance:

E tanti e tali attutti ufici ponga
Che non bisongni dei di que' pensare

(So put in charge only those whom you do not need to watch over), Barberino advised the widow of a prince or lord, as he unwittingly urged critical choices about new advisors on a woman whom, he believed, nature had designed without the capacity for making wise choices of that sort.[86]

Whoever was left in charge, disposal of personal property—signs, sym-

Figure 5. *Damisella Triulcia, virgincula Mediolanense.* A later woodcut, probably after an earlier portrait, showing a young woman in a circlet or crown, also wearing pearls, in the fashion of the fourteenth century. From Jacopo Filippo Foresti, da Bergamo, *De claris mulieribus* (Ferrara: Laurentius de Rubeis, de Valentia, 1497). Gift of Howard Lehman Goodhart, Goff J 204. Courtesy of Special Collections, Bryn Mawr College, Bryn Mawr, Pa.

bols, and badges of honor—moved out of the hands of those for whom the insignia had been intended and into the hands of others. Secondhand markets did brisk business in towns. The streets of Venice and Florence must have teemed with a kaleidoscope of visual images, some properly paraded, but precisely for that reason easily imitated or aped by others; worst of all, badges of all sorts could be parodied, including royal insignia and devices. Florentine law went out of its way to forbid women to wear circlets over two fingers' width in height that might otherwise, due to height and decorative trim, resemble crowns (see fig. 5). It also forbade artisans to design and twist a headdress so that it resembled a crown. But goldsmiths made and sold crowns to the general public.[87] In the same manner men and women, the great and small, those of high station or low, were forbidden to wear the fruit, flowers, beasts,

birds, and letters that conveyed messages about lineage, association, membership, profession, or occupation. Were insignia being worn, or suspected of
being worn, in full mockery of those with the right to wear them? From a
surviving *Prammatica del vestire* in 1343, Gérard-Marchant collected a daunting
collection of figures that Florentine women actually wore on their clothes
(legally, in some instances, when the gabelle to do so had been paid). Among
them frequent mention was made of *licteris* or *litteris*, that is, letters of the
alphabet. He also noted stars, crescents, styli, chains, bands, crowns, crests,
strings, coins, rings, dots, points, checks, ribbons, knots, Solomon's knots,
clouds, shields, blades, arrows, pavilions, embrasures, battlements, castles,
rocks, and mountains. There were flowers, thistles, roses, leaves, clovers,
acorns, and palms. Apparently women embroidered entire bestiaries onto
their clothes: birds, cocks, geese, dogs, foxes, lions, peacocks, stags, butterflies,
and fantastical sirens, dragons, and griffins, or exotic creatures like leopards.
Hare, boar, bear, and swallows as well as homunculi might appear.[88] Why such
a broad repertoire of images? What did women intend here?

There is little evidence left to explain why a pharmacist's wife might
choose stars and geometric shapes for the bodice of her gown, or whether her
choice held any symbolic meaning at all or merely pleased her whim. However, law enforcers were suspicious of mischievous intent when stars and geometric shapes appeared on a blue wool dress. With skill, a decent needle, and
perfectly legal silk threads, a woman could dress herself with motifs to honor
her husband's lineage or she could parody righteously displayed markers of
status worn by the town's proud citizens. Without uttering a word a woman
could insinuate a world of meaning into her stitched designs with a repertoire
so rich in images. In Italy fine needle skills were cultivated by the wealthy and
leisured.[89] When Tommasa Morelli received her trousseau in 1353 it contained
cloth for two dresses and a coat, along with two sets of silver buttons and linen
thread.[90] Seamstresses would produce her dresses, and she or her serving maids
would trim and embellish them according to her personal taste.

Instructional texts targeted the fine home-produced needlework that
embellished clothes. The Tuscan *Meditations on the Life of Christ* phrased it
this way: "If it was necessary for [the Virgin] to earn food by the work of her
hands, what shall we say about clothes, bedding and other necessary household
articles? They had no extra or superfluous or frivolous things. (These are
against poverty and even if she could have them, the lover of poverty would
not. Did the Lady, whatever she worked on make for love some fancywork?
No!) These are done by people who do not mind losing time. But she was so
poor that she could not and would not spend time in a vain occupation, nor
would she have done such work. This is a very dangerous vice, especially for
such as you."[91] The direct address of the final line leaves no doubt that leisured
women, likely literate and capable of reading this homily, were the persons

intended. The message was to dress modestly, embrace poverty, and leave the public parade of emblems and devices to those with the legitimate right to display them. In other words, do not meddle with men's prerogatives. Women played into highly charged factional debates when they adopted heraldic images or political symbols of any sort.[92] Controls over such displays were a matter of some consequence in grounding new oligarchic and seigneurial values in cities, so restraints on women who paraded messages on the streets are hardly surprising. Notions of nobility and citizenship competed for alllegiance in the fourteenth century, and women who adopted, mocked, or in some way inverted a contested political symbol fueled debates that were already hot.

A woman who sewed was in a good position to offer any number of political comments on her gown if she had a mind to. Additionally she might concoct a crown-like headdress, called a garland but constructed for all intents and purposes to look like a coronet. She could shock the neighbors and disturb decorum in church with a new fringe or tassels. She could make her own wry comment on those in authority with embroidered figures and symbols. Fashion began to serve new purposes, ones where the market played only the minimal role of supplying silk threads and some cheap beads. Fashion that conveyed timely commentary owed a major debt to clothes produced or refurbished at home.

Dressing for Intent

In a heightened atmosphere of attention to messages conveyed by women's clothes, was it possible that simple dress might ensure a woman's virtue and protect her from any association with carnality in the eyes of a critical public? Giovanni Boccaccio raised that issue in one chapter of his praise of famous women, *De Claribus Mulieribus*. In this treatise composed to please a queen, Boccaccio included one considerably less than renowned Florentine maiden, Engeldruda. On a visit from the Roman emperor Otho IV to Florence to "embellish a festival," the emperor was drawn to Engeldruda among the seated women circled about him because of "her beauty, her plainness of dress, her dignity and girlish seriousness." Engeldruda was left to protect her own virtue when her father volunteered that she give the emperor a good kiss, but her spoken refusal was so spirited that "in spite of his German barbarity and the fact that he did not know the girl, [the emperor] realized the saintly and chaste purpose of her breast." On the spot he found her a groom whom she could honestly kiss "and he gave her a noble dowry, thinking that the good and just things she had said [to him] were not merely something in the girl's mind, but were based on great veneration of virtue and uttered in just and rightful indignation, and that therefore she was worthy of an emperor's gift." In Boccaccio's story of stalwart virtue rewarded, it took Engeldruda's own spirited words to convince an emperor; indeed, her artless appearance, her simple dress, and girlish airs had aroused his interest in the first place.[93]

Engeldruda's lesson would appear to be that simplicity of dress alone would not protect virtue, nor would obedience to one's father when that father placed pleasing an emperor before protecting his daughter from the emperor's advances. Virtue only proved to be its own reward when Engeldruda took matters into her own hands and spoke up stoutly in her own cause. Engeldruda's response spoke eloquently of the multivalent meanings of dress in public venues. No woman or girl easily forged an uncomplicated link between simple dress and pure unassailable virtue.

On the other hand, neither did gold, silver, and jewels give off straightforward messages. Where treasures like bullion and jewels conveyed the sanctity of saints' relics—in Richard Trexler's words, "[a]t times, the word 'relic' was used indiscriminately to refer to the relic itself, its simulacrum, or the jewels or other signs of esteem attached to it"—they were, apparently, universally comprehensible to the devout.[94] But the Venetian Festival of the Twelve Maries demonstrates the divergence of meanings ascribed to precious materials dressing relics (or in this instance wooden statues of the Virgin Mary) and those same precious goods dressing actual women. Each wooden Mary was bejeweled and robed as gorgeously as local pocketbooks would permit, in a widely appreciated gesture of civic piety. It would appear that in a responsive act, a woman's own attire reflected her best efforts to honor Mary with gold, silver, and jewels in this city given to veneration of the Queen of Heaven. No less than their best was demanded of women; after all, Venice expected its dogaressa to dress in fine robes for civic occasions even if she were in mourning. Ceremonial functions imposed the demands of livery generally reserved for men onto a dogaressa and her retinue at least on state occasions. This notwithstanding, women gorgeously dressed to honor Mary at carnival time earned rebuke. Similarly, Florence suspended sumptuary laws for important religious celebrations like the Feast of St. John so that women could line the streets and honor the saint's procession in their best dresses and jewels.[95] Some women, the wife and daughters of Conte Porro, for example, chose to present themselves publicly in simple gowns while the men of their family dressed more flamboyantly (see plate 8). Still, those same well-jeweled women were the cause of scandal when they appeared well jeweled on the streets for more routine occasions.

Lawmakers suspected that a Venetian woman honoring Mary at the *ludi mariani* invited pursuit, a reenactment of salvation from pirates. Dress that seemed to invite lascivious thoughts, even in a playful reenactment, was highly suspect, with a gown called a *cipriana* featuring "devil's windows" or an unlaced bodice that did not fully conceal the breasts considered particularly scandalous.[96] Giovanni Villani's reference to women's "dishonest fashions" is perhaps best read as a veiled reference to provocative dressing (honest dress was modest, dishonest was lascivious).[97] Florentine law outlawed women's necklines more than two fingers' breadth from the collarbone, although fourteenth-century laws were generally less concerned with provocative cut and form-revealing costume than would be the case in later centuries.[98] Where men encountered reasonably clear rules for displaying their fine wardrobes, women faced the possibility of failing to adequately honor a saint through appearing in insufficiently fine attire, yet *luxuria* was often interpreted as *lascivia* in a well-dressed woman even if her clothes covered her modestly.[99] Getting it right, more clearly delineated for men, had become difficult for a woman. Fourteenth-century city fathers found it prudent to direct women's choices of apparel—this was, after all, the stated purpose of sumptuary law—but that failed to provide women clear signals about the meanings of dress. Nevertheless, dress became a matter of serious consequence, with townspeople paying close attention to visual clues about status, wealth, legitimacy, and propriety when they examined the clothes of women encountered in the streets.

Luxuria was also opposed to poverty in the value system of the day, creating a social expectation for married women that men encountered less often. A fourteenth-century man made a stark choice early in his life when he chose between taking vows in a mendicant order and forsaking riches, or remaining "in the world" and adopting the badges and attire that reflected his wealth and standing. Not so for women: a young girl might espouse poverty and join the Poor Clares or renounce the world to become a religious recluse, but only if her family tolerated her choice. Married women were expected to become more self-denying and devout as they aged; they earned the respect of the community when they renounced fine dress, giving an outward expression to a robust inner life of the spirit. Fourteenth-century Italian saints' lives were filled with examples of women who followed this path, an indication that for the laity at least the Franciscan ideal of poverty was more easily construed as a feminine virtue than a masculine one. In donor portraits in Padua's Santo, Caterina dei Francesi appeared without ornament in austere black next to her magnificently dressed husband, Bonifacio Lupi (see fig. 6). In the midst of wealth, to present oneself as poor was to renounce worldliness. It was a sure sign of Christian virtue, and on that rode societal expectations that a woman embrace poverty of her own volition once her obligations to parents, husband, and offspring were fulfilled. Italy was full of exemplars: Angela of Foligno, Bridget of Sweden (who took a long sojourn in Italy), Villana dei Botti, Zita of Lucca, and, somewhat later, Catherine of Genoa were among the celebrated. Voluntary renunciation of *le pompe* would of course render null and void the need for any governance by sumptuary laws.[100] To a degree it also rendered women who did not follow this pious course suspect.

Figure 6. Altichiero da Zavio, *Bonifacio Lupi and Caterina dei Francesi Presented to the Virgin*, c. 1373–77. West wall, Chapel of Bonifacio Lupi, the Santo, Padua. The elaborately armored figure of Bonifacio Lupi contrasts with the somber and unadorned figure of his wife, Caterina dei Francesi. Art Resource, N.Y.

If women's voices were ever raised on the perplexing issue of the meaning of dress, accidents of preservation have kept us from hearing them. It would take a century for Italy to produce Nicolosa Sanuti and Battista Petrucci, who came forward to defend women's right to their fine clothes.[101] In the fourteenth century Christine de Pizan took her sensitivity to the meaning of dress with her when she accompanied her father to the French court. She gave voice to her opinion on the significance of apparel throughout her career but left no opinions about costume in her native Italy.[102] When in the late thirteenth century a Provencal *trobairitz* raised a plaintive voice in defense of her right to her jewels and fine apparel, she expressed scorn and discontent with the law:

l sagramen,
car nostres vestirs ricx
an nafratz e aunitz;
qi o tractet sia marritz,
per que cascuna entenda
que non port vel ni benda
mais garlandas de flors
en estieu per amors.

(let the order be lifted, / they've harmed and dishonored / our rich clothing; / May the law's author suffer, / to see every woman resolve / not to wear veil or wimple / but garlands of flowers / in the summer for love).[103] This anonymous *trobairitz* regarded the king of Aragon's stewards as the source of her misery; her contemporaries in Italy were probably just as politically astute, but their words have not come down to us.

Italian women's voices remained obdurately silent on this issue in the fourteenth century, yet women found ample opportunity to express opinions through their clothes. Young married women might blur the distinction between maiden and matron at the Marian games at Venice; they could mimic or mock others, or indulge in playful commentary on the social scene with their embroidered figured bodices and cloaks. Because women employed materials on hand in their households, none of these endeavors represented heavy new expense, which was just as well since even the wealthiest woman did not have much discretionary cash to spend on such market goods.[104] Women's dress allowed for small acts of self-fashioning for slight financial investment, but dressing for public occasions was difficult to negotiate and full of pitfalls that might trip up the unwary.

Dressing the Body

In Italian love lyrics women are visions in *azzurrata*; Dante's glimpse of heaven in canto 31 of *Paradiso* pulsates in gold and white, then (the quite bourgeois)

Beatrice's magnificent golden crown directs his eye ever higher to spiritual truth.[105] Yearning for the beloved was expressed through reference to apparel, and if, in Elizabeth Gross's understanding of the social body, dress itself becomes an integral part of the body that it covers, then, like the love lyrics of the day, sumptuary laws that fixed distinctions by gender and age may reveal values formulated about bodies, their consequence, and even their sexual allure.[106] Searching in this direction may also help clarify the anxieties that underlay legislators' attempts to control apparel at a moment when female and male bodies began to appear more gendered due to tight fit in garments. When public presentation made anatomical differences increasingly apparent, did concern for sexual propriety increase? Were the concerns expressed in the law in any way an unanticipated result of legislation itself, since in cities sumptuary law was organized by gender that pinned the public's attention to the differences between women and men? While *luxuria* remained the *topos* through which society encountered and understood sexual vice, was sexual propriety ever even possible for a finely dressed woman (see plate 13)?

These questions are pertinent because the feminine wile *lascivia*, which was frequently paired with *luxuria*, was generally considered a root cause of evil with woman's more base or sexual nature at fault. It is perplexing then that in this century new stylish ensembles on women were viewed as masculinizing—a paradox certainly—and one complicated further by a fashionable wardrobe's capacity to obliterate a woman's sexuality. Holding these notions in the mind simultaneously required fancy footwork. In an environment of heightened attention to visual signals displayed in the streets the project of creating a fashionable ensemble rendered a woman more like a man in society's eyes, that is, her very stylishness was interpreted as forcing her to transgress her gender boundaries. This is certainly hinted at in rulings in the Florentine law of 1325, where a careful distinction was made: women were forbidden to dress in men's clothes, and men were forbidden to dress like women: "nulla mulier . . . vadat induta virilibus vestimentis, vel aliquis vir muliebribus indumentis."[107] The parallel in phrasing was less than exact: "in men's clothes" and "like women." Borrowing men's actual attire, or their fashions, was the practice specifically prohibited to women.

Contemporary observers like the chronicler Giovanni Villani identified fashion as a man's sphere, and problematic at that, but when women entered into the fashion parade along with men it gave great affront. Galvano Fiamma stated the problem in terms of gender transgression. Wearing gilded belts made women into Amazons, he noted, recalling the most aggressive and masculine women known from ancient times. In England and somewhat later in the century Henry Knighton vowed that women ruined their reputations with lewd excesses and extravagance, the worst being their silver belts worn low with daggers suspended from them, a decidedly masculine affect.[108] Through inheritance or gifts women may have come by great belts with appended daggers legitimately, but wearing them low on the hips moved waistlines from high to low, creating a more form-hugging silhouette; that distressed observers who read the result as masculine. Tight fit itself was masculine: for Knighton and Fiamma any perception of the body beneath—breast, waist, and hips—would not render a woman more feminine but more masculine *because* it relied on tight fit. This was the provocation. Stylistically both the belt and tight fit were originally components of men's fashions, so they recalled men's active, bold, and martial spirits. This was true of fashion generally. Boldness, a masculine trait, was transgressive in women, but apparently it might be regarded as titillating as well. The gendered poles of male activity and female passivity were shaken.

Rosita Levi Pisetzky has identified some fashions adopted by women that caused consternation when they were perceived as masculine. Beyond great belts with daggers she pointed to a high crowned hat with brim peaked in front and turned up behind, much like a hunting cap; she also mentioned a cape worn in the masculine manner over one shoulder such as one that appears in a fresco from the school of Lorenzetti, *Il Diavolo Tentatore Sotto Aspetto Femminile*[109] (see fig. 7). The presence of a thin veil fastened under the chin and a full skirt falling in deep folds identifies the figure as a woman, but it was the destabilizing use of male and female stylistic elements on one figure that disturbed contemporaries, earning the artist his intended ambiguity for the devil as tempter. Distinctions lay increasingly in details. The two rings allowed by law to women at Florence in 1349 were feminine adornment; however, as Filippo Lippi donor's portrait of Francesco de Marco Datini demonstrates, four or more rings on a man's hand were masculine adornment.[110] Did women simply mimic men or appropriate men's dignity to themselves by acts of accretion, trying to become more like men in dress and in the number and wealth of their ornaments? Apparently critics read such behavior as provocative.

As the Florentine law of 1325 stated, women were prohibited to dress *in men's clothes.* To an extent being stylish by way of consumer goods available in the market required dressing in men's clothes, thus a mild form of cross-dressing, but perhaps not one intended for any other purpose than to be "in fashion." Markets sold to men; goldsmiths' shops designed wares for the male customer. The alternatives for women would appear to be avoiding retail goods, shunning fashion, or, perhaps, obtaining materials for a wardrobe and producing proper "feminine" clothes at home. Since the project of fashion was itself provocative those clothes should be modest or even nondescript.

Men may have taken to the possibilities of cross-dressing with more enthusiasm than women because again, as the law noted, they were forbidden to dress *like* women, implying intent much more than women dressing "in men's clothes."[111] As time passed in Venice all male cross-dressing would be

Figure 7. School of Lorenzetti, *Il Diavolo Tentatore sotto Aspeto Femminile*, detail from *Anacoreti nella Tebaire*, second half of the fourteenth century. Fresco. Camposanto, Pisa. The devil as tempter dressed in ambiguous clothing, including a man's hunting cap, and a veil. Note the devil's claws peeking out from the skirt. Art Resource, N.Y.

outlawed: in August 1443 a man found wearing a woman's dress or other *habito desconveniente* was liable to lose the garment, pay a fine of 100 *lira,* and go to prison for six months.[112] The economic loss sustained here was significant, but the fine and the six-month prison term imposed indicate that male cross-dressing was regarded as far less serious a matter than other sexual crimes (see below).

Sexually provocative dressing and the related question of public dress that creates scandal pose serious questions of interpretation. Confusing signals from a crowd of affluent women wearing designs and devices borrowed from men prompted commentary and earned more official response in sumptuary legislation than fitted garments that were in some way designed to arouse men's sexual interest in a female body. The Florentine directive that necklines fall no more than two fingers' width below the collarbone is unusual in focusing the law's attention on dress that revealed women's bodies; significantly more attention would be paid to body-revealing, provocative dressing in later centuries. In fourteenth-century Florence prostitutes were enjoined to wear special gloves and carry a bell to distinguish themselves from "decent" women, but this cannot be interpreted as a stricture on the dress of those decent women whom the law wished to protect from misidentification. We tend to assume that tight fit in women's clothes means sexual provocation, but lawmakers approached the issue of tight fit in an oblique way through spending ceilings on fastenings like belts and buttons that created tight fit. Laws curbed expense here, without condemning the articles of apparel that created tight fit on grounds of indecency. Did lawmakers fail to link women's tight fit to the sexual, female form, and was female sexual allure expressed through dress not a fearful matter? Conduct books and sermons cried out against sexual provocation in women's dress, but phrasing in civic laws raises the possibility that women's dress created greater scandal and sexual provocation through rich materials and devices drawn on them than from form-revealing cut.[113]

Joan Kelly has spoken of a strangely asexual world for women in Italy: "The actual disappearance of the social world of the court and its presiding lady underlies the disappearance of sex and the physical evaporation of the woman" in Italian love lyrics of the late Middle Ages.[114] For the most part woman's sexual body seems to have disappeared from fourteenth-century sumptuary laws as well. The problem of visual displays that may arouse sexual responses relates to what constituted serious sex crime in the fourteenth century. Sodomy ranks high on that list, and in Venice it was punishable by death, usually by burning alive. Fornication with nuns commanded just a two-year jail sentence and a fine, and even milder penalties were meted out for adultery. Despite the law's evident horror over sodomy, Venetian law was more lenient on the passive partner in cases involving two men brought up on sodomy charges, even if the passive partner cross-dressed.[115] Is it possible the law found little seductive intent in men's cross-dressing escapades, that lawmakers believed no sexual invitation was being issued when young men or boys dressed in women's clothes? It may have been the case that men who dressed "like women" were merely thought to be ludicrous, in the literal sense of that word with all its associations of games and carnival playfulness. Indeed, men's cross-dressing could on occasion hold genuinely honorific meanings: before the Festival of the Twelve Maries was outlawed in 1379, a priest dressed as Mary had been the central figure in the procession to Santa Maria Formosa, and he would have been arrayed as a woman in the most precious jewels and fabrics that could be found to adorn him. This honor of dressing as Mary fell only to the worthiest priests; it was not an honor bestowed on women.

For medieval Italy Michael Rocke has noted that "in hundreds of sodomy denunciations to the courts and thousands of trial proceedings I have reviewed from the fourteenth to the sixteenth century, not a trace of transvestite boys has yet to come to light."[116] In Florence, at least, authorities did not immediately link youthful male cross-dressing with efforts to arouse other men's sexual interest. St. Bernardino of Siena (1380–1444) saw fancy dress on boys in a different light when he argued that boys who were too "spruced up" endangered gender distinctions. Mothers were to blame: "Oh silly, foolish woman, it appears you make your son look like yourself, so that to you he is quite becoming."[117] The problem for Bernardino lay not so much in rich materials, but in the clever combinations of fastenings, jewels, buttons, and trims that mothers lavished on their sons. These were the labor-intensive details of fashionable wardrobes that were identified as women's devices, and in Bernardino's eyes it was improper to inflict such "feminizing" tricks of fashion on sons. His grounds were that they led to confusion about gender in the streets, but, significantly, for Bernardino, primping details of costume did not tempt men to find young boys sexually attractive; Bernardino said it was the mother herself who found the fine details of costume on sons appealing.

Some recent studies suggest that women dressing in masculine costume did not stir society's suspicions about lesbian intentions either; perhaps the association of women with incapacity and passivity proved too strong to conceive of women bothering to dress to attract each other.[118] Guido Ruggiero has argued that in Renaissance Venice lesbian acts were not prosecuted crimes, and it is possible a woman's adoption of masculine-style dress did not signal sexual intentions toward other women any more than did boys or men who cross-dressed "like women."

Throughout the century, criticisms of masculine dress on women seemed to ignore the issue of explicit sexual invitation and failed to suspect women of showing off their bodies through baring and tight fit in order to arouse men. The rather prudish allegation of "dishonest fashions" may cover a host of daring cuts and revealing drapery in women's clothes, but since it was hidden behind a prim generalization it is difficult to interpret what was found titillating in garments. Masculine garb on women was dangerous, of course, but on the grounds that it reflected pretensions to man's estate.[119] I resist the thought that feminine was signed so passive that authorities failed to imagine women employing their displayed bodies, tightly dressed or even partially bared, to invite sexual attention, but there is little evidence in fourteenth-century laws to suggest that women were regarded as effective temptresses employing dress. For the most part Florentine law left the issue of female modesty alone. Dress that became an integral part of a woman's body, even dress that emphasized the sexual nature of the body, was largely absolved of prurient intent.[120] Yet *luxuria* was regarded as both scandalous and provocative by its nature. Embellishments, rich cover-ups, and layers of fine fabrics tantalized the public. What was marked masculine and bold was censured, so here there is a sure basis for assuming that fashion worried lawmakers. Engeldruda excepted, simple "feminine" dress, or for that matter any woman's costume that merely hugged the female form, tended to be regarded as rather ineffective at arousal.

Servants, the Household, and Needle Skills

The parade of fashion grew to include many inhabitants of cities, as opportunities for fashionable dressing, for parody and play, multiplied. At Florence by the law of 1355 serving maids (*famulae, servientes*) were forbidden to wear hats of or lined with costly fabrics, or ornaments, or clothing covered in mesh.[121] Serving maids were forbidden to wear gilded or silver buttons, and no buttons could be worn above the elbow. Servants' ornaments and styles were often imitations of what their mistresses wore, as the pronouncement about buttons above the elbow (forbidden to mistresses) suggests. A heavy fine for servant violations was imposed: fifty *lira* paid within fifteen days. The alternative was to be taken to prison, stripped naked, led through the city's streets to be flogged all around the marketplace, and then released. Under no circumstances were women servants to behave like, or appear to be, prostitutes, who were of course also regulated in sumptuary law. (Prostitutes could not wear slippers with heels [*pianelle*], which were popular in cities, and they were to wear gloves and carry bells to distinguish themselves from the honest women of the town.)[122] In practice serving maids' apparel was more restricted than that of their mistresses because what servants wore inside the house as well as out of doors was regulated in the law. Regulation invaded homes when maids' working costumes were prescribed·(this was also true where the law regulated behavior at wedding festivities or the food to be served at banquets).[123]

Clothing prohibited to serving maids, that is, the cast-offs they appropriated and the garments their meager wages afforded, spoke of a degree of complicity between mistress and maid. A serving maid, who might be accomplished with a needle, dressed a mistress and that maid used the leftovers from that task for her personal wardrobe. A mistress could reward her servant with her cast-off finery or provide access to the household caskets and cupboards. In particular, the prohibited mesh-covered dresses mentioned in Florentine laws warrant comment. These appear to have been labor-intensive needle-worked gowns where mesh masked rents, tears, faded places, and even holes in worn garments; most likely these worked gowns represented a refurbishing of cast-offs, turning old garments into something so they could reappear in public. Mesh-covered dresses required skill with a needle and plenty of time for execution. There was, in all likelihood, only a small technological distance between these prohibited mesh-covered garments of fourteenth-century Florence and actual lace-making, an invention that has been attributed to fifteenth-century Italy.[124]

To wear gilded or silver buttons a servant required the largesse of her mistress or a deft hand at borrowing finery from the household's cupboards. As for hats with linings, they could make use of saved remnants of good cloth. In the specificity of the descriptions of prohibited fashions lay hints about materials closeted away; a maid with skills and a strong inclination to join the fashion scene might exercise her ingenuity and create a striking appearance. As the high limits set in sumptuary law reveal, the intent of the law was to curb consumption among the wealthy who could afford luxuries. It is significant that the first signs of displeasure with displays of fashion outside the circle of the most affluent families fell on women servants. Their spending power was negligible, particularly when serving maids worked for a set term and received their wage as a final lump sum that provided a dowry for marriage. Of course slaves of the household had no spending power at all. In these cases the laws restricted servants' access to household goods probably because an inventive and skilled servant girl could dress well enough to cause confusion about her social status in the streets. This is revealing about deepening the market for fashion in towns: the thin wedge that opened the way for lower social orders to participate in fashion were the large corps of personal servants who sustained urban households—at least this is what sumptuary regulation of women servants' clothes would have us believe. If a serving maid could dress well in cast-offs it might encourage the laboring classes to visit second-hand markets and obtain used garments, refurbish or trim them, then pass them off as fashion. What legislators had feared—that fashion would cause confusion in the streets—had already begun to happen by the middle decades of the century.

In pursuit of fashion, mistresses turned sewing, cutting, stringing, and embroidering, perhaps even tatting (a skill from the eastern Mediterranean world), into assets for embellishing and refurbishing wardrobes. Elements of high style like circlets for the hair, veils, fastenings of all kinds, fine gowns, silk flowers, beads, and remnants of fine fabrics (even when worn or damaged) provided a repertoire of materials that could be recombined and worked to produce a fashionable look. Some of the most offending elements of female apparel—figured motifs, pleats, ruffles, elaborate headdresses, trims, borders, and incised sleeves—were little more than labor-intensive sewing projects produced from standard rather than luxurious materials. These attest to the possibilities for self-fashioning among wealthy women and their serving maids.

If by mid-century serving maids were implicated along with their mistresses in transgressing sumptuary laws, then it is quite certain that through their combined efforts in the home some of the more offensive items in current fashion saw the light of day. In Genoa a gold thread export industry had been built on the labor of women household servants, who received pay from their entrepreneurial mistresses for their skilled labor.[125] Other skilled servants, including slaves with sewing skills, were prized additions to households elsewhere in the Mediterranean region. Iris Origo noted of a ship sailing from Venice to Majorca that nine Turkish slaves worth 360 *lira* appeared on the ship's lading. Among them was a slave woman who could "sew and do everything." It is significant that she was not sold at Majorca with the others but taken on to Valencia where a wealthy household would pay more for her because of her skills as a needlewoman.[126]

Europe had a long tradition of employing servant women in the textile and needle trades. In *Opera Muliebria* David Herlihy argues that on great estates *gynaecea* (servant women's workshops) answered the need for labor in fine textile making by employing female slaves.[127] In the tenth century St. Liutbirg began life as an unfree member of such a textile workshop, as did her many students who learned skills from her, which eventually won them their freedom.[128] When the slave trade was revived in the western Mediterranean region in the thirteenth century, the price of women slaves increased as they learned household skills and were resold as highly sought-after skilled domestics. Ragusa supplied some trained household slaves to Venetians out of their own households, but other young women who had been captured in Bosnia were entirely unfamiliar with the ways of Italian towns and households; Florence drew on this source as well. Writing to Piero Davanzati in Venice in 1392, Rosso Orlandi of Florence stated that he wanted two slave girls between the ages of twelve and fifteen from Dalmatia. He wrote, "I don't care if they are pretty or ugly, as long as they are healthy and able to do hard work."[129] He was not concerned with the domestic training they had received, so presumably these young girls were among the cheapest slaves on the market. They would be trained in his household.

The average price of a young female slave was ten *hyperperi* or five ducats when purchased in the port town of Ragusa; presumably this was the going rate for a recently captured and untrained young slave girl.[130] After the voyage to Venice the price of a slave with some skills likely doubled, particularly if she had served some time in a household and learned the rudiments of Adriatic dialect and some domestic skills.[131] Add further training like needle skills and that figure could double again or rise even higher. In Florence, Romeo di Lapo, who was listed as a vagabond with no fixed residence, sold Ciaola of Albania, a baptized Christian and a "free" person, to Ser Stefano di Rainieri del Forese of Florence for forty-nine florins, under the false pretense that she was a heretic and unbaptized (she was later freed). Romeo di Lapo made a profit of close to thirty florins from the transaction before he was apprehended and convicted as "a thief and vendor of women and Christians."[132] Even unskilled slaves rose in price when they were sold into slavery in the towns of the interior where they remained a scarce commodity. Slaves of any level of training and skill were luxuries.

By 1439 a wealthy Venetian like Andrea Barbarigo would pay sums as high as 147 ducats for three slaves: Agnese, Catarina, and Jacomo. Agnese, costing somewhat less than 50 ducats, seems to have been supernumerary in his household because in 1442 Andrea rented her out to Piero Paxeto for eight ducats a year and a pair of shoes. Since he possessed a fortune of 10,000 ducats, these three slaves were a bargain when Barbarigo purchased them, and Agnese provided him a full return on his capital in six years' time when he rented her out at the going rate.[133] In the Adriatic world this increase in the price amounted to considerable inflation, although Agnese was likely a trained slave to bring such a high rental fee. While a luxury, slaves were affordable for a wealthy family and well within means, particularly when they could be taught valuable skills; slaves cost not much more than a fine wedding dress and might serve a family for decades. In addition, when slaves acquired a skill like needlework they more than earned their purchase price and might be sold for much more than their original purchase price.

Beyond the obvious advantage to an owner of a slave's lifetime of work, skilled slaves from the East (particularly Tartar slaves) were prized because they had a reputation for being skilled in needlecrafts and embroidery. They became precious assets and probably bore some degree of responsibility for the clever displays that made their mistresses' fashion statements. Again, the records are largely silent on this question, and mistresses seldom revealed how they achieved the novel and startling effects of their decorated costumes. By contrast, contracted serving maids took any needle skills they learned in a wealthy household with them, deploying their skills in workshops as seamstresses. Contracted serving maids, little more than children when they began their terms of service, plied their skill for wages after years of domestic training. Through them secrets about embellishments could filter out into workshops and in this way novel fashions could achieve wider circulation.

Does Self-Fashioning Promote Fashion?

If there is any discernible progression in sumptuary laws over the course of the century it lay in increased concern with specific fashions like figural displays on garments. While spending or *sumptus* was the primary concern of the laws, over time laws identified fashions that lawmakers considered disorderly but not expensive with increasing frequency. This was true throughout northern Italy, particularly in large towns that attracted numerous foreigners to their markets. The meanings of design elements produced in homes may remain mysterious, especially when they were part of sewing projects carried out by women in the privacy of the household.[134] What is more certain is that in towns where both a mistress's and a maid's fashionable costumes earned repeated censure, new forces were at play that hastened the pace by which one fashion replaced another.

Since a woman had little opportunity to express herself through selections she made in the market, and since clothes and jewels were often purchased for brides, wardrobes signified much about family status and lineage but less about the woman herself. Mistresses and maids entered into the creation of fashion at a later moment, when they transformed apparel with their needles and ingenious designs. A woman might exert her taste and preferences by combining elements of the rich wardrobe she had received as a bride. When those purchases were made she had only controlled the material or color of her dresses and mantles and the design and value of her jewels by influencing the market choices of others, by pleading with her husband, or by influencing the choices of her natal kin. In Venetian noblewomen's wills Stanley Chojnacki found gifts of money or clothing or jewels designated for particular daughters, granddaughters, and nieces.[135] These gifts provided one way for a woman to accumulate personal possessions, but even the wealthiest women were not entrusted with discretion over the large sums invested in *corredi* or wedding gifts. In Florence, when Tommasa Niccolini married Michele da Barbarino with a gorgeous trousseau, the choices of design and color were not hers but her guardians'.[136] In Venice, women frequented San Polo and San Marco to buy needle cases and small luxury items, but they did not go to the Rialto where there were enticing displays of gold and silver wares and jewels.[137] "Notions," the term later applied to women's small transactions in the shops for needles, thread, and beads, seems to have been a component of the world of fashion from the beginning.[138] Women bought brightly colored silk threads used in embroidery, *littere*, small gilded buttons, small stamped ornaments from a goldsmith, or veils and ribbons from silk shops. Women could exchange some of their jewels, pawn them, or beg to inherit jewels from their kin, but the opportunities to make the original and expensive purchases that composed a fashionable wardrobe fell largely to men.[139] In regard to luxuries the role of consumer was as gendered as any of the other roles associated with fashion.

Rich apparel that came to a woman was likely to be a display of spousal generosity—a groom's inclination to please his bride and new in-laws or *parentado*.[140] The bridegroom, not the bride, ordered, paid the gabelle on, and presented nuptial wear as a gift in Florence. Ambitious bridegrooms marrying into old, distinguished families outdid themselves in buying finery, but it was their taste and not their brides' that was exhibited. Alessandra Strozzi boasted in 1448 that her daughter Caterina wore the exorbitant sum of four hundred florins on her back as rich wedding gifts from her bridegroom, Marco Parenti.[141] In Venice, arguments were made to replace increasingly impressive grooms' gifts into cash award to keep them from disappearing—wastefully, it was argued—into a splendid wardrobe.[142] Costly wedding dresses at Venice were generally gifts from parents, patrons, or other donors who could bear their great cost.

According to Christiane Klapisch-Zuber's careful reading of Florentine *ricordanze* (record or memory books), a bride's most luxurious presents, such as jewels, might not remain with her through her lifetime because a husband's gifts to his bride could be recalled. As other women entered her husband's lineage those jewels would be passed to a newer bride.[143] Carole Frick has found that wedding finery was as likely to be pawned or sold as kept by the early decades of the fifteenth century.[144] Jane Fair Bestor argues that this conformed to the intent of the law since husbands who presented jewels to brides did not bestow actual gifts but only shared with a wife what was in their power.[145] At times even proud families rented jewels for special occasions. Jewels and clothes were understood to be familial wealth that could be repossessed or pawned to meet financial crises. Petrarch's and Boccaccio's Griselda, who entered and left her marriage with only her chemise to cover her nakedness, was perhaps the most celebrated story attached to early Renaissance marriage rites. She was a figure highly relevant to the immediate economic roles assumed by the groom and bride on the occasion of a marriage, at least in regard to the groom's wedding gifts, and as such her story was considered a fitting subject for the decoration of wedding caskets.[146] But the story relates narrowly to the groom's adorning of his bride. It obscures that other more important economic truth—the major transfer of wealth at marriage was the bride's dowry from her natal family to the groom.

Self-fashioning for brides was not likely to be part of marriage celebrations but occurred later when, in complicity with her maid, a married woman transformed her basic wardrobe into new ensembles. Married women earned the most fines for breaking the sumptuary laws at Florence; clearly enforcers were on the lookout for their transgressions. Through day-to-day administration of a household the raw materials of style lay at a matron's disposal, even if they were buttons snipped from her husband's cloak. In Venice, married women appeared alongside maidens in their best clothes during pre-Lenten festivities; they so cleverly disguised their matronly condition that they, too, were chased and "freed from pirates" by enthusiastic saviors. Blurring the distinction of single or married, a distinction monitored by sumptuary law, the married possessors of *corredi*, more than their single sisters, took advantage of luxuries at hand to create fetching novelties for their public appearances.

Women engaged in reclamation projects of all sorts. Remnants, fastenings, and jewels were transformed into new and fashionable effects. Incised fabrics held great potential: elaborate sleeves, as well as separate elements set into garments or sewn onto them, often cut from a contrasting fabric so they complemented the gown to which they attached. Gowns could be lined with another fabric and turned outward, or an undergarment pulled through incised bodices or sleeves. Old and torn mantles and gowns could be cut up to provide a contrasting pair of sleeves or linings for sleeves if the needlewomen of the household were skilled. If trains were ripped, they were still too valuable to be discarded and could be recycled into a new fashion. Long sleeves with incised hems could make use of torn trains, and these could be lined with other remnants. Ingenuity was rewarded by creating a stir in public. The growing list of fashions forbidden to women reads like a summary of what a resourceful seamstress could create within her home.

In the last analysis, the corner of the world of fashion in which women and their maids played a role was only tangentially related to retail markets. By designing new fashions and apparel from old materials a woman could pass for something she wished to be: wealthier, better connected, or freer in her self-expression. In turn legislators responded to this display of homemade ingenuity with new provisions. Without uttering a word fashionable women's presence in the street drew attention and signaled playful intent, parody, presumption to higher status, and boldness, that is, if a woman could get the knack of it.

Reservations and Repudiations

In the matter of public apparel, however, a very different possibility presented itself to women: repudiation of the entire fashionable endeavor. Much as Francis of Assisi had cast aside the rich robe given him by his wealthy father, a fourteenth-century woman might refuse to dress richly for the salvation of her soul. Angela of Foligno (1248–1309) provided her own coda to St. Francis of Assisi's stripping away of familial wealth: in the Franciscan church in Foligno the wellborn and wealthy Angela stood before a life-sized crucifix and publicly removed her clothes. Naked before the crucifix she pointed to her "members," promising for each of them that they would not sin. She cast aside her clothed—social—body with its connotation of wealth and vice; her soul, embodied in her unadorned naked flesh, rid itself of encumbering *luxuria*.[147]

Over the course of the fourteenth century, some women in towns grew to mistrust the very project of fashion. Samuel K. Cohn, Jr., has pointed out that from the generation of the revered St. Catherine (1347–80) the women of Siena grew more austere, devoting substantially greater portions of their willed estates to charity than outward expressions of wealth.[148] The example of Catherine, who remained in the world as a tertiary and attracted a circle of likeminded people around her, provided lessons about sacrifice in a life too full of service to others to bother with outward appearance. The century produced a circle of saintly women throughout Italy who referred to themselves as *ancillae dei* (slaves or handmaidens of God). These women dressed in the poorest garb, adopting the humble roles of serving others although they were often wellborn and wealthy.[149] St. Zita, a venerated thirteenth-century saint of Lucca, as well as the more recent figures of Margaret of Città di Castello, Sibillina Biscossi of Pavia, Veridiana Attavanti of Castelfiorentino, and Jane of Orvieto, demonstrated an alternative mode for self-fashioning.

Of all the saints or the beatified who perceived clothes, *luxuria*, and the sin of lasciviousness as pernicious, perhaps the Blessed Villana dei Botti of Florence (1336–60) speaks loudest. After a most pious childhood Villana acquiesced to her father's wishes and married a wealthy man of his choosing. According to her vita, she found herself thoroughly enjoying her worldly life and her husband's embraces, becoming a whorish Magdalene in the pleasure of it all. One day, after dressing in fine clothes to attend a festival at church with her husband, "[she] perceived as in a glass darkly how deformed her interior fullness of soul was in relation to God; and indeed, when she anxiously fixed her eyes again and again, she grasped very clearly, in those very clothes, an image of a most loathsome spirit, not a human being, presenting itself."[150]

Guilt overwhelmed Villana through the flawed image she saw in her small peer glass. The Blessed Villana threw off her finery and rushed to Santa Maria Novella in contrition. For the rest of her short life she wore a hair shirt and under it an iron chain drawn so tightly around her breasts that it could hardly be separated from her body at her death. Villana spent her remaining years in meditation and prayer, ignoring, to a remarkable degree, the worldly distractions around her. For sheer drama her choice for self-fashioning outdistanced the fashionable women around her.

Chapter 5
Costs of Luxuries

The turn to fashion in the fourteenth century began in what would be the last decades of a three-century-long era of expansion in the medieval economy. As such, Fashion's influence on demand may be treated as a late-added feature of the emergence of the European market economy.[1] In 1955, Frederic C. Lane suggested that "a consumers' theory of economic growth would ask whether part of the amount previously spent on goods no longer in demand now went into capital accumulation or some form of 'consumption' which might be so reclassified."[2] Reclassifying did occur in the fourteenth century: staple textiles were finished into luxury goods and reclassified, silver coin became silver "plate," glass paste was made into false pearls, and fine enamels that once graced church altars now served as dress accessories. This resulted in conspicuous consumption, suggesting that new preferences drove the reclassification and were likely to promote demand. This matters in the ongoing debate begun by Robert S. Lopez and Carlo Cipolla a generation ago about whether an economic depression occurred in the latter half of the fourteenth century or instead the economy weathered dislocations like bank failures, the Black Plague, and numerous costly land wars with some success.[3] The northern Italian towns stand at the fulcrum of this debate—Venice, Florence, and very likely Genoa, Bologna, Milan, and smaller communities prospering from an upturn in conspicuous consumption. These towns promoted shopping for fine goods, improved their retailing efforts over the century, and turned local production to goods consumers coveted.[4] Siena and Lucca, marvels of thirteenth-century luxury manufacture and trade, stand with these retail success stories in their creativity and output, although devastating political and financial blows did not allow them to benefit as much as their prospering neighbors.

Studying consumption patterns in fifteenth-century Florence, Richard Goldthwaite dismissed arguments about a late medieval depression, at least for northern Italy. He regarded the demand for goods among renewing elites, who were the product of political upheaval, as one among a number of factors that kept the market for luxury goods buoyant—each new elite in power vied to consume as well as or better than those preceding them.[5] Frederic Lane believed the late medieval retraction of long-distance trade with the East was overestimated in the evidence marshaled for a depression; indeed, arguments have challenged the evidence on a number of fronts.[6] The great expense of luxury goods, a cost wealthy customers paid with little hesitation, along with the conscious efforts of townspeople to promote shopping among customers with discretionary cash suggest that economic exigencies met with deliberate programs to encourage demand wherever possible. Promoting luxury trades indicates that the market economy catered to elites, but even this generalization requires some qualification. Fashions spread swiftly in cities as markets deepened and the circles of consumers buying cheaper versions of fine goods broadened to include less affluent persons like domestic servants. Secondhand markets did brisk trade and luxury goods were recycled. Long-distance traders promoted locally produced luxury items like brocades and gold thread to foreign customers. Even members of royal courts, who were accustomed to buying fine imported fabrics from the East, did not turn up their noses at the excellent work of Lucchese weavers who continued to turn out gorgeous fabrics in whichever town they relocated. If economic dislocations plagued towns, citizens did not stand idly by and risk shrinkage of their markets without some spirited responses.

For these reasons it is valuable to estimate the costs of luxuries on markets in relation to a trustworthy index of the cost of living in towns; it would be particularly valuable to do so for 1300 or 1310 and compare these results with the figures for the end of the century. However, an estimate of costs for the early years of the fourteenth century is difficult given the fragmentary nature of surviving evidence. This chapter will make a few sporadic forays into the costs of luxury wares for the early years of the century and, where possible, compare those with fuller evidence from later decades in the century.[7] Since more adequate documentation supports the study of costs of luxuries and the cost of living for the second half of the fourteenth century, this chapter will focus on those decades. A less certain economic climate characterized European markets by then, and some communities suffered major setbacks. With disruption of traditional businesses, population loss, plague and return of plague, the financial burden of buying off mercenaries, wars, and even the first intimations of a bullion famine in Europe, the era was not peaceful, nor did traditional business practices meet all current exigencies. Uncertainties beset markets, but there were plenty of prosperous patrons to cultivate if a retailer was willing to take the risk of stocking high-cost luxury wares. By no means did luxury trades present broad opportunities open to many; this was not a mass market with the capacity to reverse major underlying trends like population retraction. Rather, retailers were wise to understand changes in purchasing power like the funneling of wealth into the hands of a few heirs in the aftermath of the Black Plague. It is doubtful that conspicuous consumption could return northern Italian towns to the halcyon days of population growth and steady expansion that had characterized the European economy in previous decades, but, as a program based on human ingenuity, retailing efforts helped.

Fourteenth-century promotion of retail trade in luxuries had long-term consequences for markets in Italy's cities and in cities and towns all over Europe. Luxuries focused people's attention on shops and the urban marketplace, and markets assumed greater cultural consequence when ownership and display of luxury goods became important constituents of status. Through investments in luxuries and willingness to pay the often exorbitant prices demanded, wealthy consumers exhibited increased acuity to the meanings of market exchange, the connotations of luxury goods, and the demands of fashion (see fig. 1). In time this increased attention to the world of goods would become a significant feature of European life; however, it was a process that was only beginning in the fourteenth century.

The latter decades of the fourteenth century have been analyzed from the point of view of exchange, monetary history, and the history of money markets and banking, all factors central to developing retail trade in luxury wares; there have even been some courageous forays into the difficult terrain of estimates of cost of living. For two cities that prospered in this era, Florence and Venice, this analysis is rewarding. Charles de la Roncière's immense *Prix et salaires à Florence au XIVe siècle (1280–1380)* appeared in 1982; Richard Goldthwaite carries forward its analysis of salary structure into the fifteenth century. Posthumously, in 1996, Donald E. Queller's "A Different Approach to the Premodern Cost of Living: Venice, 1372–1391" has provided a point of comparison with de la Roncière's study, particularly when supplemented by Louise Buenger Robbert's earlier article, "Money and Prices in Thirteenth-Century Venice," and Susan Connell's *The Employment of Sculptors and Stonemasons in Venice in the Fifteenth Century.*[8] Through the pioneering work of Raymond de Roover and the research efforts of Armando Sapori, the formation of Florence's banking system and the fourteenth-century banking crisis of the Bardi and Peruzzi banks have been analyzed, and this work has been expanded by a new generation of scholars.[9] More recently Frederick C. Lane and Reinhold C. Mueller's major research project *Money and Banking in Medieval and Renaissance Venice*, which has now reached two volumes (the second the work of Mueller alone), has transformed general understandings of the development of banking and the financial networks that stretched across Italy and beyond. This study reveals the crucial role played by the five integrated financial markets centered on the Rialto in the luxury trades.[10] Peter Spufford's *Money and Its Use in Medieval Europe*, published in 1988, has linked bullion, luxuries, and currency to the monetarization of Europe.[11] Alan Stahl has produced a detailed study of the Venetian mint and its policies.[12] John Day, John Munro, and others have investigated the bullion famine of the fifteenth century. Their work allows some speculation on the inroads that fabrication of precious metals may have had on that event.[13]

For the fourteenth-century consumer of luxury wares, prices stated in florins or ducats were probably interchangeable "on the contemporary assumption that one gold ducat (of Venice, of Rome) equaled in value one gold florin (of Florence, of Pisa) wherever it circulated."[14] This makes comparing costs for luxury products, which were routinely stated in gold coin, simple—misleadingly so, since the knowledgeable Italian "calculation community," in Sir Stanley Jevons's phrase, tended to be important players in the luxury trades, and they, of course, understood currency, the price of bullion, exchange rates, and the *agio,* and they knew better.[15] Such men were aware that even in the simple relation of gold to gold currency rates differed by time and place. They made their living by understanding that when, say, ducats were traded and rated above par the quotation was given at Venice as a percentage, *meglio questi,* and when they were below par ducats would be quoted as a percentage *peggio questi.*[16] Bankers caught on swiftly to even a slight change in the bullion content of coins and adjusted their prices accordingly. These men were also in a position to understand that a poorer grade of silver than the standard of the mint was employed in fabricated silver wares, as would any practicing goldsmith. However, ordinary consumers, even very wealthy ones, likely missed the subtleties of a differential in exchange rates when purchasing luxury wares, particularly when prices tended to be given in round numbers in gold coin. Indeed, even an astute banker might be lured into paying an undiscounted price or purchasing at a premium when on impulse he bought an attractive gilded medallion, dagger, or belt to add to his wardrobe. Francesco de Marco Datini's agents stationed abroad—on whose quotations Reinhold Mueller has figured the exchange rates of Italian cities, Bruges, Paris, Barcelona, and London—reasoned in highly complex ways about money and precious metals; they were capable of allowing different considerations to govern their discounting of commercial paper and their pricing of luxury wares for retail sale, both for themselves and for others.[17]

For these reasons, valuations as perceived by the general run of wealthy consumers will be used in this study, and the rough approximation of the florin and ducat will be assumed in order to compare the values noted in inventories and in sumptuary laws, as well as prices listed on commissions and sales. Even these imprecise comparisons suggest that an enormous gulf existed between routine cost of living expenses in cities and the cost of luxury goods.[18]

Venice

By any reckoning Venice was an expensive city in the fourteenth century, and Donald Queller's study of Venetian cost of living indicates that a major war like the War of Chioggia added substantially to living costs, especially for the nobility. An *estimo* of wealthy Venetians, nobles and some non-nobles as well, whose forced loans sustained the war effort (Queller notes quite appropriately so, since the republic was theirs, particularly so for the nobles among them) was drawn up for 1379.[19] Based on this and records of the *procuratori de San Marco*, non-noble and noble grants of *victus* and *vestitus* (living allowance), which were overseen by the procurators, indicate that a person could live modestly on 35 ducats a year in Venice in the later decades of the fourteenth century. Queller augmented the grants of *victus* and *vestitus* with a 16 percent allowance for housing to obtain this figure. A noble son might pay for some basic schooling out of that grant, and a widow, non-noble or noble, could afford a servant at 3½ to 5 ducats in wages, the going rate in Venice for a servant who lived in. However, that noble son or noble widow would live simply. In the same era, an illegitimate daughter of a well-to-do man was given a small allowance of only 12 ducats a year; the grantor evidently believed she could get by on that amount.[20] The *estimo* enumeration of noble and other wealthy families' assets for 1379, while it likely underestimated private fortunes, contextualizes this allowance in useful ways. For example, it demonstrates that the estates of nobles possessing both great and small fortunes provided comparable allowances for dependents, with a few exceptions.[21]

The poor lived quite differently. Brian Pullan has noted that by the early fourteenth century, and of necessity, the Scuola di San Giovanni Evangelista dispensed charitable meals while the Scuola della Misericordia distributed charity to the poor every year.[22] In this compact city rich and poor rubbed shoulders in the street, making the visual contrast of the well-dressed rich and the ragged poor impossible to miss. The genteel poor, sometimes members of *scuole grande* themselves, relied on the charity of their confraternities, relatives, and neighbors to survive. The poor might even on occasion represent the same great lineages that successfully asserted rights to noble status and membership in the Senate in this century, such was the intimacy of the Venetian world.[23] At some level of their deliberations the senators who designed sumptuary law had to keep in mind that social and political privilege did not necessarily bestow wealth on all, and that a proud family could lose a fortune and become destitute in the risky climate of the fourteenth-century economy. In this environment manifest distinctions of wealth, made all the more evident by the display characterized locally as *le pompe*, could become a chronic and worrisome political concern.

Costs like a servant, housing, and, significantly, clothes in a moderately wealthy or well-to-do household warrant close attention. Queller was surprised to learn that one commoner, Vittorio Valentino, gave his daughter the great sum of forty ducats for a dress in 1374, that is, even before the inflation caused by the War of Chioggia had set in. Valentino could have instead purchased a young female slave, who could serve his household for many decades (see Chapter 4). Another Venetian, Giovanni Cavazza, a wealthy nobleman, gave his former wet nurse, who cared for his orphaned granddaughter, forty ducats for a gown and a summer fur. It gives some pause that the *Guidici dei Procuratori* assigned an orphaned grandchild of a well-to-do family only twelve ducats a year for support when gifts of clothes as lavish as these were given.[24] In comparison to the costs of food and housing, clothing was very expensive, Queller concluded. However, what he found here may not be ordinary dresses but celebratory clothes, possibly gifts of wedding dresses that would last a lifetime and perhaps be willed on to others.

Venice continued to compose sumptuary laws throughout the fourteenth century even while, like most other known attempts at creating limits on personal expenditure, the laws were more often flouted than respected. The law still in effect in the 1370s had been the one passed on May 21, 1360, and its valuations provide a point of comparison. For a bride with a trousseau at the highest allowable limit, a ceiling of 40 *lire di grossi* for clothes and other gifts was in force. Within the first four years of marriage a husband was not to give his wife further dresses or jewels exceeding 30 *lire di grossi* in value; thus the law took in all gifts from a bride's natal family and from her husband.[25] At an exchange rate of 1 *lira di grossi* to 10 ducats in the decades following 1360 (a period of some monetary stability at least until the War of Chioggia), brides faced a generous limit of 700 ducats for trousseau and further gifts of clothes and jewels from husbands in their early years of marriage. These gifts constituted bridal wealth, furnishings for the home, and a bride's lifetime wardrobe, or at least what a woman wore for important occasions until she donned mourning clothes. Dowries had crept up over the century from about 650 ducats to 1,000 ducats or more, and in the fifteenth century aristocratic dowries would seldom fall below the figure of 1,000 ducats and sometimes rose much higher. This dotal award, while high, conforms to expectations for *corredo* and counterdowry at a bit less than three-quarters of the dowry itself.[26] But in contrast to a modest cost of living allowance of 35 ducats a year for housing, bed, and board, this limit was extraordinarily generous, twenty times the amount of a year's living costs.

Ever since the sumptuary law of 1299 had passed, a bride had been limited to four good dresses in her wardrobe, and these were expected to last.[27] From 1334 forward Venetian brides were allowed two dresses for the wedding day itself, which could double the cost of wedding clothes for generous donors like Vittorio Valentino or Giovanni Cavazza mentioned above, if they were inclined to go to the limit.[28] Hypothetically then, not 40 but 80 ducats would be the sum spent on special dresses to be worn at the wedding celebration, and the bride might still remain within the limit of the law. This does not even broach the topic of jewels, headdresses, mantles, veils, and the other accoutrements of a fashionable bride's wardrobe.[29]

Individual fastenings for clothes and the jewels a bride might wear were specified in the law of 1360. A woman might have a belt or girdle up to the value of 20 ducats. If she were fortunate enough to have one for each wedding dress, 40 ducats of her 700-ducat allotment for wedding gifts would be used up. A woman was forbidden to wear a head ornament called a *bocheta* and beaded ornaments referred to as *drezatores perlarum* (ornaments woven into the hair) in 1360. These clauses of the law did not work, like so many other of the failed restrictions on specific fashions, so in 1403 after much controversy, the Senate capitulated to the style by merely setting a limit on *bocheta* and headdresses, precious stones and pearls included: women could wear such headgear up to 30 ducats in value.[30] This suggests that head ornaments had been in use all along in defiance of the law; they had certainly been brought up as matters of debate often enough.

A belt up to the value of 20 ducats and a headdress up to the value of 30 ducats set off the hypothetical 40-ducat wedding dress, and perhaps two full ensembles composed of these elements were placed at a bride's disposal. Laws were enforced on what was displayed but what remained at home was less easily regulated; members of a household often shared luxuries. *Le pompe* for the bride with two very fine ensembles could amount to 180 ducats, which approaches a third of a married woman's sumptuary limit of 700 ducats for her trousseau and all other wedding gifts. It appears that a bride's generous allotment for gifts could be used up quite easily by articles of fashion and dress, that is, if she and her kin had any intention at all of staying within the law. Jewels and luxurious fastenings, taken together, were regarded as likely to be even greater expenses than the hypothetical fine dress or bridal gown at Venice, while special bridal dresses were themselves expensive enough to cost more than a modest yearly living allowance. All jewels and accessories were significantly more lavish expenditures; indeed, given their secondary function in the wardrobe, accessories were exorbitantly costly items of personal apparel. Men likely wore even more wealth on their backs than women.

Fines tended to be set high; when a limit on the cost of *drezeria perlarum*, pearls woven in the hair, was set at one hundred solidi in 1299, the penalty attached was also one hundred solidi.[31] Venice soon hit upon a more expedient system of punishment: it fined the miscreant but also confiscated the offending garment, fastening, or jewel that contravened the law. This amounted to a stiff penalty, given the cost of clothes and accessories, one more onerous than the fine itself. And it meant that a stylish wardrobe was subject to the same treatment as contraband. Officers of the Levant, who examined imports, were given an increase in salary and more staff to police the streets when ordered to examine wardrobes for forbidden articles of apparel and excessive expense. Enforcement would, of course, place the republic in the position of salvaging, storing, and disposing of private wealth in the form of clothes, accessories, and jewels confiscated on the city streets. In enforcing the law officials became second-hand dealers of a sort when they disposed of confiscated goods.[32]

The law of 1360 initiated a new phase in sumptuary lawmaking in Venice by placing a few limits on the cost of adult men's apparel. Women, children, and young men up to age eighteen (sometimes twenty-five) had been restrained parties in the laws prior to this time, but a new restriction passed in 1360 placed a twenty-five-ducat limit on the price of a man's belt; while this was a comfortable five ducats over the limit set on all of women's fastenings for clothing, it signaled to adult men that they would not be completely exempt from regulation hereafter. The law forbade costly furs like ermine to young men under twenty-five years of age. Boys under twelve could wear only those buttons that were made twelve or more to the ounce. After twelve boys could wear buttons of whatever size and weight they could afford. A hierarchy of age and gender informed the legislation of 1360, but within a complex formula that required careful monitoring in the execution of the law. Beyond these specifications the law prescribed that all dowries, those above 30 *liri di grossi* (300 ducats) must be presented to the *Avvocatori di Commune* for review before donation. This enactment permitted surveillance of even modest dotal assigns. A notary also had to keep in mind the limits on gifts to a bride when drawing up the will of a parent or grandparent with unmarried daughters.[33] Venetian lawmakers had begun to think in terms of the entire package of wealth transferred at marriage.

Luxuries had always cost dearly. In 1333, the Florentine Duccio Puccii had spent 30 ducats for a silver belt which he purchased when he visited Ragusa; clearly his belt would have transgressed the law of 1360 had it been worn at Venice after that date.[34] In fact this single belt equaled one-tenth of a modest but respectable 1360 Venetian dowry of 300 ducats. If Duccio had purchased or worn that same belt in his own hometown of Florence, he would have escaped any interference from the law, and in all likelihood he took that belt back to Florence. But by the 1370s Florence had begun to legislate on men's accessories as well, in this instance by weight rather than cost. Thereafter a man might wear a great silver belt but it could not weigh more than two Florentine pounds. (In all likelihood Duccio's belt would have contained more than two pounds of silver, but neither the quality of that silver nor its weight was specified in the sales agreement.)[35]

Ragusa, where Duccio Puccii purchased his great silver belt, had few limits on luxury consumption.[36] In 1347, two great silver Ragusan belts cost over 88 ducats or, in the local money of account, 177 *hyperperi*.[37] These were the sort of ponderous, ostentatious artifacts that Venice and Florence targeted in their first specific restrictions on adult men's attire passed in the 1360s and

1370s. From commissions and sales it seems fairly certain that the largest and most decorated among silver belts increased in size and value over the course of the century. Some belts were substantially more expensive than the limit of 25 ducats set in 1360 at Venice, and most likely they contained more than the Florentine limit of two pounds of silver. Still exceptionally large belts sold earlier: in 1313, one very expensive belt with filament silver costing 143 *hyperperi* (over 71 ducats) appeared in the record.[38]

When Venice finally imposed limits on men's great belts in 1360, all of the examples of the goldsmith's art mentioned above were beyond the limits set in the law. In other words, there is evidence that very expensive items for luxury consumption appeared on the market and, regardless of the law, men could and did purchase them.[39] The earliest restrictions on men's apparel quite properly fell on the great silver belt, a signature item of fourteenth-century masculine fashion. However, it is important to keep in mind that men's other luxuries remained unrestricted. The gilded chains, medallions, rows of buttons, eyelets of silver or gold, plaques, daggers, jeweled scabbards, spurs, silver aglets, brocades with gold and silver thread, furs, leathers, fine fabrics, and jewels of affluent men's wardrobes continued to be purchased and worn without restrictions.

In thirteenth-century Venice the disparity between a relatively modest cost of living, on the one hand, and wardrobes of the wealthy, on the other, seems to have been great as well. In comparing prices and salaries in thirteenth-century Venice, Robbert found that a mantle or cloak was valued at 4.5 *libra denariorum venetialium* in 1222 (stated in the money of account then in use), but a string of pearls cost 25 *lib. den. ven.*, over five times as much, while a gilded silver candelabrum at 225 *lib. den. ven.* cost many, many times more.[40] Educating an orphan cost merely 6 *lib. den. ven.* in 1225, while an ordinary belt, not a great belt of silver, could be purchased for 1.1 *lib. den. ven.* More significantly a boat (*barca*) of first quality, which might help a family earn a living, was valued at 4.5 *lib. den. ven.* and one of lesser quality could be obtained for as little as 3 *lib. den. ven.* Furthermore, food cost only a fraction of the going prices for durable goods.[41] The costs of the early thirteenth century figured in a money of account are not directly comparable to price limits set in sumptuary legislation in a later age, when cost limits were expressed in gold ducats or lira; but they are instructive in themselves. They suggest that the disparity between the cost of living and the high cost of luxuries was long-standing and that the wealthy possessed discretionary funds to spend on luxuries because, at least in part, the cost of living remained low. Moreover clothes, known to be relatively heavy expenditures throughout the medieval era, never quite matched the heights of outlay for ornaments, gold and silver accessories, jewels, and precious plate.[42] In the fourteenth century legislators would have had no trouble recognizing that living expenses could be kept low in towns by simply foregoing the consumption of luxury fabrics and materials. Lawmakers would be acutely conscious of the fact that once the affluent embarked on programs of consumption of fine or precious goods that outlay escalated quickly. Dismissing important purchases like a great silver belt or a silver gilt brooch as mere trinkets that perked up a wardrobe seriously undervalues their relative consequence in terms of expenditures, even among wealthy people with discretionary funds.[43]

Some evidence about a spiral in the costs of luxuries over the decades may be obtained by tracing sumptuary law limits that continually edged upward. The total of a Venetian bride's finery for embellishing her two wedding dresses (as specified by law in 1334) added up to 9 *lira di grossi*. By 1360 limits set on embellishments or bridal jewels had risen to 40 *lira di grossi*, with a belt and other fastenings allowed at 20 ducats—up from 12 *solidi di grossi*. (This earlier limit, at the exchange rate of 20 solidi to 1 *lira di grossi*, would have amounted to 6 ducats.) The law of 1360 appears to have been designed to accommodate substantial increases in the cost (or perhaps number and variety) of bridal accessories; the same would hold true for the law passed later in 1403, when that chronically troublesome fashion, *drezatores*, was finally permitted but restricted in value to 30 ducats, a high limit. Assuming consumption patterns were a driving force for shifting limits ever upward, at the high end of the market, luxury wares were becoming more expensive. Nonetheless, wealthy consumers continued to buy them.

To return to the Venetian sumptuary law of 1360, by the stipulations of the law a girl aged eight or under might have one ornament for her hair worth ten ducats.[44] By comparison to allowances for cost of living for that era, the most expensive child's hair ornament could keep a commoner, or even a member of a noble family, modestly—but apparently not in want—for almost three months. Great distinctions in wealth existed in late medieval Venice, not only within the ranks of patrician families but, as the *estimo* of 1379 makes clear, among wealthy commoners and their poorer neighbors. For a strapped but perceptive observer in the streets, a child so richly dressed might appear an affront to traditional values.

Limiting the cost of a child's hair ornament to what might keep an adult sheltered, fed, and clothed for almost three months underlines the emotion expressed in the Senate's own rhetoric: it was necessary to create limits in order to restrain consumption for a people—albeit a small, affluent segment of Venetian society—who consumed "more than the rest of the world." Laws revealed that Venetians were a people remarkable, even unique, in their opportunities to consume. But did these laws have the added effect, unintended or unwitting, of alerting Venetians with discretionary income to the opportunities to buy luxuries that lay out there in the markets? Could these efforts at lawmaking in some sense have served as a means for focusing the attention of those with discretionary funds on the allures of consumption? Certainly sumptuary law fixed the public's attention on the display of wealth in the streets. By being publicly pronouced in full every six months, laws alerted casual passersby to fine gradations in the costs of fastenings and headdresses and robes seen in the streets: Was that jewel in the hair of a young child worth less or more than ten ducats? Was there jewelry in excess of thirty ducats displayed on that woman? What was the precise worth of that great silver belt? Whether by intent or inadvertence, sumptuary law could induce the public to examine and perhaps rank individuals walking the streets by what they wore.

Florence

Surviving fourteenth-century documentation of costs, prices, and wages is never commensurate, nor do scholars figuring cost of living or prices follow the same assumptions. Charles de la Roncière, working on Florence from the 1372 budget of the charitable hospital foundation of Santa Maria Nuova, estimated that food would consume 28.4 percent and fuel, clothes, and housing another 16.7 percent of a budget. This was a significant decrease in food costs—from over 56.6 percent in 1340 to only 28.4 percent—that is, since the first visitation of the Black Plague.[45] A rise in wealth and monetary stability, leading to a lowering of costs for essentials, has prompted economic historians to regard the later decades of the fourteenth century as stable, an era of "fat years" for the working classes in Florence.[46] Nominal wages for masons, gardeners, weavers, and other laborers increased almost threefold in these years, compared with wages in the years before the Black Plague of 1348. As a result this was a period of comparatively high consumption for at least some skilled wage earners.[47] A mason earning 16 solidi a day for the summer season and 15½ for the winter took home in silver coin what amounted to just over a florin for a five-day workweek at an exchange rate of 67 to 77 solidi to a florin.[48] If he worked most or all of a 260-day work year he earned in silver coin the equivalent of something in the range of 50 florins a year. However, even skilled workmen were seldom fortunate enough to be steadily employed. Somewhat later, in 1427, the Florentine Catasto officials would allow 14 florins for a living allowance for a citizen, so this wage estimate of 50 florins a year for the latter years of the fourteenth century is probably not out of line in this long period of monetary stability that Florence enjoyed. Out of his wage, presumably, a mason supported at least some others, most likely members of his own family.[49]

Based on a comparison with the earlier work of de la Roncière, Richard Goldthwaite estimated that the wages of a foreman in the building trades in the early years of the fifteenth century might rise as high as 72 florins.[50] This figure stood considerably below the salaries of 100 to 150 florins paid to government officials, who would live quite well on their incomes. By comparison, a late fourteenth-century skilled mason's wages, estimated at 50 florins, provided some discretionary income for a small family, such as decent clothes and some modest household furnishings.[51]

The issue of cost of living in towns is clouded by the problem of silver coinages. Wages paid in depreciated Florentine silver coins, where the blackened and thin silver coins in circulation did not form a single integrated monetary system with the gold florin but fluctuated independently, left the petty silver coins in circulation exposed to inflationary pressures. In the meantime the gold florin itself, the medium of international trade, was protected by strict government standards and circulated with its own money of account for calculating purposes.[52] Carlo M. Cipolla has characterized the dilemma for those wage earners who were paid almost entirely in debased silver coin with these words: "[T]he *denaro* from any mint in Northern Italy had been reduced in size and appearance to a totally wretched and ugly little disk of metal, very thin, of low fineness, easy to lose, and easy to break."[53] Wealthy citizens decked out in silver in the streets must have been a difficult sight to bear for those whose wages were paid in debased, thin, black, wretched silver coins. Wage earners might be conscious of the fact that the same silver, conveyed to the mint and coined at full weight, could improve the purchasing power of their wages.

Cipolla arrived at the figure of 20 florins a year as an average cost of living figure for Pavia in 1376, but his sample was not large and smaller cities like Pavia probably cost less than Florence in terms of routine living expenses.[54] On the basis of more examples, Christiane Klapisch-Zuber estimated that a single female domestic servant might expect to earn the equivalent of 14 florins in wages in the half century after the first visitation of Black Plague—that is, when wages had begun to be figured, if not paid, in florins (in general a stabilizing influence on wages).[55] A live-in servant working at 14 florins a year and a skilled mason earning near 50 florins would suggest a modest standard of living required somewhat more than 20 florins, the figure Cipolla suggested for Pavia.

Certainly in Florence the affluent and the poor lived in conditions of stark contrast despite the benefit of monetary stability. Alessandro Stella has noted that people with family members on whom they could rely, or people who owned some property, could expect to get by, even if their wages were low, or they worked only sporadically.[56] When access to even a small amount of personal property made a significant difference in the lives of the poor, the display in the streets of luxurious personal property would occasion awe and possibly resentment.

Some of the prices of goldsmiths' work produced in Lucca were stated in florins so the cost of luxury wares may be compared to cost of living in the general vicinity of the city of Florence. In the account book of 1354/5 for the Lucchese goldsmith Forniano Frediano di Barone, a certain Forteghuerra gave 2½ florins to purchase a gold ring with a great pearl in it, and he paid in installments. Puccinello Turchi purchased a gold ring with a fine set-in diamond for 11½ florins the same year.[57] A servant would need to work for over two-thirds of a year in Florence to purchase that diamond ring, and a skilled mason about a quarter of a year. However, if gold rings appealed to government officials earning 100 to 150 florins a year, they could most likely save up for the less expensive one at 2½ florins.

In 1356, an extensive new sumptuary code in Florence limited women's consumption largely through prohibiting specific fashions; for example, the law stated that a woman might wear a robe with a train but it must be less than one *bracchi* in length. A woman could not wear cloth of gold or velvet but she could wear silk, and she could wear a girdle or belt but it had to be limited in value to 15 florins (in 1360 in Venice the limit was 20 ducats).[58] Apparently a woman might walk the streets of Florence in the mid-fourteenth century wearing a belt that cost more than the wages of a servant for a year, and this on a robe of silk that featured other pieces of jewelry, and she might also wear an expensive headdress. Unlike its Venetian counterpart, Florentine law was more given to absolute prohibitions on various articles of apparel and styles, while it set fewer upper ceilings on the costs of luxury wares. But lawmakers could not prohibit fastenings like belts although they recognized that a belt was a prime opportunity for ostentatious display; instead they tried the expedient measure of limiting the cost of this one item to 15 florins. A simple garland was permitted to the sum of 2 gold florins in 1318. (A servant would have to work nearly two months to afford this garland.) Heavy outlay for a simple garland suggests why a circlet of this nature was sometimes identified as a crown. When Florentine legislators set a limit, they set it high, as did their Venetian counterparts.

No absolute upper limit on what might be spent on wedding gifts was set in Florentine sumptuary law. An important exchange of gifts between brides' and grooms' families characterized the weddings of the wealthy at Florence, and specific provisions of law regulated wedding festivities. In an unusually generous example of a groom's countergift to his bride, Luca di Totto da Panzano spent 550 florins to clothe his betrothed in 1350. Luca noted in his *ricordanze* that the gabelle had been paid so the bride might wear the prohibited finery.[59] Since Luca di Totto had received only a modest 450 florins in dowry from his father-in-law, Bindo, his gift was a very rich one, in fact, ostentatious. Perhaps this is best explained by the hypergamy characteristic of some ambitious Florentine men of Luca's day. The figure of 550 florins for wedding chests, the bride's clothes and jewels, the wedding celebration itself, possibly home furnishings, and the fine paid to allow his wife to wear her new apparel indicates that at Florence, as at Venice, luxurious wedding clothing and gifts came at high prices in comparison to the cost of living.[60]

The commissions for the goldsmith Giovanni di Bartolo of Siena, which have been studied in detail by Ippolito Machetti, provide some points of comparison to current cost of living in Tuscany. In the later years of the century Giovanni di Bartolo traveled between Siena, Avignon, and Rome, establishing himself as a premier master of the goldsmith's art, one who enjoyed the patronage of popes. He had major business dealings with wealthy Florentines as well. When Giovanni began his ascent at the papal court, he received 25 florins, 6 solidi for making silver bowls in 1363. He pleased the court with this commission because two years later, in 1365, he fabricated a gold rose of the sort bestowed upon princes for their service and devotion to the Holy Father, and received 122 florins, 22 solidi for it. The following year a commission brought him 264 florins, 6 solidi *pro cella regali de festa deaurata*. This may have been *c'é il regalo di festa aurata*, or a gilded holiday gift.[61] If so, it was no small token since it brought Giovanni a very high price. Generally goldsmiths received 20 to 30 percent on their commissions, although commissions for the most celebrated artists could rise much higher. Giovanni received 5 to 8 florins for his bowls, then 25 to nearly 40 florins for his first gold rose in 1365, and the princely sum of 50 to 80 florins for the rich gift he fashioned a year later. In one commission, Giovanni could earn more than a skilled mason made in a year. Most fees and commissions earned by Tuscans in the professions could not match this. The famous doctor of law Bartolus de Sassoferratto (1313/4–1357) was assigned a fee of just 4 florins by a judge when, with the consent of the concerned parties, he was entrusted with the responsibility of offering one of his learned legal opinions or *consilia*.[62]

By way of comparison, a goldsmith who became a famous artist patronized by the great and powerful did better than a goldsmith employed at a mint, if a cross-reference from Florence to Venice is attempted. In 1394 Marco and Laurencio Sesto, goldsmiths of Venice, were granted wage increases from 20 to 30 ducats, presumably for a year's work.[63] Later, Marco would receive a raise from 30 ducats to 70 ducats, which went toward the important work of producing the dies for the colonial Venetian coinages of the *soldini, mezzanini*, and *piccoli*. This income from the mint was steady, although with a stipend of only 30 ducats a year the brothers each earned less than a modest Venetian cost of living allowance (35 ducats). Presumably the brothers could afford to do so because they also served with Bernardo, their brother and a master goldsmith, and possessed rights in the family business. Other goldsmiths might make better livings at Venice, but Marco and Laurencio were members of a large and successful shop of goldsmiths, which most likely augmented their mint salaries. The Sesti produced some very important works on commission.[64]

Price differentials among luxury goods were great: Giovanni di Bartolo of Siena continued to hold papal favor, and he contracted more lucrative commissions for gold roses and other items like a *turribolo* (censor) he fashioned in 1367. A particularly noteworthy papal rose for Queen Joanna of Sicily in 1368 required in the original order more than fourteen ounces of gold and three sapphires. But that did not prove sufficient, so more precious stones as well as some silver were added to the commission; this produced an extraordinarily rich artifact. However, as Machetti has observed, amid all this grandeur Giovanni di Bartolo did not disdain to fulfill a small commission of 4½ florins.[65]

The inventory of Bonaccurso de Vanni and Geri di Andrea, preserved among Francesco de Marco Datini's personal papers, records the same disparity between the highest-valued luxury wares and more modestly priced goods, and striking differences among the valuations set on consumer goods, in the general run. A "good" miter (weighing 8 marks and containing 7 ounces of silver) at 280 florins, 2 pearl buttons at 40 florins, and 3 silver rings valued at 1 florin, 12 solidi reveal substantial differences in the cost of goods amassed for sale to the wealthy of Avignon.[66] In supplying the papal court, goldsmiths' commissions varied from a mere florin or two to many hundreds. Perhaps this wide range of price indicates an attempt on the part of luxury purveyors to set out a diversity of objects that served ritual and ecclesiastical demands, as well as items that appealed to the personal tastes of prelates, like fine rings and plate for their dinner tables.[67]

It was unusual for the inventory of the charitable gift of Madonna Margherita Vanni degli Spini (Acciaiuoli) to include valuations, but a few are included: in 1380 one ring Margherita owned was valued at 10 florins and another at 35 florins.[68] The latter ring could pay a Florentine skilled workman's salary for almost nine months. Clearly the lady and her kin had collected many fine luxury goods; this was probably part of an estate that had funneled significant wealth into her hands as a result of decimation by the plague. She appears to have held within her coffers some rich bits and pieces of finery left over from her husband Niccolà Acciaiuoli's tenure as grand seneschal to the king of Sicily.

This inventory containing goods from a king's court distorts the picture of what a citizen, in contrast to a high-placed nobleman or prince, might own. However, in number and description, the inventoried articles reveal that men's luxury consumption tended to be greater than women's. Two dozen great belts, articles men would wear, amounted to superfluity. Plate, household furniture, and linens were included in this inventory, as were some books, mementos, banners, and weapons. At the pinnacle of wealth consumption was

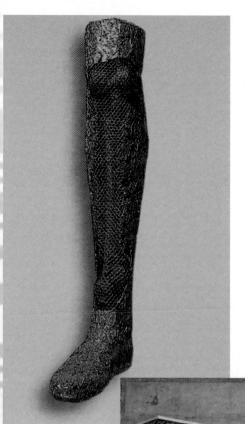

Plate 1.   Reliquary for the foot of St. Blaise, probably eleventh century. Dubrovnik Cathedral, Dubrovnik, Croatia. Work in gold sheet decorated with gold filigree, with an enameled medallion of the coat of arms of the republic of Dubrovnik. Silver disks were stamped with this likeness and circulated as ex-votos. Courtesy of the Dubrovnik Cathedral, Dubrovnik.

Plate 2.   School of Giotto, *St. Francis Renounces All World Possessions*, 1298. Mural, Upper Church, S. Francisco, Assisi, Italy. St. Francis disrobes, handing his fine clothing to his aghast but well-dressed father. Art Resource, N.Y.

Plate 3.   Giotto di Bondone, *Ognissanti Madonna*, c. 1305. Uffizi Gallery, Florence. Rich borders and gilt adorn the Virgin and Child and the retinue of angels. Art Resource, N.Y.

Plate 4.   Giotto di Bondone, *Expulsion of Joachim from the Temple*, c. 1305. Scrovegni (Arena) Chapel, Padua. This may well be the most compelling juxtaposition of classical and contemporary dress in fourteenth-century painting and fresco. To modern viewers the dress of the two figures may appear similar, but a fourteenth-century viewer would recognize that Joachim is robed in classical drapery while the bearded priest who expels him from the temple wears a fine contemporary coat with set-in sleeves. The shortened overgarment is trimmed with gold embroidery bordering seams, the set-in sleeves, and the hem of the coat. Art Resource, N.Y.

Plate 5. Guariento di Arpo, detail from *Angelic Orders,* c. 1350. Painting. Musei Civici, Padua. The angels wear identical embroidered and pleated short tunics with epaulets and display diadems on their heads. Striking reiteration is created with red shields on fields of gold, arrow-headed spears, gold halos, and large, linked gilded belts, which exhibit individual design in contrast to the otherwise uniform dress of the figures. Alinari/Art Resource, N.Y.

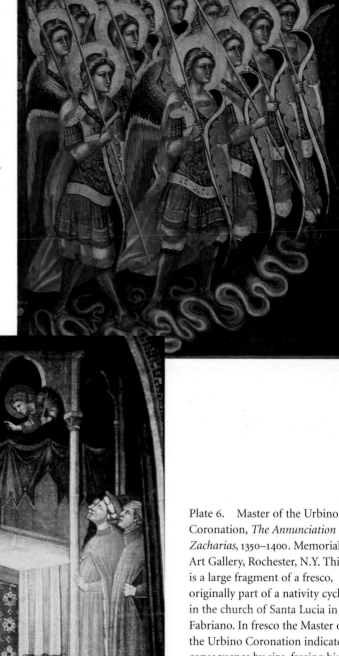

Plate 6. Master of the Urbino Coronation, *The Annunciation to Zacharias,* 1350–1400. Memorial Art Gallery, Rochester, N.Y. This is a large fragment of a fresco, originally part of a nativity cycle in the church of Santa Lucia in Fabriano. In fresco the Master of the Urbino Coronation indicated consequence by size, freeing him to dress the three witnesses in contemporary luxury apparel without detracting from Zacharias. Courtesy of the Memorial Art Gallery, Rochester, N.Y.

Plate 7. Center medallion of a twelve-medallion necklace, fourteenth century. Cleveland Museum of Art. Gold, encrusted enamel on gold, precious and semi-precious stones, and pearls, diameter 1¾ inches. The medallion is a rare surviving example of *en ronde bosse* enamel. Purchased from the J. H. Wade Fund, 47-407. Courtesy of the Cleveland Museum of Art.

Plate 8. School of Giovanni da Milano, *La famiglio del conte Stefano Porro*, 1370. Fresco, Oratoria di S. Stefano, Lentate sul Seveso. The count is dressed in military garb, which his sons' costumes echo, while the daughters' dresses reiterate the mother's robes. Art Resource, N.Y.

Plate 9. Nicolò da Bologna, *Madonna and Child Enthroned between Saints Petronius and Alle (Eligius), Christ in the Initial A,* after 1383. Rosenwald Collection, National Gallery of Art, Washington, D.C. Miniature on vellum. The frontispiece of the *Statutes of the Goldsmiths' Guild,* Siena, featuring St. Eligius, the patron saint of goldsmiths. Courtesy of the National Gallery of Art, Washington, D.C.

Plate 10. Master of the Madonna of Mercy, *St. Eligius Working a Gold Saddle for King Clothar,* Italy, late fourteenth century. Prado Museum, Madrid. First panel of a diptych. Tempera on wood with gold-leaf ground. St. Eligius works between two goldsmiths; all three wield goldsmith's tools; Clothar stands with companions just outside the workshop. Behind St. Eligius, under the archway of the workshop, ready-made gilded silver belts and chains are displayed for the public. Art Resource, N.Y.

Plate 11.   Master of the Madonna of Mercy, panel detail from *Commission from King Clothar to St. Eligius*. Prado Museum, Madrid. Second panel of a diptych. Companion to *St. Eligius Working a Gold Saddle for King Clothar*. Italy, late fourteenth century. Tempera on wood with gold-leaf ground. This detail presents the same goldsmith's shop as in the companion panel, with customers in contemporary dress gathered around. A goldsmith behind the counter weighs gold in a balance. Art Resource, N.Y.

Plate 12. *Crucifixion*, England, c. 1395. Berger Collection,
Denver Art Museum. Tempera and oil-based paint with gilded
tin relief, part gold ground on Baltic oak panels. This is one of
the largest and best-preserved surviving English Gothic panel
paintings. The Roman soldier to the right of the crucified
Christ wears a gilded and hinged silver belt with a sheath and
sword appended. His doublet is embroidered, and he wears a
fashionable cone-shaped hat. Another soldier facing him is
dressed in an embroidered doublet with a great belt and sword,
gold in appearance but probably silver gilt. Courtesy of the
Denver Art Museum, Denver, Colo.

Plate 13. *Wisdom Personified*, miniature, cutting from a Bible Historiale by Guiart de Moulins, Paris, c. 1400. Wisdom wears gold embroidered figures on her red gown. The maidens accompanying her wear less adorned robes. Courtesy of the Free Library of Philadelphia, Philadelphia, Pa.

Plate 14. Lippo di Vani, *Priest*, Siena, mid-1340s. Leaf from a gradual. Historiated initial "S" with a very richly adorned figure of a priest offering the Eucharist. Courtesy of the Free Library of Philadelphia, Philadelphia, Pa.

splendid—and endlessly repetitive. Bangles, brooches, belts, rings, jewels and jewel settings, purses, enamels, and buttons proliferated. Madonna Margherita would have been hard-pressed to find enough members of her household to wear these precious ornaments, particularly the masculine fashions included on the list in endless repetition. All manner of other goods including goblets, censors, linens, plates, pins, worked leathers, hangings, gloves, and decorated saddles were gifted to the church.

Comparing Margherita Vanni degli Spini's possessions to what would have been allowed in Florentine sumptuary laws provides some useful context. Men could wear as many rings as they wished, but walking out in Florence a lady might wear only two of her inventoried rings; she could not risk wearing the others and being written up by a scouting officer of the *Ufficiale delle donne* and fined 100 lira (unless, of course, she could prove a gabelle had been paid to wear three or more rings). Fortunately, for such a wealthy woman, a fine figured in a money of account pegged to silver that steadily depreciated in relation to the gold florin would hardly figure a heavy financial burden. If fines were paid on time they were halved, giving the wealthy who broke the law and could pay on the spot another break. It was the practice of the day for affluent families to pay gabelles as a gesture commensurate with their status and wealth; a small lead seal would be attached in plain view to any above limit garment or jewel for officials and the general public to observe. In this way wealthy persons, who often effectively sidled out of bearing their share of government expenses, were compelled to pay a luxury tax of sorts.

Given what the rich possessed it was sound fiscal policy for governments to allow citizens to pay gabelles to wear their finery; it brought in a stream of income to a frequently strapped government. There was less likelihood of grumbling about this luxury tax than about most levies that affected the wealthiest in the community since a luxury gabelle was regarded as an optional expense based on personal priorities. While the sumptuary law of 1373 granted immunity of ten years for clothing already owned, the sixteen-man commission drawing up the law had "been selected to discover way and means by which money will accrue to the Commune . . . [c]onsidering the Commune's need for revenue to pay current expenses."[69] The result was that all women and girls wearing precious ornaments or silk brocade had to pay 50 florins a year to the treasury for that privilege. More likely their husbands and fathers paid the gabelle.

The very rich who could afford an extra tax are a far different matter from serving maids who did not fare well at the hands of the state when they broke sumptuary laws. The fine of 50 lira payable within fifteen days for a servant's infraction of sumptuary law in 1355 amounted to a little less than a 17-florin fine. If the salary a servant might expect for a year came to 14 florins, no servant could hope to pay the fine, which meant facing the alternative of being stripped and beaten around the marketplace unless a generous employer or friend intervened.[70]

Gino Corti gathered some useful evidence about the fourteenth-century art market for finished paintings in Florence that helps illuminate further the cost of luxury items. The prices paid suggest why a skilled goldsmith might remain with his craft rather than enter the more precarious career of painting pictures for a living. In 1383 Monna Uliva, mother and heir of the estate of her painter son, Doffo di Bandino, sold the religious paintings completed by her son before his death. In a few instances she received 14 or 16 florins apiece for her son's paintings, but these were top prices; other finished works went for less. The prices on the open market for paintings did not approach the major commissions paid to a successful goldsmith like Giovanni di Bartolo of Siena. However, a householder could pay a servant a full year's wages for the price paid for one of Doffo's paintings. By yet another comparison, one painting of the Madonna by Doffo di Bandino in the 1380s brought 14 florins, just four florins more than the value set on one of Madonna Margherita Vanni degli Spini's many rings.[71] If compared with her "good" ring at 35 florins, the top prices for Doffo di Bandino's paintings came to less than half the cost of that one costly piece of jewelry.

The price of slaves in Italy, which rose steadily over the fourteenth century, also shows the disparity between the cost of living and the cost of luxury items. A slave from Albania sold to Stefano di Rainieri del Forese of Florence cost 49 florins by 1399.[72] Roughly speaking, prices had tripled for women slaves over the century and skilled slaves were likely sold at even higher prices. Nevertheless, articles of jewelry like diamond rings cost about two-thirds the price of a young slave, who could provide decades of labor to a household.

A Salvage Economy

Inventories of personal items provide opportunities to assess attitudes toward the value of luxury articles when notaries described goods in a variety of conditions from poor to excellent. In Margherita Acciaiuoli's list of articles destined to endow a church, there are goods in remarkably poor repair and some damaged items. One belt with a buckle of silver was described as broken; a silver cross lay in two pieces; and another buckled and gilded belt was described as worn, as was a headband. Both a fur and a large purse or sack were described as "old," and among the fabrics was a piece described as merely a remnant.[73] A notary was obligated to describe inventoried items with accuracy, even in unflattering terms if necessary, but the notary's record reveals something important about prevailing attitudes toward value. Ragged and broken items were judged worthy of being gifted along with precious jewels and plate in top condition. There is a presumption of value implied by including such objects in inventory lists: even damaged luxury wares maintained some worth and market value. The old and the damaged were expected to find future uses, to be recycled or adapted; they were certainly passed on into the hands of others.

If not suitable for refashioning, articles in less than perfect condition may have been destined for the secondhand market. Much earlier, in 1176, the inventory of the wealthy Gratianus Gradenigo, citizen of Venice, included old boots in such poor shape that they were given to charity, but an old rabbit jacket covered with green silk was kept and included in Gradenigo's estate, as were a jacket and a dark blue gown, well-worn, and another pair of boots described as old. A torn shirt was inventoried as was a ripped leather case. The value assigned to these items, a fraction of the value assigned to Gradenigo's best clothes (thirteen *solidi* for a linen shirt but only six for his old gown of dark blue), tells its own story. These garments were judged worth saving for resale or reuse although they were significantly less valuable than Gradenigo's best possessions.[74] Secondhand markets flourished when the wealthy disposed of their possessions in this thrifty way, supplying a market for fashion among less wealthy persons who were encouraged by what they glimpsed of fashion in the streets to buy secondhand.[75] Even among the well-to-do old fabrics were valued. In 1353 Tommasa Niccolini's impressive trousseaux included fine new green cloth for a cloak and fine new crimson for a dress, but her second dress was to be sewn from an old green cloth.[76] In the *Zibaldone* owned by Martin da Canal, composed in the fourteenth century, among 104 listed textiles appeared the item "old cloths"; they had market value alongside the variously enumerated new fabrics. (If not good enough to be recycled as garments they could be used as rags to make paper.)[77] A household inventory of the wealthy Datini family from 1397 listed old napkins, torn tablecloths, and twelve table-cloths that were just worn out.[78] If those who could afford all the high-priced goods they desired insisted on saving their worn goods and passing them on or reselling them, clearly they attached value to them.

Notaries also listed valuables that were held as pawns, which were, of course, capable of being redeemed and thus a tangible part of an estate.[79] Of course, pawns that were forfeited became secondhand goods for sale in the market. This thoroughness in inventorying is understandable when the tools of a workshop or charters that recorded debts, continuing partnerships, valuable pawns for loans, and outstanding sums owed to an estate were at issue, but even personal articles for wear or use, so-called baubles or 'trinkets, along with lists of worn clothes and odds and ends of personal possessions warranted itemization in notaries' case books.[80] Inventories from all over Italy tell a similar story, as Maria Giuseppina Muzzarelli's study of late medieval wardrobes reveals.[81] Even among personal possessions so magnificent in their variety and number that they defy count—for example, the inventory of goods left by Venetian doge Francesco Dandolo in 1339—one old overcoat with a tunic of red cloth *desfornita incisa et non completa* (an incised or slashed tunic no longer whole) made an appearance.[82] Condition notwithstanding, the tunic was judged worth a line of text in the inventory; it was passed along to the doge's heir.

Contemporary dress was composed of many different components, including separate sleeves, tunics, under- and outer garments, linings, fastenings, veils, scarves, jewels, mantles, weapons, trims, hose, laces, and shoes. These were, in whole or part, the bits and pieces described in inventories, and documenting the costs and condition of personal possessions reveals one important element of fourteenth-century attitudes about the value and inheritability of goods. While fashions came and went over the course of the century—for example, sleeves might be tight to the elbow, tight to the wrist, open and flowing or cut in points that hung down to the ground, slashed to show an undergarment, lined with fur, trimmed with ribbon woven of silver and gold thread, or trimmed with gilded buttons in a line to the elbow, in a line to the wrist, or in numerous rows—the basic material elements of fashion were remarkably stable. They were enduring deposits of personal wealth owned by a family. Fashion was created from the bits and pieces found in an estate inventory; these goods were categorized as "movables" and they would be passed on to others.

Two processes appear to have been at work simultaneously in fourteenth-century Italy. Luxury goods were preserved as repositories of value and passed on from generation to generation in families. However, each new generation employed what it had inherited to concoct new fashions designed to show off finery; this wealth in movables may have been accumulated through inheritance and gifts but it could be reworked or combined with something newly purchased to produce a fashionable look. The preserving step helped maintain a family's wealth, with some anticipated losses from the processes of recycling, like melting down old plate or cutting up old fabrics. A second and different step, creating new styles and new ensembles, occurred when inheritors used what they had on hand to keep up with the changing demands of fashion. Designers of sumptuary law, who raised limits upward over the century, appear to have been conscious of the consequences of both steps. Fashion making was the ingenious or creative component of reuse, but it should not mislead us: affluent people and lawmakers alike understood the value of the wealth held as movables and passed on in estates.

When new, higher limits were set in sumptuary laws—in Venice every thirty years or so and in Tuscan towns and elsewhere sometimes more frequently—a generation may have passed and its wealth funneled to another.[83] Laws responded to this transfer of wealth with new statutes that allowed higher limits. In some families decimated by plague, wealth concentrated in the hands of a few survivors created a unique opportunity to consume. While sumptuary laws tended to be accommodating to people with privately held wealth, a perplexing challenge arose with the few individuals who, through no fault of their own, possessed remarkably large collections of luxury goods. As with the case for Madonna Margherita Acciaiuoli of Florence, too many duplicated objects in an estate added up to superfluity, which prompted persons to donate items to charity rather than pass on luxuries to heirs. Many rings, many brooches, and two dozen precious belts belonged to Margherita, many of them of silver gilt with jewels or enamel, others of silk with pearls and ornaments of silver and gold. Who could absorb such a collection and make use of them? Too many goods chasing after potential wearers may be read into her inventory.

Italians recognized the asset value of their accumulated luxuries even while they chased after novelties and new fashions. Through their wills and inventories fourteenth-century people recorded the worth of what they owned and regarded as family assets; consumer goods, especially those of precious metal, were listed as one component of a private fortune. Richard Goldthwaite rates the consequence of collecting very high when he noted of fifteenth-century Florence, "[I]n a sense the city's artistic achievement is partly a consequence of the enormous accumulation of wealth in its most concrete form—gold and silver."[84] This wealth had built up over successive generations as affluent Florentines accumulated private wealth, including stores of money, plate, and other inherited goods.

Despite the increasing cultural consequence of pursuing fashion, new trends had not convinced fourteenth-century consumers that it would be wise to cast aside the old and just buy new. The basic ingredients of a fashionable wardrobe remained remarkably constant; they were goods that could be preserved and recycled.[85] Because contemporary painters possessed acuity in recording the changes in fashions of dress in the early Renaissance, there has been a tendency to assume that fashionable ensembles relied on constantly renewed wardrobes.[86] The written evidence points to the contrary. Dexterity with a needle, the aid of servants who could improvise, as well as the services of skilled craftsmen who repaired and refashioned one's inherited precious possessions abetted a saving ethic already at work. Purchasing new goods was not always necessary, and this was especially true in an era of shrinking urban population in the latter half of the century. Remnants could be used for linings, and set-in sleeves could be removed and restyled, remade, or relined from old gowns and robes. For a fashionable woman, the complex headdresses required by the changing styles of the day could be produced out of ribbons, jewels in settings, pearls or false pearls, flowers, veils, and garlands—some of these were likely to be inherited goods. Men willed their cloaks, long full gowns, belts, furs, and jewels as a significant component of their personal estates. The wealthy Doge Francesco Dandolo had six overcoats and at least a dozen tunics to pass on to his heirs.[87] The frugal Benci del Buono even kept his father-in-law's old and dirty hat liner (see Chapter 7).

The appeal of preserving some of one's wealth in the form of luxury wares, whether fine velvets and brocades, silk, gold, silver, or jewels, was strong, and certainly among the affluent the choice to hold wealth in artifacts was not determined by any lack of alternatives. In Venice, the office of the *procuratori de San Marco* provided for the preservation of family wealth by opening treasury facilities for use by the citizenry. Venetians knew how to discriminate among forms of private wealth—movables and immovables, investment instruments, real estate, and forced loans. Procurators advised citizens when necessary as a component of their obligation to preserve the wealth of Venice. Rather than keep the family fortune invested in the pepper trade, Giovanni Corner of S. Felice ordered his executors to invest in real estate in Treviso and Padua in his will of 1348, while Margherita da Mosto left 100 *lira di grossi* for each of her four daughters but ordered it invested with the Corner banker where it could make money in local *colleganze*.[88] These were prudent choices for underage heirs in all likelihood, but still others left their jewels as repositories of value, all bundled up and sent off to the procurators for later distribution to heirs. Choices abounded for preserving wealth, and Venetians viewed the opportunity to accumulate luxury wares as an attractive alternative when balancing an estate. Movables were wealth that would not be invested in a currency that was subject to fluctuation or devaluation. It was wealth that was not invested in land and subject to crop failure, or in overseas or overland trade with their known risks, or in banks that might fail. Possessions held their value rather well and they were regarded as an honorable way to uphold family prestige and preserve the family fortune.

At the pinnacle of the luxury market in Europe, the gold and silver consumed by the royal uncles of Charles VI unsettled bullion markets in France and caused such scarcity that the royal mint could not fill its requirements for coining.[89] Harry Miskimin has argued that after visitations of the Black Plague reduced population, wealth concentrated into fewer private fortunes, which in turn stimulated a brisk trade in luxuries; as a result mints everywhere were undersupplied with bullion. His model may work for France, where royal consumption of the finest grades of silver and pure gold led to loud and apparently justified complaints from mint officials.[90] The Valois royal family was enormously wealthy; they could afford precious metal of the fineness of the mint, and they lavished it on plate, jewel settings, and great table fountains. It may also be the case that the finest grade went into cups weighing precisely one mark of fine silver in the Toulouse region of France, suggesting the cups were intended to be functional objects but also useful in lieu of currency if necessary.[91] But in northern Italy the market for luxury goods was largely built on lower grades of silver, then gold leaf or foil was applied to create the impression of precious gold. For this reason, urban consumers tended to own far less fine silver than kings and princes, and sometimes it was bullion of a lower grade. To further confuse matters, it was seldom clear even to possessors themselves (save astute bankers and goldsmiths) what the precise amount of bullion in their plate was unless reliable hallmarks appeared on them.

As the bullion famine of the later Middle Ages set in, it is difficult to assess accurately how much these more modest stores of bullion in private hands affected minting, because private wealth in silver and gold was of varied fineness and both its quantity and quality was somewhat of a mystery or, in some cases, a well-guarded secret. In fourteenth-century Genoa, where silver coinage had to be suspended after 1365, a head tax was imposed based on estimates of wealth, but citizens provided their own figures for the value of their movable possessions, including luxuries made of silver and gold.[92] In hard-strapped Siena the *dazio* (direct tax), continued to be collected along with higher gabelles, mandatory salt purchases, forced loans, voluntary loans, and *preste a balzi* (forced loans), yet it was still necessary to pawn land and readmit exiles and rebels to pay off mercenaries. Taxes and loans were based on estimates of wealth, but citizens provided those figures themselves.[93] When surveyors made an attempt to estimate private wealth at Venice, the *estimo* seriously undervalued the total for many of the wealthy, who made their own reports on the worth of their movable property as well. Collections of plate were among the easiest possessions to misrepresent or pass off as something else, although assessors at Venice required that *boni denari* (household goods of gold and silver) be included in Venetian returns (*condizioni*) after 1280.[94] But assessors did not enter noble households and clip off a bit of silver from a platter or chain to subject it to cupellation, which was the reliable way to ascertain the fineness of silver in objects; valuation of silver objects rested on the honesty of the declarer. This was generally true in returns except for real estate, which was estimated by assessors. One cannot even be certain that all precious objects possessed hallmarks, especially if they were imported, so some possessors may have been honestly confused about the value of their holdings.[95]

It took extreme circumstances for the Venetian mint to raise the problem of silver in private hands. In May 1379, during the crisis of the War of Chioggia, new standards were adopted for silver coinage at the mint. Any merchant possessing free (unworked) silver was ordered to take it to the mint, and Venetians were encouraged to melt their household plate "with a provision that any silver with Venetian hallmarks could be coined free of the *quinto* [the one-fifth brought to the mint of all imported silver]."[96] Presumably hallmarked silver could be weighed to determine its worth without resorting to more costly assessment methods. Mint masters and wardens received special incentives for examining and coining this plate and unworked silver, as it was likely a difficult and contentious obligation. Hallmarks on objects provided assurance, but the project was still full of pitfalls. A merchant offering his plate in this monetary emergency would not be pleased to learn that it was less precious than he believed it to be. Both his worth and his patriotic gesture would be challenged.

In Florence, the designers of the Castasto of 1427 simply threw up their hands at the challenge of assessing the private wealth tied up in homes and furnishings; this included collections of clothes, accessories, decorations, and plate. The surveyors lumped all together as *massarizie di casa* (household goods) and did not estimate each item's value.[97] Yet Giovanni Rucellai noted, "The citizens have never had so much wealth, merchandise, and property, nor have the *monte*'s [fund's] interests ever been so conspicuous; consequently, the sums spent on weddings, tournaments, and various forms of entertainment are greater than ever before. Between 1418 and 1423 Florence's wealth was probably at its height."[98] Men wore hoods of scarlet cloth out riding and possessed great wealth in their homes, he added.

Both incidents—Venice's resorting to calling in plate and Florence's refusal to use assessors to value citizens' privately held plate—argue for general awareness of stores of gold and silver in private hands, but the problem lay in the difficulty of estimating worth. How much faith may be placed in Sir Stanley Jevons's "calculation community"—those who set monetary and fiscal policy, plus knowledgeable mint masters and wardens, and the bankers who advised them both? These experts may have believed that silver plate in private hands was a cushion of sorts in the years when silver began to drain out of Europe. Nonetheless, their refusal to call it in to sustain currency or to assist in fiscal emergencies (except in rare circumstances) suggests that private stores represented serious problems for authorities. Were officials comforted by the generally held opinion that because of collections of plate some bullion remained in Europe, even if its full extent remained a mystery? Were authorities reticent to inquire too deeply into private affairs on this sensitive issue related to wealth and standing? Mints and governments, even when strapped, shied away from calling in bullion stores, yet these stores were widely known to be components of private fortunes. Officials appear to have made conscious choices in this regard, but they have not left a record of their reasons for their choices.[99]

Despite the hesitancy to call in private plate, it is reasonable to expect that governments capable of limiting the precious metal displayed in the streets could have written laws that required a record of the number, weight, and fineness of silver objects held as private possessions, if they so wished. Urban sumptuary laws specified a ceiling on the value of owned accessories of silver, and in certain instances, for example in Venetian law on brides' gifts, on total sums to be spent on a wardrobe (inclusive of silver, jewels, and gold). On the other hand, Venetian men were free to accumulate as many precious objects as they desired and could afford, as long as they conformed to specific limits on a few articles of apparel worn out in public. In other words, there is reason to believe that legislators recognized that bullion in the form of silver artifacts resided in homes because they recognized that men collected them. Authorities knew this but the quality and extent of holdings remained hard to pin down. Sumptuary laws, increasingly accepted as legitimate intrusions of the state into the private domain, were tools for controlling consumption within wealthy circles. There is little reason to doubt that had city governments wished to extend the purview of the law they could have assessed, recorded, and even limited the precious metal in private hands, even if this would have been a difficult law to enforce.[100] City-states took on other arduous surveying responsibilities in this age. Venice assumed the daunting task of its *estimo,* and by the early decades of the fifteenth century the Florentines followed suit with their exhaustive survey, the *catasto*. But insofar as the record shows, authorities shied away from limiting or even counting privately held bullion.

The bits and pieces that made up *le pompe* held value fairly well over time, and objects could be refashioned in new ways that would uphold a family's prestige. Precious wares were attractive investments and they possessed the added advantage that their owners seemed to genuinely enjoy wearing them. Commissions and sales at the high end of the luxury market created a good living for a goldsmith, tailor, or merchant who followed those trades. And fourteenth-century people loved being seen adorned with their costly possessions, outshining, if they could, their rivals and neighbors.

Chapter 6
Shops and Trades

In a fourteenth-century *bottega* the retail business of the front room gained some leverage over the demands of the back room with its focus on production.[1] The old understanding of *apotheca*, warehouse, or magazine (*in sua apotheca vel domo* in the statutes of the secondhand clothes dealers of Florence) was largely supplanted by a new apprehension of *apotheca* as an apothecary shop open for browsing to customers.[2] For thirteenth-century Venice it has been argued that patrician merchants and shopkeepers alike served as mere brokers of services to the city's inhabitants.[3] By the fourteenth century, stiff competition for advantageous stalls in the great marketplaces of Venice required reallocation of prime sites by guild officers on a monthly basis as merchants and guildsmen competed for those locations.[4] None of these changes was sudden; they represented instead subtle shifts in emphasis from a time-tested focus on production toward a more deft hand at displaying ready-made goods in an environment conducive to spending money. Nor was there anything genuinely new in trying to promote sales since peddlers had long since mastered tricks for displaying goods to the public. The peddler's pole that served as a staff for traveling and then dangled wares before wide-eyed customers needed only to migrate inside for a shop to take on the character of a retail outlet (see plates 10 and 11; fig. 1). Even the shop as display space was not new. By long custom an astute artisan—glover, painter, or hatter—kept some examples on hand to demonstrate skill, while a shop's masterpiece was always on display to impress customers, even if business consisted entirely of commissions and served a bespoke market (see fig. 8).

Still, the nature of work within some trades changed in response to a greater emphasis on retail sales, although this is not always easily perceived from guild statutes. Martin Warnke argues in *The Court Artist* that the best way for artists to escape a guild's stranglehold on creativity was to seek an appointment and stipend at a royal court.[5] Perhaps court favor was the best path to take for the most creative and talented artists, but in this century some painters and sculptors gained stature in their fields by forming their own sub-guilds with statutes adapted to their specific needs for both production and selling. Some painters even sold ready-made works directly to the public. There were five subgroups of painters in Venice: painters of shields, painters

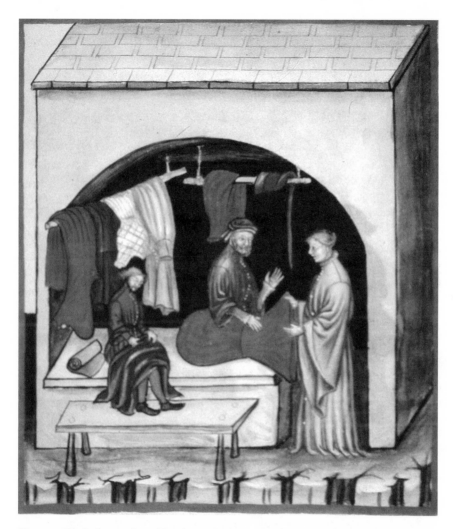

Figure 8. *Vestis de seta,* from Tacuinum Sanitatis, northern Italy, late fourteenth century. Codex Vindobonensis, s.n. 2644. Österreichische Nationalbibliothek, Vienna. Tailors at work creating garments out of silk. The process of tailoring and sewing clothing was separated from purchasing textiles in fourteenth-century Italian towns. Art Resource, N.Y.

of saddles, painters of chests, painters of pictures, and painters of furniture, all working to attract audiences.[6] This hiving off into specialized branches looks very much like a response to demand as well as production; it suggests at least a degree of flexibility within guild structure that could respond to the necessities of retailing. Like Venice, Genoa added specializations in the luxury trades over the century, and by the early decades of the fifteenth-century Pisa had 151 different professional categories among its trades.[7] Florence with its 21 guilds and Bologna with 13 responded to demands for increased specialization in other ways, but this was more a reflection of unique political configurations within guild structures in towns rather than weak consumer demand.

Flexibility was demonstrated as well by the disposition of artisans overseen by their own statutes to work together in cooperative manufacture. In building the luxurious Ca'Oro, sixty-four separate crafts were represented among the workers.[8] Catherine King has asserted that religious art, particularly reliquaries, demonstrated the success of cooperating groups of craftsmen producing a single piece of art; it bears repeating here.[9] The most popular secular products required teamwork in manufacture and apparently received as positive a response from separate trade groups. An ornamental sheathed dagger required fine leather, likely carved and gilded, possibly painted, sewn, and fitted with a silver dagger, which was also gilded, and perhaps supplied with a jeweled and ornamented hilt. Half a dozen or more artisans with different specialties may have contributed to the creation of such a dagger, given the specialization in the trades. Meeting demand encouraged both flexibility and joining of talents among artisans governed by separate regulations, suggesting that guild rigidity did not necessarily stifle the capacity of artisans to respond to the challenges of stepped-up demand.

In turning *bottege* into retail shops certain trades, in particular the cleaner finishing trades, lent themselves to opening their doors to customers; primary processes, more laborious, possibly dirtier and even odiferous, did not.[10] Certain trades were vertically organized, like the famous Lucchese silk manufacture, and when silk workers from Lucca established themselves in a new town they arrived with all necessary personnel, from the women who processed the silk bolls by hand at home (*cocitori*) to skilled weavers and merchants who presented finished cloth to customers.[11] The weaver's lovely figured damask was placed before the public, but the complex processes that produced it were obscure. Silk shops that sought customers did so through jobbing the finished product to long-distance merchants, selling through a retail outlet (Marco Polo's emporium in Venice comes to mind), or welcoming in the public to view the finished product in the front room of the local silk shop.

But even here there were impediments to retail sales. Locally produced fine fabric like good cotton, linen, wool, and silk were merely bolts or pieces of cloth when presented to the public, and while they were Italy's chief claim to fame as a center of industry and qualified as finished goods ready for purchase, they were not fashion in any recognizable shape or form when retailed to customers. A customer chose fabric, possibly on the advice of his tailor or doublet maker, then took the product to another shop where his clothes were fashioned to his measurements, specifications, and taste. Only this last transaction produced the fashion so widely sought by urban customers (see fig. 8). Few trades transcended this time-consuming and fragmented retailing procedure to appeal directly and immediately to customers' desire for fashion. Tanners dealt directly with the public out of their shops and then their customers chose their own shoemakers, at Venice selecting between *calegheri* (shoemakers) and *zavateri* (sandalmakers) for type and style of footwear according to the materials used.[12] Furriers presented finished skins for public sale, but any purchased fur had to be directed to a garment maker of any one of a number of different subspecialties to be turned into trim, a lining, a cloak, or any of the other imaginative fourteenth-century uses for fur, such as hat making.

One luxury trade could appeal directly to the public's demand for fashion: goldsmiths, and they warrant some close study for that reason. In this century goldsmiths learned well the lessons of retailing goods to local audiences and wealthy visitors. Their story is particularly relevant for understanding retailing, the ready-made, and fashion as forces driving demand in fourteenth-century Italian towns.

As an industry goldsmithery could be as vertically organized as silk manufacture, from sweating gold beaters to elegantly dressed master goldsmiths and jewelers who met the public. Conditions of incorporation and organization of the trade varied greatly in Italy's cities so it is difficult to generalize about shops, but the very diversity of roles and organization argues for goldsmiths' pivotal position in urban life.[13] Training was arduous and required mastery of a broad complex of skills. Goldsmiths had to be able to assay gold and silver, serve as experts on currency and mint coin, advise on or conduct trade in bullion from mine sites, and in many instances provide guild affiliation for their close associates, sculptors and painters. Goldsmithery demanded abstract thought and mathematical calculation, practical business and administrative skills, mastery of technical processes, artistic creativity, and very skilled hands. It also demanded a fortune in the trade's required raw materials of bullion and jewels.

Illustrations and paintings indicate that wealthy customers patronized goldsmiths' shops throughout the century, but literary analysis of the trade's retailing innovations was delayed until the middle of the next century when it appeared in the merchant manual of Benedetto Cotrugli, sometimes referred to as the first theoretical business manual for the Western economy (see plates 10 and 11).[14] Even at this advanced date Cotrugli struck an apologetic note when discussing sales techniques. In his *Il libro dell'arte di Mercatura*, Cotrugli argued that setting jewels was a noble art and the jeweler would do well to be both eloquent and affable since he was in constant conversation with lords and gentlemen. He concluded his comment with these words: "Et questa per cierto è gentile arte, et ogni gentilomo se ne doverria intendere" (And certainly this is a noble craft, and every gentleman ought to understand that).[15] For "every gentleman" read every wealthy patron or client. Jewel making and goldsmithing were distinct specialties but also associated, overlapping trades practiced in the most distinguished goldsmith establishments. To Cotrugli nobility connoted honor, and it followed that the "gentle art" of the jeweler ought to be carried out with scrupulous attention to quality, with guild standards buttressed by a gentlemen's code of honor. In such a shop the finest manners were displayed and the customer was treated as a welcome guest. Thus this idealized *bottega* cultivated wealthy customers and relied on the acumen of jeweler-tradesmen, who were gentlemen by education and training, so eloquent and noble in conduct as to qualify as social peers and fit companions for all gentlemen frequenting their shops. Cotrugli's retailing advice was to create an exclusive environment shaped to comforting the wealthy, while exuding a strong sense of shared privilege.

These *orefici* or *aurifici* of fourteenth-century Italy reveal how a craft could transform itself in response to consumer preferences. Artisans and artists alike—this industry epitomizes the predicament of drawing distinctions between craftsmen and artists in this era—followed a surprisingly mobile trade with patterns of migration that followed both supply lines capable of bringing precious metal to Italy and the markets for consumer luxuries. At times goldsmiths, like silk workers, used their craft as a path of escape from civil upheavals, wars, and heavy taxation, permitting some enterprising *orefici* to survive the economic dislocations that plagued towns in northern Italy.[16] Siena, located on the north-south Francigena highway leading to Rome, shone in the fame of its goldsmiths while the ecclesiastical market for goods remained strong, but over the course of the fourteenth-century many Sienese goldsmiths fled their homes in fear of violence or the punishing levies that paid off mercenaries. There would be little other choice open to them in a trade requiring stores of precious bullion to conduct business. Florence not only challenged and triumphed over its neighbor Siena but also absorbed a selection of Siena's most talented goldsmiths and prospered accordingly. By the fifteenth-century Florentine production of silver and gold, which was often directed toward private consumption, export, and Siena's former ecclesiastical markets, challenged and surpassed Siena.[17]

Florence's more northerly neighbor Lucca had flourished as well as a center for goldsmithing that complemented local silk manufacture. In the late thirteenth-century Lucca supported a number of masters in the goldsmith's craft; then, in a serious setback caused by war in 1306, of twenty-four previously active masters only thirteen survived. More political calamities and the sack of Lucca in 1314 disrupted workshops further, but in the aftermath of these struggles the master goldsmiths who remained, or returned, reoriented their workshops toward luxury objects and apparel. Buttons and gold- and silver-shot silk thread that enhanced locally manufactured silk and brocaded fabrics were particularly important manufactures.[18] This transition to fashion goods was never complete; the great workshops of Frediano di Barone and the

Cerlotti family continued to win commissions for ecclesiastical goods. Nevertheless, a scrutiny of routine Lucchese commissions and sales, particularly the account book of Foriano de Frediano di Barone for the years 1354–56, indicate that on a daily basis small orders for personal use had become the bread-and-butter income of the goldsmith shop.[19]

One ploy favored by goldsmiths from smaller communities was to job out ready-made goods to merchants or merchant networks. Francesco de Marco Datini contracted for the supply of an extraordinary variety of plate (by definition any and all luxury goods of precious material like ivory, gems, rock crystal and jasper, as well as gold and silver). Along with his more reliable trade in staple goods he brought luxury goods into Avignon for the resident papal court in the fourteenth century.[20] When the century ended, the bulk of the transalpine trade in precious goods was more likely to travel further north toward Paris and the courts of the royal kin of King Charles VI, while Avignon's resident goldsmiths and importers turned toward Rome to serve the papal court on its return there.[21] But this was only one sign among many of volatility in luxury markets. In search of work goldsmiths traveled to mining centers to assay and work silver and gold. The royal courts at Milan and Naples attracted goldsmiths and merchants selling luxury wares. The same may be said for the royal courts of northern Europe and for cities where court influences were significant, such as Buda, Prague, and London.[22]

Artisans who worked primarily in silver were still goldsmiths by trade. In their apprentice years they learned a variety of techniques for applying gold to silver that rendered the production of the age so bright with gilt that this was a veritable gilded age. Trained goldsmiths could no doubt produce wares of solid gold if a patron demanded it, but gold was seldom more than sparingly applied to luxury wares and was never used in any quantity approaching silver.[23] From the Certosa di Pavia ivory altarpiece with lavish gold trim to less lavish gilded pins, buckles, coronals, and buttons, goldsmiths' skill at stretching precious gold to give the impression of higher worth figured prominently among the talents they offered to customers. Perhaps only the Murano *veriselli*, the guild of imitators of jewels in glass, competed with goldsmiths in tricks of the trade that made objects appear more precious than they really were.

As a craft guild goldsmithing was known for its exacting standards for determining purity or fineness, and a goldsmith's stated opinion and his hallmark were reliable gauges of value. Goldsmiths were entrusted everywhere with the currency of the state or the realm, so an expert in applying parcel gilt to silver also stood behind the tested weight and purity of the florin or ducat in another dimension of his trade.[24] The goldsmith's mark was a trusted symbol whether it appeared on bars of silver or the base of a *moelium* (a deep bowl, often of silver). Fourteenth-century goldsmiths relied on time-sanctioned, widely shared standards of value that encouraged public trust even while, on a daily basis, they might bend their considerable skills to gilding, which was essentially a deceptive practice, albeit a widely understood and accepted one.[25] An inventory of the English goldsmith Walter Pynchon dating from 1398 listed £600 (English pounds) worth of goods of which only £15 were silver. His gems and brooches and rings of gold, although few and small in bulk, far outran his more bulky candleholders, ewers, salts, and spoons of silver in terms of assessed market value.[26] Nonetheless, silver was the staple of a goldsmith's business.

No doubt visits to goldsmiths' shops and close observation of the precise measuring carried on in them reassured customers when shops became popular gathering places for the fashionable. But is it merely irony or a revelation about the perspicacity of master goldsmiths that the most trusted assayers of bullion also promoted the sale of ready-made gilded wares designed to fool the eye? The stress on honor found in Cotrugli's laudatory comments on the trade arouses some suspicion that the goldsmith's skill could outrun the public's ability to distinguish what was apparent worth from what was real, that is, what was genuine fine gold or pure silver of the standard of the mint or what was gilded or silvered.[27] And this was only the tip of the iceberg. A bronze smith could gild less precious metal to enhance its appearance. All sorts of baser materials could be trimmed with gold or silver to give them the appearance of opulence and to allow goldsmiths to spread their gilding expertise deeper and deeper into the growing market for consumer goods. In gilding and silvering, goldsmiths had discovered a deception that pleased the public.[28]

In popular legend the goldsmith's patron St. Eligius, who had served the Merovingian ruler Dagobert II (674–79) as goldsmith and mint master, stood for the age-old obligation of goldsmithing as a public office entrusted with preserving the wealth of the royal fisc. Dagobert was the last of the Merovingian rulers to strike gold coins, and Eligius, who after Dagobert's death was elevated to the bishopric of Noyon, struggled with the collapse of royal currency and magnates' privileges of immunity from taxation. In order to maintain a sound currency he coined through his church office, and from that time forward the names of bishops and abbeys would appear on Frankish coins, an indication that churches had assumed regalian rights.[29] St. Eligius was a remarkably popular saint in the fourteenth century: painters (perhaps members of the goldsmith guild) depicted him melting down royal plate and creating church vessels in symbolic preservation of communal wealth now stored in ecclesiastical treasuries. In a fourteenth-century painting now attributed to the Master of the Madonna of Mercy, St. Eligius displays a saddle of gold being worked for Clothar II surrounded by the precise instruments and tools of his trade. The painting's companion piece features a gold merchant measuring on a miniature balance (see plates 10 and 11).[30] Measuring devices and tools served as symbols of the faith entrusted in Eligius as keeper of accurate standards and protector of the wealth of the Christian community.[31] While Europeans maintained their faith in the inherent value of precious metals, St. Eligius stood as guardian for the secular as well as the sacred responsibilities invested in goldsmithery.[32] His legend contained all the components that ensured the guild's prominence in the fourteenth century: public trust, preserving treasure, minting, and forging ecclesiastical and secular wares.

St. Eligius may be found smithing, weighing gold, delivering gilded thrones, serving as mint master, forging a gold saddle, presenting it to the king, receiving the offices of mint master and bishop, overcoming the devil, saving and resuscitating a hanged man, healing, and exorcizing demoniacs. A bronze stamp preserved at Siena displays a nimbed St. Eligius holding his hammer and a piece of precious metal above his anvil.[33] In an illuminated manuscript attributed to Nicolò da Bologna that is now in Washington, D.C., at the National Gallery, a mitered St. Eligius in bishop's vestments decorates the *Statutes of the Goldsmiths' Guild* (1383), in fitting dignity (see plate 9).[34] *Légende de St. Denis* features a Parisian goldsmith working with his tools in a portal under the Pont du Change, while bankers gather above him to conduct business.[35] In *Le Jeu deséchecs moralisé*, translated into French from Latin by Jean de Vignay, a goldsmith sits working, front and center among chess pieces personifying trusted leaders in the community.[36] On a reliquary for St. Simeon in Zara, a goldsmith kneels with his tools, presenting the saint with a gilt casket in a gift commissioned by Elizabeth I of Hungary.[37] A goldsmith found his way into the decorative border of the fourteenth-century illuminated manuscript known as the Luttrell Psalter.[38]

In Italy goldsmiths served as civic bureaucrats and officials with responsibilities for conducting the business of the mint and on occasion oversaw markets and ports where they monitored the circulation of foreign and domestic coin.[39] Their mint functions, commissions from affluent patrons, both religious and secular, and expertise in assaying the value of precious metal placed goldsmiths among the elite trades (see plates 10 and 11). From the late Middle Ages to the end of the sixteenth century, R. W. Lightbown contends, jewelry making figured as the most lucrative specialty of goldsmithing, substantially enriching those who followed that path.[40] In a pattern of adaptation to new economic forces, trust in the integrity of the goldsmiths' profession carried over from civic function into jewelers' and goldsmiths' fabrications, and customers relied on the shops of well-known and trusted masters to forge their personal treasures.

The connotations of gold as scarce, beautiful, and lustrous, yet soft enough to be shaped into pleasing objects, scarcely needs rehearsing here because it endures today. But silver, a much more highly valued commodity in the fourteenth century than it is now, warrants some comment. Gold was understood to be both sacred and regal while silver was frequently united with gold in metaphors of preciosity, silver representing the wealth and prosperity of the people, gold the treasure of heaven, the church, and kings. Those who read or heard Bible stories, or saw those lessons in church decoration, knew that King Solomon was no sooner granted wisdom by God than he realized that he should fortify his cities and secure both silver and gold, which soon became as "plenteous as stones in Jerusalem."[41] "Happy is the man that findeth wisdom and the man that getteth understanding: for the merchandise of it is better than the merchandise of silver, and the gain thereof than fine gold," from the book of Proverbs, captures a popular distinction between the two metals. Silver was understood as a liquid asset in economic life, a medium of trade, precious to the folk who relied on it for exchange but nonetheless a familiar commodity, while fine gold inhabited a higher echelon and served as an absolute standard of value.[42] But Proverbs also explained, rather grandiloquently, that "[t]he tongue of the just is as choice silver"; so silver was perfectly adequate for rendering a high compliment.[43] In a medieval retelling of the Pentateuch's Joshua and Ruth histories, known as the *Bibbia istoriatea Padovana*, the text explained the reembellished Temple in terms of silver and gold, and a goldsmith's shop illustrated the text.[44]

For fourteenth-century people connotations of great value fit silver because this was an age in which bimetallic ratios fell as low as 10:1, as they did in Florence and other northern Italian towns in the late decades of the fourteenth century.[45] Precious in its own right, silver was still a commodity and it lay within the experience, if not the actual grasp, of ordinary townspeople whereas gold was very precious and redolent of supreme power. Thus in the thirteenth century the republic of Genoa's decision to coin gold, soon imitated by Florence and later Venice, was in its own way presumptuous given gold's regal and sacred connotations. By the same token fourteenth-century citizens acquiring gold, even as mere gilding on their silver plate, were committing presumptuous acts that challenged hierarchical assumptions about value. Gold recalled the King of Heaven and his supreme agents of church and state on earth; silver was certainly precious but society at large used it on a daily basis.

In the long term, illusions of greater apparent worth in gilded wares had the capacity to disturb assumptions in a society convinced that gold and silver were inherently valuable. Perhaps more knowledgeable customers recognized that techniques that created an impression of greater worth (as in gilt silver) might be used to fool customers just as wearing gilded accessories deceived the public at large. Town governments and trade guilds regulated the output of goldsmiths using time-tested standards. In Venice regulations forbade "falsifying" for all the luxury trades, not just goldsmithing but glassmaking and work in (genuine) rock crystal as well. Yet statutes also recognized techniques like gilding and making "false jewels" as legitimate ones.[46] In Lucca the Communal

Statute of 1308 forbade buying gold or silver thread from any but a recognized merchant or broker in good standing, presumably because it was so easy to produce thread of inferior quality, although it was difficult to spot.[47] Siena, Florence, and Bologna also regulated the goldsmith's craft.

Nevertheless, "genuine" held different connotations in the fourteenth century than it does today. Along with the *veriselli*'s glass beads, *gioie false* (false jewels), and gilded silver, recognized counterfeits like coins that imitated other currencies held less negative connotations than they do today. When Dante spoke of the Serbian ruler Uros II, called Milutin (1282–1321), as "he of Rascia who falsified" silver coin of Venice, Dante probably understood that the coin in question was not underweight and inferior (it was not) but shaped and stamped to resemble a Venetian coin, and as such a challenge to Venetian sovereignty.[48] Condemning foreign coin as counterfeit allowed Venetian officials to collect Milutin's foreign coins as they entered the city and reissue them as Venetian *grossi*. This brought revenue to the mint and supplied Venice with silver; thus "falsifying" was not so much a comment on the malfeasance of a neighboring power as an expedient move to assert rights of sovereignty and acquire silver for Venetian purposes. In the same vein, "false" jewels were often valued in their own right as both beautiful and splendid examples of an artisan's skill and therefore not to be disparaged. The "false" were routinely set along with precious or semi-precious gems in decorative work, with the public fully cognizant that false gems were just glass paste. The taxonomy of preciosity differed substantially from ours: rock crystal was precious before the manmade crystal of the fifteenth-century surpassed it in clarity; horn and bone found places in the repertoire of precious materials that would be lost in later centuries. Indeed, the scale of value from semi-precious to precious altered over the course of the fourteenth century itself, sometimes right before a consumer's very eyes.

Workmanship

The earliest preserved statute of the Venetian guild of goldsmiths dates from 1233. Local workmanship in the traditional style of the eastern Mediterranean favored designs of spun wire. Filament, or filigree, was already a well-established technique in the city by this day. This manner of working was suited to the production of luxury wares because light and airy designs made an impressive display out of small amounts of extruded silver wire, and it could be gilded. Wire making was an ancient art where short rods of cast metal were drawn through sets of diminishing holes in a draw-plate designed for that use. As the goldsmith's essential handbook, composed by (Presbyter) Theophilus (probably a Belgian or German monk from the early twelfth century), described the process, "There are two iron implements, three fingers wide, narrow at the top and bottom, shallow throughout and with three or four rows of perforations; through these openings wires are drawn."[49] In Ragusa/ Dubrovnik filament work was popular among trade goods: *unam centuram de filo de argent* (a belt of filament silver appears) along with sixteen other belts in an order in 1319 (see plate 1).[50]

Silver wire could be worked and so could gold. The malleability of both allowed wire to be drawn until it was very thin, and then it was hammered and worked into designs or wound around silk thread to produce silver and gold threads that were then woven into fabric or embroidered onto textiles or through ribbons. Gold thread could also be produced by beating gold into foil, or beating gold foil into silver foil, and winding it around a silk core. In England this was often called "Venice" gold or "Lucca" gold by the fourteenth century, although by this date gold and silver thread were prized exports from Cologne as well, and what the English bought may have only circulated through Italy before arriving in England.[51] Gut could also form a base for beating gold and silver into flexible threads and then winding these around silk threads.

The *battilori* (beaters of gold) were a recognized subguild in precious metal work in the thirteenth century.[52] The work of pounding to create foil or leaf was often performed by apprentices who learned the technique as a primary component of goldsmithing; as the luxury market prospered apparently more and more men spent their entire careers as *battilori*. In Lucca the gold thread for which *battilori* produced their beaten foil came under the supervision of the government first in 1308 and then again in 1369.[53] In this town known for its output of fine silk fabric a secondary industry in gold foil to wrap around the threads employed in embroidery, woven borders, and the silver- and gold-shot ribbons that weavers of Lucca's silk shops turned out was a logical addition to production.

Battilori carried on the exhausting, tedious, but essential task of creating foil, then it fell to more skilled craftsmen to assemble goods out of their processed material. Unfortunately, the account books of Lucca do not survive for the period before 1371, and even after that they give little information on gold beaters. But the putting-out system employed at Lucca—where great merchant companies maintained control over materials and paid workshops or domestic workers by the piece—likely characterized the work of *battilori,* as it did the work of silk throwers. In some towns gold beaters organized into their own guilds. In Cividale, on the route into Italy from the German silver mines in the north, a confraternity of *battuti* (gold beaters) existed by 1365. Similar associations were organized to improve the lot of beaters elsewhere, but their guilds did not figure prominently in the higher echelons of the trades.[54] It is impossible to know today how many gold beaters were necessary to support

foil and leaf making in this century, but it was most likely a significant number, because one feature of the new luxury industries was the increasingly lavish use of foil and gold and silver thread. Time-consuming processes of
manufacture demanded a high ratio of the semi-skilled work necessary for
beating metal to skilled techniques like annealing foil to silk thread then weaving it into a fabric. Beaters, of whom dexterity and care were demanded, might
expect to labor at piecework while high rewards were earned elsewhere. Where
battilori remained pieceworkers for a lifetime, they became a proletariat of
sorts for the luxury trades. In fourteenth-century Venice twenty-four goldsmiths, but not one gold beater, served as trusted civil witnesses chosen for
membership in the prestigious *scuola grande* of St. John the Evangelist. Venetian goldsmiths, not *battilori*, became masters, presented their masterpieces,
and established their own shops.[55]

In Lucca a close parallel to the work of local *battilori* may be found within
the ranks of the hundreds of women known as *incannaresse* (reelers), who performed essential labor for the silk-making industry.[56] Merchants often
employed subcontractors or factors to negotiate terms with these domestic or
pieceworkers: factors delivered raw materials to women reelers at their homes
and collected silk thread on bobbins after it was wound. Working from their
homes, women reelers would be paid by the piece for a task that was essential,
delicate, and perhaps most labor intensive of all the major steps in silk making.[57] The rest—more reeling, throwing the silk, boiling, dyeing, and finally
warping and weaving silk fabric—was less demanding labor and paid better. A
woman reeling thread composed of four or five filaments, using the *caldara
alta* process (high kettle, referring to the warm bath that softened cocoons for
unwinding), required an assistant and produced about a pound of silk a day
in her home. A second or *caldara bassa* (low kettle) process produced silk that
was less uniform and therefore poorer in quality but it allowed the reeling of
four or six threads at once, and a woman reeler with her assistant might produce six to eight pounds of silk a day.[58] The great water-powered throwing
machine (*filatoio* or *torcitoio*) that took this thread was mechanized, placing
great demand on the initial hand-reeling processes performed by *incannaresse*.[59]

Gold and silver thread were never demanded in great quantities like
simple silk thread, which was the very foundation of the silk industry. Nevertheless, in making gold and silver thread comparable demands of hand production fell on gold beaters and silk reelers. Applying silver or gold foil to silk
thread or pounding it into ox guts and then winding it around silk thread were
delicate and tedious hand-performed steps, and were therefore bottlenecks in
elaborate production processes. The demand for silk thread as well as gold and
silver threads increased substantially with the rise in demand for luxury goods.
Initial and essential steps in luxury manufacture like these involved extraordi-

narily delicate but repetitious work since silk thread broke easily while foil was intentionally fragile—as thin as human skill could make it—because it was so precious. These labor-intensive processes fed into either well-mechanized loom weaving or skilled jewel making where the high profits in the luxury trades lay.[60] Generally speaking luxury industries relied on unwieldy combinations of time-consuming hand steps and advanced technological processes employing ingenious machinery, mechanical inventions, and precision tools as well as great skill. Pressures played out most heavily on workers relegated to the labor-intensive initial steps involving hand labor, for which no known mechanized processes could as yet be substituted.

Siena, whose statutes of goldsmiths dated from 1361, produced enameled objects in a style often associated with Gothic influences from the north. On the authority of Ippolito Machetti, writing in 1929, the primacy of Siena goldsmiths in Italy from the thirteenth to the end of the fourteenth century has been accepted by other authorities.[61] He traced the Sienese architectural style, based on Gothic influences characterizing church enamels of the trecento, to a more plastic form that emerged over the following two centuries. The master goldsmiths of Siena captured the pope's attention with their reliquaries and statuary; Machetti claims that the very idea of a commissioned work of art developed in Siena before it spread to other centers of artistic production in Italy.[62] It is remarkable that 130 goldsmiths could find work in such a small city; it is even more noteworthy with the shrinkage of Siena's population due to plague and war to perhaps fifteen thousand inhabitants by the end of the fourteenth century.[63] Siena's goldsmiths' shops trained generations of skilled workmen who spread their techniques in enamel and thus their reputation for artistry throughout Italy and beyond the Alps. Meanwhile, the tradition of production for the ecclesiastical market created fame for a few masters at the pinnacle of the trade. These talented craftsmen worked in a style both Byzantine and Gothic, more often turning east rather than north for their inspiration, according to Machetti.

Between 1365 and 1395 the celebrated Giovanni di Bartolo of Siena created at least eleven papal gold roses, precious and exquisite objects that were traditionally bestowed upon princes who had rendered particular service to the papacy. Giovanni's fellow Sienese, Giovanni Maurini, produced at least two papal roses as well between 1379 and 1386, but it fell to Giovanni di Bartolo to capture numerous commissions that demonstrate the artistry that might result when great talent caught the eye of the mighty.[64] Giovanni had followed the pope to Avignon; indeed, his artistic productivity may be divided into three periods through tracing his itinerancy in search of commissions. From 1364 to 1368 he resided in Avignon and worked in the established Sienese enamel tradition with his father's assistance. By 1372 he was living in Rome, where he carried out a commission for a great reliquary to house the heads of the apostles

Peter and Paul. This was a work stylistically distinct from the small enamels that were generally associated with the architectural style. From 1373 to 1385, he lived again in Avignon, where he returned to the Sienese tradition of producing small enameled gold objects. During this latter period he also produced enamel work for a jewel-encrusted bust of Saint Agatha as a commission from Catania. This has become, perhaps, his most celebrated work of art, but Giovanni did not disdain lesser commissions for articles of personal apparel over his prolific career. In 1376 he produced a gilded silver belt worth 4½ florins, along with another small belt ordered in conjunction with a small cross of gold. Even an artist patronized by popes and princes filled mundane orders in the days between great commissions.[65]

Fine, sacred objects decorated with enamel characterized the output of Siena, although the enameling process on gold and silver was also conducive to producing luxury goods. The enameled drinking cups, brooches, buckles, crosses for wear or home altars, buttons, and belts described in Giovanni's work records and in private inventories make this clear. Over the fourteenth century enameled goods of silver, copper, and bronze, and occasionally of gold, grew in popularity. The term "limoges" so often applied by scholars to this work betrays French origins for enameling, although the word "limoges" was increasingly applied to enameling irrespective of origin. For goldsmiths there were a number of techniques for enameling precious metal wares. Flint, sand, and other materials received metallic oxides as coloring agents once they had been heated to a clear liquid. When cooled and solidified, the colored material was ground, then the metal surface to be enameled was prepared by any one of four techniques; after this the ground powder was applied and it was dried and fired, perhaps more than once. The last step was to polish the enamel to remove imperfections and add luster.

The techniques for preparing metal surfaces to accept the enamel were the classic cell-work technique or *cloisonné*; *champlevé*, which was achieved by gouging out the metal and laying in the enamel; and *basse taille*, which was a variant on *champlevé*, where a design was engraved onto a base of silver or gold to produce the effect of translucent enamel. The technique of *basse taille* only came into use over the course of the thirteenth century. Finally, in the fourteenth century, goldsmiths invented a fourth technique, *email en ronde bosse*, a method of encrusting a curved or irregular shape with enamel. A roughened surface was prepared to anchor enamel, and this method was highly effective for high-relief sculpting. The enameled buckles and heraldic arms worked onto medallions and belts, curved surfaces of enameled drinking goblets, and enameled jeweled settings resulted from this exacting and difficult technique.[66] Later Giorgio Vasari (1511–74) would describe another new enameling technique, but disparagingly: "Another sort is made by hand, and polished with tripoli plaster (powder) and a piece of leather." He described this method as more akin to painting on metal than true enamel. This may be the "Venetian" enamel that was in use in Vasari's own day and had been developed to place enamel work more within the reach of less affluent consumers. It was a form of opaque enamel painted over copper, decorative but coarse in comparison with the more elaborate processes designed to produce brilliant color in translucent enamels on a foundation of precious metal.[67] Yet it is significant as one in a line of late medieval technical innovations that brought a valued and costly form of embellishment more in line with the purchasing public's means.

Fourteenth-century secular goods were greatly enhanced with the translucent enamel produced by *baisse taille* enameling. William Milliken noted it was a "process which consisted of engraving, in more or less relief, plaques or restricted areas of metal, usually silver. Upon this, the translucent enamel was applied, and the engraved surface gave sufficient purchase so that the enamel did not flake off easily. Despite this, its hold on the metal ground was slight at best, and few translucent enamels are now in perfect state."[68] This enameling flaked easily, but a gold medallion with a small white-enameled female figure, set off by a green stone, has managed to survive from the fourteenth century and it reveals how lovely work in *baisse taille* might be (see plate 7).[69] A rare survivor of Siena's brilliant craftsmen is the Cleveland belt, over ninety inches long, gilded, run on a flexible ribbon, and studded with enamels of musicians and fantastic creatures against azure backgrounds. There is wear at the belt holes at thirty-six inches, suggesting a robust figure wore the belt, with a tongue of fifty-six inches falling toward the ground. The enamels reorient to appear upright in this "tail" section, as belts were worn in that age. The long-style belt was at least two centuries old by the date of its fabrication, another indication that expensive fashion goods need not be innovations when Sienese craftsmen produced them (see fig. 2).

Enameling all but displaced niello in the fourteenth century, at least for decorating secular goods.[70] The older decorative technique of niello relied on a metallic substance consisting of silver, copper, lead, and sulfur. An engraved or incised design was filled with this amalgam to create a pattern. In earlier times it had been a popular device for creating borders on silver and gilded objects, even on gold. It was still used on occasion, for example, to emphasize the intaglio of a coat of arms for dramatic effect. According to the major medieval text on goldsmiths' techniques by Theophilus, niello itself was a natural product of separating gold from silver, so if a goldsmith's shop stocked copper and lead, niello was ready at hand for use from a goldsmith's own refining processes.[71]

Gold continued to be prohibitively expensive for all but a tiny group of customers. However, goldsmiths could stretch their small supplies and even tint them to make them appear redder and more opulent. Beaten gold leaf for gilding silver provides an illustration of stretching the ducat, quite literally. According to Cennino Cennini, in the fourteenth century Italian gold beaters could obtain 145 leaves, similar in size to modern leaf (80 millimeters square) from a Venetian ducat, which, at this time, weighed about 3.5 grams.[72] The method today remains essentially that of Cennini's day. Gold is pressed between rollers to give a ribbon. Two hundred squares (50 millimeters square) may then be cut from the ribbon and interleaved with parchment. Once bound the packet or "cutch" is pounded until the gold extends to the edges of the parchment. The pieces of gold are then quartered and pounded, and quartered again. This yields roughly 800 pieces, which are then placed in gold beaters' skins and beaten three times. A final beating, this time in very thin skins, with a cleaning in gypsum powder completes the process and the gold may be cut into pieces 80 millimeters square.[73] Francesco de Marco Datini made a business of importing ox guts from Provence and Lyons for Italian goldsmiths to use as their "skins" for pounding gold leaf.[74] Apparently there was sufficient business in gold leaf production, and in the production of silver and gold foil to wrap around thread, to make ox guts a lucrative trade.

Once gold leaf was pounded thin it could be applied to silver through a number of different techniques. Most simply gold leaf might be hammered onto silver, although it would tarnish. Any number of adhesives (or bole, in the parlance of the trade) could be used to apply gold leaf to surfaces of metal, wood, and even of fabric. Both water gilding, which can produce a burnished surface, and oil gilding, which cannot, were known in the Middle Ages. The preparation of a surface gessoed to accept gold leaf constituted one of the most laborious and time-consuming instructions in Cennini's *Il libro dell'arte*: after many hours of pounding and grinding to create *gesso sottile* from *gesso grosso*, the result was painted on the surface to be gilded. "Then give it another coat in the other direction. And in this way, always keeping your *gesso* warm, you lay at least eight coats of it on the flats. You may do with less on the foliage ornaments and other reliefs; but you cannot put too much of it on the flats. This is because of the scraping which comes next."[75] What follows are time-consuming instructions for scraping, tempering, and grinding to perfect the *gesso sottile*.

Gold and silver leaf could be applied to glass as well. Venice would become famous a century later for mirrors where silver, mercury, and tin were painted on the new invention of colorless glass called *cristallo*. In the fourteenth century rock crystal workers produced a few highly prized small mirrors in Venice. Although rock crystal contained flaws, it could be shaped and polished and backed with foil, producing a better reflection than metal, which had been the traditional material for making peer mirrors.[76] Venetian goldsmiths also produced silver forks that gained popularity over the century. In Tuscany the inventory of Bonaccorso di Vanni and Geri di Andrea (1362–65) included five forks of silver, along with knives and bowls, salts, goblets, and candleholders for the tables at Avignon.[77] Rock crystal objects, mirrors, and forks were goods that goldsmiths, working in collaboration with other luxury craftsmen, had identified as marketable. In another instance of close collaboration between glassmakers and goldsmiths, gold and silver leaves were embedded between sheets of glass to produce tesserae for mosaics, an important trade good from the Murano glass works. Angeliki Laiou has argued that the thirteenth century had introduced mass production to the luxury trades at Venice with the manufacture of glass medallions featuring pictures of saints (sometimes gilded or flecked with gold or silver) embedded in the glass; these were destined for the pilgrim market. Goldsmiths found market-oriented artisans among the Murano glassmakers who became allies in turning production toward wider audiences.

Luxury objects were traditionally the result of collaboration among craftsmen, as a rare early inventory (1265) of the goods of the Venetian Pietro Vioni, who traveled to Persia, attests.[78] Vioni had among his trade goods a backgammon set carved of crystal and jasper, a chess set, a fine bottle, two candelabra, three cups, one saddle decorated with crystal, jasper, silver, pearls, and green silk, as well as one jeweled gown. These were fabulous luxury wares, but it is significant that the silver dress accessories and fastenings, like buttons and belts, that would dominate fourteenth-century production were not yet present among Vioni's trade goods. By way of contrast, in 1332 the Venetian Senate authorized export to the king of Rassia (Serbia's Stephen Dusan, 1331–55) 67 bales of cloth, 36 silver belts, 33 silver cups, 200 fustians (cloths), as well as arms, military gear, and other trade goods.[79] An emphasis on fine fabric, luxury fastenings for tight fit (probably in a military style for Dusan), and silver wares characterized the trade with kings by 1332.

In 1265 it had been common practice for a trader in luxury goods to set a minimum value on his trade goods. Laiou remarks of Pietro Vioni's wares: "It is not stated that they were manufactured in Venice, but this can safely, I think, be posited."[80] Relying on the secular character of the goods to back her assumption, Laiou stresses close links among Venetian craftsmen, who enjoyed a tradition of collaborating to produce trade goods like chess sets or jeweled saddles. Jointly undertaken projects continued to be a mark of Venetian craftsmanship and trade, and marketing conditions stimulated this cooperation.

Inventories of goldsmiths' tools supply evidence that stamping was popular, particularly in producing small objects like buttons or plaques. Stamping tools show up in numbers in the inventory of the Cerlotti workshop in Lucca, along with inventoried hammers and finishing tools ranging in size from miniature to large.[81] Inventories from Venice include stamping tools and molds as well.[82] For stamping, silver and gold were poured into molds to create standard shapes and into specially molded casts; matched sets of silver buttons or plaques produced in molds were then gilded. Fastenings of all kinds were fashioned in a standard mold or by a stamp; no doubt the alternating plaques of a celebrated classical motif, the *gorgoneion* (a woman's face and a flower), set in relief on a belt in the fourteenth-century Treasure of Colmar, came from standard molds.[83] In Lucca accounts from 1354–56 for the *bottega* of Frediano di Barone note that there were orders to be filled for matched sets of 53 buttons, 20 buttons, and 36 buttons, respectively.[84]

Maria Giuseppina Muzzarelli stresses that the transformation of costume in northern Italy began with the introduction of buttons in the last decades of the thirteenth century.[85] Figure-hugging clothing became the mode and differentiated the silhouettes of men and women. The button's capacity to create a snug fit emphasized difference, convincing Muzzarelli to weigh the button as even more significant than the set-in sleeve for bringing fashion to cities. It seems safe to assume then that buttons helped initiate the trend toward applying precious metals to wardrobes. Bodies' contours were outlined, drawing attention to sexual features; thus buttons also tightened the link between vainglorious dressing and the twin vices of *luxuria* and *lascivia*.

Turning out sets of buttons, gilding them, setting semi-precious stones on them, or enameling them became increasingly important in workshops; this was the bread-and-butter work of a goldsmith's shop. By contrast, sculpting from casts represented the high end of a *bottega*'s business and was undertaken only when wealthy customers commissioned unique pieces and selected a chosen subject. Lorenzo Ghiberti imagined that his future as a goldsmith lay in a career sculpting precious metal for wealthy patrons. Much later Benvenuto Cellini (1500–1571) would define sculpting as the epitome of a goldsmith's artistry, and who would doubt that claim given his extraordinary output? But in the prestigious workshops where casting unique objects of art was carried out, customers also expected to find more mundane cast, molded, and stamped goods, some produced in sets from standard designs. Reputation became a force to be reckoned with in the fourteenth century when great works of art promoted sales of standard goods.[86] Some *puntali* (imprints or goldsmith's marks) have survived from the medieval era, most of which derive from the fourteenth century or later, an era that saw marked increases in production. Nevertheless, hallmarked objects are likely to be the unique cast masterpieces that have been preserved in church treasuries. Goldsmiths' shops also turned out beaten gold for thread, buttons from molds, drawn wire, and polished plaques. Renowned goldsmiths' marks lent prestige to the production of a widening circle of workers who specialized in ready-made goods for sale to the public. With time apprentices could learn to fabricate objects like buckles, jointed purse clasps, and chains of silver or silver gilt. These would be displayed in a shop to entice casual customers much as the St. Eligius diptych featured ready-made goods in the background. St. Eligius holds out his monumental gold saddle in the foreground, but coiling over a rod behind the saint's shoulder are eleven gold (more likely gilded) belts and chains, presumably wrought by lesser members of the workshop, who hover in the background as well. The ready-made could be artfully displayed, and these objects sustained workshops.

Among the technical skills of goldsmiths, intaglio was a true test of talent. Engraving required a stylus or perhaps a punch that was tapped lightly with a hammer. A surface could be indented with tools to form designs, or pushed out (*repoussé*). Both processes could be used on gilded surfaces, producing various designs and shapes. A gilded surface might also be painted or glazed to create other decorative effects. Among engraving techniques, *pointillé* was the most delicate because the design was created by pricking out a series of tiny dots. Goldsmiths generally placed a 20 or 30 percent premium on their workmanship, that is, above the cost of precious metal and jewels. Engraving commanded the highest premium and the greatest loss when, with the bulk of other fourteenth-century goldsmiths' production, it was melted down for its bullion content.

The growing array of techniques for working precious metals and embellishing fabricated wares helps explain why goldsmiths were primarily workers in silver. Increased consumption of luxury goods rested heavily on the rising popularity of this metal for secular use; it was dear but not entirely out of the reach of urban customers. Fourteenth-century Italy still imported silver from the Harz Mountains region (hence the rather large community of goldsmiths and gold beaters in Cividale, which sat on the route from Germany to Venice), silver and some gold from Hungary, as well as silver from the Balkans. Freshly mined silver sustained the production of ready-made goods but shortages did occur. In 1328 Venice experienced a significant shortage of silver, while Genoa and other northern Italian cities faced major shortages of silver in the last years of the century. The financial demands of warfare meant sporadic raids on plate in landed realms north of the Alps. Significant as well was Italy's conversion to gold as the currency of long-distance trade because it freed imported silver for use in fabricating goods. Goldsmiths, familiar with local currencies and trusted mint employees, were generally the first to learn whether silver was plentiful or in short supply, that is, its availability to goldsmiths for uses other than coining.[87] Factors conspired to place goldsmiths in strategic positions to assess bullion's supply.

Silver bullion could be adapted in a variety ways to fill demand for secular goods; for example, four grades of silver ore came out of the West Balkans. Standards for these grades were fixed by a law of the Great Council in Ragusa in 1327. The highest grade was termed *argento de glama,* which was gold-laden silver, produced from the mines at Nova Brdo. Next came *argento fino,* followed by *argento biancho.* At the bottom of the scale stood *argento plico,* which contained a substantial amount of lead.[88] As long as a goldsmith specified quality, work in all four grades of silver was permissible. Graded standards operated across the Adriatic in Venice, where the Silver Office specified different standards for worked silver different from the fineness required for the mint.[89] It was expedient for goldsmiths to use silver in varying grades of fineness since silver alloyed with baser metal permitted fabrication of sturdier mechanical parts, like joints, buckles, pivots, hinges, or screws, or reinforcement with wires or rods. Also silver leaf "gilding" on a baser metal, produced in much the same way as gold leaf on silver, could stretch the available supply of silver and produce a less expensive product. Since silver is a highly malleable and ductile medium, it has strength and fluidity that facilitates working and annealing. In the fourteenth century it was stretched in lead alloy for silver wire and for "luxury" goods that were, in actuality, not very precious at all. Silver was hardened by alloy with copper for production of large plate such as platters. Its reflectivity was exploited when it was applied as a coating to rock crystal disks to produce mirrors. Silver's beauty lay in its whiteness, at least in medieval eyes, and the discerning customer did well to learn to assess the quality of silver in objects they purchased, as well as how to distinguish gilding from fine gold. Alloys and highly polished surfaces could fool the eye, but alloys also permitted the fabrication of a cheaper or more durable product.

A silver town like Ragusa regulated the use of this highly ductile medium that was so easily annealed to baser metal, and the Great Council valued the town's reputation as exporter of silver wares. In Venice official standards for assaying gold, silver, and alloy were long-standing, and they were reiterated and adjusted periodically.[90] This was true as well for Florence, Siena, Bologna, Genoa, and Lucca. Goldsmiths policed standards of fineness and stood by their marks. Guild records reflecting exacting standards have survived in sequence in Bologna, and notarial records of goldsmiths' regulations exist for both Lucca and Siena. Goldsmiths' touchstones, essential testing tools for fineness, survive, and sleuthing down the marks of leading workshops has become a scholarly quest, as Pietro Pazzi's *I Punzoni dell'argenteria e oreficeria veneziana* and Costantino G. Bulgari's great five-volume *Argentieri* attest.[91]

A Restless and Shifting Trade

A surprising pattern of itinerancy may be found in Bulgari's and Pazzi's studies of goldsmiths. Where names of fourteenth-century goldsmiths survive, a significant pattern of movement from city to city emerges. This was the case despite the propensity of local guild statutes to favor stability. Family ownership within the trade and an awards system and honors that were parceled out to old established businesses also favored stability. The high costs associated with materials, that is, the gold, silver, and jewels that were raw materials for carrying on the trade, would seem to indicate that goldsmithing would be the most sedentary and stable of all the medieval trades. But powerful incentives could induce a skilled goldsmith to pull up stakes and establish himself in a new community.

Information about opportunities for goldsmiths circulated freely in the fourteenth century: the wealthy patron Louis d'Anjou knew of the reputation of Master Gusmin of Cologne and hired him on the strength of his fame; the Florentine Lorenzo Ghiberti also knew of this talented northern artist's work through examining the casts of his sculptures. At the highest levels of the craft a long-distance network of information aided any goldsmith willing to make his fortune in foreign parts.[92] The most reputable craftsmen were widely recognized through circulating casts of their work, their goldsmith marks were renown, word of mouth fed reputation, and possibly merchants' letters and even craft manuals spread fame (see Chapter 2).[93]

In Lucca, when after a tumultuous first half of the trecento more settled conditions prevailed, some of the city's long-exiled luxury craftsmen returned to their native town from Venice or from north of the Alps. They reestablished workshops in their trades, namely silk production and goldsmithing. In reorienting production toward secular objects the returned Lucchese achieved an impressive success, sufficient to require the assistance of goldsmiths trained elsewhere. Over the course of the century Lucca provided work for six goldsmiths from Siena, four from Pisa, four from San Miniato, three from Florence, two each from Venice and Pistoia, and one each from Padua, Perugia, Arezzo, Ravenna, Piacenza, Paris, Ghent, and Basel. Even greater diversity of origin may be found at Lucca among practicing goldsmiths later on in the fifteenth century.[94]

By contrast, the rich city of Bologna kept the goldsmiths it trained in its own workshops and took fewer opportunities to incorporate goldsmiths trained elsewhere into the *Società degli orefici*. Two men, possibly related, were welcomed to Bologna: Giovanni di Bondideo, *orefice orginario de Canetolo* (Parma), and Marco di Giacomo, also noted as *orefice originario de Canetolo*, from Parma.[95] Since there were at least eighty-seven goldsmiths active in Bologna from 1298 through 1400, the town sustained a community of goldsmiths of about the same size as Lucca's (where close to one hundred may be identified over the course of the fourteenth century). However, the few surviving references to wares produced in Bologna's goldsmith shops suggest that commissions for the ecclesiastical market still dominated the precious metal trades. Native-born and trained goldsmiths were employed as trusted officers of the mint or as civil servants, so the continued prosperity of Bologna assured goldsmiths more traditional outlets for their work. Nevertheless, as Maria Giuseppina Muzzarelli has noted, in Bologna as elsewhere, consumer goods became more consequential over the century.[96] In 1399, the Bolognese Giovanni Papazzoni, *orefice,* received payment from the commune of Bologna of 92 *lira,* 16 solidi for a sword ornamented with gold and silver inlay, and for a belt of gold and silver, as well as for several other ornaments intended to be worn as apparel.[97] This certainly hints at production for secular use, particularly since Bologna found it necessary to limit luxurious apparel by new sumptuary codes in 1389 and again in 1398.[98]

Bulgari's to-date incomplete but still immense reference work on Italian goldsmiths and Pazzi's study of goldsmiths in Venice and the Veneto indicate that many northern Italian communities provided work for non-native goldsmiths. In 1344 Pietro Paolo di Bettino, a goldsmith from Bologna, had become a resident who practiced his craft in Faenza, while in 1312 Raphael de Bononia, *aurifex,* was practicing his craft in far-off Candia in Crete.[99] While Bologna did not accept many foreign goldsmiths into its guild, it trained some who left town to pursue their trade elsewhere. Francesco, *orefici di Cividale* in the Veneto, also hailed from Bologna.[100] In the 1300s Vicenza began its career as a center for the goldsmith's trade, which it still is.

Some goldsmiths traveled farther afield to establish themselves. In 1397 Rimini provided a living for a goldsmith named Giovanni Albanese dell'Albania.[101] His Albanian roots suggest he was a goldsmith trained at one of the newly opened West Balkan mine sites that sat on the mountainous border between Albania and Montenegro. A certain Melsa, *orefici de Cattaro* (Kotor), was active in Zara, where he created a reliquary bust of St. Silvester; he was assisted by Rodoslav, another goldsmith from Kotor.[102] Kotor was Montenegro's window to the sea, and its goldsmiths worked the precious ore that had traveled overland to the coast from mountain sites. The six huge silver lamps in Kotor's church of St. Triphon attest to the training and artistry of local goldsmiths.

Zorzi Ragusino, a premier Venetian goldsmith active somewhat later, employed fellow Ragusans Marco and Nicolò in his shop and became a major supplier of refined bullion to the mint. He capped a line of Ragusan-trained goldsmiths who had migrated to Venice over the course of the fourteenth century in exchange for the Venetian goldsmiths who made the opposite trek to seek work at Ragusa. Zorzi's success did not keep him from being 40,000 ducats in debt at his death, demonstrating that the transfer to Venice, while it was the hub of the Italian luxury market, could still be a risk-filled venture.[103]

The opening of Balkan mines and a program of production for export had attracted a community of goldsmiths to Ragusa by the late 1280s. Cvito Fisković found fifteen goldsmiths mentioned in the earliest extant registers of the chancellery at Ragusa that dated from the last decades of the thirteenth century.[104] From all appearances these craftsmen were trained locally in the established tradition of eastern, that is, Byzantine, goldsmithing, and they had most likely arrived in town from other parts of the Adriatic world.

The mines of the West Balkans continued to open as the older thirteenth-century mine sites like Brskovo were worked out. A steady pace of mine openings promoted the goldsmith craft in Ragusa and neighboring communities like Kotor that lay even closer to the mine sites; both communities welcomed numerous foreign-trained goldsmiths over the course of the fourteenth century. As Fisković has argued, most immigrant goldsmiths at Ragusa bore Slavic names, suggesting that the burgeoning goldsmith industry in town was primarily a magnet for migrants from the West Balkans and the islands on the eastern shore of the Adriatic Sea. But word of silver strikes reached across the sea as well. Immigrant Venetians moved to Ragusa to practice their craft, suggesting that Ragusa's traditional trading partners in northern Italy had learned of the opportunity for a career across the Adriatic. By 1367 a Phillippus de Flora had become an active goldsmith in Ragusa; the word had spread to north-central Italy and to Florentine workshops.[105] Fisković's review of fourteenth-century notarial registers turned up 165 names of goldsmiths. This list may contain duplications of names but even taking this into account, goldsmithing represented a large and growing industry.[106] Ragusa numbered about 7,000 inhabitants within its walls in this century, with possibly 25,000 more inhabitants in the countryside or Astarea.[107] Civic authorities monitored immigration closely, so it is all the more significant that goldsmiths were welcomed, especially after the Black Plague of 1348, which had decimated the ranks of tradesmen in the town.

In real numbers, Ragusa supported fifteen or sixteen goldsmiths in the last years of the thirteenth century; sixty-six new names were mentioned in the notarial charters over the first half of the fourteenth century, almost half of which were new immigrants into town in 1349 and 1350 after the first visit of the Black Plague. Nearly one hundred more new names of goldsmiths may be found in the registers in the second half of the fourteenth century. The Street of the Goldsmiths ran parallel to *Stradun* (*Platea*), the main concourse of the town, and eventually grew into a crowded warren of workshops. Ragusan merchants added the new export of worked silver to the traditional luxury exports of candle wax, leather, and fur. A glass industry grew up, probably in imitation of Murano, and an industry in arms and armor.[108] Over the century Ragusa added more furriers, pelters, and leather workers.[109] Once the preferences of the luxury market in Venice and elsewhere in Italy had been assessed, local merchants fed those markets with ensembles of luxuries; for example, fur trims for men's robes along with great belts, and attached daggers decorated with precious or semi-precious gems, encased in embossed leather hilts.

Other evidence points to an Italian-Ragusan connection in the production and sale of luxury wares. In 1313 the Venetian-appointed count of Ragusa inventoried the possessions of a Venetian goldsmith named Blasius who had died while in Slavonia. Blasius had carried with him two *specula* (magnifying glasses) and quicksilver (used in refining)—presumably these were tools of his trade (the magnifying glasses suggest he may have worked in engraving as a pointillist). Blasius would have impressed local residents with his other possessions, including his trade goods: an ivory-handled knife trimmed in silver, various gemstones, and seven purses worked with gold.[110] After his death his treasures were packed up, reached the coast safely, and were sent back to Venice. In Tuzla in Bosnia, grave goods discovered in 1881 included fragments of a beautifully crafted silver belt, rings, and other accessories. These were likely the possessions of a traveling merchant or a goldsmith (not royal treasure, as was first assumed). The long sinuous belt found here was in the style of Siena rather than the wide, hinged silver belt popular in the Adriatic region.[111] In a similar manner Italian-trained goldsmiths traveled to Buda and to mining sites in the kingdom of Hungary. Pietro Gallico of Siena, resident of Buda, produced a remarkable gilded silver crucifix with panels of translucent enamel for the king of Hungary in 1333.[112] When visiting Buda, Buonaccorso Pitti, gambler extraordinaire, boarded with the Florentine goldsmith Guido Baldi, mintmaster to the Hungarian king and supplier of luxury wares to the court.

Just as predictably goldsmiths flocked to Avignon while it was the residence of the pope. "A census of 1376, taken after the final departure of Gregory XI from Avignon reveals that in the parish of St Pierre alone there were 48 goldsmiths. Twenty-two were Italian, six being from Florence, four from Siena, . . . one each from Brescia, Piacenza, Forli, Parma, Arezzo, Rome, Milan, and Lucca, while the rest were of unspecified origin."[113] Presumably after 1376 this colony of diverse origins dispersed to secular courts, returned home to work in cities in Italy, or, more optimistically, relocated to Rome to take up trade with their old customers. In contrast, out of the thirty-nine goldsmiths active in Perugia in the fourteenth century none appears to have been of foreign origin. Possibly Perugia followed an older pattern of sedentary goldsmith shops under close local supervision.[114]

Venetian Goldsmiths

Venice was recognized near and far as the heart of the luxury trade in the fourteenth century.[115] The city possessed a renowned community of goldsmiths, men with the charge of embellishing the *pala d'oro*, who held close associations with the mint, or who worked the luxury trades with the glassmakers at Murano.[116] When the diaspora of exiled Lucchese goldsmiths occurred in 1306, and again after the sack of the city in 1314, Venice became one of their preferred destinations and apparently Lucca's hardworking and adaptable craftsmen prospered there. Much later, in 1368, the Lucchese colonies of craftsmen in Venice contributed a substantial portion of the 50,000 florins demanded of the town's citizens by Emperor Charles IV to serve as protector.[117] By this date the sons and grandsons of those earlier Lucchese migrants were the active masters in relocated family shops, but a half-century exile had not broken their ties of loyalty to home. In the meantime the long Lucchese exile helped promote the reputation of Venice as a center of luxury production. The association in the minds of northern Europeans of "Lucca" gold and "Venice" gold (both terms referred to gold thread) was probably not coincidental, given the comingling of talent and shared knowledge among the skilled craftsmen of Lucca and Venice.[118]

An open welcome extended to political exiles further enhanced Venetians' ability to promote the luxury trades and build local fame. Florentine craftsmen following the luxury trades, men like the merchant Baldassare Ubriachi and his goldsmith kin, had been welcome at Venice when their families fell out of favor at home. Messer Manfredo degli Ubriachi, a cousin of Baldassare, established new homes in both Venice and Verona in the mid-fourteenth century. His son Maso married a Venetian woman of good family, Bianca Contarini, and their two older sons, Giovanni and Antonio, shared equally in their father's business, adopting what surely by this date was recognized as a winning division of labor: Giovanni became a long-distance merchant resident in Paris, while his younger brother Antonio was trained in goldsmithing and remained in Venice to run the family workshop. Antonio's marriage to his cousin Ginevra, Baldassare's daughter, sometime between 1395 and 1398 reunited the Ubriachi family lines, and Antonio soon represented Ubriachi interests in Venice while both Baldassare (his father-in-law) and Giovanni traveled abroad for the business. Antonio's tasks included overseeing "Giovanni di Jacopo master of my [that is, Baldassare's] works of bone, who lives in my house with me. And I want him to live in the house with [my family] until they, my sons, are of age."[119] Between them these two branches of the Ubriachi, along with a Florentine compatriot, Giovanni di Jacopo, created a preeminent workshop in luxury wares, which in turn trained Baldassare's young son, Benedetto, who in time became an important goldsmith and artist in his own right.[120]

The immigrant Florentines of Venice were by no means all exiles, and many who came to Venice were attracted simply by the opportunity to make a good living.[121] Venice, more immune to the political calamities that affected the other communities of northern Italy, often served as a preferred city of exile for the well trained, as a place to learn banking and the bullion trade, and as a city in which to practice a luxury trade. Among the more famous master goldsmith shops was the prestigious establishment of Mondino da Cremona (1316–34); he added to Venice's fame by constructing a great clock purchased by the king of Cyprus for the steep sum of 800 ducats. Giovanni Boninsegna Toscano worked among the goldsmiths of Venice and participated in a refurbishing of the *pala d'oro*; his Florentine family had supplied at least one other member, Philippo, factor of the banking house of Acciaiouli, to Adriatic banking and trade.[122]

Paired goldsmiths and long-distance merchants or bankers, sometimes related by marriage or blood, overcame the structural opposition inherent in guild affiliation and created winning partnerships in the luxury trades. Reinhold C. Mueller brings to light a pair: "Alessandro degli Agolanti of Florence was active at the Rialto from 1348 to 1356; he was naturalized by special privilege in 1349. His compatriot Donato Alemanni was active as a *campsor* (money changer) from 1350 to 1353 and as a refiner of silver, and the two merged their operations [at Venice] about 1352."[123] Donato's elder kinsmen, Alemonno and Giannino, had become naturalized citizens at Venice twenty years earlier. The network of Florentine goldsmiths and merchant bankers extended further to Giovanni di Filippo Talenti of Florence, a naturalized Venetian citizen like Donato. In liquidating his business Donato had called on Talenti to settle his entire base of operations: banking, commerce in bullion, and operation of a shop for refining precious metals.[124] Like the merchant banker and goldsmith brothers by the name of Pardo from Pistoia, these pairings confirm that banking operations, the bullion trade, and luxury production traveled well together.

Earlier, in 1213, the corporation of Venetian goldsmiths had established itself at the church of San Salvador. Thereafter they transferred to the church of San Giacomo di Rialto, and later on in the fifteenth century they would move again to the church of San Giovanni Elemosinario. Three specialized *arti* came under the authority of the local organization, the *Scuola dei Oresi: gioiellieri da falso* (those who worked with margaritas or false jewels of glass paste); *diamanteri da duro* (diamond setters); and *diamenteri da tenero* (those who worked in other precious stones).[125] Goldsmiths and silversmiths, as well as other specialists, came under the supervision of the mint. Until October 23, 1335, all worked silver was first to be conveyed to the mint to receive the imprint of St. Mark, after which it might also receive the mark of an individual goldsmith's shop.[126] The explosion in secular production of silver wares may safely be dated to the demise of this policy: after 1335 mint officials apparently judged production of precious metal for secular use simply too extensive to continue their civic surveillance and guarantee. With the earlier demise of a bimetallic standard for currency, Venice had relaxed controls over silver bullion, without, apparently, suffering appreciable ill effects; however, the Silver Office never relinquished oversight entirely. The mint permitted fabrication of silver wares below the standard of purity of the mint within the city of Venice, and while it tolerated the export of silver to the Levant, the office still continued to monitor all movement of silver and gold.[127]

Vibrant market conditions favored expansion, but goldsmiths' initial forays into the retail space at the Rialto met with resistance; bankers demanded goldsmiths be excluded from setting up their own stalls. In March 1331 the Great Council reconfirmed the right of bankers to the exclusive right to trade in gold or silver from their benches there. This relegated goldsmiths to their own street in San Silvestro near the Rialto, but this was not, apparently, as advantageous a location for sales. The council stated unconditionally that no goldsmith could erect a "station" or display counter to sell or buy worked gold or silver at the Rialto, although presumably they were still free to sell out of their shops that stood in the *Ruga dei Oresi*. The *scola aurificum* (Venetian goldsmiths' confraternity) was co-opted into the ruling since it was specified that the *scuola* would receive a third of any fines collected for noncompliance.[128]

Through dint of effort, by 1392 or perhaps earlier, goldsmiths gained entry into the promising open-air markets at Venice. In May 1392, Abraam di Benedetto di Salamone, "Judeus de Ispania, vagabundus," was arrested for stealing rings from the counter of a jeweler who had managed to obtain a market stall in piazza San Marco.[129] In this instance a jeweler, not a money changer, was robbed, if Abraam, a recent victim of the pogroms in Spain, was appropriately charged. Abraam paid with his life for this, confirming in the process goldsmiths' entry into prime open-air markets.

Retailing silver and gold had become a contentious issue for all parties by this date. At San Marco and Campo San Polo Venetian *campsores* had long enjoyed customary privileges of selling silver and gold wares from their benches, just as bankers held the privilege of displaying gold and silver wares at the Rialto. In the 1390s bankers moved to exclude money changers from the wholesale bullion market, but an exception was made to allow them to continue to sell worked articles of silver, "which every day they display for sale at their *banchis* [benches]."[130] Meanwhile, bankers at the Rialto maintained their privileges over high-value silver and gold wares and pawns, which were displayed prominently along with the familiar carpet and funnel tray for counting coins. Within shouting distance stood the *fondacho dei tedeschi* where Germans and other northerners brought their imported silver, while just across the bridge Ragusan silver traders inhabited the Slavic quarter in the *contrata San Silvestro*. On this side, just a few steps from the Rialto Bridge, Venetian goldsmiths plied their trade in the *Ruga dei Oresi*. Mint officials oversaw them all in this close world of high finance and trade in gold and silver wares.

The *campsores* of San Marco, who exchanged currency for travelers and pilgrims, in contrast to Rialto bankers, who carried out complex deposit banking transactions, displayed small ready-made consumer goods of gold and silver as their right and privilege. In 1361, when a mint official could not persuade a money changer to pay his small fine, the officer angrily swept up a handful of his ornaments (*unum mazum frissadurarum*) in lieu of payment. Those "trinkets" probably represented a considerable outlay of capital for that recalcitrant money changer. The incident further accentuates the close connection of coin, exchange functions, and luxury sales in the mind of Venetians officials, retailers, and customers.[131]

At the end of the century the old division of responsibility between money changer as retailer and goldsmith as producer was challenged once again. With potential profits to be made in retail sales, goldsmiths renewed their attempt to challenge the money changers' near monopoly in retailing silver goods at San Polo and San Marco. Against opposition from officials overseeing guilds in 1394, goldsmiths obtained permission to set up their stalls at San Marco and San Polo on market days.[132] The *Giustizia vecchia,* overseers of guild privileges, readily acknowledged that they represented the interests of money changers when they moved to exclude the petitioning goldsmiths.[133] Remarkably in this new contest, and against entrenched interests, goldsmiths won their suit and earned the right to set up tables and benches in prime locations on the open *campi.* Venetian goldsmiths had secured a permanent place in the great public retail markets. All in all this was a significant victory in the battle for market share.

Marco and Laurencio, brothers of Bernardo Sesto, the master goldsmith, were also eminent goldsmiths, die engravers, and employees of the Venetian mint, and thus in a position to profit from the more open retail market created by the ruling of 1394. These brothers supported a family workshop as well. Their shop received the most choice commissions, such as the sculptural decoration of the iconostasis of St. Mark, which can be viewed today in the Treasury of St. Mark, and a large silver processional cross for the Cathedral of Venzone in Friuli, signed and dated 1421. The Sesto brothers straddled two worlds: private production out of a family shop and highly skilled die engraving and medal making for the mint.[134] Between these two poles of activity the family apparently prospered.

Goldsmiths in Florence

Florence presents a comparable picture of impressive growth in the luxury trades but one for which there is, unfortunately, interrupted documentation in the fourteenth century. Goldsmiths were listed among the guilds of Por Santa Maria from 1322 onward and their statutes date from 1335. Beginning in the 1320s and through the end of the century, 258 goldsmiths can be identified at Florence. Since most did not request the reduction in matriculation fees allowed to those with relatives in the guild, there is a good probability that some of these men were immigrants.[135] In these decades Florence trained gold-smiths who would establish the city's reputation throughout Europe; this was famously true given the renown of artists of the fifteenth century, but a century earlier the foundations were being laid for future greatness. Fourteenth-century Florentine goldsmiths often produced ready-made goods for retail sale and built their success on the strength of their skill and the absorption of craftsmen from Siena and other neighboring towns. Cennino Cennini's *Il libro dell'arte,* composed in the 1390s, may be read as an exercise in the filial piety inspired by a Florentine workshop tradition. Cennini acknowledged Agnolo Gaddi as his mentor, the son of Taddeo Gaddi, who in turn had served as assistant to the great Giotto di Bondone himself. When Cennini said that "painting calls for imagination, and skill of hand, in order to discover things not seen, hiding themselves under the shadow of natural objects, and to fix them with the hand, presenting to plain sight what does not actually exist,"[136] he spoke of a guiding vision shared with his predecessors. The organization of Cennini's handbook illustrates the senselessness of trying to separate this painterly vision from the highly technical skills of goldsmithing in the early phases of the Renaissance. *Il libro dell'arte* affirms an aesthetic ideal but soon gets down to the practical matter of explaining techniques in mosaic gold, gilding parchment and velvet, mordants, burnishing—indeed, how to do just about anything required in the fabrication of luxury goods. Cennini did not despise the techniques that pleased the public; he employed them with careful deliberation. But then the same may be said of his entire artistic genealogy back through the Gaddis to Giotto himself.

Prior to the earliest documentation of goldsmiths in the Arte de Por Santa Maria, all luxury craftsmen, goldsmiths among them, had been censured by an ecclesiastical statute. Indeed, the law could have jeopardized their liveli-hoods had it been enforced. The 1310 synodal legislation of Bishop Antonio d'Orso Biliotti recommended punishing the manufacturers as well as the wear-ers of luxury apparel. In condemnation of women's ostentatious dress, the bishop held artisans who had manufactured the finery, indeed all those who sold or provided forbidden luxuries to women, responsible. No less a sentence than anathema was to be brought to bear against an artisan who produced and sold such wares to Florentines. Synodal sumptuary law inspired a civic response, and sumptuary law borrowed the idea of punishing the producer as well as the wearer of luxury goods when it adopted the provision.[137] In laws regulating goldsmiths in 1318 and in the sumptuary statutes written from 1322 to 1325, goldsmiths were prohibited from selling any forbidden ornaments to Florentine women. One exemption was included in the statutes: goldsmiths could sell freely to foreign women visiting Florence.[138] It is difficult to imagine the office enjoined with enforcing the sumptuary laws of Florence, the *Ufficiale delle donne*, which registered apparel above the limit of the law and levied fines on women, undertaking this wide-scale oversight of local industry and trade. It is telling, perhaps, that subsequent sumptuary laws focused solely on the consumer; the prohibition on producers was not repeated, apparently because it was difficult to enforce and, quite possibly, because legislators realized it damaged the local economy. From the 1330s onward Florence was well supplied with all sorts of the finery prohibited to its women.

The Black Plague and its subsequent visitations drastically reduced Florence's population, but it maintained its master workshops. By the early decades of the fifteenth century, when the population of the city had dropped to about 37,000, there were 105 identifiable goldsmiths, jewelers, gilders, and engravers working in the various quarters of the city. In the Castasto of 1427 goldsmiths represented an active and wealthy community.[139] But some Florentine goldsmiths did travel elsewhere: Constantino, goldsmith of Florence, was active in the region of Perpignan from 1300 to 1333.[140] Nicolò, son of Bartolomeo of Florence, "nunc Padue habitans," became an engraver in the principality of Carrara in 1376.[141] Rome, once the papal court returned, provided opportunity for some of the most renowned Florentine goldsmiths.[142] There had been at least six Florentine goldsmiths known to be working the ecclesiastical market in the parish of St. Pierre in Avignon in 1379, that is, before artisans packed up and followed the court to Rome.[143] Florentines sometimes traveled farther south: Queen Joanna of Naples appointed Giovanni Siri Giacobbe of Florence as her court goldsmith in 1350, breaking the line of goldsmiths from France in the hire of the crown.

Fourteenth-century Florence provided goldsmiths for many communities, including Bologna, Umbria, Naples, Milan, Lucca, Venice, Ragusa, Cividale, and Udine.[144] Florentines sought wealthy patrons abroad, or they traveled to cities with luxury manufacturing, reconfirming a pattern where a strong reputation in the luxury trades created opportunity for craftsmen to find work abroad.

A few major commissioned works by goldsmiths have survived in Florence. A sculpted silver figure of Herod from *John the Baptist before Herod* (c. 1367), which decorated the altar of San Giovanni, attests to the fine artistry of the city's masters. Andrea Arditi's bust and reliquary of St. Zenobius stands as a fine example of fourteenth-century Florentine enamel work over silver. A highly ornate reliquary of St. Reparata by Francesco di Vanni, an artifact gilded and enameled, dates from the second half of the fourteenth century. It demonstrates, as do many other religious works, that preservation favors the survival of ecclesiastical goods.

And Florence had discovered a valuable new source of silver bullion. An ambassadorial report from Florence to Rome in 1403 claimed that silver imports to Florence from Ragusa had reached such heights that Florence might "purchase Pisa," a project never too far from the minds of the *signoria*.[145] Malaria-stricken and war-torn Pisa may not have brought any great ransom price by 1403, but imported Balkan silver characterized in such a way would certainly produce numerous reliquaries, as well as many belts and brooches for a consuming public.

The written record of fourteenth-century goldsmiths is anecdotal and fragmentary at best while the surviving samples of goldsmiths' work are seldom the objects for secular use of which notarial records often speak. This results in a significant gap in knowledge, but even the scant information that may be gathered speaks resoundingly to creativity in design, of technological brilliance, and of lively attempts to innovate. In that context goldsmiths, like contemporary embroiderers, glassmakers, and silk weavers, appear to have been in the forefront of innovation in the luxury trades. Goldsmiths moved beyond the confines of a world stifled by guild and civic restrictions. The Florentine propensity to take locally manufactured luxury wares to their customers, whether to northern courts or to markets elsewhere in Italy, speaks to self-conscious promotion of secular production to encourage retail trade.

A Place for the Ready-made

Itinerancy, mingling of goldsmiths trained in different traditions, and collaboration with other luxury craftsmen helps explain much about the early phases of selling ready-made goods. Considerable ingenuity and talent went into producing consumer goods, even if the production for this market did not achieve the artistic heights of the singular works commissioned generally by churchmen. But even that judgment is subject to qualification since wares for secular use have seldom survived; medieval consumers melted down their plate and redesigned in new styles every generation or so.[146] The prestige of the trade was considerable. Cyril Bunt, working from the papers of Sidney Churchill, noted that "in the fourteenth-century every boy, who in any way showed a leaning towards artistic talent was, almost as a matter of course, apprenticed to a goldsmith. Almost all the famous painters, sculptors, potters and decorative artists of Florence were enrolled as members of the *Orafi*." He went on to claim the artists Lorenzo Ghiberti, Paolo di Dono (Uccello), Antonio Pollaiuolo, Botticelli, and Dominico del Ghirlandaio as talented men who saw in the goldsmith's trade the best opportunity to express their talents.[147] Even the most creative artists were trained to make secular goods on the path to greatness.

Artists who were goldsmiths were sometimes small rather than great talents, but they matter as well. Manno di Bandino, whose career probably began as a painter in Siena where a Madonna dated 1260 has been attributed to him, settled down in Bologna sometime after 1298. Once established as a goldsmith in the parish of San Damiano, Manno di Bandino was enrolled in the *matricola degli orefici*. In 1301 he completed a statue of Pope Boniface VIII in gilded bronze. Later in his career, in 1312, he produced a reliquary for St. Floriano that survives today in the church of St. Stephen at Bologna.[148] Rated as a minor artist today, his commission work and his travel in executing them related back to the old guild tradition of goldsmithing but also pointed forward to a new era of changing residences and resettling in quest of work. Somewhat later the great and talented Lorenzo Ghiberti served his goldsmith apprenticeship at Florence under the tutelage of his stepfather, the goldsmith Bartoluccio, and matriculated in the goldsmith's guild in the early quattrocento, producing his great works of sculpture in gold, silver, and bronze over the following decades. He forged both secular and religious objects worked in precious metals both for commission and for direct sale to customers. He epitomizes the heights to which goldsmiths might aspire.

Artists celebrated their brother goldsmiths. A fourteenth-century master goldsmith might be pictured with shelves behind him, as in the *Treatise on the Seven Vices* (Genoese) from the second half of the fourteenth century (see fig. 1). John Cherry describes the scene with these words: "The goldsmith, standing behind a table, concludes a bargain with a customer, using elaborate finger gestures. The customer's servant waits in the doorway while the goldsmith's assistant notes down the details of the purchase in a book. Behind and on the table are spread the rich products of the goldsmith's art as well as gold and silver coins. It is these that encourage the vices of luxury and avarice as well as discord over their price."[149] Those trained in the craft of goldsmiths had care for each other: in Venetian-colonized Crete Georgius Rosso, a successful goldsmith, left land to his children but all the tools of his goldsmith's trade went to his pupil (*discenti meo*), where that gift would help perpetuate the reputation of his shop.[150]

Italian goldsmiths produced for both local and foreign markets. In England, or perhaps in southern France where he spent much of his life, the Black Prince dealt with a merchant from Pistoia, Martin Parde, and through him with his goldsmith brother, Hanekyn.[151] Edouard Tadelin's merchant's account book from Paris, which contained some early evidence of royal spending, presents the career of a Lucchese merchant at the French court dealing in luxury goods forwarded to him from workshops in his hometown.[152] The luxury trades at Lucca, both goldsmithing and silk manufacture, relied on merchants like Tadelin, who is representative of a network of Lucchese merchant companies that sold Italian wares abroad. According to Florence Edler de Roover, Lucchese companies did not specialize exclusively in the sale of silk despite its significant role in the local economy. "Diversification, not specialization, was the rule," she states. Lucchese companies combined international trade in luxury goods with foreign banking, and employed bills of exchange; the Ricciardi, Guinigi, Balbani, and Rapondi companies all promoted diversification, trading in spices, fruit, silverware, Flemish cloth, and other commodities as markets dictated.[153] Diversification in retail goods was a way to hedge risks for merchant companies and for their allies the goldsmiths, who also diversified to produce and sell ready-made goods throughout northern Italy.

Across the Adriatic Sea in Ragusa the principle of diversification drove trade in luxury wares as well. Merchants commissioned goldsmiths to produce trade goods, specifying what those objects were to be: for example, knives, belts, or bangles. Traders frequently combined these wares with other luxury goods for transport to Venice, which suggests that they might have been sold together. In contracting with a long-distance merchant, a Ragusan goldsmith generally specified the quality of the silver or gold entrusted to him, the number and type of objects to be made from it, and when they would be completed. Goldsmiths in this silver town, remote from the fast-paced retail markets of Italy, often shied away from selling their wares themselves, although they readily sold to foreigners who visited Ragusa. They often relied on Italian merchants to present their wares in foreign markets.

In Venice, any imported product made from precious metal would be inspected at the waterfront by the *officiales denariorum de Rascie*, and one-fifth of the value would be paid to the mint. Merchants were then free to present their goods on the market.[154] A dozen knives, or a set of thirteen spoons (very possibly Apostle spoons, which were popular in this century), a brooch, a belt, and a crown might make up a shipment, and it would likely reach the table of a money changer. This may be the reason for the *nappum de argentum* that accompanied so many commissions to goldsmiths, that is, this may be unworked silver accompanying the order to settle the account for one-fifth at the mint before retail sales reached the market.

Throughout Italy and the Adriatic region the close links among goldsmiths and merchants cemented ties at the highest levels of the luxury trade. Lucchese merchants and goldsmiths were brothers and cousins; Florentines exiled in Venice were often both kin and partners; and Pistoiese who traveled north to Provence and England in pursuit of royal customers were kin as well. When goldsmiths pulled up stakes and moved, they figured among an elite, cosmopolitan coterie with a marketable craft that allowed them to make alliances and prosper wherever they settled. Through enterprise, links among merchants and goldsmiths, and increasing fame for premier artists in the trade, a market for ready-made works in silver and gold emerged. "The art market was never altogether freed from the commission nexus, and retail trade did not develop to the extent that it could sustain the luxury shops that later grew up in London and Paris," Richard Goldthwaite has argued for Italy. But in Italy goldsmiths who moved to a new town, whose shops gained favorable reputations, and who even employed agents who took wares abroad could operate successfully and prosper.[155] Known for their resourcefulness, goldsmiths numbered in the vanguard of trades who repositioned themselves in promoting retail sales.

In 1312 Lando, a Sienese goldsmith who had been sent to serve Henry VII in Milan and had recently presented an Iron Crown to him, joined the retinue of the emperor and received a horse as a token of favor. "He was probably the first artist known to have been permanently engaged in the entourage of an emperor," Martin Warnke notes.[156] As such Lando set a course future artists would aspire to: through obtaining gifts or a stipend from an imperial, royal, or noble patron, artists would become court favorites, leaving behind guild restrictions and the uncertainties of relying on commissions. Lando's was a most attractive path to follow, but it was also the case that the new culturally consequential and widely frequented Italian markets selling ready-made goods provided a path for aspiring goldsmiths. By the end of the fourteenth century the workshops of Italian goldsmiths sustained a retail market oriented toward luxury, and by the 1390s in Venice, goldsmiths had successfully challenged their old collaborators, the money changers, and gained access to open-air marketplaces.

Consumer markets were transformed by some small innovations, which reduced cost. For example, new methods for enameling large-scale production of hinge and buckle mechanisms, varied techniques for gilding, and silver and gold thread making saw small improvements. Rock crystal workers created a superior peer glass by backing small pieces of rock crystal with foil (perhaps an inspiration to the glassmaking industry). The number of products for personal and domestic use increased significantly. Forks for table service augmented spoons and knives. Goblets and glasses, sometimes gilded, augmented cups at the table. Belts not only grew in size but developed flexibility and elaborate designs. Experts specializing in embroidery used gold and silver thread in a highly sculptural fashion, like the embroidery of Jacopo Cambi of Florence, who produced an altar frontal cloth for the Strozzi chapel in 1336, or Geri di Lapo of Florence, who embroidered a crucifixion cloth with gold and silver thread for the Cathedral at Manresa in Catalonia sometime between 1322 and 1357.[157] Murano glassmakers developed their own style for etching glass they termed *embrici* because it imitated fine embroidery work. Ingenuity characterized the luxury industries, and as an independent factor influencing markets, ingenuity, tastefully displayed before customers who were already in love with luxury goods, stimulated demand.

In the time of Theophilus, who wrote on goldsmithing in the late eleventh or early twelfth century, glass had been sufficiently scarce to be judged a rare medium, and it received precious stones as ornaments when molded into windows. By the thirteenth century glass had become a more commonplace material, and authorities like the *Giusticza vecchia* of Venice protected rock crystal sculpture from cheap imitations in glass paste. But rock crystal was not destined to remain precious in the eyes of consumers for long; as it became more available it lost this advantage. Craftsmen in the luxury trades hastened the transformation from precious to more readily available. Glassmakers of Murano were particularly sensitive to demand. Because of their efforts "pearl-encrusted" came in time to mean decorated with glass beads rather than decorated with genuine pearls. This was certainly the case in the production of ever popular hair ornaments, or fancy borders on dresses and cloaks, and it was true as well when "false pearls" or beads were used in lieu of gemstones in jewel settings for the hilts of men's knives. Goldsmiths used their ingenuity to create thinner leaf or foil, or more dilute precious metal in alloy with baser metals. Substitutions became commonplace; exotic materials like ivory were expensive but the Ubriachi workshop of Venice also worked in bone, which, when polished, could create a handsome effect and was much cheaper to obtain and closer at hand than imported ivory. Readily available shell and mother-of-pearl could be worked into a number of luxury products, replacing more precious materials. Ascending and descending scales of cost, based on scarcity on the one hand and the ingenious invention of substitutes on the other, crossed in craftsmen's rush to meet demand. In the extensive examples that R. W. Lightbown collected from the inventories of French nobility, prelates of the French church, and the French bourgeoisie, the most precious wares appeared alongside the merely gilded, and gemstones studded the same objects as semi-precious stones and glass beads. The same pattern may be found in the extensive inventory of luxury goods with which Margherita Acciaiuoli endowed a Carthusian church in the 1380s.[158] Fourteenth-century consumers found value in a broad range of luxury wares and demonstrated readiness to change their scale of relative value, so tastes changed and trends affected markets.[159] Cheaper versions often triumphed over more expensive wares.

In their rush to stimulate demand, goldsmiths and their associates in other luxury industries inhabited one of the most regulated corners of the guilds yet one open to market forces. Regulations demanded that they state the quality and weight of their precious medium with accuracy, and goldsmiths who made a living from jewelry and plate in a world turned to fashion continued to uphold this responsibility. But market opportunity opened new avenues to goldsmiths. The trade operated in a society that rewarded ingenuity, particularly where customers had direct access to luxury and "art" goods in cities. Consumers understood that goldsmiths possessed tools and techniques to make the most ostentatious display from the smallest shreds of precious metal and they bought accordingly. In this retailing environment some extraordinary wares were gradually brought within the reach of urban customers who might never have presumed to wear a piece of jewelry or to own gilt silver in earlier days. "Mass" produced, as long as it does not connote production for the masses, characterized production in the luxury trades. In turn the display of ready-made wares stimulated demand.

Almost the entire collection of fourteenth-century dress accessories dredged up from the bottom of the Thames, now on display at the Museum of the City of London, are of baser metal. Silver is notoriously vulnerable to saltwater and unlikely to survive in the river's silt.[160] But the collection is a valuable reminder that any market good that could be made of silver could be made in baser metal and gilded. Goldsmiths could forge bronze, and they worked in copper and in any base metal that could be alloyed with silver. An entire range of wares from belt buckles to candleholders could be produced in less expensive media and sold to less affluent customers. The deepening of markets through production of less expensive editions of luxury goods was barely beginning in the fourteenth century. It was most definitely encouraged by imports of belts and crowns described as "white," which were probably alloys of lead with a little silver.

In the last analysis this was a gilded age, and people were dazzled by the work of goldsmiths because it shone brightly and often appeared more precious than it was. Despite goldsmiths' market-oriented assaults on inherited perceptions of value, fourteenth-century goldsmiths did not dislodge one abiding feature of medieval economic thinking: faith in the inherent value of precious metals. Stretching it, annealing it, or beating it to leaf did not diminish its prestige. Gold and silver were worth possessing because they were understood to be repositories of value in whatever guise they appeared, and this was a significant force driving the market for luxury consumption: consumers operated on the assumption that their luxury wares were repositories of value. To own, use, or wear gold and silver was also to hoard. If a silver cup was fabricated out of precisely one mark of fine silver, then it was likely its owner looked upon the cup as only a little less liquid an asset than silver coin: the cup was potentially a medium of exchange. However, fabricated wares were not only understood to be repositories of value, they were also deemed worthy of display in public as personal adornments. These were the objects that came into greater use over the century and characterized the fourteenth-century turn to fashion. The inherent value in precious metal rubbed off on the person wearing it. This same principle may have operated for domestic plate, but since plate was much less likely to be seen in public, it did not serve as well as a marker of prestige. European consumers who could afford to do so conveyed a sense of themselves as worthy of their treasures by appearing in them in the streets, on occasion risking condemnation by civic or church law or by the public as avaricious for doing so. An increasingly high premium placed on public display of wealth was one consequence of the turn to fashion, and goldsmiths fed this trend.

Chapter 7

Marketmakers

Italian banking and long-distance trade had developed hand in glove in Europe, so a prominent role for banks and currency handlers in marketing luxury goods in Italian towns was an extension of earlier joint enterprises conducted farther afield. Notwithstanding, the banker's bench or the money changer's stall as a spot for selling silver, gold, and jeweled wares has earned little comment until recently in the scholarly literature. This small bypath on the road to building complex financial networks warrants some attention, however, since it reveals a different facet of retailing, one that helps explain how precious metals and jewels came to be viewed as repositories of value, even at times as means of exchange in lieu of currency. Exploring sales of silver and gilded wares sheds its own rather unexpected light on the bullion famine of the late fourteenth century. In regard to the trade in bullion, supplying city-states was a straightforward endeavor, if risk laden, in contrast to the complexities of encouraging customers to consume bullion in the guise of fabricated goods. It is this latter issue that comes to the fore in the late medieval era when people grew enamored with silver and gold as adornments for themselves and their households. On the supply side, merchant bankers who were bullion traders brought refined ore to mints and could also provide silver and gold to craftsmen, who then fabricated accessories and domestic plate; this was perfectly legal in Italian towns once the proper fees were paid to the mint. More significantly, perhaps, imported precious goods could move directly to bankers' benches, money changers' stalls, or other outlets where they were sold directly to customers. This was the case in Venice where, fortunately, adequate documentation affords at least cursory information on this nascent traffic in ready-made luxury goods. On the demand side, in order to suit customers' preferences, retail bankers and money changers needed a steady supply of fabricated luxury goods, resulting in an unusual sideline to their usual financial services. When demand for luxury goods increased bankers and money changers, who dealt directly with customers possessing discretionary funds for luxuries, were in a position to affect attitudes about what constituted wealth as well as ideas about the liquidity of fabricated wares.

Venice had long served as a point of embarkation for crusading pilgrims, and to attract this influx of foreigners and their funds, money changers began retailing luxury wares from their stalls at some point in the thirteenth century. As Angeliki Laiou has noted, money changers sold glass-encased images of saints, sometimes embellished with silver or gold foil, that served as icons for pilgrims who exchanged coins at their stalls.[1] These were certainly "low-end" luxury goods, but they exhibited the mixed media approach associated with the trade: an advanced technology like glassmaking turned to new and unfamiliar uses combined with painted images supplied by artists and foil supplied by gold beaters. Laiou believes these icons were the first Venetian instance of a mass-produced luxury product, and one can readily grasp the opportunistic nature of sales of glass-encased icons at a money changer's stall. A pilgrim's funds on hand favored impulse purchases, at the possible risk of inadequate budgeting for the remainder of the pilgrim journey.

The possibilities in this line of trade were promising. After the Jubilee of 1300 small ex-votos circulated widely throughout Italy as aides-mémoires and identification badges for devout pilgrims. Although an "art" good, a typical small lead *vera icona* added to a pilgrim's sack was of small material value, so it scarcely qualified as a luxury, but an ex-voto made from a silver disk that fit in the palm of a hand, stamped with a miniature of a revered relic, was an object of considerable resale value that might qualify as a luxury product (see plate 1).[2] These circulated to money changers' stalls when a hard-pressed pilgrim preferred the price of the homeward journey over a silver replica of a holy relic. Some ex-votos that were offered to a church as acts of piety have survived.[3] In circulation as trade goods ex-votos were popular and relatively inexpensive items that were likely to appeal to devout persons and pilgrims; they inhabited a liminal category—part prized holy object and part trade good because they served as repositories of material as well as spiritual value.

In San Marco and San Polo, where money changers offered wares, exchanged coin, and served pilgrims and other travelers, a market for "low-end" luxury goods grew up over the fourteenth century. An incident reported in 1361 captures the scene: a Venetian official of the mint tried unsuccessfully to collect a fine from a reluctant money changer and the frustrated officer finally scooped up a handful of silver ornaments from the money changer's stall in lieu of proper payment. Because the encounter ended in a scuffle and a suit, it found its way into the record books, where it serves to document money changers—dealers in small exchanges of foreign coin—displaying ready-made luxury goods for sale.[4] *Campsores* (money changers), bit players in the world of finance, dealt in transactions with the public at large: this included pilgrims, travelers, and the mercenaries who appeared with increasing frequency in Italian towns over the course of the century. Of course local customers visited these stalls as well. Merchandise presented in this venue gives an idea of the increasing depth in the market for ready-made goods.

When goldsmiths and retailers of jewelry demanded their own stalls for selling wares to the public, Venetian authorities were inclined to grant them that privilege. Goldsmiths claimed this right by long-standing custom, but money changers, who enlisted the *Giustizia vecchia* as overseer and advocate, claimed an older and exclusive privilege in the custom of selling small luxury goods. In the interests of money changers, officers of the *Giustizia vecchia* stated their opposition to the goldsmiths' petition in strong terms.[5] Neverthe-less, when a final ruling came down, goldsmiths had won access: market days were to be open to all, and goldsmiths were not to suffer from discrimination on any account. San Marco and San Polo became open markets for purveyors of small luxury goods, even jewels, and the exclusive privilege money changers had enjoyed over two centuries came to an end.

But craftsmen had already found opportunities at the great Venetian mar-kets of San Polo and San Marco by this date. When, in May 1392, according to a criminal indictment, Abraam di Benedetto di Salamone was arrested for stealing rings from the counter of a jeweler with a market stall in piazza San Marco, a jeweler selling from an open-air stall in this public market was plain-tiff in the suit.[6] Goldsmiths and jewelers entering this space by the last years of the fourteenth century mark a coming-of-age of sorts; henceforth public markets would be open to all purveyors with fine goods to sell. Highly compe-tent Venetian record keeping allows this rare glimpse of a milestone in retail-ing luxury goods, but it is likely that other towns saw comparable competition for prime retailing space in open markets, as well as comparable changes in the manner and means of presenting luxury goods to customers.

Margaret Newett has argued that decent women of Venice shopped at San Marco because they would not frequent the Rialto with its notorious neigh-borhood of prostitutes and loose women.[7] The street of the goldsmiths ran directly from Rialto Bridge, and apparently decent women's reticence applied to frequenting that street as well. By contrast, the open-air stalls at San Marco and San Polo in residential neighborhoods attracted fashionable women along with the traffic of foreigners and pilgrims. This certainly raises the possibility that small trade goods displayed at San Marco and San Polo were secular as well as religious in nature: women tended to make only incidental purchases for their wardrobes from among petty goods since the major articles of their fine wardrobes were supplied to them by their natal families or their husbands. Here, finally, at the money changer's stall, the overused word "trinket" is appropriate to the emerging luxury trade, whereas in so many other instances applying it diminishes the inherent worth of retail luxury objects. Even the wealthiest of women sought only small items that were pleasing to the eye like bangles, silver *tabulae* to hang from headdresses, small buttons, or silver trims. Luxuries have at times been defined as unnecessary rather than expen-sive goods, and that characterization seems appropriate for the trinkets obtained at money changers' stalls for small outlays of cash. Yet trinkets appealed because they carried an unmistakable aura of luxury about them: engraved aglets, small embossed silver plaques, needles, or thimbles could be stocked by an enterprising money changer to augment the religious items displayed for the pilgrims' trade. If women enhanced their wardrobes with trims, borders, buttons, and elaborate headdresses, small, relatively inexpensive items that could be obtained at market stalls, they had found a way to become consumers of luxuries, if on a small scale. Less wealthy townspeople had the example of foreigners and wealthy Venetian women crowded around stalls to instruct them in the art of shopping. As such, open-air retailing promoted greater depth in the market for luxuries, and trinkets revealed a capacity to lure in less affluent customers. More significantly, money changers' new sideline represented a purely retail endeavor in presenting small luxuries to the public. In a real sense they evolved into merchandizers while disengaged from the production houses that had dominated medieval marketing heretofore.

If money changers represented the low end of retailing luxuries to the Venetian public, then bankers exemplify the high end since they sometimes dealt in ready-made luxury goods intended for Europe's wealthiest customers. More than exemplary record keeping and the accidents of preservation pertain when this study proposes that Venetian banking played a role in luxury marketing. Venice was known as a silver town because it had sustained its silver *grossi* through imports of silver well into the fourteenth century, long after other Italian cities had ceased to mint their traditional large silver coins. Silver flowed into Venice from late medieval finds at Freiberg, Iglau, and Kutna Hora in rapid succession and from the newly opened mines of the Balkans, which constituted the last nearby and easily accessible silver strike of the medieval era. Additionally Venice imported a certain amount of bullion to sustain its own industry in luxury manufacture or for export to nearby towns. A loosely federated corps of long-distance merchants and bankers, Germans, Florentines, and Ragusans prominent among them, as well as Venice's own bankers, staffed and managed this well-articulated supply system.

Banking, bullion, and luxuries were linked historically. Merchant bankers from Lucca, the Ricciardi, Guinigi, Balbani, and Rapondi companies in particular, had taken banking services north and advertised their readiness to do business with Lucca's fine silks and jewels, illustrated beguilingly by merchant bankers' own luxurious wardrobes.[8] Lombard and Tuscan merchant bankers followed this path and by the end of the thirteenth century spread their networks from Ireland to east European principalities. Italian bankers to the great and powerful accepted pawns of jewels, gold, and silver for surety wherever they set up business. A secondary market perched on a far-reaching banking network—trade in luxuries prospered wherever Italian merchant bankers set up business. Meanwhile Venice carved an exceptional place in this system if only because its bankers were the fortunate few who, if they wished, could afford to stay home and allow others to come to them: such was the power of reputation. Bankers from northern Italian towns were fully aware of Venice's position in the bullion market and the drawing power of its luxury trades, so agents from Lombard and Tuscan firms sought a presence on the Rialto.

The Tuscan merchant Paolo de Certaldo counseled his sons that when traveling abroad to secure the friendship of powerful (and wealthy) people for protection and in order to enter local markets.[9] Wisely, nonresident merchants and bankers, Florentines in particular, followed this dictum at Venice. Individuals seldom succeeded in setting up successful banks and trade alone, but networks of merchant bankers sustained by chains of allied personnel and powerful local patrons did. In a story narrated below, that of Benci del Buono of Florence, the list of requisite traits for a merchant banker active at Venice would place ease with his fellows, geniality, and affability almost as high as a shrewd head for a deal.

A long career helped as well. The Florentine Baldassare Ubriachi left his grown and married offspring at home in Florence and Venice while he made his rounds of courts and markets north of the Alps and in Naples, probably well into his seventies. Again, old ties and friendships mattered, particularly ties to ranking members of royal, ducal, or ecclesiastical courts. Neither Ubriachi's sons, nephews, or sons-in-law could be as effective abroad as the aged Baldassare himself because it was he who had won a noble title from the Holy Roman Emperor Charles IV of Bohemia, which helped him move about with ease in royal circles.[10]

The most elusive traits of merchant bankers, ones that must be imagined because they left little discernible mark in records, were worldly sophistication and fast talking. Bankers appear to have been persuasive talkers with conspicuous skills for promoting new ways to spend. Social ease in a foreign setting also relates to a certain cosmopolitan frame of mind, which was a valuable trait for a dealer in luxury goods. The most successful among these entrepreneurs learned to work as comfortably and effectively abroad as at home—perhaps at times they were more at ease abroad given their sometimes troubled relationships with their native communities. The cooperation of Venetians and Florentines at the Rialto epitomizes this spirit.

Benci del Buono

Newly opened Balkan silver mines provided one powerful reason for Florentines and Ragusans to work together to transport bullion from the Balkans to Venice. Benci del Buono de Flora settled in Ragusa (Dubrovnik) a few decades after silver first appeared at nearby Brskova mining sites; this silver strike led in short order to opening other mines nearby, and apparently the word spread to silver-hungry Italy. Benci was active in the Balkan trade from 1318 until 1340 or 1341, and was something of a jack-of-all-trades, sending couriers to Constantinople for Florentine bankers, arranging grain sales from Barletta for the city, and sending off funds to Florentine bankers who had set up in business in Venice.[11] An ambitious young man willing to travel across the Adriatic Sea to make his fortune, Benci entered the precious metals market, where merchant bankers traded bullion and provided "free" silver to be turned into luxury wares.[12] He became an agent in the bullion trade, probably because of his association with the partners and factors of Florentine banks who visited Ragusa (in particular Nerio Balducci of the Bounacursi bank at the Rialto) and his good relations with Ragusans who brought silver from the Balkan interior to the coast.[13]

Florentines like Benci, his associate Lorini Rici, and another agent in the Balkan trade named Johannes Fici de Flora handled bulk shipments of silver by sea from Ragusa to Venice without, apparently, worrying much about the risk of sea transport. The Adriatic had become a reasonably safe place in these years when Venetians referred to it as *mare nostrum* (our sea). Transactions worked this way: a Ragusan silver merchant like Pale de Rasti placed 58 Ragusan pounds, 8 ounces (Ragusa used a 328-gram pound weight) of silver worth 763 *hyperperi* and 6 *grossi* ($382^3/_4$ ducats) with Benci in January 1327. The silver was to be sold in Venice at a price no less than that specified in the contract when it arrived at market (setting a minimum price on contracts was common in both the luxury and precious metals trades). That same day Benci turned around and secured two agents to see to the safety and transport of the silver onboard ship and through the port of Venice.[14] From other comparable contracts, Venetian mint records, and the Venetian *Grazie* (a judicial record), it is fairly simple to reconstruct the path of the transported silver once it reached Venice. Agents on the Venetian market like Nigri de la Resa (a Venetian?), Marinus de Volcassio, a Ragusan, or perhaps Nerio Balducci would see to the sale of the imported Balkan silver.[15] Transactions that failed to convey the required fifth of all imported silver to the mint at Venice appeared occasionally in the *Grazie,* and the entries suggest that silver sales on the open market were commonplace; indeed, *Grazie* references specify on occasion that imported silver was destined for the market rather than the mint.[16] All trade in bullion at Venice continued to be overseen by officials of the Silver Office, but by the end of the third decade of the century sales on the open market were routine.[17]

In this era Ragusan shipments of silver from Balkan mines were not large in comparison with German and Hungarian imports, suggesting one reason mint officials tolerated sales of Balkan silver on the open market. Somewhat later in the same year, Benci del Buono negotiated to send a little more than sixteen pounds of silver to Venice, but this was silver of Nova Brdo, and thus of some distinction. On occasion, silver from the mines at Nova Brdo was labeled *argento de glama* (silver with shine?) because it contained some gold, so Nova Brdo silver was, potentially at least, a valuable cargo to place on the market.[18] It may be the case as well that Balkan silver was known to be of uneven quality, which would also determine its disposal. In any event, once a fifth was delivered to the mint as the law required, sales of Balkan silver on the open market were not opposed by the Silver Office. This was not generally the case for imported silver; indeed, the *fondacho dei Tedeschi* had been established with the intention of keeping the mint supplied with silver imported from Germany. Officials kept a close eye on imports of bullion from Hungary as well.

Terms that describe Ragusan silver shipments are suggestive of the bullion's disposition once it arrived in Venice. Rather incongruously, Benci's silver was measured simply in Ragusan pounds and ounces, whereas other transported silver described as "eighteen marks of good silver of the fineness of the mint" had been tested and vetted for delivery to the Venetian mint.[19] The same may be true for *tantum argentum bonum et legatem* (an amount of good and legal silver) shipped to Venice that same year.[20] Silver coin from Rascia (Serbia) marked *de cruce* or *de lilia,* when transported to Venice, would be picked up by harbor officials called *super denariis grossi de Brescova,* who would confiscate it and convey it to the mint.[21] Benci's first trade in silver, measured in pounds, was possibly inferior silver, perhaps *argento biancho* or lead-laden *argento plico,* still useful for making goods.[22] On the other hand, Benci's Nova Brdo silver might fetch a better price than silver at the fineness of the mint since it was likely to be gold laden. Perhaps then quality variation influenced the disposition of Balkan bullion and that is the message to take away from these Ragusan trade contracts.

Argento plico was suited to producing an object like a "white" crown (heavily leaded); this serves as a valuable reminder that only trade goods explicitly labeled *argento fino* or bearing hallmarks were verifiably silver of the fineness of the mint and exchangeable at prices established at the mint.[23] Benci and other merchants transporting less fine silver (or gold-laden silver) to Venice were actively pursuing a new market for mined bullion and new uses for silver bullion outside of coining.

In these decades, Venetians disbanded their "defense of the *grossi*"— support of their great silver coin. The rerouting of German silver westward rather than across Austria to Venice acted as a contributing factor.[24] The effort to attract newly mined foreign silver to Venice continued, but the mint now demanded only what was necessary to sustain smaller silver coinages, and even these coins were for the most part destined for use in Venice's overseas ports of call rather than for circulation at Venice.[25] Outside the required fifth, Balkan silver circulated freely and Venice, a magnet for silver imports, in turn exported silver to the Levant. According to Frederic C. Lane and Reinhold C.

Mueller, Venice was flooded with silver as a direct result of minting policies in the middle years of the century.[26] Significantly, in this period, Balkan silver arrived at the port already fabricated into accessories, jewelry, utensils, and vessels, with gold applied sparingly for embellishment. These goods had been produced at Ragusa in numbers that suggest trade goods: a dozen knives, sixteen belts, and a dozen pair of bangles, for example.[27] This new supply of luxury goods was probably regarded as beneficial by Venetian authorities on many counts: silver in goods stimulated luxury sales; it helped ensure that silver remained in Italy as goods, and it attracted customers from all over Europe and was less likely to drain toward the East. By the 1330s and 1340s, Hungarian silver and gold output had increased as well, with a portion of the newly mined metal funneling directly to Italy.[28] Yet it was demonstrably Balkan silver, a brisk trade in silver goods absorbed into the Venetian market as fabricated wares, that represented the new use for silver.

Both Ragusan exporters and Florentine factors of banks representing those exporters brought fabricated wares to market. Very small amounts of gold, aided by techniques for stretching gold to make a show—gilding, foil, gold wire trim—added a bright glint to any display of silver wares. Articles of crafted bone, ivory, rock crystal, coral, semi-precious and precious stones from the East and from Africa (which also supplied gold) might appear alongside silver wares.[29] Glassmakers at Murano stepped up their production of *veriselli* or glass facsimiles of precious stones that were also displayed alongside the genuine article. Luxury goods were amalgams of precious and nonprecious materials and sold all the better for it.

When a Venetian businessman was challenged on failing to pay required import fees in his dealings with Florentine agents selling imported Balkan silver *zonas* (belts), he identified himself as a link in this supply chain. When Ragusans were fined in the Venetian *Grazie* for failing to pay the impost on *zonas* (silver belts), they identify themselves as part of this new supply network as well.[30] Decades ago Frederic Chapin Lane noted, "Jewels played a consistent part in the bankers' reserves, for they were extensively used as securities for loans."[31] Apparently precious metal in fabricated wares did as well. There was a further incentive for exhibiting jewels and fabricated wares of silver or gilded silver on a banker's bench. An investor collecting profit took his interest away in currency or, perhaps, he might on impulse purchase some object that tempted him, while, quite marvelously, retaining its liquidity as a fungible asset. A heavy chain with a jeweled medallion, a silver dagger with a gilded hilt, or a great linked belt with gold inlay were desirable on many counts. Perhaps this trade followed naturally from bankers' role in dealing in pawns, which on forfeit could be resold. More to the point, luxury objects displayed on a banker's bench were appealing because of a widespread belief in the inherent value of precious metal. In times past fine accessories had possessed liquidity only a little less reliable than coin (provided, that is, fineness of silver was specified or hallmarks provided). Luxury wares could be melted down if a need arose, they served in lieu of cash to secure loans, and their appearance as fungible goods on bankers' benches tacitly reinforced assumptions about inherent worth. Silver wares even paid bills: when Simone del fu Giovanni da Prato gave *una cintura di argento dorato* (a gilded belt) in restitution for a squandered dowry, he employed a valuable fabricated object to serve in lieu of currency.[32] In this regard the luxury market was bonded to money and bullion markets, and this built trust. At the very moment when silver of lesser quality began to arrive at Venice to be sold as goods, goods lacking the hallmarks of recognized Venetian goldsmiths, other forces conjoined to encourage trust.[33]

Shortly after Venice ceased to sustain the silver *grossi* (1327), the Great Council reconfirmed the exclusive right of bankers to buy and sell gold or silver wares from their Rialto benches. As the preceding chapter noted, at about the same time petitioning goldsmiths demanded access to selling space at the Rialto for their own fabricated silver wares. In March of that year gold-smiths demanded their own Rialto counters, presumably because it was galling to watch fabricated wares move into customers' hands from bankers' benches within a few paces of their own shops. Worse yet, imported fabricated wares were among the goods displayed on those benches. Nevertheless, a 1331 ruling reconfirmed bankers' traditional monopoly for selling at the Rialto, relegating goldsmiths to their own street. The council stated unconditionally that no goldsmith could erect a "station" or display counter to sell or buy worked gold or silver at the Rialto, indirect but trustworthy evidence that bankers were dealing in such wares. The *scuola aurificum* was co-opted by the council's rul-ing by specifying that the *scuola* would receive a third of any fines collected from goldsmiths for noncompliance.[34] This echoed earlier Great Council rul-ings issued in July and September 1325 forbidding goldsmiths to set up stalls for selling silver and gold at the Rialto.[35]

The first three decades of the fourteenth century had brought together a network of Venetian and Florentine bankers, as well as Ragusan and other for-eign suppliers, who created a new retail outlet for fine goods. Then the expul-sion of all Florentines from Venice in 1340–41 after the Scaliger War affected the livelihoods of all foreign bankers at Venice and threatened banking services generally. Reinhold Mueller explains just how disruptive the sudden collapse of Venetian-Florentine ventures could be. Two Florentine partners of Benci del Buono, known to us in a story Benci's son Franco Sacchetti related later, were Tosco Ghinazzi de Flora and Noddo d'Andrea de Flora, merchant bank-ers active in Venice; they may be identified as such in the Covoni ledger, still extant in the Florentine archives. Tosco Ghinazzi represented the Venetian firm of Dino Guidi and Jacopo Guardo, while Noddo d'Andrea was a partner in Branca Guidaloni's company, also a Venetian bank. Both banks suffered

major setbacks when Tosco and Noddo withdrew their assets, a necessary pre-
caution on their part since as Florentines they were threatened with expulsion.[36]

Because Venice declared Tosco Ghinazzi a citizen *de intus* in 1344, it is
safe to assume the banking disruption of 1340–41 had been at least partially
repaired—at least Tosco Ghinazzi was willing and eager to return to Venice
and start all over again.[37] Noddo d'Andrea received the privilege of citizenship
de extra in 1358.[38] Apparently both men accepted Venetian citizenship, which
demonstrates the appeal of the Rialto, where the rewards were as great as the
risks, as both men knew. Bankers' endeavors to offer precious wares to customers developed at this risk-filled juncture in Venice's emerging financial networks. Benci del Buono, who served as an agent of the Bardi and Peruzzi,
Buonacursi, and Acciaiuoli at various times, made his fortune within this loose
federation of Florentine and Venetian bankers. Insofar as the record shows,
Benci did not trade between his native city of Florence and the port of Ragusa;
the evidence suggests he worked the market at Venice from across the Adriatic
and returned to Venice in his later years to pursue more trade despite the risks
represented by joint banking and trading ventures.[39]

Having linked his future at least in part to silver, Benci became a market-
maker in the high end of the silver market. At Venice, once the *aurifici* established retail shops in the *Ruga dei Oresi*, near bankers' benches on the Rialto
just a few steps away, the city sustained a premier luxury market, which was
further augmented by sales of small items from money changers' booths on
Campo San Polo and piazza San Marco. Hungarians brought their precious
metals here; Germans from the Harz Mountains mines still brought silver to
the *fondacho dei Tedeschi*.[40] Goldsmiths in Ragusa produced ready-made articles for the luxury market to transport to Venice along with shipments of bulk
silver. A small corps of Ragusan traders, like Marinus de Volcassio and Vita de
Goce, worked and lived near the Rialto, in the *contrata San Silvestro* nearby.[41]
A number of Venetians followed the trade in Balkan silver as well: members
of the Quintavalle family of bankers and Giovanni Stornado's bank did business with Ragusans and between Ragusa and Venice.[42] Marco Stornado did
business there as well. The trade in Balkan bullion and fabricated wares was
well organized and generously staffed.

Venice's evident success in capturing the luxury trade had much to do
with the emergence of integrated financial markets in the city. By mid-century
Venice had become a "city of finance" in five areas: as a city with a system of
local deposit and *giro* (transfer banks); as a center for maritime insurance; as
a money market for short-term loans; as a financial market for "forced" loans
or long-term government bonds that were negotiable; and, most significantly
for this investigation, as the premier bullion market of Europe. Values from
all five sectors of this interrelated financial network were quoted daily at the

Rialto. This financial system displays signs of maturity, and it was widely frequented and efficient.[43] But why would Benci and other Florentines trade Balkan silver, and luxury wares made from Balkan silver, with Venice primarily when all of Italy went begging for bullion? Florentine agents went so far as to supply the Venetian market with silver even to the point of slighting their own native Florence. Politics likely played a role since relations were far from cordial between Guelf Florence and aristocratic Ragusa, the chief source of Balkan silver. The realities of Venetian political dominance of the Adriatic meant that Ragusa, while it remained under Venetian lordship until 1358, exported to Venice.[44] The case was significantly altered a century later when, according to commentary from the Florentine *signoria*, enough silver flooded Florence from Ragusa to "purchase Pisa."[45] By the middle of the fifteenth century Ragusa had rethought its policy of avoiding direct trade with Florence, in part at least in response to Florentine military aid to Milan, and had freed itself from Venice. Balkan silver then flowed to Florence as well, where, at least partially in response to assured supplies, a lively industry in silver production flourished.[46] Peter Spufford believes that this Serbian silver ameliorated the bullion famine for northern Italy for at least a few decades in the middle of the fifteenth century.[47]

Returning to the fourteenth century, Florentine compatriots working at Venice—Giovanni Ducci, Testa di Lippi and Piero di Lippo Buonagrazia, Giovannozzo di Bartolo Fede, Noddo d'Andrea, and Michel Cini, as well as Benci del Buono (all known to us from Novella 98 of Sacchetti's *Trecentonovelle*)—were active on the Venetian markets all through the banking crises of the 1340s. Florentine authors of the early Renaissance seem to owe a significant debt to Florentine bankers active at Venice: Giovanni Boccaccio was the son of a Florentine father who represented the Bardi bank at Venice in 1334; the father's name was Boccaccini and he was nicknamed "Gallini."[48] Benci del Buono was himself father to Franco Sacchetti, who, despite his constant moralizing, is a useful source on how the resident Florentine banking community in Venice conducted their businesses and their lives.

According to Sacchetti, his father played a joke at the expense of his fellow Florentines at Venice, yet he did not give offense. In Sacchetti's tale of a joke played on Testa Ghinozzi, an ancient, and none too clean, leather hat liner was slipped into Testa's cooking pot by a servant in place of a delectable bit of tripe, all at Benci's behest. The liner had come from a big soiled hat left over from among Benci's father-in-law's possessions; thus Sacchetti characterized his father as a man not only affable but of a saving nature. This old hat in his wardrobe—in his son's words, "[Benci] had played a dirty joke because that hat was very dirty"—suggests a certain lack of concern for appearance, perhaps even of personal fastidiousness.[49] Even with its facetious tone Sacchetti's portrait of his father recalls Dante's more sober description of his revered ancestor, Cacciaguardi, in whom nobility of character was accompanied by simplicity of taste and dress and a most unostentatious manner.[50] Benci's earthy humor and simple, if rough, taste harked back to an idealized time in Florentine history, a time recalled with nostalgia by Sacchetti, who wrote during the more tumultuous years at the end of the fourteenth century.

Benci's joke played at Venice may have done more than provide an engaging memory for his son. Franco Sacchetti, a proud member of an old lineage, used more than one of his stories as a vehicle for expressing values consonant with his heritage of a noble Sacchetti lineage. In this way he was able to take some sharp jabs at pretensions, and he saved some of his best bits, even his dirty bits as Carol Lansing notes, for those who pretended nobility: *cavalleria* or knighthood has become no more than *cacaleria*, he quipped, an aside that deserves celebration as among his very best.[51] Because Sacchetti also derided usurers posing as knights, some have taken his concern with true nobility to be hostile to the commercial spirit, but with his story about his father, Sacchetti set that matter straight. Tolerant goodwill among Florentine traders abroad allowed Benci's joke to be taken in stride and appreciated, even by the man on whom it was played. This story captures the spirit of an early fourteenth-century generation of Florentine merchants, their noble or common origins notwithstanding. He wanted his readers to understand that his father's generation formed such a tight community abroad that they might enter each other's homes, enlist each other's servants, and play a "dirty" joke. In Novella 98 he concluded sadly that in this tolerant way merchants used to amuse themselves, whereas in the divided and strife-torn Florence of his own day (the 1390s), such a joke would lead men to kill each other. Sacchetti's nostalgia for a better time when a merchant's trust was tested by joking and found durable highlighted the ways in which Florentines had relied on close connections with each other. He praised marketmakers like his father who had forged close-knit ties that permitted Florence to prosper.

Still the market these men served was a risky one and subject to sudden dislocations. In the 1340s, the bank of Donato Quintavalle failed and, soon after, that of Giovanni Stornado failed as well. The Quintavalle family had a major presence in Ragusa and dealt in Serbian silver, whereas Giovanni Stornado had trade contacts in Ragusa and been both a refiner of silver and a banker since 1328. As Mueller expresses it, "Stornado was very active in mediating payments among Florentine merchant bankers especially as dealers in bills of exchange; in that specific role the banker profited from the oscillating *agio* [spread] between bank money and specie."[52] When in 1341 the republic of Venice exiled all Florentine traders from the Rialto because Florence had not repaid a small fraction of its debt incurred in the joint pursuit of the Scaliger War, these banks collapsed. This banking crisis foretold the better known collapse of great Florentine banks that followed; in fact the collapse of 1340–41 represented little more than a portent of that greater event. Wildly fluctuating grain prices, overextended loans, and repudiated loans to kings figured more heavily in that major collapse of banks from 1343 to 1345. But no sooner was a collapse over than this network of bankers began to rebuild their financial liaisons at the Rialto. The collapse of branches farther afield in Naples and England (occasioned by massive defaults on the part of royal debtors) created long-term damage to the European-wide banking system, but the financial markets of Venice, with the luxury market pegged to them, rebuilt swiftly. To a great extent the repeated rebuildings of financial networks rested on trust and cooperation among merchant bankers. After each collapse Benci's circle of Florentine associates returned and re-formed their joint banking enterprises with Venetian partners when conditions permitted. Mutual trust and goodwill compensated for the often frustrating structural weaknesses of fourteenth-century banking ventures.

Still, the inherently unstable nature of fourteenth-century banking revealed itself far too often at Venice. In 1343 in Florence the Peruzzi failed, as did the Acciaiuoli soon after that; the Bardi failed in 1346. At Venice five banks survived the Black Plague, and Florentines returned to the Rialto. However, the economy had been thrust into full economic crisis: population loss, the fall of gold, some famine, and a tendency to speculate on bullion, all of which precipitated further bank failures. Venice's mid-century war with Genoa added more burdens to financial and bullion markets. Despite this Florentines reentered the Rialto banking, but only to experience failure again. Francesco Guida, an immigrant Florentine in partnership with his noble Venetian father-in-law, Pietro da Mosto, failed next.[53] During the War of Chioggia another banking crisis occurred although no major Venetian banks defaulted.[54] In Florence there was an average of six bankruptcies a year from 1366 to 1370, and seven a year occurred from 1371 to 1376.[55] The bullion market also experienced difficulties: a silver shortage at Venice occurred after 1327 and increased its price in relation to gold, but unevenly. By the last decades of the fourteenth century the phenomenon now known as the great bullion famine in silver was beginning to make itself felt in Italy.[56]

Like his father, Franco Sacchetti spent some early years traveling for business but he soon settled in to a political career, serving as a magistrate in Florence and an ambassador abroad. He knew the important personages of his day and he could write knowledgeably about kings and popes for his local audience. There were always eager readers for his stories about the famous men of earlier generations like Dante Alighieri and the painter Giotto di Bondone. Florentines were justly proud of their great men and any small detail or gossip about their lives drew in the curious. In Novella 63 Sacchetti told one of his anecdotes about the renowned painter Giotto, making reference to a commission given him by an artisan who had, apparently, become the custodian (castellan, probably watchman) of a castle outside town. The artisan wished to have his shield decorated with his coat of arms. In Sacchetti's story Giotto accepted the project despite his disdain for it, and he decorated the artisan's shield with a helmet, a neckpiece, bracelets, gauntlets, breastplates, leg armor, a sword, a dagger, and a lance. He had quite literally painted the artisan's "arms," in fact his full weaponry onto the shield. When the artisan saw this he protested and took Giotto to fair claims court (*Grascia*) but lost his case, which meant he had to pay Giotto six lira for the painted shield.[57]

Franco's appended moral turned on an aphorism: *cosi costui, non misurandosi, fu misurato*—loosely, those who cannot estimate their own worth will have their worth judged by others.[58] Then he added a comment that was more biting: all sorts of men wish for a coat of arms and to create a great family or house, even foundlings from the orphanage. From the height of his own prominence in Florentine life, from the serenity of being an acknowledged son despite his illegitimate birth, Franco Sacchetti condemned upstarts, his own origins forgotten. He expected his audience to have forgotten the circumstances of his low birth as well, if indeed that story had ever gotten out in Florence. His humorous anecdote about Giotto relied on an audience that shared his sense of social entitlement based on lineage, wealth, and talent, none of which the poor aspiring castellan could claim. In one generation the Sacchetti family had moved a vast social distance from Benci's early years, when he had risked much for a living in a strange place, relying on his own wits, and without family backing.

These are the bare bones of a merchant family whose fortune was built on banking at Venice and the emerging luxury trades of the fourteenth century. However, with the aid of recent studies of late medieval Florentine society, most particularly of the magnate families of Florence in the years after the passage of the Ordinances of Justice (1292–95), it may be possible to view Benci and the Sacchetti in a wider social context.[59]

While the Sacchetti have been listed as *popolani* by a few scholars, Gaetano Salvemini identified the family as magnates of the late thirteenth-century city; more recent scholars, Gene Brucker and Carol Lansing among them, have followed his lead.[60] It would be difficult to deny Benci noble antecedents in any event since in canto XVI of the *Paradiso*, Dante Alighieri listed the Sacchetti along with the Giuochi, Fifanti, Barucci, and Galli as the old noble lineages of Florence.[61] In the interests of civic reform, the rule of law, and an end to violence, magnate families were taxed and their roles circumscribed by a series of laws from 1292 to 1295.[62] The Sacchetti, whether guilty of any civic offenses in Benci's own line or not, were caught in the same net as other magnates, which created a crisis for the generation born near or at the turn of the trecento. At the very least traditional family career choices would have been closed to young sons of magnate families like Benci's; a number of magnate lineages faced exile and loss of their fortunes. Apparently Benci was thrown back onto his own capacity to make his way in the world and he left for the far shores of the Adriatic Sea.

Benci's place in the Sacchetti lineage is not disputed, given the affirmation in his son's writing, but the father never used his noble name in his career abroad. Other Florentines active in Ragusa—Duccio Puccii, Fortebracchus Charmontesis, and Lorino Rici, to name a few—broadcast their surnames proudly in their business dealings while at Ragusa. A generation later Franco Sacchetti would again wear his lineage name proudly, as would his nephew Forese Sacchetti, who followed his uncle into civil service. The Sacchetti family's probable dip in fortunes after 1295 was likely responsible for Benci's many decades abroad and his focused efforts to make a fortune on his own; it may also account for the fact that Benci did not employ his old and noble surname in business. Other evidence suggests a certain discomfort with his circumstances. He never allied himself permanently with any of the great banking firms, dominated as they were by *popolani* families except in the case of the Bardi. He did not marry into one of the fine old lineages of Florence, although his son Franco would later wed a well-connected Strozzi bride. His years abroad and his apparent single-handed rebuilding of a family fortune may represent a response to a personal crisis for a man compelled to go off on his own and refashion a way of life at odds with the Florentine magnate privileges of birth and position. It would appear that he amassed a sizable private fortune over his lifetime and that he launched his sons and grandsons into civic careers that in turn resurrected his line's status. By the second half of the fourteenth century his offspring had made the name Sacchetti honorable in Florence once more. In the meantime Benci lived much of his life abroad and avoided politics. He appears to have been well pleased with his nickname, del Buono or "the good," which was given to him by his Ragusan associates. This nickname signified popularity among his foreign hosts and the reservoirs of goodwill that accompanied him on his travels.

To all appearances, and in these circumstances, Benci developed an eye for the good chance. Residence in Ragusa and established contacts with the local patriciate, as well as cultivated contacts with a broad spectrum of Florentine banks, placed him in an excellent position to enter the trade in silver on the ground floor, so to speak. In the years when the Balkan silver mines were being reopened, when Venice had given up its policy of defending its silver *grossi*, that is, after the second decade of the century, he served as a middleman in "free" silver trades to Venice. Insofar as the record shows, he did not trade between his native city of Florence and Ragusa, although, of course, there are gaps in the documentary evidence. The evidence suggests that he traded on the luxury markets at Venice exclusively, then returned to Venice in his later years to pursue more trade.[63]

Banking Clients at Venice

From a banker's standpoint, the ideal customer was a wealthy foreigner visiting Venice (or his agents) who wanted to invest large sums. Such a customer was also prone to taking away some profits from investments in the form of luxury goods. Merchant bankers with luxury goods on display could thank their integrated financial markets for attracting a man like Paolo Guinigi, lord of Lucca, as Mueller relates his story.[64] Paolo Guinigi had been overlord of Lucca for a dozen years when he approached Venetian authorities with a request to invest 25,000–50,000 ducats in either Venetian government bonds or the Grain Office. He was already an honorary citizen of Venice, a cultivated foreign customer so to speak, and he had little fear of being refused. He was able to secure investment for his vast wealth with generous terms allowing his personal heirs to inherit free from "interdict or sequester on the basis of any claim whatsoever, be it individual or institutional."[65] In other words, Guinigi's family fortune would be safe from any seizure or coup like the one he had recently weathered at Lucca. When, after lengthy negotiations, he transferred about 40,500 ducats to Venice, he stationed his own representative on the market to watch over his investment. He prospered through his calculated risk: collection of interest over four years (1412–16) amounted to over 7,000 ducats. His investment rose to 114,000 ducats in bonds by 1427. With much to celebrate and now more discretionary funds on hand, Paolo Guinigi ventured into the local luxury market and bought gems with some of his profits: "16 rubies and a *balas* ruby cost [Guinigi] 220 ducats, . . . a sapphire and pearls cost 400 ducats [report of January 1417]; an 8-carat ruby was purchased cheap [*buono marchatto*] for 500 ducats."[66] Guinigi also purchased books and sugar, a thoroughbred horse, and a bulldog that could hunt. A prudently contracted and, perhaps more important, relatively safe investment had in the end tempted Paolo Guinigi toward consumption. The sugar he bought would be consumed, and his new acquisitions of a horse and a dog would die in time, but the books and gems he purchased had a good chance of enduring and appreciating in value. These were high-end consumer goods, so here he proved himself a prudent customer by the standards of his day, and as such he qualifies as a preferred customer at a banker's bench.

These goods could have been obtained from a wide variety of Venetian purveyors, but bankers were still likely to play a role in encouraging Guinigi's luxury consumption. By displaying wares bankers could whet the customer's interest in luxury goods. Bankers could also encourage their customers to visit the shops of reputable goldsmiths. They could discuss with customers how to judge the value of jewels, and how gold and silver wares stood up to the market over time. Promoting consumption was a financial service of sorts offered to the clientele of Venetian banks.

Mueller has identified more than forty foreign customers investing sums in Venetian financial markets from the 1330s until the first decade of the fifteenth century, when Paolo Guinigi began investing his great sums. This was only the first phase of growth, since wealthy and powerful people continued to patronize Venice's financial markets throughout the fifteenth century. Taken together, foreign investors represented both the great and the small—persons who ventured from 50 to 100,000 ducats (the latter from Caterina Visconti, wife of Giangaleazzo of Milan). A scriptor's widow, a physician, and a canon represented the smaller folk among foreigners seeking investment returns at Venice. Since the great included John I, king of Portugal, as well as many of the most powerful princely families of northern Italy, the reputation of a safe and attractive investment opportunity had circulated to even those living at a great distance. Each foreign investor represented future earned interest that might be spent on luxuries, especially if they were laid out temptingly on the very bench from which an investor drew interest.

It was significant for the development of consumer markets that by the mid-fourteenth century both the bankers of the Rialto and the money changers at St. Mark's offered ready-made luxury goods as a sideline. For a banker or a money changer a silver object displayed on a bench meant that a customer might take away dividends in wares rather than coin, creating the additional profit of a second transaction. There was a role for Jews on this market because the closely interconnected families of Jewish traders supplied Italian luxury markets with gems, but Jewish moneylenders enjoyed less opportunity than their Christian counterparts to enter this retail trade. Outlawed in Venice in the thirteenth century, Jews were readmitted in 1382 to help Venetians over the money famine brought on by the crisis of the War of Chioggia. Thereafter Jews were again exiled, this time to Mestre. Their role in trade and lending was restricted in any event because the poor with whom they dealt tended to borrow against pawn whereas rich borrowers in Venice, who dealt with Christian bankers, could provide written promises of repayment or notarial deeds. Uncollected pawns were fungible assets, but because the poor pledged only clothing, hammers, and other tools against their debts to Jewish moneylenders, there was small resale value in the pawns collected.[67]

Open markets and ready-made luxury goods were becoming a potent force in the economy, and Venice was certainly not alone in discovering how to retail ready-made luxury goods. Monna Uliva, mother of the Florentine painter-goldsmith Doffo di Baldino, lost her son in 1383 and, along with his estate, acquired some completed works of art. She set about finding customers for these finished works, all of which were religious in nature and ranged from images of the Madonna to depictions of the Four Evangelists; however, the most she received for any one of these religious works of art was sixteen florins. Still, their presence in Doffo's estate suggests that the artist had been prepared to sell finished works of art out of his workshop to customers interested in the ready-made.[68]

Benedetto Cotrugli, who characterized long-distance trade as a pursuit fit for a nobleman in 1458, included among the noble trades jewelers (*de gioiellieri*).[69] A new aspiring community of luxury craftsmen and retailers had emerged by his day; they were masters of their trades and as adept at discerning and influencing the taste of affluent customers as they were at producing beautiful ready-made objects. Successful goldsmith establishments and banks at the Rialto shared this high end of the luxury market. Here, where the stakes were very high, competition for market share emerged as early as the 1330s, a decade to remember as one in which the retail trade in luxuries came alive.

The Luxury Trade Travels on Financial Networks

Renato Piattoli discovered an unusual feature for the transport of small luxury goods in his research on the art market at Avignon. Enamels that decorated plaques, buttons, or brooches traveled across the Alps from Italy to France in the pouches of bank couriers.[70] While bankers avoided transporting currency whenever possible, some shipments of specie were unavoidable, and an excellent service designed to transport currency could also handle small bulk high-value wares like enamels. Carefully constructed financial networks meant relatively safe transport for Italian luxury goods because bankers understood and managed risk skillfully.

Early in the century Amerigo and Bettino Frescobaldi, Florentine bankers, appear to have been among the most adept at handling the safe transport of luxury goods when abroad. In 1312 King Edward of England had ordered the arrest of agents of the Frescobaldi bank who were in residence in London, among them Amerigo and Bettino. The king, in serious debt to the bank, feared his merchant bankers would flee the realm without giving an accounting, an ominous sign, and one not likely to be misconstrued by a family of experienced bankers. The Frescobaldi had the unfortunate example of the Riccardi bank's earlier quick expulsion from England, so they would have given some forethought to the crisis. Wisely, by 1312, the Frescobaldi had begun an orderly program to quit England. Amerigo and Bettino managed to slip a hoard of gold and silver objects estimated at £500—their plate and very possibly pawns held in surety—by the Tower guards. As part of their exit plan these possessions were hidden in ordinary bales of wool, which were referred to, in a deft exercise in periphrasis, as "Il balle della decta lane ove entrò nostre care cose" (bales of fine wool with our very nice things) (see plate 12). By a circuitous route these "very nice things" made their way back to Florence safely, an impressive accomplishment in this era of hazardous travel.[71] The Frescobaldi plate amounted to a small fortune.

While in England the Frescobaldi had maintained a household suitable for bankers to the king, and its riches may have been augmented by pawns collected from English debtors. This household was the provenance of the fine things the brothers secreted in bales of wool when they departed under a cloud of royal suspicion. Within that cache of luxuries would have been vessels and utensils of silver and silver gilt; there would have been items of personal apparel suitable to wear at court or to give as gifts to the king and to men in high places. Luxurious gifts were time-honored tools for cultivating financial networks abroad since opulence symbolized the stored wealth of successful banks and helped establish a banker's credentials. But appearances befitting great wealth represented a serious game of chance, as this close call with the Frescobaldi plate reveals. Over and over again Italian merchants and bankers were ready to take this risk, which confirms the value they placed on luxuries for keeping up appearances.

Perhaps there was a special Frescobaldi knack for protecting "very nice things" when traveling. Lionardo di Niccolò Frescobaldi solved his problem of taking gold coin on pilgrimage to the Holy Land in 1384 in this fashion: "And from the said small chest we detached one of those bands which are set in the lower part of the cover, and with a bodkin we emptied a part so that inside we hid six hundred brand new ducats, two hundred for each of the three of us; and I carried two hundred ducats of silver Venetian grossi and a hundred gold ones." He and his companions also carried letters to Alexandria and Damascus on behalf of the Portinari company. In Frescobaldi's small chest were other useful things like books "and silver cups and other delicate things" to provide comforts for the journey.[72]

By the last years of the fourteenth century the Florentine Baldassare Ubriachi made his fortune in the trade and transport of luxury goods based on his own role as arbiter of taste and beauty.[73] Although he had been enrolled in the *cambio* (banking and money changers' guild) at Florence from an early age, he did not immediately turn to luxuries for his living but traveled to Avignon where he was coproprietor of a hostel or warehouse, then he went farther afield as a dealer in pedestrian goods. In England Ubriachi was licensed to supply wine from New Rochelle. Later he attempted to recover cotton at Venice from the estate of his kinsman, Tommaso Ubriachi.

In 1318 at least one, possibly two, individuals from the Florentine magnate lineage of Ubriachi had been expelled from Florence for political reasons, so this old family fell victim to the reforming ordinances of the Florentine *signoria* in the early years of the fourteenth century. One of these, Ugolino, Baldassare's uncle, a fabricator of luxury goods, had the good fortune to obtain citizenship in Venice.[74] Over the decades this branch of the Ubriachi created a well-respected workshop, in which Baldassare would later take on a role of long-distance trader.

As for his own childhood and early education, Baldassare, son of Simone Ubriachi, appears to have lived in Florence where he joined the *cambio* in 1365, setting him on a similar path to other Florentines discussed above. His early life is not well documented but it is likely that his immediate family branch did not undergo exile from Florence and were sufficiently well connected to launch Baldassare in a business career. He traveled in his youth and developed a network of contacts in long-distance trade and banking which, apparently, lasted him a lifetime, proof of his capacity to forge and maintain the friendships critical to the success of merchants.

Rare information about his early days appeared much later in 1395 in Ubriachi's correspondence with Francesco de Marco Datini. Speaking of his early years at mid-century, Ubriachi wrote to Datini: "I do not think, Francesco, that you have forgotten the fine friendship we had in Avignon from the time we were boys. That was forty-four years ago, [yet] we have preserved [our friendship] and made it better wherever we have been. Nothing less than death can separate us."[75]

Baldassare survived the Black Plague and found a place among suppliers of goods to the papal court and to the ecclesiastical households resident in Avignon. Datini's own trading company would have been the source of valuable business contacts for Baldassare, although the more humbly born Datini was the son of a taverner who had died during the plague, and was no more than sixteen when he befriended the well-born Baldassare. Avignon was probably Europe's most prosperous center of consumption at mid-century, and enterprising young men sought it out for its well-heeled customers.

Baldassare Ubriachi learned banking and trade abroad. Building on this experience in the prescribed manner of the day, he became in time an established banker, a member of the Italian confraternity in Avignon, and partner in a company with the Florentines Jacopo di Gherardo de' Giuochi and Giovanni d'Andrea Segnini Baldesi.[76] For a quarter century he pursued long-distance ventures, but by 1376 Florence was at war with the pope, and this interrupted his relations with Avignon's ecclesiastics. Baldassare's career, like those of other Florentines before him, was vulnerable to the political fallout from the century's wars, but Baldassare had ingratiated himself with the Florentine *signoria* so that measures were taken on his behalf when his goods were confiscated. In February 1376, Florentine officials wrote to the lords of Pisa and Sicily to protest a seizure of his goods.[77] It is to his credit that even in the difficult political climate of the day Baldassare was able to enlist the aid of Florentine authorities on his behalf.

After having traveled abroad as a merchant in his early life, Baldassare was able to rehabilitate the political fortunes of the Ubriachi in Florence. Baldassare's prosperity, coupled with his cultivation of the current regime, counted heavily. Now married and the head of a family, he returned to Florence though this was not to be his permanent residence. No sooner did he return than he made known his ambition to be accepted as a wealthy patron of the community, a role in keeping with his distinguished lineage. Baldassare commissioned a chapel at Santa Maria Novella dedicated to the Three Kings, completed by 1378. Soon thereafter he also constructed a great house outside the gates of the city at Porto San Frediano. Both projects undertaken in the same decade suggest Baldassare had amassed a considerable fortune and that he was determined that his fellow Florentines be fully cognizant of his family's restored fortune and consequence in the life of the city.

The foundation of a family chapel proclaimed Baldassare's restored political status in his hometown. In tracing Baldassare's career as an early promoter of the cult of the Magi in Florence, Richard Trexler has asserted that the Ubriachi heraldic ducks that decorated the two large coats of arms painted on the east wall of the chapel differed from other Ubriachi ducks carved elsewhere in the chapel (the addition of a red cross: "on their folded white, shield-shaped wings, each cross on its side").[78] More to the point for his career, Baldassare understood the importance of a symbol. His new chapel at Santa Maria Novella celebrated the visit of the Magi, an iconic assertion of noble status since it implied his personal association with the Kings. So also with his fine new residence, identified later as the place "where the Kings are" because of the use of that theme in decoration. The Magi carried rich gifts and dressed in splendor; they served as a moral sanction for luxury both worn as adornment and given in charity. With their fine gifts to the Christ Child the Magi transformed luxuries into sacred gestures, to be emulated by only the most affluent and distinguished among the faithful. While the republican regime in power in the 1370s supported Baldassare Ubriachi, even considering him as one of their own, that is, an honorary Guelf and *populano* and a "good merchant," in establishing his prominent chapel Ubriachi revealed himself under his preferred colors. He was to be understood as a noble person and a distinguished donor worthy of associating himself with the cult of the Magi.[79]

Baldassare did not settle down and enjoy his new prestige in Florence but soon traveled to the north once more. Apparently the imperial family had taken his service as a great favor and, upon a royal visit to Italy and while residing at Lucca, Emperor Charles IV made Baldassare a Count Palatine, thus *nobilis vir* and a titled gentleman. Not long after this Ubriachi traveled to England, where he benefited in turn from the protection and patronage of King Richard II, son-in-law of the emperor. Since Richard II and his queen, Anne of Bohemia, were as enthusiastic consumers of jewels and elegant fashions as Anne's parents (Elizabeth of Bohemia had bought pearls worth 1,200 ducats from Ubriachi), he encountered opportunities at royal courts. A count by decree of the emperor, Baldassare moved smoothly through the courts of Europe and began to supply luxuries to men like Jean, Duc de Berri.[80] If he looked the nobleman at home, abroad Ubriachi now looked and acted the prince. In the climate of late fourteenth-century luxury trades, in court settings, nobility was not seen as inimical to a commercial spirit; a titled purveyor of gems and precious goods, dressed like a prince and possessing cultivated manners, was welcome in the best circles. Throughout his travels north of the Alps Baldassare could rely on the assistance of a community of resident Florentines who had settled in major trading cities or near courts. His task was to approach the royal or noble customer while a network of agents supplied luxury goods, saw to transport, and arranged for security.

Access to courtly circles was key for merchant bankers' success abroad. So what could be more useful to traders than a boon companion for nobles and princes at court, one who could share royal pastimes, invite royalty to dinner, dance like a courtier, and, of course, gamble? In the feckless Buonaccorso Pitti Florence possessed such an ambassador, if one without any pretension to business acumen. In his diary, Pitti was candid to a fault about his shortcomings and admitted he was a high roller and spendthrift. As he traveled from the court of the king of Hungary to royal and ducal courts in France, the Low Countries, and England, occasionally taking up a diplomatic mission, Pitti spent his time gambling—extravagantly so, according to his diary. He was daring, reckless, and restless, thus an excellent link to courtly circles, who valued that in a "lombard." Resident Florentine traders and goldsmiths, like Guido Baldi of Florence, master of the royal mint at Buda, could make use of a man like Pitti, and as it happened Baldi housed Pitti during his stay in that royal capital. Wherever he traveled Buonaccorso Pitti maintained contacts with Florentine businessmen in much the same way; on occasion they bankrolled him just as he had been supported by Guido Baldi in Buda—on the grounds that he opened doors with his easy manners and gambling forays. With his entrée at court, it was frequently worth a merchant's investment to support Pitti's expensive lifestyle, even his gambling debts. Pitti recounted: "I had been commissioned by Bernardo di Cino [of Florence] to play against the Duke of Brabant in Brussels, where he and many other great gentlemen were beguiling their time with tournaments, jousting, dancing and the gaming tables. A few days after reaching Brussels, I had already lost 2,000 gold francs belonging to Bernardo di Cino with whom I had gone into partnership on the understanding that he was to supply the money and I my poor skill."[81] Like a number of his other escapades, this one ended surprisingly well, largely because of the friendship and largesse of the duke. But presumably Bernardo di Cino gained benefits even as Pitti's heavy gambling debts mounted. Through Pitti's contacts Bernardo di Cino would gain an advocate in the duke of Brabant's circle, so the investment in Pitti was apparently worth the price. Social and business contacts reinforced each other in the luxury trades.

Baldassare Ubriachi apparently had no such marketable vices as gambling to ingratiate himself at court but certainly by the last decades of the century he moved smoothly in the same court circles, if less flamboyantly. He did not return again to his native city of Florence until the late 1380s. Over the following years he petitioned the court to legitimate his two young sons so they could inherit his estate, and he reentered banking after a hiatus of seven years; however, he did not enter Florentine politics. The suits of his two well-connected sons-in-laws, Recco di Simone Capponi and Piero di Bernardo Chiarini Davanzati, for unpaid dowry precluded any active political career for Baldassare with the *signoria*. Why he did not pay the contracted dowries is not at all clear; it could have been a matter of a setback in his private fortune or merely a falling out with his sons-in-law.

By the 1390s Baldassare had settled in Venice and pursued the luxury trade in partnership with the Venetian branch of his family. Apparently he had moved away from earlier trading ventures in cloth and other staples pursued in conjunction with members of the confraternity of Florentine merchants in Avignon. By this decade he was firmly established in finance and concentrated on the trade in gems, ivory, and bone, a business open to him through the workshop of his Ubriachi kin, who had transferred their citizenship to Venice earlier in the century.[82] In this decade he married his third daughter, Ginevra, to his kinsman and a citizen of Venice, Antonio di Tommaso degli Ubriachi. This Antonio, along with a brother, had inherited "all the coins, silver, pearls, rings, gems, jewels, bonds, cloth, tools, and goods of their father's estate"—in sum, the working capital of the highly esteemed Ubriachi workshop.[83]

A link to this eminent luxury-producing establishment sent Baldassare to northern courts once more. With Baldassare as purveyor of wares, the Ubriachi workshop could approach the greatest art patrons of the day. In this phase of his career the Certosa di Pavia paid Baldassare's agent for a great triptych fashioned out of hippopotamus teeth, heavily gilded, which decorated the altar of that great monastery, perhaps the finest work in ivory of the century. Baldassare had a hand in its design and theme, if not an even larger role in its execution. The triptych presented a full exposition of the myth of the Three Kings, in its highly elaborated late medieval version. Highly detailed reliefs, outlined in gilt, told an elaborate story about the Magi's long and circuitous journey. The great triptych provided an unparalleled opportunity to exhibit the wide variations of apparel and jewels appropriate for great kings embarked on a quest to find and honor the Christ Child.

This triptych was a sacred icon and as such represented the old established market for luxury wares. Far more numerous were the decorated coffers, home altars, set jewels, and bridal gifts produced by the Ubriachi workshop and sold by Baldassare and his agents. Ready-made items that were high in value increased in importance; these were often small in size or, if larger, capable of being concealed and transported reasonably safely. For transporting goods, a *goffano* (large chest) with a deeply arched lid, a *cassa* or *casseta* (box-like chest), and *forziere* (metal-bound and painted or decorated chests) came out of the Ubriachi workshop. Chess sets, portable altars, and wedding finery including jewels could be packed in such coffers and they provided the bread and butter of luxury production. According to Robert Brun, ready-made coffers rivaled paintings in popularity at Avignon while that city remained the seat of the papal curia. Coffers were generally sewn into leather casings for transport from Venice then sold along with the goods they held.[84] The Ubriachi workshop also designed jewels, gem settings, small statuary of bone, ivory, and precious materials, and luxurious brooches and other expensive accessories.

Jewelry and other objects created on speculation of future buyers' taste sustained the workshop, that is, filled the gap between great commissions like those for the Certosa de Pavia and royal customers. Ready-made goods represented major outlays for raw materials and labor, but they were not as risk-laden ventures as great ecclesiastical or royal commissions and thus were reliable sources of income.[85] Smaller wares, the so-called minor arts produced in the workshop, were excellent advertising as well. Concealed in bales or under nondescript leather coverings, rich accessories and other fine goods were transported by mule or cart to the north, while lightweight enamels were sent through the courier system with coin and bankers' letters of exchange. The communication system that connected European bankers also brought luxuries to the affluent.[86]

Through an effective set of contacts with Florentine agents spread from Spain to Germany, Baldassare Ubriachi satisfied the demand for beautiful and costly things among the wealthiest consumers in Europe. He always seemed to work with other Florentines: "in Barcelona Ubriachi relied on [Simone d'Andrea] Bellandi, [a partner of Datini stationed in Barcelona] in Montpellier on the Saulli, in Pavia upon Francesco di Maso, in Venice upon Giannino di Jacopo Giovanni, maestro Giovanni de Jacopo Giovanni and Antonio Ubriachi, and in Paris, [less certainly] upon Giovanni Ubriachi."[87] Some time in the first decade of the fifteenth century Baldassare Ubriachi died while on his travels. He had gone south to Naples, another city with a royal court filled with wealthy consumers, making his circle around Europe's western realms more or less complete.

This brief sketch of his life contains some parallels with the earlier career of Benci del Buono Sacchetti. Both Florentines descended from magnate lineages; both lived the majority of their lives abroad and appear to have been content to do so. Both were active on the Venetian market and returned to

Florence sporadically. They succeeded as pioneers in establishing trading networks for precious materials, but less fortuitously both men encountered mixed results in their political dealings with their native Florence. Neither established permanent residence in Florence, although Benci's sons and grandsons entered civic careers there and Baldassare's descendants through his two older daughters did so as well. Both men experienced some setbacks brought on by political strife; the pattern of success abroad in trade despite political vicissitudes appears to repeat itself. Benci traded bullion to Venice; Baldassare Ubriachi's kin manufactured luxury goods at Venice that employed precious bullion, and that he took to customers abroad. Both men relied on an interrelated network of Florentine agents who lived abroad as they did. Both began life in business dealings with more pedestrian products: grain trades in Benci's case and cloth and wine for Baldassare; both ended their careers connected to Venetian financial markets and dealing in luxury products.

But the homely Benci of simple tastes was no match for the princely and titled Baldassare Ubriachi. Ubriachi's chapel at Santa Maria Novella dedicated to the Three Kings reflects the donor's pretensions; Richard Trexler has identified Baldassare himself as the model for the figure presented by the middle king on the lintel of the chapel. How readily this gentleman ascended to eminence! This was not a man of simple tastes: he was a titled nobleman, a cultured gentleman who owned a library, and an accomplished courtier at northern courts. As such he was appreciated for his taste, his knowledge, and the products he brought to his royal customers. Most likely he was recognized in court circles as an arbiter of fashion, and certainly few would have appeared at court equipped as well as he with the most modish and well-fashioned goods. In name and demeanor Baldassare stood for all that was lordly, so the Ubriachi workshop wisely relied on him, well into his old age, to present their luxuries at courts throughout Europe.

The fourteenth-century English court, where Baldassare enjoyed the patronage of Richard II until that unfortunate king's loss of his throne at the end of the century, provides a good example of why a trader would be tempted to enter the market for Italian-designed luxury goods. T. F. Reddaway has noted that fourteenth-century English royalty—the likes of the Black Prince, son of Edward III, for example—had little use for London's own resident goldsmiths. The prince "was frequently abroad and, particularly in his purchases of jewels, had no need of Londoners, little skilled in such matters. He dealt largely with Martin Parde of Pistoia in Italy and Hanekyn, Martin's goldsmith brother."[88] Reddaway's opinion must be taken with a grain of salt because London goldsmiths prospered in this century much like their Italian counterparts. Notwithstanding, Italian merchant bankers did fill some impressive orders at royal courts, and their wares did influence taste at court. The Black Prince gave the following New Year's gifts in one year: an enameled gold cup to his father; jeweled rings to family members; an enameled silver-gilt tabernacle to the bishop of Winchester; a gold mug to the lord of Castelnau of Burgundy; silver gilt cups to German knights who had brought the news of Edward III's election as emperor; and a comparable cup to the nurse who guarded the cradle of William, the prince's brother and godson.[89] These fine wares, probably the work of Hanekyn Parde or wares imported directly from Italy by the Parde brothers, stand in marked contrast to the consumer goods commissioned in London by an earlier English ruler, Henry III. Local London artists and craftsmen had produced Henry's luxuries almost exclusively.[90] Some time between the mid-thirteenth century and the fourteenth century, royal taste changed and the English turned to Italy for fashion. A continuously replenishing network of Italian merchant bankers active at English courts suggests that luxury trades flourished with the constant encouragement of Italian agents. Only death, in the case of Anne of Bohemia in 1396, or loss of a throne in 1399, as in the case of Richard II, prevented English royalty from further consumption of the favored Italian fashions. Purchases had been so constant and varied over the years that Henry of Lancaster, Richard's successor, immediately ordered an inventory of 359 pieces of fine jewelry and plate that the royal couple had collected prior to 1399.[91]

As a general rule long-distance Tuscan merchants and bankers, men like Francesco de Marco Datini of Prato, who more than once in his career took on heavy risk, relied on the tried and true trade in staples to make their fortunes. This course held less risk than the luxury trades, but even Datini, who over a lifetime rose from humble origins to become one of Italy's richest merchants, moved beyond the trade in wool and leather and entered the luxury market. By the end of his life he had become a member of the Florentine silk guild, in addition to the wool guild, where he had been a member from the early decades of his career. By the late years of the century he traded in brocades and velvets along with more common cloth, when he could find a market for better goods. Datini appreciated and could afford luxuries for himself, as the elaborate inventories of his personal possessions and homes prove. He was a patron of artists, albeit one who drove a hard bargain. Upon his death he not only left a fortune for good works to his hometown, he also left twelve great silver lamps to burn perpetually to adorn the *Capella del Sacro Cingolo* in the Cathedral of Florence. In his portrait as Prato's benefactor, created a half century after his death by Filippo Lippi, Datini was painted by the artist as an imposing figure in splendid dress: he is beautifully robed in red from head to toe and adorned with four large rings on his right hand.[92] Datini was a man well versed in the value of precious wares.[93]

But while Francesco de Marco Datini provisioned the wealthy papal court at Avignon and established branches at Valencia, Majorca, Genoa, and Barcelona, that is, at centers of wealth, he dealt by preference in spices, iron, wool, and slaves, all of them expensive but directed toward a broader market than jewels, wares of silver gilt, and brocades. Not until 1399 did Datini take the next logical step in a successful merchant career by opening his own bank. Once he had taken that step, however, he could be expected not only to loan money and negotiate bills of exchange, but to increase his position in bullion and gems as well.[94]

An inventory of Bonaccorso da Prato and Geri da Pistoia numbers among the most remarkable business records in the extant Datini collection.[95] As Renato Piattoli has remarked, the predominance of sacramental vessels marked this inventory as a collection of articles intended for the ecclesiastical market: great crosses, chandeliers, chalices, and richly trimmed miters. It required eight charters and the hands of three different scribes to record it all. Among the predictable sacramental goods were ready-made luxuries like gloves, buttons, and rings, augmented by a collection of precious and semi-precious stones that included rubies, emeralds, and a truly remarkable assortment of sapphires. The cups, forks, goblets, and *nave* (*nefs*, or silver containers for the table fashioned as ships, sometimes used for utensils or for salt) that appeared in the inventory could furnish as many stately homes as the corresponding sacramental vessels could furnish great churches. The inventory contained even more rich items strictly for personal use, and sometimes weights were added to the descriptions, as well as a value assigned in Florentine currency. Articles were embellished—intaglia or inlay, *dorato* or gilded silver—and described in detail: "XXXIIII taze dorate et lavorate et vare" (thirty-four various gilded and decorated cups).[96] The fourteenth-century transformation of goldsmiths' production to suit new market preferences is evident here: the old market for ecclesiastical goods remained strong at Avignon but it was augmented through the inclusion of ready-made personal luxuries, both apparel and domestic objects.

Despite his inclination to follow a safe route by trading in staples, Datini was well placed to serve as purveyor of luxuries to the wealthy because he was so thoroughly established in the Avignon market. Nevertheless, luxuries remained a high-risk venture that tied up capital in a manner clearly repugnant to Datini, and as he knew well, some among his associates had met failure in the luxury trades. Neither the affability of Benci del Buono nor the princely mien of Baldassare Ubriachi aided Datini in his efforts to become a market-maker in the luxury trades; he lacked easy manners, and courtliness was, apparently, beyond him. Despite the increasing luxury of his own appointments in Prato, he was too concerned with the bottom line to spend his days languidly chatting with wealthy patrons, tempting them to spend their wealth.[97]

Leaving sales to others, Datini purchased luxury goods for his company, and artists felt his sting the most when he specified fine gold (*oro fine)* or a silvered casing, a bit of gilt here and there, and a well-drawn figure (*boune fighure*) in a painting, all for a cheap price (*di piccollo pregio*). Clearly he understood the taste of the buying public but resented the expense of securing objects to suit it.[98] Six and one half florins as the top price for a picture that was "the most beautiful picture obtainable" were Datini's stated terms when buying from one artist in 1373. His associate Boninsegna di Matteo told agents somewhat later to buy only when a painter needed money so that the firm could get the best price.[99] The artist's rendering, even when fine, was not good enough for the Datini company; paintings needed a splash of gold or silver or ultramarine blue. So the market for the ready-made reached into the artist's studio by way of a hard-bargaining middleman; Datini and his company bought on speculation based on what they knew about customer preference even if to the point of garishness.

Datini's partners in Avignon, Barcelona, and other great cities appear to have been better suited to approaching affluent customers than was Datini himself, so he left the job of presenting fine wares to his smooth-talking agents. Agents on site promoting sales of luxuries allowed Datini to be a sedentary, if never silent, partner dealing with supply.[100] From correspondence and inventories it is evident that in entering the luxury market Datini dealt with a sensitive consumer market for high-priced goods, a market requiring precise knowledge of personal preference and a customer's ability to pay. Datini understood that customers needed to know the provenance of goods since they trusted established Italian manufactures and tended to purchase according to locale and known manufacturers.[101] Discerning consumer taste for luxury goods in foreign capitals was a more sensitive task for Datini's agents than the earlier supplying of West Balkan iron to the forges of Spain. So Datini's agents dealt with wealthy buyers, and Datini wisely limited himself to the acquisition of ready-made "art" and luxury goods when he was certain of customer preference.

Consequences

Italian merchants and bankers erected both an import and a distribution system for the luxury trades over the course of the century. This did not result in a sudden reorientation in markets: in the case of Venice merchants merely augmented their pepper and spice trade with an increasing array of luxury wares, some imported and some manufactured locally; apparel and exotic, expensive accessories figured importantly on this list. Francesco di Balduccio Pegolotti's famous list of "spices" included gold and gold leaf as well as turquoises, coral, pearls, and ivory in the form of elephant tusks.[102] Skeptics have challenged Marco Polo's *Travels*, but his will was authentic enough, and his wife and three daughters inherited from Polo enough by way of velvets, silks, and fine accessories to fill a substantial shop.[103] As his critics have alleged, every bit of the expensive exotica inventoried in his will could be found in the city of Venice or in the Levantine ports with which Venetians traded regularly.

But for all their grandeur, the manufacture and presentation of luxuries remained high-risk ventures. Even if transport systems grew safer, market conditions for precious materials remained uncertain. Lest Benci del Buono, Baldassare Ubriachi, and Francesco de Marco Datini make the luxury trades appear the means for easy gain, the Venetian merchant banker Giovanni Stornado, who had followed the silver trade and whose bank failed in the 1340s, warrants mention. Stornado died in 1347 shortly after making a will. His estate for his underage heirs lay in the hands of the *procuratori de San Marco*, who, along with four of Giovanni's own kin, were to speculate in silver with an inheritance for Giovanni's young sons. Over three years these agents were to buy silver within two months of the time when galleys left Venice, and sell that silver a month before the last galley departed the following year. Timing the market would presumably allow them to buy cheap and sell dear, and Stornado hoped for a 6 percent return on this speculation. He also listed terms if 6 percent were not obtained (this was routine practice in the bullion and luxury trades where minimum values were set as a matter of course). Stornado had apparently overestimated the demand for silver. The *procuratori* were unable to obtain his commission and actually lost money on this speculation.[104] Earlier in his career Stornado had turned to the Council of Ten to help him collect what he was owed by Jacopo Quirino, whose investments in pepper had been financed by Stornado, but failed.[105] The Quirini as well as Marcus Stornado had trading interests at Ragusa, and apparently through investing in the high end of the Venetian market, that is, in imports of pepper and silver, they prospered. But Giovanni Stornado's career serves as an instructive example of how a daring and talented family of traders in bullion might still get the equation wrong.

Taking a glimpse at fifteenth-century market conditions for the luxury trades, some anecdotal evidence suggests that bad news lay ahead. In 1456 Pigello Portinari, a brilliant banker who operated out of Milan, encountered such a significant narrowing of the market for his luxury goods that he ultimately catered to a single client, the Lord Duke and his family. According to Raymond de Roover's account, outside the court and court circle, there was little if any demand for luxury goods. When queried about selling brocaded silk cloth at Milan, Portinari replied that the merchandise would find no buyers there, "except for the Duchess, who was very particular and purchased only what appealed to her taste."[106] Narrowing the luxury market so drastically, if even for a brief time, placed Portinari's firm at the whim of too small a customer base, in contrast to earlier luxury markets in their expansive phase.

Widening and deepening markets in the process of incorporating new custom-ers were far more attractive to prudent traders.[107]

In the mid-fifteenth century risks in trading precious wares that had become popular in the previous century were less worth taking, if the career of Andrea Barbarigo is any indication. In his successful career as an overseas merchant, Barbarigo invested only sporadically in luxury wares except, of course, for the mainstay of his trade, Levantine pepper, for which the market was steady. He traded some in cloth where most of the English cloth he pur-chased was obtained through Bruges. In turn, he sent Bruges his pepper and spices from the East, since it was the best market for the distribution of spices in the north. Outside of his high-value, small bulk trade in pepper and spices, Barbarigo favored goods for the general consumer rather than high-end luxu-ries for the affluent. For example, in 1431 he purchased tinware and pewter from England. He intended the pewter for the "local" market, by which he meant, apparently, the *inter-culfum* or Adriatic region. He sold his pewter in Francaville in Apulia, Ferrara, and Verona.[108] Along with pepper, luxury items occasionally found a place in his business: accompanying Barbarigo's six bales of pepper traveling north by galley in 1430 were "glittering jewels," which came in handy for bribing the Castilian fleet that patrolled local waters. Frederic C. Lane speculated that these jewels might have been nothing more than glass, but the pepper traveled through safely to Bruges because these "jewels" were available for bribes when the Catalans boarded.[109] Still, such bribery was a long stretch from pursuing trade in luxury goods, even if Barbarigo's galley crew wisely stocked glittering jewels for buying their passage through troubled waters.

Like Benci del Buono and Baldassare Ubriachi, Andrea Barbarigo built his family's fortunes, but he did not always play a relatively safe game of trade in everyday goods. At least twice he was tempted into the luxury markets. He purchased gold thread on the market in Constantinople and transported it to Venice. This was very likely gold thread of excellent quality since Constantino-ple was known for fine production. In 1432 Barbarigo was determined to pur-chase twenty English cloths of the sort that sold well in Syria. He would have to borrow for this investment and he financed the transactions in part by remitting bills of exchange and in part by sending the gold thread he had pur-chased at Constantinople overland.[110] Again, in 1438, he tried to ship gold thread from Constantinople overland, but, as Lane notes, "The market for gold thread was a very tender one, according to Andrea's references to the wide price fluctuations produced by small shipments."[111] Both cheaper "Lucca" gold thread and "Venice" gold thread sold well in the north, and while these may have been inferior to Barbarigo's genuine Constantinople gold thread, it is doubtful that customers really cared very much (see Chapter 5). Neither the gold thread nor a piece of fine silk he had obtained in Spain years before, and had been unable to sell, were worth the risk of heavy investment. Aside from pepper, Barbarigo returned to his trade in less precious, and less risky, wares.

In general Andrea Barbarigo espoused the view that silver was best employed as a means of exchange rather than a medium for luxury production. He often sent silver in the form of coin to Levantine ports in payment for the wares he imported to Venice for shipment to the north; at least twice he purchased silver bullion in bars, which he used in exchange for grain and hides.[112] Andrea's sons Nicolò and Alvise exported silver from Venice as well: "For some years their commercial operations were limited to exporting wares and above all silver from Venice to North Africa and exchanging most of it there for gold," Lane noted.[113] But Barbarigo and his sons also acquired valuables for themselves along the way; precious silver, gold, and jewels were components of their private fortunes. Much later, in 1538, the reckoning of the estate of Andrea's grandson Antonio Barbarigo amounted to somewhat over 5,000 ducats in government bonds, over 8,000 ducats in real estate, but almost 2,000 ducats in jewels, furnishings, and cash.[114] Movable goods acquired over three generations had become a repository of wealth and a component of the family's estate.

Antonio Barbarigo's jewels, cash, and furnishings represented well over a century of collecting for this affluent Venetian family, and this asset category of "movable goods" provides an indication of how wealthy families valued accumulated precious wares obtained through purchase and preservation.[115] A preference for investing at least a portion of the family fortune in luxury goods was, apparently, even more noteworthy at Florence. The fifteenth-century Pucci family estate listed wardrobes of eleven members of the family worth almost 40 percent of the total of inventoried family property.[116] Traders in luxuries dealt in consumables that laws classified as movable goods. If fabric, even fabric described as worn or tattered, was routinely inventoried, gems, ivory, silver, and gold were unlikely to escape the eye of a vigilant notary recording family assets. By the fifteenth century jewels, gold, and silver were common holdings among the affluent.

Although fifteenth-century merchants accrued luxuries for themselves and their heirs over the course of the century, their business activities often contrasted with the eager pursuit of the luxury trades evident earlier. The cumulative effect of generations of affluent consumers preserving their valuables and passing them on to heirs, of estates of the wealthy funneling into a few hands due to the Black Plague and its frequent return, may have discouraged those with inherited wealth from making major new purchases of luxury goods. Tastes changed, too. People became interested in new categories of goods like books and paintings, and a person might now look modish in high-quality but unadorned black cloth instead of the more extravagant tastes of earlier years. Consumers were increasingly prone to save their finery and recycle it into new fashions, so fully furnished palaces and inherited articles of apparel likely meant dampened demand. Local goldsmiths were all too willing to melt down plate metals and create new fabricated articles for use or wear when called upon to do so by their wealthy customers. The wealthy willed their clothes, jewels, silver, and gold, so luxury goods represented an increasingly important and recognized category of wealth and capital accumulation as it mounted up in family coffers.[117] Closeting away luxuries may have become as appealing as wearing wealth about the person once was. Madonna Margherita's vast collection of goods, which were too numerous in regard to belts, cups, plates, and buttons for an individual's or even a family's consumption, suggests that the most tempting luxuries of one generation could in time also lose their appeal. Craftsmen developed merchandizing expertise to adapt to changing tastes, but an increasingly important component of their business lay in melting down or refashioning the luxury items entrusted to them by the wealthy, as was the case with Madonna Margherita's treasures.[118] Luxuries had not lost their cachet, but even if luxuries remained attractive holdings this did not necessarily mean that the production and presentation of more editions of fourteenth-century fashion goods represented the growth opportunity they once had.

Changing tastes is another theme that runs through this study—that a fifteenth-century aesthetic revolution reformed market preferences. Michael Baxandall, echoed by Richard Goldthwaite, argues for a transformed aesthetic that affected luxury markets in decisive ways in the fifteenth century. Baxandall writes of a general shift away from gilt splendor as the result of a pervasive and complex change in taste that affected what people would buy in the market. According to Baxandall, the "conspicuous consumption of gold and ultramarine became less important and its place was filled by the conspicuous consumption of something else—skill." Markets were transformed because as always they relied on canons of taste. Within this new aesthetic there was less of a place for middlemen like the Florentines of Venice selling silver belts, or Baldassare Ubriachi with his gilded ivory, or Francesco de Marco Datini, who insisted on gilt and ultramarine "everywhere."[119]

Perhaps the most elusive matter of all is the question of bullion consumed in fabricated wares during the bullion famine that began in the 1390s. Conditions for mints that had felt this initial sting ameliorated somewhat after the turn of the fifteenth century, but the silver famine returned by mid-century. There are more than enough factors to account adequately for the onset of a late medieval silver famine: working out of mines, loss through use, export of silver to the Levant, the ascendancy of gold currency, and greater reliance on paper in exchange, among others. Ever since John Day posited a bullion famine for the late medieval era scholars have seen some role for consumption as a factor in creating shortages of bullion, but the general run of scholarly opinion suggests that royalty and high nobility amassed enormous collections of plate that cut significantly into supplies of precious metals, especially gold, a form of hoarding that could affect royal mints. For example, Peter Spufford cites in evidence Arnoul Braque, who gave up his position as head of the Paris mint in 1397, declaring that there was no gold because princes of the blood had turned it all into plate.[120]

The famine in silver was of course a different issue, although it was a particularly severe problem since it was felt throughout Europe and affected both royal and urban mints. In England Edward I (1272–1307) had been able to remint some one hundred tons of silver in his total recoinage, but Henry IV, in his similar effort in 1412–14, was able to recoin only two tons.[121] Italy's mints were hard hit, and some simply ceased minting silver coins in the 1390s altogether, with Genoa and Florence hit particularly hard. Would the consumption of silver by ordinary citizens cut into silver supplies and add to the silver famine in Italian towns? This is a matter that has received less attention from monetary historians and there are a number of uncertainties that make it difficult to provide definitive answers. *Avoirdupois* pounds and ounces were measurements specified in numerous sales agreements when accessories of silver were sold to the public in the fourteenth century. These were rough and untrustworthy measures of the fineness of silver bullion. At least some silver in private collections was of this unknown fineness and probably inferior to the standard of mints. Of course any silver in private hands could be melted down and refined. To test fineness in silver cupellation of a portion of that silver (smelting a bit of it under precise conditions), had to be performed.[122] This test was not appropriate for worked, ready-made silver and silver gilt goods. Reliable hallmarks from reputable goldsmiths did guarantee fineness when they appeared on goods, but imported silver did not always have them.[123] Goldsmiths and merchant bankers openly acknowledged that lesser grades of silver were used in fashion goods.[124] Society at large condoned this since alloy with lead or another base metal was often necessary to provide the tensile strength to hold shape and wear durably.

Pricing structures for precious goods also obscured the fineness of bullion. A silver belt that cost thirty ducats was traded not for its exchange value of fine silver to gold, but with the cost of workmanship (generally 20 to 30 percent) with, possibly, a further retail markup to what the luxury market would bear, factored into the price. Moreover, gilding and comparable techniques altered perceptions of value, as they intended to do. Luxury accessories were sold at steep prices and in round numbers, pricing practices that tend to be found at the high end of markets and favor the seller. When one's jeweler or merchant banker was deemed a gentleman, thus honorable and beyond reproach as Benedetto Cotrugli suggested he should be, it further strengthened the retailer's advantage over the terms of a sale.[125] As a result of these factors the balance of power between retailer and consumer might easily tip to the retailer. It is possible that whenever a ready-made accessory caught the eye of the consumer the retailer gained an advantage: as purveyor he might simply demand on the spot a price he thought he could extract, relying on his quick estimate of a customer's degree of interest. This was not a novel marketing strategy by any means but it covered more transactions and increasingly involved a variety of high-priced ready-made objects. A customer could gaze upon and heft a belt, but without precise information about the precious bullion contained in it, information only available by using the precise scales, touchstones, and cupellation processes authorized by mints, or through reference to trusted hallmarks, a customer was left in the dark. A reckoning occurred later when the object was melted down to recover its value, or resold to a goldsmith or banker, that is, to a member of Sir Stanley Jevons's aptly termed "calculation community." A goldsmith or banker could assess an object's value precisely because it was his business.

But who is to say the customer did not receive good value in the transaction? The very idea of purchasing accessories of silver, gilded silver, or jewels lay in anticipation of making an impression on others. If that occurred, a consumer should be satisfied—up to a point. In the fourteenth century consumers still put faith in the possibility that the silver and gold in their wardrobes and on their tables were recoverable. Like kings and the high nobility, citizens of cities put some faith in their precious goods as a hoard against hard times, not just fashion, and in an age of plague, war, economic dislocation, and population retraction, it was prudent to diversify private holdings, sequestering away some wealth in precious objects. Any time customers made purchases of goods fabricated from precious metals they had to consider whether this investment was capable of future recovery. That they willed these possessions, traded them, pawned them, and used them in lieu of coin for payments all argue for the expectation that precious wares would maintain some degree of their inherent value and some liquidity. Persons wealthy enough to purchase luxuries had to assess a number of factors to avoid being duped, that is, they needed to ensure that their precious wares were investments as well as luxury goods that enhanced their appearance.

More was at stake than an individual bewildered about the precise value of his accumulated plate. One of the tasks of late medieval town governments in Italy was to make accurate estimates of private fortunes so that forced loans, the preferable means for raising revenue among the affluent, could be levied. As greater portions of estates were held in purchased or inherited luxury goods, this task became more difficult. Thus governmental responses to hoarding by way of amassing luxury goods, especially those made of silver, jewels, and gold, offer some insight into luxury consumption among townspeople and its effect on economic life and values. Here some evidence suggests that individuals holding stores of wealth in goods cut into available supplies of bullion that would otherwise flow to urban mints; this was a genuine problem for Venice with its disastrously expensive fourteenth-century wars. An official estimate of private fortunes held by both wealthy patrician and nonpatrician families (the *estimo*) was mandated in order to allocate forced loans or *prestiti*.[126] Venetian authorities required a statement about the worth of precious goods in these returns, but if the *estimo* permitted underestimation of fortunes generally, here the opportunity for misrepresentation of wealth was capacious. Hallmarks should have represented a reliable standard of value for precious household goods, but not all luxury wares owned in Venice bore hallmarks. There was room for honest confusion on the value of private holdings in goods and likely a tendency for citizens to overestimate the worth of their goods, given all the factors that had entered into their purchase and preservation. The best that might be expected was that an individual or a family could provide an estimate of their major dress accessories or vessels by weight, description, and perhaps hallmark. Not all individuals or families could or did provide adequate estimates, nor did civic officials enter homes and paw through a wealthy family's possessions to obtain the necessary information.

Venetian officials did recognize that citizens possessed collections of plate of substantial worth, however. For the dire monetary emergency in 1379 brought on by the War of Chioggia, Venetian mint masters called in private collections of plate on a voluntary basis. This was very likely a tacit admission that the extent of private plate was known to exceed what had been learned from the earlier *estimo*. In 1379 the mint merely directed citizens to turn in their silver goods, but the difficulty of assessing the silver in luxury objects on this occasion proved great, demonstrating what a prudent policy it had been to let the precise extent of private holdings in bullion lie unexamined in the past. That same year, special officers were enlisted to estimate the value of surrendered plate; still, mint officials ran the risk of insulting worthy citizens in giving their estimates of value that were more accurate than the opinions of owners. In addition the initiative of 1379 required that imported silver be sent to the mint, but here as well serious difficulties in collecting silver and establishing its value arose. This attempt to turn luxury objects back into bullion and coin was not repeated once the emergency was over, suggesting that the inherent difficulty of the project was recognized.

Florence refused to even estimate the value of privately held plate when assessors catalogued citizens' wealth for the Catasto of 1427. The clear omission of this category of wealth from the estimates of private fortunes seems all the more remarkable because fifteenth-century Florentines have been credited with a significantly more opulent lifestyle and finer luxurious possessions than their counterparts in earlier times. As Giovanni Rucellai boasted, "Neither the city nor the countryside ever had such an abundance of household goods: there are plenty of tapestries and materials to cover chairs and chests, and more female servants than ever before. The production of textiles has never been greater, nor have such precious silk clothes luxuriously adorned with golden embroideries ever been made."[127] Apparently the difficulty of making adequate estimates of this new kind of wealth outran the capacities of the most determined Florentine civic authorities. This is not an indication, however, that they were unaware of the valuable plate held in private hands.

Familial wealth held as precious goods was in a certain sense condoned by city-state governments when they shied away from the daunting task of estimating its true value or failed to call in plate to answer the increasing need for silver in bullion famine years. Inventories, the best guides to stores of private wealth, described precious wares in detail far more often than they provided a putative market value; so even here doubts arose over how much wealth individuals or families owned. With this significant category of private wealth left uncounted, the extent of privately held fortunes could not be assessed easily or accurately. Luxury goods became an increasingly mysterious category of wealth and as a result there was much greater room for pretense in urban society. Display of inherited and purchased luxury goods was a significant marker of status, but the messages about wealth that such goods provided were anything but clear. Was that vessel fine silver or silver of lesser quality? Could that brooch or belt be genuine gold or was it merely gilded silver? And in the last analysis perhaps this uncertainty was significant for the economy as well. Precious wares allowed a person to pretend, even to dissemble, and the extent of privately held wealth was increasingly open to miscalculation, a mystery to all but one's closest associates.

In regard to the bullion famine of the 1390s, especially for the towns of northern Italy, it appears that one must proceed on the assumption that mints went undersupplied despite genuine, if less than perfectly clear, information about the bullion that sat in local hands. It seems reasonable to assume that mints knew this wealth existed and could ameliorate communal shortages, yet plate was not tapped except in the instance noted above at Venice, insofar as the research for this study indicates. Would privately held bullion have made a difference for the mints of northern Italy and could it have ameliorated shortages? Certainly it would have made a great deal of difference in Florence, where minting silver coin ceased completely in 1393. Milan felt serious shortages at its mint; it was so difficult to pay bank depositors cash in Genoa that the city government authorized bankers to make a 4 percent charge on withdrawals in cash, and individuals could withdraw only fifty florins of coin in any one day.[128] In these instances governing councils and officers of urban mints appear to have been content to ignore currency needs. In Carlo Cipolla's words regarding Florence, "the relative value of the gold florin and the local silver currency was not one of interest only to the bankers and a few big merchants. It was, on the contrary, a question of preeminent general interest with all the potential of causing widespread tension and unrest," at least when the florin was strong and silver currency very weak.[129] Consumption of bullion was clearly understood to be a form of hoarding, but it was, apparently, condoned hoarding in Italian towns where communal governments possessed the authority to call bullion in and did not do so. In the 1390s priorities at the mint favored affluent collectors and governments left silver held as consumable goods—silver that might have alleviated the silver bullion famine—in private hands. This silver was much less likely to drain toward the Levant than coined silver or silver in ingots, so in a sense it functioned as a cushion against future needs. But this does not change the fact that late fourteenth-century urban economies condoned more elitest uses for that scarce resource. It is possible to speculate that in the "fat years" of high urban wage earning in the latter half of the century less pressure had fallen on mints to create a sound silver currency, but that hardly explains the dearth in silver that led to small mint runs or no minting of silver coin at all in the 1390s.

There is greater certainty that economic priorities favoring the most affluent had come to the fore in towns where fashion dictated that silver bullion be consumed and worn, rather than coined. The robust market for ready-made luxuries reflected the designs of Italy's most wealthy and powerful urban families as they moved away from traditional communal priorities and toward economic values more consonant with seigneurial rule. While religious and political upheavals of the fourteenth century accurately identified luxury and ostentation as harmful to the polity and inimical to the common good, popular movements were unable to reverse this pervasive trend among rich consumers.

Hypothetically, if at least a thousand families in Florence possessed five pounds of silver in plate—a modest figure by any standard given the consumption of the day—there would have been at least 5,000 pounds of precious metal, predominantly silver, in private hands in this city alone.[130] This would have helped out at the local mint: in 1391 Florence, which minted coin in half year cycles, produced at its peak 2,880 pounds of silver coin in one semester; the semesters preceding and following saw minting of only 136 pounds and 72 pounds of silver, respectively. These figures represent the cycle of surfeit and dearth that characterized urban minting in the later Middle Ages. By contrast there had been an annual production of 18,617 pounds of (silver) *grossi* minted in 1350–51, then 1,313 pounds of silver minted into *grossi* two years later.[131] The relative size of coinages had decreased precipitously by the end of the century, so much so that 5,000 pounds of bullion, predominantly silver, would have made a difference.

The features of a market driven by fashion emerged simultaneously, with the century providing a reasonably coherent time frame for those changes. Stella Mary Newton's pinpointed date of 1340 for the coincident emergence of fashion all over western Europe is probably too abrupt an advent; Braudel's less specific mid-century mark does find the salient features of a retail market for ready-made goods with heightened consumer interest driving demand largely in place. At Venice milestones in this market occurred in 1325 and 1331, when goldsmiths petitioned for retail space at the Rialto in order to compete with bankers. Apparently by then Venetian goldsmiths were sufficiently adept at creating ready-made luxury goods that they saw real benefit in displaying wares to the buying public in this most excellent location.[132]

Also by this time the diaspora of talented artisans from Lucca and Siena was making a substantial contribution to the quality and variety of precious goods available in market towns throughout northern Italy and beyond. Later in the century, by the 1370s at least, significant stores of wealth lay in private hands in the form of precious goods so that the wills of the affluent became unwieldy with the enumeration of hoarded luxury objects. In 1379, Venetian authorities acknowledged this wealth through an experimental program to draw on it to finance war with Genoa, but the program was not a success that bore repeating. By 1394, a market open to all suppliers of precious goods had come into existence at San Marco and San Polo in Venice, while at the same time severe bullion famine had set in in the rest of northern Italy and beyond. In city-states that minted silver coins the silver famine might have been ameliorated by drawing on private stores of wealth in the form of plate, but this did not happen.

Francesco Petrarch (1304–74) in *De remediis utriusque fortune* understood the embellished, *ornatu*, to be "knowledge of things and the improvement of moral conduct," rather than the display of precious wares and rich color. He expressed what would become a more acceptable aesthetic once the fourteenth-century riot in bright colors, massive ornament, and gilt had played itself out.[133] Still, Leon Battista Alberti (1404–72) argued many decades later that rich fabrics and gold actually increased the dignity and the pious mien of a man at prayer, so a good man's luxurious appearance remained well regarded, a worthy goal for affluent citizens. Over time Alberti's traditional aesthetic, grounded as it was in fourteenth-century taste and values, lessened its hold as Petrarch's prophetic and sparer aesthetic gained ground. Consumer preferences for luxuries would prove themselves to be as amenable to transformation as other cultural preferences that affected people's choices in the marketplace.[134]

Chapter 8
Conclusion

Although there was little that was genuinely new in the fourteenth century when fashion began to affect consumer preferences and influence demand, fashion was a new economic phenomenon and thus uncharted territory, and there was no template for retailers, merchant bankers, luxury tradesmen, or for that matter urban customers to use for predicting how fashion would affect markets and influence daily life. John Day has noted that "by mid-fourteenth century, merchant capitalism had already perfected the instruments of economic power and business organization that were to serve it for the next four hundred years: foreign exchange, deposit banking, risk insurance, public finance, international trading companies, commercial bookkeeping."[1] Fashion was merely a late addition to the fundamental features of early capitalist development. Still, those who sold in luxury markets or followed fashion by purchasing fine goods that enhanced their prestige soon discovered that fashion was baffling and confusing—a slippery business. Fashion held appeal for retailers and consumers alike but it was just as likely to get out of hand as serve the purposes intended by its trendsetters.

There was a template for social values consonant with purchasing, displaying, and wearing fine luxury wares, one that was firmly grounded in traditional notions of hierarchy and entitlement. These values in turn informed the sumptuary laws written for the towns of northern Italy. Class was a negligible factor in the earliest urban laws, but hierarchical notions about age and gender played significant roles in creating a taxonomy for what was purchased, worn, and consumed, or how celebrations were conducted in towns. An imagined and highly idealized pyramid of consuming behaviors figured among utopian ideals in medieval times, and Franciscan preacher, lawmaker, and pater familias alike regarded markets as dangerous when they tempted townspeople to consume above their allotted place. If not amenable to promptings of Christian conscience, then ostentation of a scandalous nature was to be curbed by the imposition of laws that were directed toward the goal of reestablishing a seemly order.[2] Nevertheless, wise, grave leaders saw a role for fine wares for townsmen of means like themselves, since luxuries helped men dress for success and move with confidence within wider circles of power and influence. This constituted a more elitist use of materials like silver; still, those who dressed for success justified their new consumption patterns as bestowing fame and fortune on the entire community. Affluent townsmen encountered enhanced opportunities for "leveling upward" through fine dress, especially when traveling abroad, or when royalty, the nobly born, or their agents traveled to Italy with shopping on their minds. Fine clothes created occasions for pleasant exchange and mutual admiration whenever leading citizens of towns mixed with Europe's richest and most powerful personages. Dressed to the hilt, as the saying goes, townsmen promoted fine fashions and supplied the materials for dressing well to others.

Fine clothes bestowed another, more elusive, benefit on leading citizens. Dressing richly and fashionably allowed men to exhibit themselves as peers of rich and powerful: men who were active at court, bore grand titles, held high office, and enjoyed great landed estates. There was every reason for affluent citizens of city-states to forward a claim to membership in exclusive circles. It was commensurate with their recently won honors and wealth, and town leaders were, in any event, swiftly undergoing their own transformation toward greater seigneurial weight within their respective communes. Arguably early aspirations toward such authority were better expressed through silent acts of dress rather than through bold verbal flourishes. Despite this, in busy Italian marketplaces, seigneurial ambitions, high office, or birth did not deter men from participating in commerce. Fashion goods demonstrated to all why this was proper and beneficial. Noble and non-noble businessmen and bankers mingled together and promoted retail trades. Men of fortune celebrated in mutual accord and joined together in the cult of the Magi, appearing confidently and unabashedly dressed as wealthy kings bearing rich gifts for the Christ Child. Fine clothes created a new, more exalted social coterie out of well-turned-out and fashionable men. Italians belonged to that circle by right of affluence and their carefully cultivated taste for rich goods.

A new set of conditions prevailed where fashion took hold in towns. When fashionable women of wealthy families encroached on men's prerogatives, it opened the door for others to experiment, to try their hand at attracting attention in public places. This was certainly the case with household servants who used cast-offs to construct their own fashionable ensembles. Affluent women had discovered how to create new fashions at home with their own needle skills; there was no reason why less affluent people could not do the same. Markets accommodated deepening demand for apparel by producing fashion goods in less expensive editions, secondhand markets did brisk business, and, perhaps most important, innovation itself became an increasingly consequential component of dress. At the Festival of the Twelve Maries, all of Venice turned out to celebrate, not just the most affluent. If the open houses held by great families were exclusive affairs, new styles could still be presented by the less affluent outside in the streets and on the canals. In Florence, fines were collected from women who could afford to wear only plain wool dresses, dresses they had sewn into parti-colored patterns or embroidered with figures.[3] Bold two-color displays or bodices covered with figures and exotic symbols comprised the offense against sumptuary laws, not the high cost of the wool dresses. Fashion had become an urban pursuit with any number of players, any of whom could make fashion statements using less than opulent materials. Labor-intensive trims like glass beads substituted for rich materials and achieved eye-catching effects; what looked like gold was often gilt. Fashion was a new pastime with a widening circle of participants, and as such it was increasingly difficult to regulate. New ideas fed fashion: the path of adoption for new styles would continue to be crucial and reliant upon adoption by an acknowledged urban elite, but almost anyone could introduce a new visual idea into the mix and draw attention from the crowd. There was always a chance of presenting a daring new idea that would catch on.

Even a drab wardrobe could be transformed by means other than a fat pocketbook. Experimentation and a discerning eye for novel effects flourished. An urge to participate—what economic behaviorists today refer to as a negative averse response—animated sensibilities.[4] Urban lives flourished in a perpetual present, with fashion a vital, if fleeting, part of that moment; fear of being left out provided a powerful incentive for dressing up and consuming. It was not so much a question of keeping up with one's wealthy neighbors, that is, envy, that drove fashion, but rather the fear of exclusion from the suddenly great matter of seeing and being seen. Affluent women led the way by showing others how to direct attention toward themselves and away from their fashionably and richly dressed fathers, husbands, and sons. The boldest women wore provocative symbols on their clothes and embroidered playful designs, borders, and trims on their robes, sometimes in parody of others. It became apparent that the fashion game was open to all who had the temerity to try something new. Outside sumptuary law (which urban people seemed to enjoy breaking), there was little reason not to join the fashion parade.

So while well-dressed leaders of cities ascended toward more exalted circles of power and influence abroad, at home, other townspeople broke into the now more riveting social scene by means of fashion. The increasing pace of fashion following fashion thwarted attempts at control because challenges to order and decorum were mounted from just about every quarter of the town. People seemed to delight in flaunting novel effects before the eyes of crowds in the streets; indeed, crowds were the catalyst for the effervescent mix of market and nonmarket stimuli that encouraged the extreme dressing so decried in sermons and sumptuary laws. Yet fashion was a genuinely medieval phenomenon because it revealed a corporate spirit: it relied on a strong impulse to see and be seen by one's neighbors. Fashion expressed a new way to belong in urban settings. A startling new effect was only valued when it attracted an audience and imitators.

Scholars label the fourteenth century as a threshold of sorts out of a stable, ordered medieval world into the energetic early Renaissance with its strong impetus for dynamic growth, yet there is little within this interpretive construct to help explain the effects of fourteenth-century fashion and the acceleration of economic exchange that attended it. From the evidence of this study of fourteenth-century town life in Italy, Burckhardtian individualism was not the inspiration for fourteenth-century people who chased headlong after fashion.[5] Rather, group values and catching the community's attention and interest created the milieu for fashion's spread; the impulse to join in fashion and impress one's neighbors was corporate in nature, a sign that fashion remained consonant with an essentially medieval set of values. The pleasure of joining in lay behind the more playful components of fashion, and impressing the neighborhood with one's luxurious dress was not merely a haughty assertion of personal superiority. It was a declaration about the consequence and wealth of the entire community; it broadcast to all: "Look what we have become—we are princes in our own right."

Yet it was Burckhardtian individualism that became the historical cornerstone of Werner Sombart's popular economic explanation of the advent of fashion in the Western world.[6] He regarded fashion as a bourgeois replica of more illustrious courtly style, and most subsequent explanations follow him in this line of reasoning. Styles of the courts trickle down to the town, creating fashions that rely on individuals' envy of social superiors; this supplies motive for adopting fashion. For Sombart styles authorized by royal courts were inspired by women's taste, and here as well Sombart followed Burckhardt closely. The new interest in dress and culture was a feminized taste and it required considerable time for fashion to affect men's taste and behavior. Baldassare Castiglione's *Il libro de cortegiano* (1528), cast a long shadow over this opinion as well, although his commentary relates more properly to its own early sixteenth-century context than to the manners and taste of the fourteenth century when fashions first caught on.[7]

This early fourteenth-century fashion was a social pastime that encouraged spending and infected collectivities; as such, it was a broader social phenomenon than court style. To become a force driving consumption fashion required complex urban environments in which to thrive and grow. The idea of hierarchy that informed early fashion did not dwell on the social distance between court personages and affluent townspeople—long-distance merchants and noble customers mingled together, submerging their differences, and they were more likely to exchange ideas about dress than arrange themselves by rank based on envy. In towns following after fashion, infected crowds, who were given to sudden infatuations and town fashions, gathered in a broad spectrum of visual ideas, with courtly style merely one influence among many. Style remained a prerogative of royal courts where there were ample resources to support its heavy expenditures. Indeed, courtly style sometimes accepted ideas from fashions popular in towns, which of course was actively encouraged by long-distance merchants. At court there were powerful pressures to stamp culture with the style of the ruler; urban fashions were less easily controlled by any power. They appealed to crowds, to seeing and being seen, and townspeople followed fashion so as not to be left out. A style once favored at court like the long, sinuous belt displayed on the effigy of Queen Berengaria (d. 1230) would not wait a good century to infect fashionable taste in Italian towns. Rather, the belt interpreted in precious metal figured as part of a repertoire of ideas from which medieval dress ensembles were traditionally created. That it was appropriate to the costume of the day, handsome, dramatic, and enhancing, that goldsmiths knew how to manufacture and market it, all figured in its adoption by the fashionable in the fourteenth century. On balance, fourteenth-century fashion goods were not particularly novel, although clever details might make them suddenly conspicuous and therefore popular. As it happened fashion turned playful at the least excuse while court style was construed as a solemn exhibition of power and authority. Joining the fashion parade was remarkably easy for wives, children, and even the servants of fashionable men, hence its rapid spread and the imposition of the restraints in sumptuary law. Tradesmen encouraged the spread of fashion by making cheaper versions of fashion goods. Fashion was dynamic, whereas style was intended to move at a stately pace or even remain static.

Retail markets prospered where fashion reigned, and market players grew rich on the luxury trades. Over the century, textiles increased in variety and the market for luxury cloth diversified and deepened. As Luca Mola has noted in regard to Venetian silks, this trend would continue for many more centuries.[8] Cloth was the very foundation of the luxury trades, as the necessary ingredient for creating a visually more compelling presentation. But luxury textiles served a bespoke market. Expert tailors and skilled seamstresses advised affluent customers on a textile's quality, weave, the stability of a dye, finishing, and the fall or drape of a fabric, then they tailored and fitted garments from the purchased fabric. There was little that was, or could be, ready-made about the marketing of new textiles; secondhand markets were the more likely purveyors of ready-made clothes. Fine new garments were constructed to fit individuals and were expected to last decades, if not a lifetime. A discerning gentleman could take his tailor with him for advice when he purchased expensive fabric. Husbands and fathers purchased then gave bolts or lengths of whole cloth to their wives and daughters; women's dresses were often fitted at home by seamstresses, as decorum demanded. Fine cloth was expensive, clothing was designed and sewn to last, and better garments were willed to heirs.

This manner of retailing textiles out of workshops encouraged deliberative choice on the part of consumers, so merchandizing fabric remained to a large extent what it had been in earlier times: a market exchange where the consumer maintained some control over the quality and suitability of his purchase and the terms of the trade. The pace of economic exchange possessed a brake of sorts when impulse buying was inhibited by marketing conducive to making slow, deliberative choices. That is to say, customers still had time to inspect textiles with a critical eye for quality and suitability; then they could query a retailer about manufacture or provenance and expect the retailer to stand behind the product.

Meanwhile the market for accessories of jewels and precious metal was transformed into a market for ready-made wares where, significantly, the fineness of bullion in fabricated objects was obscured at times. New lessons in merchandizing goods were learned in this venue. It should be noted that this study has made no attempt to give precise values for retail goods in the ancient and highly accurate systems for determining fineness or purity of bullion (marks of fine silver, for example). Frequently recorded sales and valuations for silver belts, bowls, chains, and other precious plate were expressed in less precise terms. *Avoirdupois* pounds and ounces were routinely employed in sales agreements when accessories of precious metal were sold to the public; even sumptuary law in Florence limited men's belts to two pounds of silver by weight in 1355. Pounds cannot be trusted to provide a reliable measure of quality or fineness of bullion.[9]

In the market for ready-made accessories of precious metal lay a unique opportunity to stimulate markets and accelerate exchange. Advantage tipped to the seller whenever ready-made objects encouraged impulse buying; this type of exchange, like weighing in pounds, was conducive to only a vague apprehension of an object's true worth. Customers were less prone to examine ready-made objects carefully and slowly when an impulse to put on and wear a proffered object affected selection. Some of these objects displayed hallmarks attesting to silver content, but certainly not all did. Valuable accessories and jewels were pawned and sometimes forfeited and sold to others, and farther along the chain of sale or resale knowledge about an object's provenance would be lost. Some luxuries were rented for special occasions and, here again, the quality or fineness of an object could be obscured. Customers who were avid for accessories of jewels, gold, and silver were more likely to be at the mercy of retailers than were customers for textiles, so accessories were a wedge of sorts that could open up consumption markets and encourage sales. Whim and fancy enjoyed greater play wherever customers acquired ready-made goods.

The pace of economic change relied not only on market factors like new methods for retailing fashion goods but also on the pace at which one fashion replaced another; fashionable women played their own unique and significant role here. Urban women seldom frequented luxury retail shops or bankers' benches so husbands and fathers mediated women's direct impact as consumers to a large extent. Women's influence on fashion was exerted in a different venue since it stemmed from women's dramatic displays in public. Sumptuary laws and arguments about a woman's place in the scheme of things had acted in concert, sidelining women from the marketplace. In affluent households where luxuries were affordable, that deprivation was not absolute by any means but rather relative; it did not mean women did without by any stretch of the imagination. Nonetheless, a sidelined position with few opportunities for selecting goods in luxury markets appears to have distressed some women, at least when measured by their acts of dress. On occasion their discontent expressed itself through devising and wearing extreme fashions crafted at home. As consumers, wealthy women may have been marginalized but their fashions created at home riveted all eyes in public, winning them the attention they sought.

This helps explain the more exuberant examples of figural motifs on women's garments, where some adventurous souls at least were determined to exploit rare outings—at mass, at saints' day celebrations, at festivals—to create a stir. It was left to others who were market players to interpret the fashions that women invented and to adapt those ideas to market goods. Fashions that did catch on could be transformed into new consumer wares, or shopkeepers could lay in provisions for creating newly popular fashions. With successive rounds of experimentation in dress on view for all to observe—a new cut of sleeve, a new headdress, border, or trim, new embroidery of fantastical creatures on a bodice, new mesh or "tatting" over a garment—women inhabited a unique niche in the new world of fashion. Affluent, well-provisioned households supported their homemade innovations. Leisure time spent in the company of other women of the household and women servants provided opportunities to create. Incentive was derived from their liminal position in economic life. Social mores and sumptuary laws aimed to keep women retiring and modestly dressed, but with little success. Instead women's experiments with fashion added to the acceleration of one fashion following another, and encouraged new tastes and stimulated exchange.

"Without [fashion] nothing would have changed so fast," Fernand Braudel asserted a half century ago. He pointed out the long-term consequences of a quickened pace for economic life but he did not explain how acceleration, his key to capitalist development, was manifested in a society that had been content with traditional garb for centuries. While well-supplied markets were necessary for the sudden turn to fashion, without the non-market innovations that women introduced out of their homes it would be hard to imagine the pace of change picking up as briskly as it did. It appears that when visual signals gained consequence some women insisted on their right to dress conspicuously, that is, to find a way to be fashionable, impress others, and thus influence taste. In subsequent centuries other persons or groups would enter the world of fashion from the sidelines and help determine the taste and market preferences of the consuming public in a comparable way.

Braudel tended to view the emergence of fashion as some new configuration of cultural, social, and economic behaviors, and he never assumed that markets alone created the accelerated pace of fashion replacing fashion that characterized the fourteenth century. It lay outside the scope of his investigations, but it is no less the case for this reason—the pace of change accelerated at least in part because of the ostensibly trivial matter of nimble fingers that rearranged buttons, pulled out old embroidery threads, and added some new outrageous design to a cloak or a bodice. The social pastime of dreaming up fashions, executing them, and wearing them in public bolstered urban people's already strong inclination to pay attention to visual signals in the streets. Women became innovators because, like the men of their households, they were convinced that appearances mattered and that people had become what they appeared to be; so women improvised and the public rewarded their efforts by paying attention. Markets caught up with what fashionable women introduced by supplying the sets of buttons, *veriselli*, mother-of-pearl, gold and silver-shot ribbons, and endless other accessories that fed fashion. In towns and cities, the circle closed: women were sidelined by law and custom; they joined the fashion parade by inventing eye-catching new fashions at home, which in turn influenced the preferences of those who were customers in markets, which then adapted to suit new consumer preferences.

This acceleration in market exchange served as a stimulant to the economy in what became an increasingly difficult environment for trade in the latter decades of the fourteenth century. Due to the Black Plague and its periodic recurrence, population retraction occurred periodically throughout Italy, especially in towns. Wars grew in number and intensity in the second half of the century, bringing their own plague of mercenaries down on town and countryside alike. Bank collapses grew in number and cost as the century progressed. The fourteenth century saw more cold and rainy seasons with bad harvests, and some eastern trade routes were jeopardized. A bullion famine set in by the last decade of the century.

Robert S. Lopez and Harry Miskimin believe these factors set off a serious depression in the late fourteenth century, one that the European economy was unable to shake off until the sixteenth century.[10] This has proved to be a controversial idea, and while the market for fashion cannot resolve the issue by any means, it adds weight to those who doubt a severe depression occurred in these decades. Carlo M. Cipolla has argued that high per capita wealth remained an essential feature of urban economies through the early Renaissance, and in Italian towns, this wealth sustained market exchange because there were new opportunities to spend on luxuries. In these circumstances, the accelerant of fashion played a role by encouraging robust markets and attracting the consumers who still possessed discretionary income.[11] Stronger consumer demand served as an antidote to contraction in the urban marketplace so some of the more serious effects of population retraction were relieved. New fashions encouraged spending while tastes continued to evolve, making it possible for new market preferences to emerge and in turn stimulate sales. A luxury market was an opportunity to sop up the private fortunes that resulted when inheritances funneled wealth to a few heirs during the high mortality years of the plague. For the short term, that is, through the second half of the fourteenth century, purchasing luxury products acted as a stimulant to the market, although the proclivity to acquire could lead to hoarding. For one, it contributed to the onset of a bullion famine by the 1390s. Nevertheless, once fashion unleashed a wellspring of creativity in towns, securing consumers' close attention, taste in goods proved to be amenable to change, and in turn this initiated new rounds of consumption because fashion was reliant on constant change. Luxury markets provided motive and opportunity to spend, and spending on the part of wealthy individuals helped sustain market activity through unsettled times. Consumers diversified their private wealth through accumulating jewels, silver, and gold in collections of plate. Born during the decades of the greatest of medieval prosperity in the early decades of the fourteenth century, fashion proved to be a stimulant for the market and an antidote of sorts for the economic exigencies that followed.

Did fourteenth-century fashion contribute as well to the civilizing process of which Norbert Elias spoke so eloquently? His ideas apply more appropriately to consumers of a later era, who regarded their project of self-fashioning in a thoughtful and self-conscious manner, but they are provocative ideas and certainly worth trying on for this first age of fashion. In this regard it is significant that townspeople pursued fashion as a collective project rather than a way to distinguish themselves competitively from others. While men of fashion were seldom presented identically dressed (with the exception of family members, or the liveried angels in plate 5), richly dressed men most likely differed in their wardrobe's details, color, or trim. Men participated in a corporate endeavor to promote their own and their community's status, local industries, and local trades and dressed in similar fashion, favoring the same fashion goods, which could be recycled on occasion. If new hats or hoods came into fashion, men wanted some version of the new fashion, not something entirely different. Additionally, men and women alike judged their own dress largely through observing others; they lacked mirrors that might encourage self-reflection and any benefits that might bring. The fashionable dressed in similar outfits and the well-dressed moved out into the streets sporting clever details on recognizable ensembles that drew admiring—or sometimes shocked—responses from crowds.

The highly self-conscious behavior that would characterize the manners and clothing of the sixteenth century, when Erasmus could cite examples of the manner of dress that corresponded to this or that mental condition, had yet to dawn.[12] "In order to be truly 'courteous' by the standards of *civilité*, one was to some extent obliged to observe, to look about oneself and pay attention to people and their motives. In this . . . a new relationship of person to person, a new form of integration is announced," Elias argued.[13] Fourteenth-century people aspired to the social and economic benefits of fashionable dress, or to the adventure and playfulness of dress, but as yet they did not participate in self-conscious and thoughtful debate about the meaning and consequence of their fashions. To an extent, fashion had caught them unaware and drew some of its strength from doing so. The polemics of dress were subsumed under the rubric *luxuria*, thus not yet sufficiently acceptable to society at large so that fruitful debate might lead to edifying presentiments about self-fashioning. Fashion statements were silent acts presented in the streets of towns that insinuated themselves into urban life and were launched without comment. The debate on dress was held elsewhere, in legislative bodies or among Franciscan reformers. Critics of fashion dominated that debate just as surely as fashionable dressers dominated the streets and turned heads. It would be many decades before reflections on dress would subject dress to discussions about the meaning and consequence of self-fashioning. Moreover, fashion was gendered, leading men and women toward very different acts of dress. Women's acts of fashionable dress could be disruptive and fashionable women, even the less audacious among them, were often condemned since the very act of dressing "in fashion" was regarded as masculine. Men saw fashionable dress as their proper arena and a widely exhibited proof of their social consequence and standing within the ever-widening circles of power and influence to which they had gained access. Fashion held a central place in medieval townspeople's social aspirations but it had yet to figure in intellectual debate.

The protean nature of fashion, its emergence as a social phenomenon in towns even before those who participated in fashion grasped its broader meaning and consequence, is a feature that marks fashion as medieval in its sensibilities. Similarly, a reliance on noble metals to convey a sense of one's self-worth as a noble being by wearing those metals or exhibiting them in the home is consonant with traditional medieval values, an inherited system linking a person's value to perceived material worth. A late-added feature of capitalism, fashion was medieval in its swift evolution in towns. Novelty helped forge new fashions and townspeople struggled to keep pace, comprehend, and interpret the fashionable scene around them.

Perhaps sun-drenched cityscapes, our prized artistic legacy from the early Renaissance, give a false impression of fashion, for the summer portrayed in painting and fresco was not the season for donning fashionable wear. The heavy woolens and brocades that composed an elegant wardrobe would stifle all but the hardiest on a summer's day. Pounds of silver that belted in garments, heavy beading, or fur that weighed down a gown or cape meant acute discomfort under the hot summer sun. Linens and cottons augmented by other tissue-weight fabrics from the Levant suited this season. Summer was a time to dress in light, airy garments and leave town for the pleasures of the cooler countryside. "One can immediately observe the beauty of the Mugello [in the Tuscan countryside] through looking at its inhabitants," Giovanni Morelli enthused. "The women are attractive, friendly, pleasant, amorous, merry, and constantly dancing and singing, . . . organiz[ing] elegant gatherings, filling the region with a constant resounding of joyous voices and beauty."[14] Summer in the countryside was delightful by itself, with little need for fine fashions and embellishments.

In Italy, proper fashion came into its own during the winter season. Heavy layered garments provided warmth while belts hugged clothing tight and held in body heat. Gaudy fourteenth-century fashions suited dull, gray days and brightened the saints' days, festivals, and carnivals that punctuated the season before Lent. On a winter's day, fashion was best displayed at dawn or dusk: the heavy, garish effects favored in this century worked magic at those moments. A well-dressed woman slipping out her door to attend mass in the first light of day caught the faint early rays of a winter sun and shimmered as the beads, buttons, and silver and gold thread of her ribbons, trims, and headdress moved in rhythm with her steps. A gentleman done out in his gilded belt, silver dagger, chains, furs, rich borders, and trimmed hat could catch the last glimmer of the afternoon sun or, better still, give off glints of bright silver and gold in a lantern's light. In poorly lit streets and fog-bound pathways fashion became part masquerade; a garment, elegantly trimmed, might be hardly glimpsed, but its meaning was grasped well before the wearer's identity was known. Clothing held powerful connotative meanings in this milieu. Fourteenth-century clothing's expressiveness was novel for a public that was unprepared for its visual impact, so a brief sighting or fleeting glimpses increased fashion's assault on sensibilities. Clothing "allows a culture to insinuate its beliefs and assumptions into the very fabric of daily life," Grant McCracken has argued.[15] In this century when fashion was still fresh, this may have been more overwhelming than in later centuries because it was so startling and new. For a people who had yet to develop tools for interpreting fashion's hold on life and mores, an unexamined acceptance of the messages encoded in clothes might occur.

As it is often depicted in fourteenth-century painting and fresco, the simple leather strap holding in place John the Baptist's rough hair shirt conveyed the vital iconographic meaning in Christian art attached to a belt circling the waist. Was there any opulent edition of a gilded and enameled belt that could compete for significance with this highly evocative Christian symbol embodied in John's rough leather fastening? Unpredictably the answer is yes. Near the end of the century, even the Baptist's belt underwent one striking transformation. In a remote gallery of the Correr Museum in Venice, a rather undistinguished work sometimes attributed to Jacobello di Bonomo (active 1370–90) presents the figure of John the Baptist. He is flanked by St. Paul and an accompanying panel presents Saints Peter and Andrew. Originally these four saints on two panels formed the predella of a now lost polyptych.[16]

As strange as it seems, John the Baptist stands barefoot wearing his distinctive hair shirt, over which hangs a fine cloth cape with a gold-trimmed border. Despite the poor condition of the painting it is evident that the saint's cape possesses a gold (possibly gilt?) clasp, and, even more remarkable, underneath that cape the Baptist's coarse hair shirt is cinched in at the waist with a gold-embossed belt. Even this most ascetic of New Testament figures has donned the signature item of fourteenth-century fashion, a gilded belt (see fig. 9).

Figure 9. Jacobello di Bonomo (attributed), *John the Baptist*, c. 1370–90. Correr Museum, Venice. Courtesy of Museo Correr, Venice.

Notes

Chapter 1

1. In jewelry production gold ducats could be pounded into gold leaf for gilding. See Chapter 5.

2. On measures, see Bruno Kisch, *Scales and Weights: A Historical Culture* (New Haven, Conn.: Yale University Press, 1965), 150–55, and Ronald Edward Zupko, *Italian Weights and Measures from the Middle Ages to the Nineteenth Century* (Philadelphia: American Philosophical Society, 1981), 81–83. For bullion in the Mediterranean region, one *exagia* = 24 carats (0.9 grams); 1 carat = 4 grains (0.0475 grams).

3. Edwin S. Hunt and James M. Murray, *A History of Business in Medieval Europe, 1200–1550* (Cambridge: Cambridge University Press, 1999), 169.

4. Giovanni Villani, *Chroniche de Giovanni, Matteo e Filippo Villani,* ed. A. Racheli (Trieste: Austriaca, 1857), vol. 1, bk. 12, chap. 92, and Peter Spufford, *Profits and Power: The Merchant in Medieval Europe* (London: Thames and Hudson, 2002), 65–67.

5. It is difficult to estimate Venetian wealth before the 1420s, when Venice amassed a land empire in Italy. Spufford argues that "by the 1420s it [Venice] was possibly the richest capital in Europe" (*Profits and Power,* 66).

6. Catherine Kovesi Killerby, *Sumptuary Law in Italy, 1200–1500* (New York: Oxford University Press, 2002), 26–40. See also Curzio Mazzi, "Alcune leggi suntuarie senesi," *Archivio storico italiano,* 4th ser., 5 (1880): 133–44. Siena was unusual in forbidding some ornaments to men as well as women as early as the thirteenth century.

7. Luciana Frangioni, *Chiedere e ottenere: L'approvvigionamento di prodotti di successo della bottega Datini di Avignone nel XIV secolo* (Florence: Opus Libri, 2002), 41–42. Florence produced wares "alla senese," swords in the style of Siena, and "alla guisa di Bordello," in the style of Bordeaux, and weaponry in the styles of Hungary and Milan.

8. Killerby, *Sumptuary Law in Italy,* 28.

9. For comparison of Genoese and Venetian trade in the fourteenth century, see Benjamin Z. Kedar, *Merchants in Crisis* (New Haven, Conn.: Yale University Press, 1976). Kedar frequently employs Genoese *commenda* agreements preserved in the city's colonies.

10. William N. Bonds, "Genoese Noblewomen and Gold Thread Manufacturing," *Medievalia et Humanistica,* old ser. 17 (1966): 79–81. Unfortunately Bonds specified no names of Genoese noblewomen who manufactured gold thread.

11. See Luigi Tommaso Belgrano, *Vita privata dei Genovesi* (Rome: Multigrafica Editrice, 1970), 194–288, for discussion of Genoese wardrobes in medieval times.

12. Giovanni Boccaccio, *The Decameron,* trans. Frances Winwar (New York: Modern Library, 1955), The First Day, Eighth Story, pp. 31–33. See discussion in Steven

A. Epstein, *Genoa and the Genoese* (Chapel Hill: University of North Carolina Press, 1996), 214.

13. Luca Mola, *La comunità dei Lucchesi a Venezia: Immigrazione e industria della seta nel tardo medioevo* (Venice: Istituto Veneto di Scienze, Lettere ed Arti, 1994), 26–27, 139–96. Gold thread workers in residence would add to the appeal of Genoa for the Lucchese.

14. Epstein, *Genoa and the Genoese,* 276.

15. See discussion in John F. Cherry, *Goldsmiths* (Toronto: University of Toronto Press, 1992), 69, for women entrepreneurs in the gold thread business.

16. Luciana Cocito, ed., *Anonimo Genovese: Poesie* (Rome: Ateneo, 1970), poem 136, ll. 79–81, p. 546, and poem 138, ll. 121–40, p. 563.

17. Belgrano, *Vita privata dei Genovesi,* 244, citing *Archivio di Stato di Genova,* Foliatium Notariorum, Ms. Della Civico-Beriana vol. 3, pt. 2, p. 256.

18. Maria Giuseppina Muzzarelli, *Guardaroba medievale: Vesti e società dal XIII al XVI secolo* (Bologna: Il Mulino, 1999), 148.

19. See William Caferro's forthcoming *John Hawkwood, English Mercenary in Fourteenth-Century Italy* (Baltimore: Johns Hopkins University Press, 2006).

20. Bruno Thomas and Ortwin Gamber, "L'arte Milanese dell'armatura," *Storia di Milano* (Milan: Alfieri, 1958), 11:698–841, and Lionello Boccia, "Ancient Italian Pieces in the Kienbusch Collection," in *Studies in European Arms and Armor: The C. Otto Von Kienbusch Collection in the Philadelphia Museum of Art,* ed. Jane Watkins (Philadelphia: Philadelphia Museum of Art, 1992), 33–65.

21. Frangioni, *Chiedere e ottenere,* 129. The request for goods was forwarded to Datini on August 26, 1368.

22. Catherine King, "The Trecento: New Ideas, New Evidence," in *Siena, Florence and Padua: Art, Society and Religion, 1280–1400,* ed. Diana Norman (New Haven, Conn.: Yale University Press, 1995), 1:216–33.

23. Francis M. Kelly and Randolph Schwabe, *A Short History of Costume and Armour, Chiefly in England, 1066–1800* (London: B. T. Batsford, 1931), and Stuart W. Pyhrr, *Arms and Armor,* exhibition catalog (New Haven, Conn.: Yale University Press, 2003). Among other works on armor, see Museo Stibbert, *Guerre e assoldati in Toscana, 1260–1364,* exhibition catalog (Florence: Museo Stibbert, 1982), Leonid Tarassuk and Claude Blair, *The Complete Encyclopaedia of Arms and Weapons* (London: Batsford, 1982), and Leonid Tarassuk, *Italian Armor for Princely Courts* (Chicago: Art Institute of Chicago, 1986). Today armor collections are the most likely place to find rare fourteenth-century nonprecious or precious metal dress accessories.

24. Luca Mola, *The Silk Industry of Renaissance Venice* (Baltimore: Johns Hopkins University Press, 2000), 4. See note 26 below for Galvano Fiamma. Bonvesin de la Riva's *On the Marvels of the City of Milan, 1288,* is translated in part in Robert S. Lopez and Irving Raymond, *Medieval Trade in the Mediterranean World: Illustrated Documents Translated with Introduction and Notes* (New York: Columbia University Press, 1955), 61–69.

25. Boccia, "Ancient Italian Pieces in the Kienbusch Collection," 33.

26. Maria Giuseppina Muzzarelli, *Gli inganni delle apparenze* (Turin: Scriptorium, 1996), 125–26; Galvano Fiamma, *Opusculum de rebus gestis,* ed. Carlo Castiglioni. *Rerum italicarum Scriptores,* ed. L. Muratori, new ed. (Bologna: N. Zanichelli, 1938), vol. 12, pt. 4, p. 370; and Ettore Verga, "Le leggi suntuarie milanesi," *Archivio Storico Lombardo* 25 (1909): 5–79.

27. See vol. 2 of Rosita Levi Pisetzky, *Storia del costume in Italia* (Milan: Istituto

Editoriale Italiano, 1964). See also her "La nuove fogge e l'influsso della moda francese a Milano," in Giovanni Treccani degli Alfieri, *Storia di Milano* (Milan: Fondozione Treccani degli Alfieri per la storia di Milano, 1958), vol. 11, pt. 11, pp. 548–94. This study deals with foreign influence on fashion in Milan but in a later era. See Frangioni, *Chiedere e ottenere*, 38, for the list of tradesmen who sold Milanese products.

28. See Philip Jones, *The Italian City-State from Commune to Signoria* (Oxford: Clarendon, 1997), 619–46, on popular demagogues in Milan and support from the *popoli* and the merchant community.

29. Mola, *La communità dei Lucchesi a Venezia*, 26–27.

30. Muzzarelli, *Guardaroba medievale*, 231. Ferrara and Naples were also known for gold thread embroideries.

31. Muzzarelli, *Gli inganni delle apparenze*, 102.

32. For the law of 1289, see Maria Guiseppina Muzzarelli, *La legislazione suntuaria, secoli XIII–XVI, Emilia-Romagna* (Rome: Ministero per I Beni e le Attività Culturali-Direzione Generale per Gli Archivi, 2002), 47–48 for statutes from 1250 to 1261; statute of 1288, pp. 50–58; statute of 1335, pp. 75–81. See also Lodovico Frati, *La vita privata in Bologna dal secolo XII al XVII* (Bologna: Zanichelli, 1928), 235–41. The Bolognese passed an early sumptuary law code in 1233 under the influence of the Allelujah movement of Fra Giovanni da Vicenze, who arrived in the city that year. He urged women to veil themselves modestly. Other details of this law are not known.

33. See, for example, Muzzarelli, *Legislazione suntuaria*, 78, statute of 1335: "videlicet frixos, chanellas, flubetas, cordellas, botonçellos aut margaritas."

34. Frati, *La vita privata*, 204–7: "Item unam robam de saia persa scura de Florentia"; "Item unam guarnacchiam de sbiaveto cum ismaltis de argento super doratis cum auxelitis de argento superdoratis foderatam de vario"; and "Item unum collaretum de ferro cum canzellis de argento" (205). Peter Spufford, *Handbook of Medieval Exchange* (London: Royal Historical Society, 1986), gives an exchange rate in 1313 of 44 solidi 4 denarii Bolognese to the florin.

35. Maureen Mazzaoui, "The Emigration of Veronese Textile Artisans to Bologna in the Thirteenth Century," *Atti e memorie della Accademia di agricoltura, scienze e lettere di Verona*, 6th ser., 19 (1967–68): 275–321. See also Mazzaoui, *The Italian Cotton Industry in the Later Middle Ages, 1100–1600* (Cambridge: Cambridge University Press, 1981). On Bologna, see Cecilia Ady, *The Bentivoglio of Bologna* (1937; reprint, London: Oxford University Press, 1969).

36. Mola, *La comunità dei Lucchesi a Venezia*, 28–29.

37. Mola, *The Silk Industry of Renaissance Venice*, 198.

38. Frati, *La vita privata*, 186.

39. Illustration of a book and stationery shop, Dalla Cronaca di Bologna del Villola, reproduced in Frati, *La vita privata*, 183.

40. Killerby, *Sumptuary Law in Italy*, 28–29 (table). Some privileges were reserved for knights and other servants of the state in Florentine sumptuary law; see following discussion. As Philip Jones argues in *The Italian City-State*, by 1300 Florentine knights were no longer a military but rather a mercantile species (208).

41. Killerby, *Sumptuary Law in Italy*, 28, 52.

42. Norbert Elias, *The Court Society*, trans. Edmund Jephcott (New York: Pantheon, 1983), 147. Elias cites the work of Joseph Lemonnier on the French monarchy.

43. James C. Y. Watt and Anne E. Wardwell, *When Silk Was Gold* (New York: Metropolitan Museum of Art, 1997), 127–63; Christine de Pizan, "Book of the Deeds and Character of Charles V the Wise," trans. Eric Hicks, in *The Writings of Christine*

de Pizan, ed. Charity Cannon Ward (New York: Persea, 1994), 208. Many of the woven luxury fabrics imported from Central Asia and China have been preserved in church treasuries. They may have been purchased by prelates of the church or have been gifts from wealthy donors.

44. Brigitte Klesse, *Seidenstoffe in der Italienischen Malerei des 14 Jahrhunderts* (Bern: Stampfli, 1967). Many scholars of medieval textiles follow her pioneering study and concur that most Italian design was eclectic and owed a debt to the example of imported Asian textiles.

45. Lisa Monnas, "Silk Textiles in the Paintings of Bernardo Daddi, Andrea di Cione and Their Followers," *Zeitschrift fur Kunstgeschichte* 53 (1990): 39–59; and Cathleen S. Hoeniger, "Cloth of Gold and Silver: Simone Martini's Techniques for Representing Luxury Textiles," *Gesta* 30:2 (1991): 154–62.

46. Elias, *The Court Society,* 150–81, examines power shifts in the sixteenth and seventeenth centuries that opened court society to new strata of people.

47. See Ronald E. Rainey, "Sumptuary Legislation in Renaissance Florence" (Ph.D. diss., Columbia University, 1985), 49, for a provision of the law enacted in March 1318 directed against artisans, goldsmiths in particular.

48. Rainey, "Sumptuary Legislation in Renaissance Florence," appendix 7, pp. 735–45, gives the entire text of the petition.

49. Spufford, *Profits and Power,* 12–59.

50. See in particular Robert Frank, *Luxury Fever* (New York: Free Press, 1999).

51. Werner Sombart, *Luxury and Capitalism,* trans. W. R. Dittmar (Ann Arbor: University of Michigan Press, 1967).

52. Frederic C. Lane, "Some Heirs of Gustav von Schmoller," in *Venice and History: The Collected Papers of Frederic C. Lane,* ed. a Committee of Colleagues and Former Students (Baltimore: Johns Hopkins University Press, 1966), 485. See also Sombart, *Luxury and Capitalism.*

53. See the older but still valuable Hans Baron, "Franciscan Poverty and Civic Wealth as Factors in the Rise of Humanistic Thought," *Speculum* 13 (1938): 1–37. Salimbene da Parma collected quotations on women's vanity and sinfulness for use in pastoral sermons. For an English translation, see George Gordon Coulton, *From St. Francis to Dante* (Philadelphia: University of Pennsylvania Press, 1972), 96–97, including a list of quotations from the Old Testament and the Church Fathers employed by Salimbene.

54. Fernand Braudel, *Capitalism and Material Life, 1400–1800,* trans. Miriam Kochan (New York: Harper, 1967), 226. See also Braudel, *The Structures of Everyday Life,* volume 1 of *Civilization and Capitalism,* trans. Sian Reynolds (New York: Harper and Row, 1979), 311. *Structures of Everyday Life* contains this argument with the addition of citations. On the treatment of costume and fashion it largely repeats the phrasing of the earlier publication.

55. Braudel, *The Structures of Everyday Life,* 333.

56. Ibid., 324.

57. Adam Smith, *The Wealth of Nations: An Inquiry into the Nature and Causes* (1776; New York: Modern Library, 1937), 385–87. On Smith's views, see Albert O. Hirschman, *The Passions and the Interests: Political Arguments for Capitalism before Its Triumph* (Princeton, N.J.: Princeton University Press, 1977), 100–113.

58. Jeremy Bentham, *Principles of Morals and Legislation* (Oxford: Clarendon, 1789).

59. In 1963, *Business History Review* devoted an entire issue to the role of fashion in business. See in particular Dwight E. Robinson, "The Importance of Fashion in Taste to Business History: An Introductory Essay," *Business History Review* 37 (1963): 5–36, and Herman Freudenberger, "Fashion, Sumptuary Laws, and Business," *Business History Review* 37 (1963): 37–48. The latter deals largely with sumptuary law in landed realms.

60. See John Brewer and Roy Porter, eds., *Consumption and the World of Goods* (London: Routledge, 1993); John Brewer et al., eds., *Early Modern Conceptions of Property* (London: Routledge, 1994); and Brewer et al., eds., *The Consumption of Culture, 1600–1800: Image, Object, Text* (London: Routledge, 1995).

61. Sombart, *Luxury and Capitalism.*

62. Hirschman, *The Passions and the Interests*; and Hirschman, "The Changing Tolerance for Income Inequality in the Course of Economic Development," *Quarterly Journal of Economics* 87 (1973): 504–66.

63. Mary Douglas and Baron Isherwood, *The World of Goods* (New York: Basic Books, 1979), 18–19. Arjan Appadurai, ed., *The Social Life of Things: Commodities in Cultural Perspective* (Cambridge: Cambridge University Press, 1986), collects together a variety of opinions on the promotion of trade in material goods.

64. Frank, *Luxury Fever*, 295–316. This bibliography gives the reader some idea of the attention social scientists have given spending and consumption over the past decade. See also Christopher Berry, *The Idea of Luxury* (Cambridge: Cambridge University Press, 1994), and Thomas Hine, *I Want That* (New York: Harper Collins, 2002).

65. Jones, *The Italian City-State,* 650, concludes about Italy on the eve of the Renaissance: "and everywhere [there was] further aristocratization of society and values."

66. Frank, *Luxury Fever,* 140.

67. Diane Owen Hughes, "Sumptuary Law and Social Relations in Renaissance Cities," in *Disputes and Settlements,* ed. John Bossy (Cambridge: Cambridge University Press, 1984), 69–100.

Chapter 2

1. Michael M. Postan, "The Trade of Medieval Europe: The North," in *Cambridge Economic History,* ed. Michael M. Postan and H. T. Habakkak, 2nd ed. (Cambridge: Cambridge University Press, 1966), 2:168–305, places trade in staples over great distances at the heart of his argument. Diverse interpretations of European economic growth follow this lead, for example, Immanuel M. Wallerstein, *Capitalist Agriculture and the Origins of the European World Economy in the Sixteenth Century* (New York: Academic Press, 1974). See also Douglass Cecil North and Robert Paul Thomas, *The Rise of the Western World: A New Economic History* (Cambridge: Cambridge University Press, 1973), 9–19. In contrast to Postan's trade in the north essay, Robert S. Lopez, "The Trade of Medieval Europe: The South," in *Cambridge Economic History,* ed. Postan and Habakkuk, 2:306–401, emphasizes luxury imports into Europe. His opinion has had less of an impact on interpretations of the origins of European economic growth. Successful retailing relied on provenance and certification of origin by the fourteenth century according to Frangioni, *Chiedere e ottenere,* 37–41.

2. Graham Child, "Mirrors," in *Dictionary of Art,* ed. Jane Turner (New York: Grove, 1996), 21:711–22. According to Filippo Villani, Giotto used small peer glasses as

a new technique for painting in the early fourteenth century. Villani, *De origine civitatis Florentie et de eiusdem famosis civibus,* ed. Giuliano Tanturli (Padua: Antenore, 1997), 411–13. This passage is translated in *Images of Quattrocento Florence,* ed. Stefano Ugo Baldassarri and Arielle Saiber (New Haven, Conn.: Yale University Press, 2000), 186–87. See example of the beatified Villana dei Botti and a mirror in Chapter 4.

3. See Manlio Cortelazzo, *Dizionario etimologico della lingua italiana* (Bologna: Zanichelli, 1979–88), 2:531.

4. Georg Simmel, "Fashion," *American Journal of Sociology* 62:6 (1957): 541–58, established the theoretical model that open societies will emulate prestige groups. However, his pathbreaking work did not deal with the fact that subjacent groups do so in order to be "in fashion" rather than as a way to emulate an elite.

5. Pegolotti, Francesco di Balduccio, *La pratica della mercatura,* ed. Allan Evans (Cambridge, Mass.: Harvard University Press, 1936), 293–97, translated in Lopez and Reynolds, *Medieval Trade in the Mediterranean World,* 109–14.

6. Metà may refer to the southernmost Atlantic port in Morocco, according to Robert Lopez, but it is more likely that "gold of metà" is a type of prepared imported gold leaf. Lopez and Reynolds, *Medieval Trade in the Mediterranean World,* 109–14.

7. David Herlihy, *Pisa in the Early Renaissance: A Study of Urban Growth* (New Haven, Conn.: Yale University Press, 1958), 145–61.

8. Bartolomeo Cecchetti, *La vita dei veneziana nel 1300* (Venice: Emiliana, 1886), 123–29.

9. Watt and Wardwell, *When Silk Was Gold,* 14, 127–36; Cocito, ed., *Anonimo Genovese,* poem 138, ll. 121–40, p. 563. See also Giulio Bistort, *Il magistrato alle pompe nella Republica di Venezia* (Bologna: Forni, 1912; reprint, 1969), 334n. 1. In the Venetian sumptuary law of June 20, 1334, the word was given as *nassicio.* Bistort relates this cloth of gold to the product from China. For discussion of provenance of fabrics, see Anne Wardwell, "Panni Tartarici: Eastern Islamic Silks Woven with Gold and Silver," *Islamic Art* 3 (1988–89): 96–115. Marco Polo believed cloth of this name came from Baghdad.

10. Assuming, as in Polo's bequest to his wife, the *lira di grossi* was in use here. Amy Frances Yule, ed., *Travels of Marco Polo* (New York: Scribner, 1926), 2:514. See Chapter 5.

11. Wardwell, "Panni Tartarici," 141: "Item, uum dosale pro altari de panno tartarico laboratum ad multas bestias, babuinos et compassus de auro." Pages 135–42 list descriptions of imported fabrics coupled with illustrations.

12. Mola, *La comunità dei Lucchesi a Venezia,* 21–72. Florence Edler de Roover, "Andrea Banchi: Florentine Silk Manufacturer and Merchant in the Fifteenth Century," *Studies in Medieval and Renaissance History* 3 (1966): 221–86, and "The Beginnings and the Commercial Aspects of the Lucchese Silk Industry," *CIBA Review* 80 (June 1950): 2902–30.

13. Mazzaoui, *The Italian Cotton Industry,* 59–71. By the fourteenth century production of Lombard fustians had already begun to decline, with increasing warfare a contributing factor. See also Frangioni, *Chiedere e ottenere,* 49–57.

14. Robert S. Lopez, "The Origin of the Merino Sheep," *The Joshua Starr Memorial Volume: Studies in History and Philology, Jewish Social Studies* 5 (New York, 1953), 161–68.

15. On thirteenth-century dress, see, for example, Ricobaldo da Ferrara, *Historia Imperatorum Romano Germanicorum a Carolo Magno usque ad annum MCCXCVII,* in Muratori, *Rerum italicarum Scriptores,* vol. 9, col. 128.

16. Muzzarelli, *Gli inganni delle apparenze,* 33–39. Lynn White places the origin

of "buttoning" buttons around 1230 in Germany in "Technology Assessment from the Stance of a Medieval Historian," *American Historical Review* 79:1 (1974): 10.

17. Stella Mary Newton, *Fashion in the Age of the Black Prince: A Study of the Years 1340–1365* (Woodbridge: Boydell, 1980). Newton echoes opinions put forward by Herbert Norris and Max von Boehn in the 1920s and 1930s.

18. Newton, *Fashion in the Age of the Black Prince*, 2.

19. Giovanni Villani, *Croniche de Giovanni, Matteo e Filippo Villani*, ed. A. Racheli (Trieste: Austriaco, 1857), bk. 12, chap. 4, in vol. 1, p. 445. Villani speaks of the clothes of young men—"si vestivano i giovani una cotta ovvero gonnella corta e stretta"—and goes on to specify the components of the new fashion in detail. Fiamma, *Opusculum de rebus gestis*, vol. 12, iv, 6–7, p. 37; Anonimo Romano, *Historiae romanae fragmenta ab anno MCCCXXVII usque ad MCCCLIX*, in *Rerum italicarum Scriptores*, vol. 3, cols. 307–9.

20. Commentary on fashion appeared in England in the second half of the fourteenth century, for example, in the writing of Henry Knighton or, for that matter, Geoffrey Chaucer.

21. Levi Pisetzky, *Storia del costume in Italia*, 2: 19, plate 3, and pp. 77–81.

22. Ellen Kosmer, "The 'Noyous Humoure of Lecherie,'" *Art Bulletin* 57 (1975): 1–8.

23. Helen Woodruff, "The Illustrated Manuscripts of Prudentius," *Art Studies* 7 (1929): 33–79. See also Adolf Katzenellenbogen, *Allegories of the Virtues and Vices in Mediaeval Art: From Early Christian Times to the Thirteenth Century* (London: Warburg Institute, 1939; reprint, Toronto: University of Toronto Press, 1989).

24. Giotto di Bondone, *St. Francis Renounces His Worldly Possessions*, fresco, Franciscan Cycle, Upper Basilica of S. Francesco, Assisi.

25. Cited by Peter Brown, "The Saint as Exemplar in Late Antiquity," *Representations* 2 (1983): 5.

26. Dyan Elliott, "Dress as Mediator between Inner and Outer Self: The Pious Matron in the High and Later Middle Ages," *Mediaeval Studies* 53 (1991): 296. Elliott cites Elizabeth's *vita* for the story. On dressing the part, see Rachel C. Gibbons, "The Queen as 'Social Mannequin': Consumerism and Expenditure at the Court of Isabeau of Bavaria, 1393–1422," *Journal of Medieval History* 26:4 (2000): 371–95.

27. James O. Caswell, *Recalling the Past: A Selection of Early Chinese Art from the Victor Shaw Collection*, exhibition catalog (Vancouver: University of British Columbia Museum of Anthropology, 1997). No. 45, "Belt plaques. Gilt bronze. Tang or Song dynasty. Overall length when joined: 49.0 cm." See later discussion for Balkan and Hungarian influences.

28. Sombart, *Luxury and Capitalism*, 39–49. See introduction by Philip Siegelman.

29. Newton, *Fashion in the Age of the Black Prince*, 27, citing Louis Douet D'Arcq, *Comptes de l'argenterie des rois de France au XIVe siècle*, and *Nouveau recueil de comptes de l'argenterie des rois de France* (Paris: Librarie Renouard, 1851 and 1874).

30. *The Writings of Christine de Pizan*, ed. Charity Cannon Willard (New York: Persea Books, 1994), 238, trans. Eric Hicks for this portion of Charles V's biography.

31. *The Writings of Christine de Pizan*, 237–38.

32. Gibbons, "The Queen as 'Social Mannequin,'" 394, argues that Queen Isabeau's opulent household could not begin to compete with the expenditures of the royal uncles at the turn of the fifteenth century.

33. R. W. Lightbown, *Secular Goldsmiths' Work in Medieval France: A History*

(London: Society of Antiquaries of London, 1978), 30. Lightbown drew on the highly detailed description in the royal inventories noted above. See H. Moranvillé, ed., *Inventaire de l'orfevrerie et des joyaux de Louis I, duc d' Anjou* (Paris: E. Leroux, 1903–6). The inventories of Charles V and of the duke of Berry and the dukes of Burgundy have been published as well; see Lightbown's select bibliography on p. 128.

34. Alessandro Guidotti, ed., *L'oreficeria nella Firenze del quattrocento,* exhibition catalog (Florence: Scelte, 1977), sec. 3, pp. 153–57.

35. Peter Spufford, *Money and Its Use in Medieval Europe* (Cambridge: Cambridge University Press, 1988), 346. See Maurice Rey, *Le domaine du roi et les finances extraordinaires sous Charles VI, 1388–1413* (Paris: SEVPEN, 1965), 131.

36. Cited by Georges Duby, *The Early Growth of the European Economy: Warriors and Peasants from the Seventh to the Twelfth Century,* trans. Howard B. Clarke (Ithaca, N.Y.: Cornell University Press, 1974), 260.

37. Ellen Callmann, "Cassone," in *Dictionary of Art History,* ed. Jane Turner (New York: Grove, 1996), 6: 2. See as well her *Appollonio di Giovanni* (Oxford: Clarendon, 1974).

38. Louis Charles Jean Courajod, *Leçons professées à l'école du Louvre, 1887–96,* 3 vols. (Paris: A. Picard et Fils, 1899–1903). For an example of the application of the phrase International Style, see Bernard Berenson, *Italian Pictures of the Renaissance: A List of the Principal Artists and Their Works* (New York: Phaidon, 1963), 1:197–200, on the Vivarini of Venice and their partnership with Giovanni d'Alemagna.

39. Martin Warnke, *The Court Artist: On the Ancestry of the Modern Artist,* trans. David McClintock (Cambridge: Cambridge University Press, 1993), 45–58. See also Henri Dubois, "Commerce international, métaux précieux flux monétaires aux confins orientaux du royaume de France," in *La moneta nell'economica europea secoli XIII–XVIII,* ed. Vera Barbagli Bagnoli, Istituto Internazionale di Storia Economica "Datini," Prato, Serie II, Atti delle "Settimane di studio," 11–17 Aprile 1975 (Florence: Le Monnier, 1981), 681–97.

40. Lorenzo Ghiberti, *Commentaries,* pamphlet, trans. the staff of the Courtauld Institute of Art (London: Courtauld Institute of Art, 1962), 40–41. For the Italian, Ghiberti, *I commentari,* ed. Ottavio Morisani (Naples: Ricciardi, 1947), 20–21.

41. Lightbown, *Secular Goldsmiths' Work in Medieval France,* 34–35.

42. Jean de Venette, *The Chronicle of Jean de Venette,* ed. and trans. Jean Birdsell (New York: Columbia University Press, 1953), 63.

43. Fiamma, *Opusculum de rebus gestis,* c. 7, "Zonas aureis supercincte amazones esse videntur," 37; see also Henry Knighton, *Chronicon Henrici Knighton vel Critthon, Monachi Leycestrensis,* ed. Joseph Rawson Lumby, Rolls Series, 92 (London: Eyre and Spottiswoode, 1889–95), 2: 57–58, for the year 1348: "in tunicis partitis scilicet una parte de una secta et altera de alia secta, com capuciis brevibus et liripiis ad modum chordarum circa caput advolutis, et zonis argento vel auro benecircumstipatis, etiam ex transverso ventris sub umbilico habentes cutellos quos daggerios vulgariter dicunt in powchiis desuper impositis." He goes on to say these women ruin their good reputations with their lewd excesses and extravagance.

44. There were many types of sumptuary legislation, and this generalization applies to civic codes only. Traditionally sumptuary legislation in the church applied a dress code that favored modesty and propriety and, incidentally, distinguished between harlots and chaste women. James Brundage, "Sumptuary Laws and Prostitution in Late Medieval Italy," *Journal of Medieval History* 13 (1987): 343–55; see also his *Law, Sex, and Christian Society in Medieval Europe* (Chicago: University of Chicago Press, 1987). For

Florence, see Richard Trexler, ed., *Synodal Law in Florence and Fiesole, 1306–1518* (Vatican City: Biblioteca Apostolica Vaticana, 1971). North of the Alps and in Spain royal sumptuary laws placed an emphasis on privilege and class distinction that cannot be found in civic sumptuary laws in Italy in the fourteenth century.

45. Margaret Newett, "The Sumptuary Laws of Venice in the Fourteenth and Fifteenth Centuries," in *Historical Essays*, ed. T. F. Tout and James Tait (London: Longmans Green, 1902), 248.

46. Louise Buenger Robbert, "Twelfth-Century Italian Prices: Food and Clothing in Pisa and Venice," *Social Science History* 7:4 (1983): 381–403, citing Venetian State Archives, *Biblioteca Nazionale Marciana*, Lat. Ms. Cl. XIV. Cod. 71. For this document, see also Cecchetti, *La vita dei Veneziana*, 113–18.

47. Robbert, "Twelfth-Century Italian Prices," 391.

48. Ibid., 396–401.

49. There is a vast literature on codpieces. See Lois Banner, "The Fashionable Sex, 1100–1600," *History Today* 42 (1992): 37–44.

50. See Pompeo Molmenti, *La storia di Venezia nella vita private della origini alla caduta* (Turin: Roux e Favale, 1880), part 1. Trans. Horatio F. Brown as *Venice: Its Individual Growth from the Earliest Beginnings to the Fall of the Republic* (London: John Murray, 1906), part 2; chap. 9, pp. 1–22.

51. Robert S. Lopez, "Nota sulla composizione dei patrimoni privati nella primametà del duecento," *Studi sull'economia Genovese nel medioveo,* Documenti e studi per la storia del commercio e del diritto commerciale Italiano, 7 (Turin: S. Lattes, 1936), 205–64.

52. The Florentine synodal constitutions of 1310 forbade priests to shorten their robes. Thus it may be assumed that priests in Florence had adapted this stylish practice. Trexler, *Synodal Law in Florence and Fiesole*, 113, 227–89. See later discussion of sumptuary law.

53. Giotto di Bondone, *Expulsion of Joachim from the Temple*, Padua, Scrovegni Chapel, Plate 4.

54. Boccaccio, *Decameron*, 366–67.

55. Andrea Lancia, "Legge suntuaria fatta dal commune di Firenze l'anno 1355 e volgarizzata nel 1356," *L'Etruria* 1 (1851): 366–83, 429–43.

56. Curzio Mazzi, ed., *Argenti degli Acciaiuoli, nozze, Lungo-Bacci* (Siena, 189?), 14, 26.

57. Klesse, *Seidenstoffe in der Italienischen Malerei des 14 Jahrhunderts.* See also King, "The Trecento," 1: 217–33.

58. Susan Mosher Stuard, "The Adriatic Trade in Silver, c. 1300," *Studi veneziani* 17–18 (1975–76): 113.

59. Molmenti, *La storia di Venezia*, pt. 2, pp. 1–22.

60. Cecchetti, *La vita dei veneziani*, 123–29.

61. Charlotte Jirousek, "More than Oriental Splendor: European and Ottoman Headgear, 1380–1580," *Dress* 22 (1995): 22–33. Rosamond E. Mack argues that portability of trade objects from Islam often determined their reception and influence in western Europe. Mack, *Bazaar to Piazza: Islamic Trade and Italian Art, 1300–1600* (Berkeley: University of California Press, 2002), 2.

62. Mack, *Bazaar to Piazza*, 73–94.

63. See Klesse, *Seidenstoffe in der italienischen malerei des 14 Jahrhunderts,* 63–71, for Persian and Chinese motifs in fourteenth-century woven silk.

64. Cecchetti, *La vita dei Veneziani*, 119; Molmenti, *La storia di Venezia*, pt. 2, p. 10.

65. John E. Dotson, ed. and trans., *Merchant Culture in Fourteenth-Century Venice: The Zibaldone da Canal* (Binghamton, N.Y.: Medieval and Renaissance Texts and Studies, 1994), 76–80.

66. Mazzi, ed., *Argenti degli Acciaiuoli,* 24.

67. In addition to his important study of fourteenth-century prices, *Prix et salaires à Florence au XIVe siècle (1280–1380)* (Rome: École Francaise de Rome, 1982), Charles de la Roncière has a great deal to say about the interiors of homes in *A History of Private Life,* ed. Georges Duby and trans. Arthur Goldhammer (Cambridge, Mass.: Belknap, 1987), vol. 2, *Revelations of the Medieval World,* 157–309. Unfortunately this study is not accompanied by footnotes. Richard A. Goldthwaite, *The Building of Renaissance Florence: An Economic and Social History* (Baltimore: Johns Hopkins University Press, 1980), discusses fifteenth-century domestic architecture and ornamentation in detail.

68. F. de Roover, "Lucchese Silk Industry," 2920–30.

69. Frangioni, *Chiedere e ottenere,* 41–42, is useful on imitations and counterfeiting.

70. Lancia, "Legge suntuaria," 373, 377.

71. Lionardo di Frescobaldi, "Fecevi grande onore, e la sua casa pareva una casa d'oro, ed havvi piu camera che poco vi si vede altro che oro e azzuro fine; e costagli dodici mila fiorini," in *Viaggio in Terrasanta,* ed. Cesare Angelini (Florence: Le Monnier, 1944), 14, cited in Paul Hills, *Venetian Colour* (New Haven, Conn.: Yale University Press, 1999), 174. Frescobaldi was attending a banquet in Remigio Soranzo's *casa.*

72. Cennino Cennini, *Il libro dell'arte,* trans. Daniel V. Thompson (New Haven, Conn.: Yale University Press, 1933), 2: xi–xii.

73. Mola, *The Silk Industry of Renaissance Venice,* 109–13.

74. This was true in regard to mourning clothes, which had their own designations for style and color.

75. Laurence Gérard-Marchant, "Compter et nommer l'étoffe à Florence au trecento (1343)," *Médiévales* 29 (1995): 97.

76. *Skarlatino* was also type of fabric in Florence and might be found in many colors. See Rainey, "Sumptuary Legislation in Renaissance Florence," 335. See also John Munro, "The Medieval Scarlet," in *Cloth and Clothing in Medieval Europe,* ed. N. B. Harte and K. G. Ponting (London: Heineman, 1983), 13–70.

77. Michael Baxandall, *Giotto and the Orators* (Oxford: Oxford University Press, 1971), 62, and Hills, *Venetian Colour,* 91.

78. *Diana's Hunt: Caccia di Diana, Boccaccio's First Fiction,* ed. and trans. Anthony K. Cassell and Victoria Kirkham (Philadelphia: University of Pennsylvania Press, 1991), 31–32, 148–49.

79. Mack, *Bazaar to Piazza,* 51–72.

80. Hoeniger, "Cloth of Gold and Silver," and Monnas, "Silk Textiles in the Paintings of Bernardo Daddi."

81. Michael Baxandall, *Painting and Experience in Fifteenth-Century Italy: A Primer in the Social History of Pictorial Style* (Oxford: Clarendon, 1972), 14–15. See also Richard Goldthwaite, "The Renaissance Economy: The Preconditions for Luxury Consumption," in *Aspetti della vita economica medievale,* Atti del convegno di studi nel X anniversario della morte de Federigo Melis, Firenze-Pisa-Prato, March 10, 1984, and Goldthwaite, *Wealth and the Demand for Art in Italy, 1300–1600* (Baltimore: Johns Hopkins University Press, 1993). On medieval consumption, see Susan Mosher Stuard, "Toward a Theory of Consumption and Exchange," *Journal of Economic History* 44 (1985): 921–25.

82. On *jaune à l'argent*, see Hills, *Venetian Colour*, 109.

83. Hills, *Venetian Colour*, 114.

84. See Frati, *La vita privata*, 238–39, for the text of the 1289 law.

85. Newett, "Sumptuary Laws of Venice," 245–77. She cites Venetian State Archives, *Maggior Consiglio, Deliberations Spiritus*, XXIV, fol. 97, an archaic reference.

86. Diana Norman, *Siena and the Virgin: Art and Politics in a Late Medieval City State* (New Haven, Conn.: Yale University Press, 1999), is important for this observation. In early fourteenth-century presentations of the Virgin surrounded by saints opulent borders appeared on all figures.

87. *Deliberationes del Consiglio dei Rogati (Senato) Serie "mixtorum,"* 1333–34, ed. Roberto Cessi and Mario Brunetti (Venice: A Spese della Deputazione, 1961), 2:323, June 20, 1334.

88. Dante Alighieri, *The Divine Comedy*, trans. Charles Singleton (Princeton, N.J.: Princeton University Press, 1977), vol. 3, pt. 1, *Paradiso*, canto XV, pp. 100–102.

89. See later discussion of medallions on heavy chains as a male fashion.

90. This motif is one of the rare identifiable Classic representations in the secular apparel of the fourteenth century. The Classical motif of a gorgoneion (gorgon head) suggests an Italian origin because the use of classical motifs from pediments may be found there.

91. *Les fastes du Gothique: Le siècle de Charles V,* exhibition catalog (Paris: Ministère de la Culture, 1981), 242–45. The treasure was found in the Jewish quarter of Colmar in 1863. It was acquired by the Musée de Cluny in 1923. On dress for Jews in France, see Michèle Beaulieu, "Le costume, miroir des mentalités de la France médiévale (1350–1500)," in *Mélanges offerts à Jean Dauvillier* (Toulouse: Centre d'Histoire Juridique Méridionale, 1979), 65–87, especially figure 9, p. 86.

92. Ilse Fingerlin, *Gürtel des hohen und späten Mittelalters* (Munich: Deutscher Kunstverlag, 1971), 310, no. 14; see illustration that page.

93. John Michael Montias, *Artists and Artisans in Delft: A Socio-Economic Study of the Seventeenth Century* (Princeton, N.J.: Princeton University Press, 1982), 7.

94. Dora Thornton, *The Scholar in His Study: Ownership and Experience in Renaissance Italy* (New Haven, Conn.: Yale University Press, 1997), and Isabella Palumbo-Fossati, "L'interna della casa nella Venezia de Cinquecento," *Studi veneziani*, n.s. 8 (1966): 109–53; Muzzarelli, *Guardaroba medievale*.

95. Mazzi, ed., *Argenti degli Acciaiuoli*, 6. (*Nozze* were celebratory publications on the occasion of weddings. Thus, inventories of household possessions were considered appropriate subjects.)

96. Mazzi, ed., *Argenti degli Acciaiuoli*, 6.

97. J. Kirby, "Gilding," in *Dictionary of Art*, ed. Jane Turner (New York: Grove, 1996), 12: 621. Ristori discusses the terminology for the techniques of gilding here, among them *metà*.

98. Mazzi, ed., *Argenti degli Acciaiouli*, 28, 24.

99. Dubrovnik State Archives, *Diversa cancellariae*, 12, fol. 238, *die xxviii Junii* 1335.

100. Dubrovnik State Archives, *Diversa cancellariae*, 5, fol. 41, *die vi Marcii* 1313.

101. Dubrovnik State Archives, *Diversa cancellariae*, 12, fol. 240v, *die vi Junii* 1335.

102. Dubrovnik State Archives, *Diversa cancellariae*, 10, fol. 106v, *die xxiii Novembris* 1333.

103. Dubrovnik State Archives, *Diversa cancellariae*, 10, fol. 27, *die xxii Madii* 1333.

104. Dubrovnik State Archives, *Diversa notariae*, 3, fol. 121, *die v Marcii* 1319 and *Diversa cancellariae*, 6, fol. 46, *die xvi Octobris* 1320.

105. Dubrovnik State Archives, *Diversa cancellariae*, 8, fol. 114, *die xxviii Octobris* 1326. The scribe crossed out "argento" and wrote "rame" above the line, possibly silvered copper that fooled his eye initially?

106. Dubrovnik State Archives, *Diversa cancellariae*, 13, fol. 49v, *die xvi Novembris* 1341.

107. Cecchetti, *La vita dei Veneziani*, 125–26.

108. Fingerlin, *Gürtel des hohen*, 334, no. 66, and illustration, no. 372, p. 335.

109. Lopez, "Nota sulla composizione dei patrimoni privati," 232. See Zupko, *Italian Weights and Measures*, 130.

110. Venetian State Archives, *Grazie*, vi, fol. 81v.

111. Fiamma, *Opusculum de rebus gestis*, vol. 12, pt. 4, p. 37.

112. Lancia, "Legge suntuaria," 370–75.

113. Knighton, *Chronicon Henrici Knighton*, 2:58.

114. Ippolito Machetti, "Orafi senesi," *La Diana* 5 (1929): 47.

115. Kelly and Schwabe, *A Short History of Costume and Armor*, 64.

116. François Garnier, *Le langage de l'image au Moyen Age*, vol. 2, *Il grammaire des gestes* (Paris: Le Léopard d'Or, 1982), 171–74; see figs. 232–39.

117. Brendan Cassidy, "A Relic, Some Pictures, and the Mothers of Florence in the Late Fourteenth Century," *Gesta* 30: 2 (1991): 91–99.

118. Jacqueline Marie Musacchio, "Weasels and Pregnancy in Renaissance Italy," *Renaissance Studies* 15: 2 (2001): 172–87.

119. Ful fressh and newe hir geer apike was;
hir knyves were chaped noght with bras
But al with silver, wroght ful clene and wel
Geoffrey Chaucer, *Canterbury Tales*, General Prologue, 361–63

120. Lopez, "Nota sulla composizione dei patrimoni privata," 257, in an inventory of the estate of Dondidio, *speziali* (a spice merchant) for April 30, 1259, pp. 251–58.

121. Venette, *Chronicle*, 63.

122. Cecchetti, *La vita dei Veneziani*, 123. "Le Gemme del Doge Lorenzo Celsi," citing Venetian State Archives, *Procuratori di s. Marco, Misti*, vol. 120.

123. Dubrovnik State Archives, *Diversa cancellariae*, 14, fol. 129, *die vii Januarii* 1345.

124. Dubrovnik State Archives, *Diversa cancellariae*, 8, fol. 176, *die primo Junii* 1327.

125. Franco Sacchetti, *Il Trecentenovelle*, ed. Vincenzio Pernicone (Florence: Sansoni, 1946), Novella XCVIII, p. 221.

126. Dubrovnik State Archives, *Diversa cancellariae*, 9, fol. 104, *die vi Novembris* 1329.

127. Dubrovnik State Archives, *Diversa cancellariae*, 14, fol. 92v, *die xi Marcii* 1344, and *Diversa cancellariae*, 16, fol. 16v, *die xxvii Novembris* 1348.

128. Sacchetti, *Il Trecentenovelle*, Novella CXXXVII, p. 304.

129. Florentine State Archives, *Esecutore degli ordinamenti di giustizia*, 83, fol. 19r, January 21, 1346/7.

130. Donald Queller, "A Different Approach to the Pre-Modern Cost of Living: Venice, 1372–1391," *Journal of European Economic History* 25:2 (1996): 441–64.

131. There were persistent efforts to prevent imitation in a less costly medium. For example, workers in rock crystal at Venice enlisted the government to keep Murano glassmakers from imitating and passing off their blown glass as rock crystal. In many cities statute law specified grades of fineness for bullion in regulation of gold-

smiths. See Angeliki E. Laiou, "Venice as a Centre of Trade and of Artistic Production in the Thirteenth Century," in *Il medio oriente e l'occidente nell'arte del XIII secolo,* ed. Hans Belting (Bologna: CLEUB, 1982), 11–33. For regulations at Venice, see Bartolomeo Cecchetti, "Le industrie in Venezia," *Archivio Veneto* 4 (1872): 212–25. See later discussion for the gradations in silver ore specified by law at Ragusa/Dubrovnik.

132. Geoff Egan and Frances Pritchard, *Dress Accessories, c. 1150–1450* (Woodbridge, Suffolk: Boydell Press, 2002), x. For examples, see Fingerlin, *Gürtel des hohen.*

133. Trexler, *Synodal Law in Florence and Fiesole,* 32–33, and Constitution of Florence, 1310, p. 244, ll. 14–23, in regard to modest apparel for higher and lower clergy.

134. Trexler, *Synodal Law in Florence and Fiesole,* Constitution of 1310, p. 289, ll. 5–19.

Chapter 3

1. Dubrovnik State Archives, *Diversa cancellariae,* 10, fol. 27, *die xxi Madii* 1333.

2. Boccaccio, Sacchetti, Fra Paolino, and Villani all criticize new fashions. Dante singled out belts as representative of the dangerous new trends in consumption. See Dante Aligheri, *The Divine Comedy, Paradiso,* canto 15, ll. 97–102, where Dante contrasts the austerity of his ancestors' generation with the ostentation of his own.

3. On the role of fashion in Sicily, see Salvatore Tramontana, *Vestirsi e Travestirsi in Sicilia: Abbigliamento, festee spettacoli nel medioevo* (Palermo: Sellerio, 1993), 149, specifically, on Nicolo Acciaiuoli.

4. Frangioni, *Chiedere e ottenere,* 37–38.

5. In Ragusa/Dubrovnik there were four grades of silver: *argento plico* (worst or fourth grade of fineness); *argento biancho* (white silver); *argento fino* (fine silver or high grade); and *argento de glama* (gold-laden silver, which was most valuable). Value differed substantially within these four grades.

6. Fingerlin, *Gürtel des hohen,* 310, no. 14. See also the Cleveland belt, p. 310, no. 66, discussed in Chapter 6.

7. Marian Wenzel, "Bosnian History and Austro-Hungarian Policy: Some Medieval Belts, the Bogomil Romance and the King Tvrtko Graves," *Peristil, Povijesno drustvo Hrvatske* 30 (1987): 29–54.

8. Frederic C. Lane and Reinhold C. Mueller, *Money and Banking in Medieval and Renaissance Venice: Coins and Moneys of Account* (Baltimore: Johns Hopkins University Press, 1985), 452. Durdica Petrović, *Dubrovačko Oruzje u XIV Veku* (Belgrade: Vojni Muzej Kosmos, 1976), illustrations on 215–17. Buonaccorso Pitti visited his fellow Florentine, Guido Baldi, royal mintmaster at Buda, in that city in 1376. Florentines had close ties to the king and kingdom of Hungary. Gene A. Brucker, ed., *Two Memoirs of Renaissance Florence: The Diaries of Buonacoiso Piti and Gregorio Dati,* trans. Julia Martines (Prospect Heights, Ill: Waveland Press, 1967), 26.

9. Newton, *Fashion in the Age of the Black Prince,* 2–6. Levi Pisetzky, in *Storia del costume in Italia,* vol. 2, sees greater dominance of Italians over the introduction of fashion in costume.

10. Robbert, "Twelfth-Century Italian Princes," and Lopez, "Nota sulla composizione dei patrimoni privata," 205–64. Both provide examples of such articles of clothing from earlier dates. See Villani, *Cronica,* bk 12, pt. 4, pp. 419–20.

11. Ludovica Sebregondi, "Clothes and Teenagers: What Young Men Wore in

Fifteenth-Century Florence," in *The Premodern Teenager*, ed. Konrad Eisenbichler (Toronto: Center for Reformation and Renaissance Studies, 2002), 27–50.

12. Altichiero, *Bonifacio Lupi and Caterina dei francesi Presented to the Virgin and Child by Saints James the Great and Catherine of Alexandria*, c. 1373–79, fresco, west wall, Chapel of Bonifacio Lupi, the Santo, Padua; and Altichiero, *Council of King Ramiro*, c. 1373–79, fresco, east wall, Chapel of Bonifacio Lupi, the Santo, Padua, in Diana Norman, "Those Who Pay, Those Who Pray, and Those Who Paint: Two Funerary Chapels," in *Siena, Florence and Padua*, 2:188–90, plate 234.

13. Davide Banzato, *Giotto e la pittura del trecento a Padova* (Venice: Marsilio, 1998), 20–27. On markings and uniforms, see Simona Slanicka, "Male Markings: Uniforms in the Parisian Civil War as a Blurring of the Gender Order, A.D. 1410–1420," *Medieval History Journal* 2 (1999): 209–44. In the fifteenth century uniforms and livery became important. Fourteenth-century records make fewer references to livery.

14. "Tunicam unam et guarnazam unam de saia blanca furnita cum frisaturis, perolis, cendato et aliis frunimentis," October 10, 1338, in Cecchetti, *La vita dei Veneziani*, 121.

15. Cecchetti, *La vita dei Veneziani*, 122.

16. Sacchetti, *Il Trecentonovelle*, 443. Some *novelli* have been translated by Mary Steegman in *Tales from Sacchetti* (New York: Dent, 1908), although the translations offered here often differ from Steegman's.

17. Venetian State Archives, *Senato, Deliberationes, Miste*, XXIX, fol. 64. For the text, see Newett, "Sumptuary Laws of Venice," 268n. 48: "et sicut notum est in civitate nostra hodie, plusquam in alique alia parte mundi, fiunt multe vanitates et expense inordinate, circa sponsas et alias mulieres."

18. Fr. Theophilus Bellorini and Fr. Eugene Hoddle, trans. and eds., *Visit to the Holy Places of Egypt, Sinai, Palestine and Syria in 1384 by Frescobaldi, Gucci, and Siglo* (Jerusalem: Franiscan Press, 1948), 34–35.

19. Goldthwaite, in *Wealth and Demand for Art in Italy*, and in "The Renaissance Economy," argues that fifteenth-century Italian consumption was stimulated by one elite's replacing another through political upheaval.

20. Françoise Piponnier and Perrine Mane, *Dress in the Middle Ages*, trans. Caroline Beamish (New Haven, Conn.: Yale University Press, 1997), argue that men generally outspent women on wardrobe in the medieval era.

21. See Warnke, *The Court Artist*, 3–74, for distinctions between civic and court patronage in the fourteenth century.

22. Giotto di Bondone, *Adoration of the Magi*, 1306, Scrovegni Chapel, Padua, Italy; Franco Mario Ricci, *Embriachi: Il trittico di Pavia* (Milan: Bondoni, 1982), 57–76. Antonio Vivarini and Giovanni d'Alemagna, *Epiphany*, c. 1440, Berlin. On the legend of the Magi, see the contemporary Joannes of Hildesheim, *The Three Kings of Cologne: An Early English Translation of the "Historia Trium Regum*," ed. Carl Hortsmann, Early English Text Society, 85 (London: N. Trubner, 1886), and Ugo Monneret de Villard, *Le leggende orientali sui Magi evangelici* (Vatican City: Biblioteca Apostolica Vaticana, 1952). See also Luca Beltrami, *La certosa di Pavia*, 2nd ed. (Milan: U. Hoepli, 1907).

23. Frank Edward Manuel and Fritzie Manuel, *Utopian Thought in the Western World* (Cambridge, Mass.: Belknap, 1979), compares the hierarchical utopia of the Renaissance with more egalitarian notions of utopia that emerged in later centuries. For the quotation, see Gene Brucker, *The Civic World of Early Renaissance Florence* (Princeton, N.J.: Princeton University Press, 1977), 30.

24. Richard Trexler, "The Magi Enter Florence," *Studies in Medieval and Renais-*

sance History, n.s. 1 (1978): 129–32. See Levi Pisetzky, *Storia del costume in Italia,* 2:19, plate 3, *La Famiglia del Conte Stefano Pooro,* Oratorio, Lentate, fresco, 1370. See Levi Pisetzky's discussion at the bottom of the page. By 1370 the long belted robe had been replaced by a shorter, sometimes pleated garment; still the belt remained an important component of costume for men. See also pp. 77–81.

25. Trexler, "The Magi Enter Florence," 139. For fuller treatment of the topic, see Richard C. Trexler, *The Journey of the Magi* (Princeton, N.J.: Princeton University Press, 1997).

26. Trexler, *Journey of the Magi,* 119.

27. Trexler, "The Magi Enter Florence," 129.

28. See M. J. Gegnano, "La bottega degli Embriachi a proposito di opere ignoto o poco note," *Arte Lombardo* 5 (1960): 221–28.

29. Boccaccio, *Decameron,* 632–48.

30. On the mercantile spirit in Boccaccio's work, see Vittore Branca, *Boccaccio: The Man and His Works,* trans. Richard Monges (New York: New York University Press, 1976), 276–307.

31. Frati, *La vita privata,* 235–41, and Mazzi, "Alcune leggi suntuarie senesi."

32. Killerby, *Sumptuary Law in Italy,* 28–29, lists over 325 pieces of legislation in the period covered.

33. This chronology follows Rainey, "Sumptuary Legislation in Renaissance Florence," 648–52, in regard to civic legislation. On synodal legislation, Trexler, *Syndol Legislation in Florence and Fiesole,* provides texts from the Constitution of 1310 and subsequent laws. See also Andrea Lancia's vernacular translation of the important civic sumptuary law of 1355 in "Legge suntuaria," 366–83, 429–43. On sumptuary law at Florence, see also Catherine Guimbard, "Appunti sulla legislazione suntuaria à Firenze dal 1281 al 1384," *Archivio Storico Italiano* 150 (1992): 57–81.

34. Alessandro Gherardi, ed., *Le consulte della repubblica fiorentina dall'anno 1280 all'anno 1298* (Florence: G. C. Sansoni, 1896–98), 1:383, 387.

35. See Villani, *Croniche,* bks. 10, 11, in vol. 1, p. 305.

36. See the recent study by Gérard-Marchant, "Compter et nommer l'étoffe à Florence au trecento."

37. Rainey has collected the major pieces of fourteenth-century legislation in "Sumptuary Legislation in Renaissance Florence," appendices 2–7, pp. 658–742.

38. Trexler, *Synodal Law in Florence and Fiesole,* 229–30, "De consuetudine, Rubrica."

39. Nicholas of Cusa, "A General Reform of the Church," trans. Morimichi Watanabe and Thomas M. Izbicki, in *Nicolas of Cusa on Christ and the Church,* ed. Gerald Christiansen and Thomas M. Iabicki (Leiden and New York: E. J. Brill, 1996), 199.

40. Mazzi, "Alcune leggi suntuarie senesi," 136.

41. Ibid.

42. Rainey, "Sumptuary Legislation in Renaissance Florence," 55, 98n. 51. "Statuti 1322–25," 2:416 (Statuto del Podestà 1325, liber V, rubr. 88, "Quod nulla mulier incedat indute virilibus vestimentis"): "Statutum et ordinetum est quod nulle mulier per civitatem, burgos vel suburgos vadat indute virilibus vestimentis, vel aliquis vir muliebribus indumentis; et quod dominus Potestas teneatur primo mense sui regiminis facere micti bannum per civitatem quod nulla mulier vel vir audeat vel presummet predicta facere, et que contra fecerit post bannum missum fustigetus per civitatem Florentie, scilicet a palatio Communis usque ad locum ubi invencta fuerit, et quotiens invenitur contra facere." The issue of cross-dressing will be taken up in the following chapter.

43. Rainey, "Sumptuary Legislation in Renaissance Florence," 200–214.

44. Ibid., 393, citing Florentine State Archives, *Esecutore degli Ordinamenti de Giustizia*, 92, fol. 5r, July 17, 1347. See also 11r and 14r for two other indictments. Rainey notes that the cases differ because the number of witnesses to the infringement of the law was great.

45. Bistort, *Il magistrato alle pompe nella Republica di Venezia*, 323–29. Cesare Foucard, ed. *Lo statuto inedito delle nozze veneziane nell'anno 1299, nozze* (Venice: Tipografia del Commercio, 1858), 8–14. See also Foucard's notes on the text (1899), pt. 1, p. 42, that placed the first legislation even earlier, in 1274.

46. Frati, *La vita privata*, 239.

47. *Deliberationes*, ed. Cessi and Brunetti, 2:323–26.

48. Samuele Romanin, ed., *Storia documentata di Venezia*, 3rd ed. (Venice: Filippi, 1973), 3:280–83.

49. "Cum sit habenda bona consideratio et matura deliberatio quando fieri volunt decreta, que generaliter et indifferenter tangunt omnes cives, subditos, et habitatores, et specialiter in rebus super quibus semper fuit vel sit difficile dari ordo qui sit cum contentamento omnium, sicut sunt vestimenta, iocalia, et alia ornamenta, tam de perlis, quam de auro et argento et lapidibus preciosis, et similiter de dotibus sive repromissis, aut coredis, vel donis: et properea, consideratis predistis, et quod sepe posite sunt partes ab improviso ad Consilia Venetiarum super quibus non est habitum pensamentum, et non redundarunt nec redundant nostro communi et nostris civibus et subditis in illam utilitatem et commodum que putantur." Newett, "Sumptuary Laws of Venice," 271, citing Venetian State Archives, *Senato, Deliberationes Miste*, reg. XLVI, fol. 99.

50. Bistort, *Il magistrato alle pompe nella Republica di Venezia*, 69–70. Bartolomeo Cecchetti, "La donna nel medio evo à Venezia," *Archivo Veneto*, n.s. 31 (1899): pt. 1, 42. Cecchetti argued that Pope Gregory X's prohibition of feminine ornaments for all the Christian world was the origin of sumptuary legislation (pontificate, 1271–76); however, Venetians did not pay much attention.

51. Foucard, *Lo statuto inedito delle nozze veneziane*, 23–24.

52. Killerby, *Sumptuary Law in Italy*, 38–39, regards the heyday of legislative controls on women's dress as the late fourteenth and fifteenth centuries.

53. See in particular Muzzarelli, *Gli ignanni delle apparenze* and *Guardaroba medievale* for insightful analysis of Bologna's sumptuary laws. The Angevin king Charles I of Naples and Sicily faced active dissent against sumptuary law from women in the Straits of Messina in 1273. Guiseppe del Giudice, "Una legge suntuaria inedita del 1290," *Atti dell'accademia pontaniana* 16:2 (1886): 121–22.

54. Rainey, "Sumptuary Legislation in Renaissance Florence," 145.

55. Gene Brucker, ed., *The Society of Renaissance Florence: A Documentary Study* (New York: Harper, 1971), 179–80. Brucker cites *I capitoli del commune di Firenze*, ed. Cesare Guasti and Alessandro Gherardi (Florence: M. Cellini, 1866–93), 2:173–74.

56. Cessi and Brunetti, *Deliberationes*, 2:314–26 for May 26, 1334–June 20, 1334.

57. Frati, *La vita privata*, p. 238: "Ordinamus quod nulla persona parva vel magna audeat vel presumat portare, vel mittere, vel portari seu mitti facere alicui presbitero de novo faciendo, vel monacho vel monache, vel fratri, vel sorori, vel alicui religiose persone cereos, vel candellas, vel fogacias, vel toaglias, vel aliquod allud dare et quicunque contrafecerit condempnetur proqualibet vice in decem lib. Bon."

58. Jones, *The Italian City-State*, 208.

59. This does not mean that enforcement would be the same for commoner and patrician. In regard to social crimes Guido Ruggiero found that nobles and commoners

were treated quite differently in the courts. Ruggiero, *The Boundaries of Eros: Sex, Crime and Sexuality in Renaissance Venice* (New York: Oxford University Press, 1985), 60–65. To compare English sumptuary law that regulated by rank and wealth, see John Scattergood, "Fashion and Morality in the Late Middle Ages," in *Reading the Past,* ed. John Scattergood (Portland, Ore.: Four Courts Press, 1996), 240–57.

60. The sixteenth century represented something of a departure, particularly in Florence where distinction by class became significant in sumptuary law. See Carlo Carnesecchi, *Donna e lusso a Firenze nel secolo XVI: Cosimo I e la sua legge suntuaria del 1562* (Florence: Cocchi i Chiti, 1902), 37. There were some intimations of class expressed earlier. Venice exempted the doge's family from sumptuary legislation, and the law of 1355 in Florence exempted the spouse of a *cavalieri* from the prohibition against fine furs. See Lancia, "Legge suntuaria," 373. In 1453 Cardinal Giovanni Bessarion, papal legate to Bologna, designed a sumptuary law that specified women's dress by class. See Muzzarelli, *Gli inganni delle apparenze,* 118, and Catherine Kovesi Killerby, "'Heralds of a Well-Instructed Mind': Nicolosa Sanuti's Defense of Women and Their Clothes," *Renaissance Studies* 13 (1999): 255–63.

61. Regulations of a secondhand market at Venice date from the thirteenth century, and that market thrived on the stepped-up consumption of the fourteenth century. See Patricia Allerston, "Wedding Finery in Sixteenth-Century Venice," in *Marriage in Italy, 1300–1650,* ed. Trevor Dean and K. J. P. Lowe (Cambridge: Cambridge University Press, 1998), 36.

62. Venetian State Archives, *Senato, Deliberationes, Miste,* XXIX, fol. 64. For the text, see Newett, "Sumptuary Laws of Venice," 268–69n. 48: "et sicut notum est in civitate nostra hodie, plusquam in alique alia parte mundi, fiunt multe vanitates et expense inordinate, circa sponsas et alias mulieres."

63. Newett, "Sumptuary Laws of Venice," 268. This occurred later in the fifteenth century.

64. Andrea Lancia apparently petitioned the Florentine government in 1355 that a copy of these proclamations be translated for use.

65. See Frank, *Luxury Fever,* 140, for an economic behaviorist view of how contemporary businessmen might regard investment dressing.

66. Cessi, *Deliberationes,* 2:324. See Bistort, *Il magistrato alle pompe nella Republica di Venezia,* 331, 334. See also Newett, "Sumptuary Laws of Venice," 263–72.

67. Trexler, *Synodal Law in Florence and Fiesole,* 230, 105. The Constitution of 1310 regulated artisans who produced luxury wares. See Rainey, "Sumptuary Legislation in Renaissance Florence," 694–706. Mazzi, "Alcune leggi suntuarie senesi," 136.

68. Newett, "Sumptuary Laws of Venice," 249–50.

69. Foucard, *Lo statuto inedito delle nozze veneziane,* 23–24, and Cecchetti, "La donna nel medio evo à Venezia," pt. 1, pp. 41–43. The papacy began regulating "immoderate ornamentation" in 1274 with an edict issued by Pope Gregory X. See Alan Hunt, *Governance of the Consuming Passions: A History of Sumptuary Law* (New York: St. Martin's Press, 1996), 26.

70. Venetian State Archives, *Deliberationi, Maggior Consiglio, Spiritus (copia),* XXIV, fol. 97. These fashions were headdresses of pearls and borders on robes of pearls. The "pearls" in question might very well have been glass beads. Murano produced these in great numbers.

71. Florentines had a particular concern over *lettere*—symbols embroidered onto fabrics, or otherwise applied. See further discussion in Chapter 4.

72. Mazzi, "Alcune leggi suntuarie senesi," 135, in particular.

73. Daniel Miller, *Material Culture and Mass Consumption* (Oxford: Blackwell, 1987), 135–36. Emulation is the favored agent of change here and thus Miller's analysis owes much to Simmel, "Fashion."

74. The Venetian law of 1299 was almost entirely directed at controlling weddings and wedding gifts. Thereafter the agenda broadened. In Florence at the end of 1290, a registry to denounce excessive dress was introduced in Florence; the earliest extant civil laws dated from 1307. See Guimbard, "Appunti sulla legislazione suntuarie," 57–81.

75. Frank, *Luxury Fever,* 140.

76. Henry Brod, "Constructions of Masculinities in the Canonical Texts of Western Political Theory" (paper presented at the Society for Women in Philosophy, Pacific Division Meeting, May 21, 1994, California State Polytechnic University, Pomona), 3.

77. (Fra) Paolino Minorita, *Trattato de regimine rectoris, nell'anno 1314,* ed. Cesare Foucard, Nozze (Venice: Pietro Naratovich, 1856), chap. 2, p. 4.

78. Rainey, "Sumptuary Legislation in Renaissance Florence," pragmatic of 1356, no. 2, p. 669, and no. 22, pp. 680–81.

79. In the fifteenth century spending on men's wardrobes among affluent Florentine families would continue to be comparable to spending on women's wardrobes, as Carole Frick notes in "Dressing the Renaissance City: Society, Economics and Gender in the Clothing of Fifteenth-Century Florence" (Ph.D. diss., University of California, Los Angeles, 1995), 458. This remained true despite the change in fashion occasioned by a revolution in taste that moved men away from silver gilt accessories and other comparable luxuries.

80. See Chapter 4. Lifetime allotment of fine dresses was four.

81. 1 *lira di grossi* = 10 ducats. See Lane and Mueller, *Money and Banking in Medieval and Renaissance Venice: Coins and Moneys of Account,* 338, 338n.15; Newett, "Sumptuary Laws of Venice," 264; and Bistort, *Il magistrato alle pompe,* 343–48. On cost of living at Venice, see Chapter 5 and Gino Luzzatto, "Il costo della vita a Venezia nel trecento," in his *Studi di storia economica veneziana* (Padua: CEDAM, 1954), 285–97, and more recently Queller, "A Different Approach to the Pre-modern Cost of Living." Queller suggests a noblewoman's median allowance for cost of living, adjusted for housing, would be forty-two ducats in 1372–77, somewhat after the passage of the law under discussion. He also notes that dresses estimated at forty ducats each were expensive items in any budget.

82. Lancia, "Legge suntuaria," 370–75.

83. Trexler, *Synodal Law in Florence and Fiesole,* 229, Constitution of 1310.

84. Lancia, "Legge suntuaria," 373, 377. On women and sumptuary law at weddings, see Christiane Klapisch-Zuber, *Women, Family and Ritual in Renaissance Italy,* trans. Lydia Cochrane (Chicago: University of Chicago Press, 1985), 241–46.

85. Newett, "Sumptuary Laws of Venice," 262; Bistort, *Il magistrato alle pompe,* 343–45.

86. Rainey, "Sumptuary Legislation in Renaissance Florence," 214.

87. Jones, *The Italian City-State,* 511.

88. Frederic Chapin Lane, "Merchant Galleys, 1300–34," in *Venice and History* (Baltimore: Johns Hopkins University Press, 1966), 216.

89. Sumptuary laws were considered, passed, collected, or revised by successive Florentine regimes over the century. Excesses of aristocratic dress remaining in the 1340s after Walter of Brienne was expelled have been claimed as one reason for creating sumptuary legislation, but this fails to explain the rare concurrence among legislators of various political leanings over the propriety of limiting consumption.

90. The closing of the patriciate in the fourteenth century raises the issue of class

at Venice. However, sumptuary law was adamant in imposing limits regardless of social or family status. See Dennis Romano, *Patrician and Popolani: The Social Foundations of the Venetian Renaissance State* (Baltimore: Johns Hopkins University Press, 1987), for a review of the debate on noble privilege and civic legislation. For Florence, see Anthony Molho, *Marriage Alliances in Late Medieval Florence* (Cambridge, Mass.: Harvard University Press, 1994), who argues that Florence possessed an intermarrying elite that created solidarity among the aristocracy. At Florence in the 1370s sumptuary laws were enacted frequently but apparently the government in power after 1378, with a large representation of the *arti minori,* had more pressing matters of concern, and no sumptuary laws were passed in this period. Only in 1384 when the *arti minori* had lost their position did the elites returned to power gather together sumptuary pronouncements in one pragmatic and again broadcast them in the city.

91. On anti-aristocratic bias in the law, see Hughes, "Sumptuary Law and Social Relations in Renaissance Cities," 69–73.

92. Jones, *The Italian City-State,* 252–53.

93. Sir William Stanley Jevons, *Money and the Mechanism of Exchange* (New York: D. Appleton, 1875), 78–80. See discussion of this principle as it applies to medieval Venice in Lane and Mueller, *Money and Banking in Medieval and Renaissance Venice: Coins and Moneys of Account,* 59. On interrelated personnel in merchant banking, goldsmithery, and the office of the mint, see Alan Stahl, *Zecca: The Mint of Venice in the Middle Ages* (Baltimore: Johns Hopkins University Press, 2000), 99–280.

94. See the classic study of Armando Sapori, *La crisi delle compagnie mercantili dei Bardi e dei Peruzzi* (Florence: Olschki, 1926), for the extent of the Florentine banking network before the crisis of the 1340s.

95. See Trexler, "The Magi Enter Florence," 163–85. See Ricci, *Embriachi;* see also Antonia Bostrom, "Embriachi," in *Dictionary of Art,* ed. Jane Turner (New York: Grove, 1996), 10:178–80.

96. Norman, *Siena, Florence and Padua,* makes a major contribution to understanding of patronage and the role of patronage and politics in artistic production.

97. Reginald Abbott, "What Becomes a Legend Most? Fur in the Medieval Romance," *Dress* 21 (1994): 5.

98. The great merchant banking houses were precipitated into bankruptcy by the repudiation of loans on the part of their royal debtors, a lesson about regal condition that does not seem to have affected the Florentine fascination with the legend of the Three Kings.

99. This does not mean that women and youths might not, in turn, attempt to accomplish their own ends through fashion. The *sapientes* did not dress in explicitly sexual clothes. Apparently at times women tended to display their shoulders and breasts more than in the past and young men appear to have challenged their elders with tight hose, pointed shoes, and, later, codpieces. See Banner, "The Fashionable Sex," 40; Patricia Simons, "Alert and Erect: Masculinity in Some Italian Renaissance Portraits of Fathers and Sons," in *Gender Rhetorics: Postures of Dominance and Submission in History,* ed. Richard C. Trexler, Medieval and Renaissance Studies and Texts, 113 (Binghamton, N.Y.: Medieval and Renaissance Texts and Studies, 1994), 163–86; and Jacqueline Murray, "Hiding behind the Universal Man: Male Sexuality in the Middle Ages," in *Handbook of Medieval Sexuality,* ed. Vern Bullough and James A. Brundage (New York: Garland, 1996), 123–46.

100. Stuard, "The Adriatic Trade in Silver," 113.

101. Diane Owen Hughes, "Distinguishing Signs: Ear-rings, Jews and Franciscan Rhetoric in the Italian Renaissance City," *Past and Present* 112 (1986): 3–59.

102. Miller, *Material Culture and Mass Consumption,* 136.

Chapter 4

1. See *Statuti della Repubblica Fiorentina*, ed. Romolo Caggese (Florence: Tip. Galileiana, 1910), 1:222–31. For other thirteenth- and fourteenth-century statutes, see Gherardi, *Le consulte della repubblica fiorentina*, and Guasti and Gherardi, *I capitoli del comune di Firenze* vol. 2. Rainey, "Sumptuary Legislation in Renaissance Florence," 292–362, provides the texts of a number of fourteenth-century sumptuary laws.

2. Sacchetti, *Il Trecentonovelle*, 303–5.

3. Like trims on robes, buttons as decoration marching down a sleeve from shoulder to wrist were a style popular among men at Florence. See Giotto di Bondone, *The Expulsion of Joachim from the Temple*.

4. This refers to Roman women's revolt against the Oppian Law in 195 B.C.E., related in Livy, *Historia*, trans. Evan T. Sage, Loeb Classical Library (London: W. Heinemann, 1935), vol. 9, bk. 34, chap. 1, pp. 412–45.

5. "fu detto per tuto l'officio a messer Amerigo, che guardasse di far quello che ben fosse e l'avanzo si stesse." Sacchetti, *Il Trecentonovelle*, Novello 137, p. 305.

6. Brundage, "Sumptuary Laws and Prostitution in Late Medieval Italy."

7. Venetian State Archives, *Senato, deliberations, Miste*, reg. 24, fol. 64. For the edited text and provisions of the law, see Romanin, *Storia documentata di Venezia*, 3: 280–82. See also Newett, "Sumptuary Laws of Venice," 268n. 48, who translates the following from the preamble (not contained in Romanin): "et sicut notum est in civitate nostra hodie, plusquam in alique alia parte mundi, fiunt multe vanitates et expense inordinate, circa sponsas et alias mulieres."

8. Salimbene de Adam, *The Chronicle of Salimbene de Adam*, ed. and trans. Joseph L. Baird, Giuseppe Baglivi, and John Robert Kane (Binghamton, N.Y.: Medieval and Renaissance Texts and Studies, 1986), 160–61, and Villani, *Croniche*, bk. 10, chap. 2 in vol. 1, pp. 301–2.

9. Newett, "Sumptuary Laws of Venice," 265.

10. Guimbard, "Appunti sulla legislazione suntuaria," 57–81. See Manlio Bellomo, *Le condizione giuridica della donna in Italia: Vicende antiche e moderne* (Turin: Eri, 1970), and Carole Lansing, "Gender and Civic Authority: Sexual Control in a Medieval Italian Town," *Journal of Social History* 31 (1997): 33–60. A sumptuary law of Orvieto in 1311 linked female dress to attempts to arouse men's desire and employed civic authority to curtail women's provocative attire (p. 43).

11. By contrast the *mundualdus* of fifteenth-century Florence was an adaptation of a Lombardic legal principle, although it scarcely resembles the *mundualdus* as defined in earlier Lombardic law. See Thomas Kuehn, "'*Cum consensu mundualdi*': Legal Guardianship of Women in Quattrocentro Florence," *Viator* 13 (1982): 309–22.

12. Mario Chiaudano, ed., *Studi e documenti per la storia del diritto commerciale italiano nel secolo XIII*, Memorie dell'Istituto Giuridico (Turin: Presso Istituto Giuridico della R. Università, 1930), l. See also Eleanor S. Riemer, "Women in the Medieval City: Sources and Uses of Wealth by Sienese Women in the Thirteenth Century" (Ph.D. diss., New York University, 1975), 70.

13. Diane Owen Hughes, "From Brideprice to Dowry in Mediterranean Europe," *Journal of Family History* 8 (1978): 262–96.

14. Ibid., and Riemer, "Women in the Medieval City," 70.

15. Christiane Klapisch-Zuber, "The Griselda Complex: Dowry and Marriage Gifts in the Quattrocentro," in *Women, Family and Ritual in Renaissance Italy*, trans. Lydia Cochrane (Chicago: University of Chicago Press, 1985), 213–46.

16. Salimbene de Adam, *Chronicle*, 160–61.

17. Constitution of 1310, in Trexler, *Synodal Law in Florence and Fiesole*, 229, ll. 4–12.

18. Susan Mosher Stuard, "Dowry Increase and Increments in Wealth in Medieval Ragusa (Dubrovnik)," *Journal of Economic History* 41 (1981): 795–811. Enrico Besta, *La famiglia nella storia del diritto italiano* (Milan: A. Guiffre, 1962), and Stanley Chojnacki, "Dowries and Kinsmen in Early Renaissance Venice," in *Women in Medieval Society,* ed. Susan Mosher Stuard (Philadelphia: University of Pennsylvania Press, 1976), 173–98. Husbands' gifts to wives are referred to here as *vestis vidualis.* See R. Corso, "Patti d'amore: I doni nuziali," *Revue d'ethnographie et de sociologie* 2 (1911): 228–54, as well as Molmenti, *La storia di venezia nella vita privata,* vol. 1.

19. Romanin, *Storia documentata di Venezia,* vol. 3, bk. 8, pp. 280–83. At Venice both families gave gifts to the bride and these were limited by law in 1360 to 400 ducats from the bride's family and 300 from the groom and his family. On wedding gifts at Venice in the fourteenth century, see Chojnacki, "Dowries and Kinsmen in Early Renaissance Venice," 173–79, and "Patrician Women in Early Renaissance Venice," *Studies in the Renaissance* 21 (1974): 176–203.

20. See Julius Kirshner, "Pursuing Honor while Avoiding Sin: The *Monte delle doti* of Florence," *Studi Senesi* 89, 3rd ser., 26 (1977): 177–258.

21. Susan Mosher Stuard, "Burdens of Matrimony: Husbanding and Gender in Medieval Italy, c. 1140," in *Medieval Masculinities: Regarding Men in the Middle Ages,* ed. Claire Lees, Thelma S. Fenster, and JoAnn McNamara (Minneapolis: University of Minnesota Press, 1994), 61–72. For the same issue from the perspective of the wife, see Stuard, "From Women to Woman: New Thinking about Gender, c. 1140," *Thought* 64 (1989): 208–19.

22. Klapisch-Zuber, "The Griselda Complex," 213–26.

23. In 1273 women's complaints about restrictions on dowries, gold, pearls, and other ornaments stemmed from the fact that the new laws of the Angevin king Charles I violated *antiche usanze,* that is, traditional rights, in this instance the rights of women from the Straits of Messina. Giudice, "Una legge suntuaria inedita del 1290," 122.

24. The phrase should be attributed to the Roman emperor Majoran, who made dowry a condition for legal marriage.

25. Gratian, *Decretum,* in *Corpus Juris Canonici,* ed. Emil Friedberg (Graz: Bernard Tauchnitz, 1911), vol. 1, *Questio* 5, cols. 1254–55.

26. Kuehn, "*Cum consensu mundualdi,*" 309–22. Historians have argued that a number of women in Florence continued to appear in court unrepresented by a man appointed to represent them despite this.

27. But women were vocal in asserting their own rights, and the formality of a male representative in court was not always respected, as numerous historians of Florence have pointed out.

28. Stanley Chojnacki, "From Trousseau to Groomgift in Late Medieval Venice," in *Medieval and Renaissance Venice,* ed. Ellen Kittell and Thomas Madden (Urbana: University of Illinois Press, 1999), 141–65; Jane Fair Bestor, "Marriage Transactions in Renaissance Italy and Mauss's Essay on the Gift," *Past and Present* 164 (August 1999): 6–46.

29. Perhaps Reinhold Mueller has stated this most explicitly when discussing the Procurators of St. Mark at Venice: "The government, however, viewed itself as a *pater familias* with a responsibility to those of its families which lacked a head, and it was this area of public service which the state conferred on the *Procuratori di S. Marco.*"

Mueller, "The Procurators of San Marco in the Thirteenth and Fourteenth Centuries," *Studi Veneziani* 13 (1971): 147.

30. Fra Paolino Minorita, *Trattato de regimine rectoris*, chap. VIII, p. 9. Also in Newett, "Sumptuary Laws of Venice," 263.

31. Ginevra Niccolini di Camugliano, *The Chronicles of a Florentine Family, 1200– 1470* (London: J. Cape, 1933), 66.

32. Bellomo, *Le condizione giuridica della donna in Italia*, 35–78.

33. Julius Kirshner, "Materials for a Gilded Cage: Non-dotal Assets in Florence, 1300–1500," in *The Family in Italy from Antiquity to the Present*, ed. David L. Kertzer and Richard P. Saller (New Haven, Conn.: Yale University Press, 1991), 184–207.

34. Ian MacLean, *The Renaissance Notion of Woman: A Study of the Fortunes of Scholasticism and Medieval Science and European Intellectual Life* (Cambridge: Cambridge University Press, 1980), 3.

35. On polarities as prerational constructs in Classical Greek thought, see G. E. R. Lloyd, *Polarity and Analogy: Two Types of Argumentation in Early Greek Thought* (Cambridge: Cambridge University Press, 1971).

36. Villani, *Chroniche*, bk. 10, chap. 11 in vol. 1, p. 305. On efforts to control sexuality through controlling women's disorderly appetites, see Pierre J. Payer, *The Bridling of Desire: Views of Sex in the Later Middle Ages* (Toronto: University of Toronto Press, 1993), and Brundage, *Law, Sex, and Christian Society in Medieval Europe*. See also Paolo de Certaldo, *Libro di buoni costumi*, ed. Alfredo Schiaffini (Florence: Le Monnier, 1945), 132, no. 183. "La donna dee essere sollicita in casa e onesta fuori e divota in chiese"; that is, modest.

37. *Aristotle's Politics and Poetics*, trans. Benjamin Jowett and Thomas Twining (New York: Viking, 1957), bk. 1, chap. 12, p. 21, and chap. 13, p. 22.

38. Christine de Pizan was a notable exception. See Liliane Dulac, "Mystical Inspiration and Political Knowledge: Advice to Widows from Francesco da Barberino and Christine de Pizan," trans. Thelma Fenster in *Upon My Husband's Death: Widows in the Literature and Histories of Medieval Europe*, ed. Louise Mirrer (Ann Arbor: University of Michigan Press, 1992), 223–58.

39. Salimbene de Adam, *Cronicle*, 1:246, "et turbavit mulieres omnes cum quadam constitutione quam fecit; in qua continebatur quod mulieres haberent vestimenta curta usque ad terram et tantum plus, quanta est unius palme mensura."

40. Villani, *Croniche*, bk. 10, chap. 11, in vol. 1, p. 305.

41. Benjamin Kohl, "Fina da Carrara, née Buzzacarini: Consort, Mother, and Patron of Art in Trecento Padua," in *Beyond Isabella: Secular Women Patrons of Art in Renaissance Italy*, ed. Sheryl E. Reiss and David G. Wilkins (Kirksville, Mo.: Truman State University Press, 2001), 19–35.

42. For bibliography of Renaissance women's writing, see Letizia Panizza, "A Guide to Recent Bibliography on Italian Renaissance Writings about and by Women," *Bulletin of the Society for Italian Studies* 22 (1989): 3–24.

43. "In the fourteenth and fifteenth centuries, licit female public appearance was, more often than not, religiously sanctioned." It might be added that it was also a rare outing. See Adrian W.B. Randolph, "Regarding Women in Sacred Space," in *Picturing Women in Renaissance and Baroque Italy*, ed. Geraldine A. Johnson and Sara F. Matthews Grieco (Cambridge: Cambridge University Press, 1997), 17–33. Sermons were often directed at women in regard to public appearances.

44. In Provence women troubadours were much more vocal about sumptuary restriction. See Matilda Tomaryn Bruckner, Laurie Shepard, and Sara Melhado White,

eds. and trans., *Songs of the Women Troubadours* (New York: Garland, 1995), 102–3. "Sirventesca" (type of lyric genre) anonymous, from the late thirteenth century.

45. See Villani, *Chroniche*, bk. 11, chap. 94 in vol. 1, pp. 419–20, on schooling in arithmetic and reading for boys and girls at Florence.

46. Iris Origo, *The Merchant of Prato* (New York: Knopf, 1957), 169–87. For Margherita Datini's correspondence, see Francesco de Marco Datini, *Le lettere di Margherita Datini a Francesco di Marco (1384–1410)*, ed. Valeria Rosati (Prato: Cassa di Risparmi e Depositi, 1977).

47. See Killerby, " 'Heralds of a Well-Instructed Mind,' " 256–58.

48. Edward Muir, *Civic Ritual Life in Renaissance Venice* (Princeton, N.J.: Princeton University Press, 1981), 135. See also Newett, "Sumptuary Laws of Venice," 255–61, and Dennis Romano, "Gender and the Urban Geography of Renaissance Venice," *Journal of Social History* 23 (1989): 339–53. On the Festival of the Twelve Maries, see Martin da Canal, *Les estoires de Venice*, ed. Alberto Limentani, Civiltà Veneziana fonti e testi, no. 12, 3rd ser., 3 (Florence: Olschki, 1972); Silvio Tramontin, "Una pagina de folklore," in *La religiosità popolare nella valle padana: Atti del II convegno di studi folklore padano, Modena, Marzo 19–20-21, 1965* (Modena: ENAL, 1966), 401–17. Giambattista Galliccioli, *Storie e memorie venete antiche* (Venice: Domenico Fracasso, 1795), 6:4–5, contains primary material relating to the festival. See also Romanin, *Storia documentata di Venezia*, 3:250–51, and Bistort, *Il magistrato alle pompe*, 16, 77–90. Bistort noted, "in XII magioni XII Marie apparecchiate si ricca e bellamente, che egli e una meraviglia a vedere" (83).

49. Muir, *Civic Ritual Life in Renaissance Venice*, 140.

50. Cecchetti, "La donna nel Medio Evo a Venezia," 69.

51. Venetian State Archives, *Maggior Consiglio, Deliberationes, Spiritus (copia)*, fols. 281–281v (fols. 355–355v), *die ultimo Novembris* 1341.

52. Ibid., fol. 381v (fol. 455v), *die xxiii Decembris* 1347.

53. Romanin, *Storia documentata di Venezia*, 3:251n. 27.

54. Muir, *Civic Ritual Life in Renaissance Venice*, 143–44.

55. Ibid., 137, for both quotations. Apparently the source was a certain thirteenth-century Marco, and the passage was published by Angelo Zon in *Archivio storico italiano* 8 (1845): 226–27. The *Zibaldone da Canal* did not mention this event although it was contemporaneous. Dotson, *Merchant Culture in Fourteenth-Century Venice*, 152–53.

56. Galliccioli, *Storie e memorie venete antiche*, 6:5, quotes a contemporary condemnation of women's ostentations at the festival and a chronicle account for 1378 justifying prohibitions and the reform of the procession to Santa Maria Formosa.

57. Romanin, *Storia documentata di Venezia*, 3:280–82.

58. Newett, "Sumptuary Laws of Venice," 262. See more discussion in Chapter 2.

59. Lansing, "Gender and Civic Authority," 43. Lansing calls the thirteenth century the great era of Franciscan sermonizing that equated women with *luxuria* and carnality. For a Venetian example of a Franciscan homily from 1314, see Fra Paolino Minorita, *Trattato de regimine rectoris*.

60. Rainey, "Sumptuary Legislation in Renaissance Florence," 303–13. The fine for this violation was 2 florins in the law, so we may assume here that six *lira* equaled 2 florins in 1347. The ratio of 1 *lira* to the gold florin had been established in 1252 but silver currency depreciated thereafter, and, 3 *lira* equaled the florin by 1347.

Fines, which were set relatively high, were figured in petty currency using the appropriate money of account. See Chapter 5 for comparative prices and further discussion of gabelles, which were, apparently, commonly paid, so lead seals were frequently seen on the streets of Florence. It is interesting that while limits were set in florins, fines were given out in petty silver coins that depreciated over the decades, reducing whatever schedule lawmakers had originally intended in comparison to the cost of the purchased ornament. Nevertheless, fines demanded at Florence remained high.

61. More than three rings were also forbidden by sumptuary law to women in Bologna. See Frati, *La vita privata,* text of *Ordinamenti Suntuari,* 1289, p. 240.

62. Rainey, "Sumptuary Legislation in Renaissance Florence," 309–10, citing Florentine State Archives, *Esecutore* 116, fol. 2v–24v.

63. Rainey, "Sumptuary Legislation in Renaissance Florence," 311.

64. Ibid., 322.

65. Hughes, "Sumptuary Law and Social Relations in Renaissance Cities," 87–88. For analysis of the Florentine registry of clothes of 1343, see Gérard-Marchant, "Compter et nommer l'étoffe à Florence au trecento."

66. Florentine State Archives, *Esecutore degli Ordinamenti de Giustizia,* 83, fol. 27r, January 23, 1346/7. See also Rainey, "Sumptuary Legislation in Renaissance Florence," 563n. 7.

67. See Slanicka, "Male Markings," 212. Slanicka argues that in the later Middle Ages badges could be chosen "almost at random" and that "the most visible form of wearing the new devices was by stitching them on to clothes."

68. Brian Spencer, *Pilgrim Souvenirs and Secular Badges* (London: The Stationery Office, 1998), 252.

69. On astrology and propitious signs for celebrations at Florence, see Richard Trexler, "Ritual Behavior in Renaissance Florence: The Setting," *Medievalia et Humanistica: Studies in Medieval and Renaissance Culture,* n.s. 4 (1973): 125–44.

70. Rainey, "Sumptuary Legislation in Renaissance Florence," 335–38.

71. Ibid., 330.

72. Women were forbidden cloth of gold in Florentine sumptuary law, but they could wear silk, and the embroidery was created with silk thread on wool.

73. Caggese, *Statuti della Repubblica Fiorentina,* 1:227–28: "Item quod nulla persona masculus vel femina, parva vel magna, cuiuscumque dignitatis aut gradus existat, fatiat vel fieri fatiat aut portet vel teneat aliquem vestem in qua sint incise, sute, fonficte vel supraposita alique ymagines vel avium vel aliarum quarumcumque figurarum, sub pena librarum centum f.p." Found in Rainey, "Sumptuary Legislation in Renaissance Florence," 95.

74. Rainey, "Sumptuary Legislation in Renaissance Florence," 72.

75. Mark Phillips, *The Memoir of Marco Parenti: A Life in Medici Florence* (Princeton, N.J.: Princeton University Press, 1987), 150–67. This became the practice in Florence in the fifteenth century.

76. Item 30, *Capitoli del Comune di Firenze* 12, fol. 48–54, in Rainey, "Sumptuary Legislation in Renaissance Florence," 68.

77. Klapisch-Zuber, "The Griselda Complex," 237.

78. Mazzi, *Argenti degli Acciaiuoli,* 6–29, with notes translating archaic terms.

79. Levi Pisetzky, *Storia del costume in Italia,* 2:69.

80. See earlier discussion. Fingerlin, *Gürtel des hohen,* 310, number 14, and illus. 314.

81. Katharine R. Brown, "Six Gothic Brooches at the Cloisters," in *The Cloisters: Studies in Honor of the Fiftieth Anniversary,* ed. Elizabeth C. Parker (New York: Metropolitan Museum of Art, 1992), 409–19. For Mary's initial "M" on a pilgrim's badge, see

Michael Mitchiner, *Medieval Pilgrim and Secular Badges* (London: Hawkins, 1986), 104. For amatory badges with letters, see Spencer, *Pilgrim Souvenirs*, 319–21.

82. See Debra Pincus, "Hard Times and Ducal Radiance," in *Venice Reconsidered*, ed. John Martin and Dennis Romano (Baltimore: Johns Hopkins University Press, 2000), 89–136.

83. Dubrovnik State Archives, *Diversa cancellariae*, 8, fol. 114, *die xxviii Octobris* 1328. There were also *frontale* or head ornaments and bangles described as *agrillanda* featuring open or cut work in silver. *Diversa notariae*, 3, fol. 110v, *die xiiii Februarii* 1319, and fol. 121v, *die v Marcii* 1319.

84. Molmenti, *Venice*, pt. 2, pp. 196–201. "Et liceat ipsi domine ducisse vendere de bonis nostris mobilibus pro solvendo et satisfaciendo sibi de sua dote et de eo quod sibi tenemus per catam, et pro satisfaciendis nostris debitis si qua forent" (197).

85. Francesco da Barberino, *Del Reggimento e costumi di donna . . .* , ed. Carlo Baudi di Vesme (Bologna: Gaetano Romagnoli, 1875), 207, pt. 2, ll. 40–42. On the plight of widows in Barberino's work, see Dulac, "Mystical Inspiration and Political Knowledge," and Catherine Guimbard, "Le reggimento e costumi di donna de Francesco da Barberino: Une Oeuvre Témoin," *Revue des études italiennes* 36 (1990): 43–58.

86. Francesco da Barberino, *Reggimento e costumi di donna*, 232–33, pt. 2, ll. 33–34. A more modern edition exists: Francesco da Barberino, *Reggimento e costumi di donna*, ed. Giuseppe E. Sansone (Turin: Loescher-Chiantore, 1957), pt. 2, pp. 23–36.

87. Dubrovnik State Archives, *Diversa cancellariae*, 16, fol. 16v, *die xxvi Marcii* 1348. A *corona alba* costing two ducats was probably not intended to adorn the head of royalty.

88. Gérard-Marchant, "Compter et nommer l'étoffe à Florence au trecento," 99–102. Compare to Susan Crane, *The Performance of Self* (Philadelphia: University of Pennsylvania Press, 2002), 12. In 1393 the earl of Mortimer's loose robe was cut from nine yards of satin and covered with embroidered leeches, water, rocks, gilded whelks, gilded mussels, and fifteen cockles of white silver, weighing twelve ounces, Troy weight.

89. Margaret Labarge, "Stitches in Time: Medieval Embroidery in its Social Setting," *Florilegium* 16 (1999): 77–96. See also *Art and the Courts: France and England from 1259 to 1328*, ed. Peter Brieger and Philippe Verdier, exhibition catalog (Ottawa: National Gallery of Canada, 1972).

90. Niccolini di Camugliano, *Chronicles of a Florentine Family*, 65–68.

91. St. Bonaventura, *Meditations on the Life of Christ*, trans. Isa Ragusa, ed. Isa Ragusa and Rosalie B. Green (Princeton, N.J.: Princeton University Press, 1961), 72–73. On the *Meditations, from St. Bonaventura's Sermons*, as admonitory literature for women, see Laura Jacobus, "Piety and Propriety in the Arena Chapel," *Renaissance Studies* 12 (1998): 181.

92. Slanicka, "Male Markings," discovers another instance when women adopted and displayed a factional emblem—in this case a simple cross band of white across the chest—in a hotly charged political environment.

93. Identified as Gualdrada, daughter of Bellinicione Berti dei Rovignani, by the editor in Giovanni Boccaccio, *Concerning Famous Women*, ed. and trans. Guido Aldo Guarino (New Brunswick, N.J.: Rutgers University Press, 1963), 237–38.

94. Trexler, "Ritual Behavior in Renaissance Florence," 130.

95. For Florence, see ibid., 144n. 67. When dignitaries entered the city sumptuary laws might also be officially disbanded.

96. Bistort, *Il magistrato alle pompe*, 167–68.

97. Villani, *Chroniche*, bk. 10, chap. 11 in vol. 1, p. 305.

98. Brundage, "Sumptuary Law and Prostitution in Late Medieval Italy."

99. John Sekora, *Luxury: The Concept in Western Thought from Eden to Smollett* (Baltimore: Johns Hopkins University Press, 1977), 43, argues that *luxuria* tends to encompass the other deadly sins in the Middle Ages.

100. See Elliott, "Dress as Mediator between Inner and Outer Self." The woman who dressed as a widow while her husband lived to mark her renunciation of the world created special difficulties for religious advisors, however.

101. For the sixteenth-century oration of Nicolosa Sanuti on the consequence of women's fine apparel, see "Orazione Inedita di Nicolosa Sanuti" (appendix) in Frati, *La vita privata*, 251–62. For a translation into English and comment, see Killerby, "'Heralds of a Well-Instructed Mind.'"

102. For example, from Christine de Pizan's *Book of the City of Ladies*, the governess to her charge, the princess: "Then she will have her mistress dress and array herself suitably, without devoting overmuch time to clothing, as some ladies do. This is ridiculous waste of time and, furthermore, an unseemly custom." *The Writings of Christine de Pizan*, Willard, 218–19. Christine created an incisive analogy with the following reference to expensive cloth: "Just like someone who has a long and wide robe cut from a very large piece of cloth when the material costs him nothing and no one opposes him, they exploit the rights of others" (183).

103. Bruckner, Shepard, and White, *Songs of the Women Troubadours*, 102–3. I am grateful to E. Jane Burns for bringing this example of anger over sumptuary law to my attention. Law in the Kingdom of Aragon as elsewhere in lands ruled by kings would make privilege or estate a much greater concern than in Italian cities.

104. Widows would be the exception here, which is one reason why Barberino paid them so much attention in his advice manual.

105. Dante Alighieri, *The Divine Comedy*, pt. 1, pp. 350–51, *Paradiso*, canto 31, ll. 70–72:

Sanza rissponder, li occhi sù levai,
e vidi lei che si facea corona
reflellendo da sé li etterni rai

106. "[Luce Iragary] specified an account of the body's *morphology*; 'the body is not considered an anatomical, biological or neuro-physiological body—a body that is the object of the sciences of biology.' Rather, her object of analysis is the body as it is lived, the body which is marked, inscribed, made meaningful both in social and familial and idiosyncratic terms, the body psychically, socially, and discursively established: the body as socially and individually significant." Elizabeth Gross, "Philosophy, Subjectivity, and the Body: Kristeva and Iragaray," in *Feminist Challenges: Social and Political History*, ed. Carole Pateman and Elizabeth Gross (Boston: Northeastern University Press, 1986), 136.

107. Archivio de Stato, Florence, *Statuti 1322–25*, 2:416 (*Statuto del Podestà, 1325*, Liber V, rubr. 88), cited by Rainey, "Sumptuary Legislation in Renaissance Florence," 96n. 51.

108. "Zonas aureis supercincte amazones esse videntus." Fiamma, *Opusculum de rebus gestis*, vol. 12, pt. 4, p. 37. See also Knighton, *Chronicon Henrici Knighton*, 2:57–58.

109. Levi Pisetzky, *Storia del costume in Italia*, 2:125.

110. Filippo Lippi, *Donor Portrait of Francesco de Marco Datini with Four Buonhomini*, Galleria Comunale, Prato.

111. On homosexuality at Florence, see Michael Rocke, *Forbidden Friendships:*

Homosexuality and Male Culture in Renaissance Florence (New York: Oxford University Press, 1996). Samuel Cohn, Jr., notes in *Women in the Streets: Essays on Sex and Power in Renaissance Italy* (Baltimore: Johns Hopkins University Press, 1996), 29–30, that over the course of the fourteenth century criminal courts transferred much of their concern over rape from heterosexual cases to homosexual cases.

112. Venetian State Archives, *Senato, Terra*, Reg. 1, p. 105, cited by Newett, "Sumptuary Laws of Venice," 206.

113. On conduct books, see Roberta L. Krueger, "'*Nouvelles choses*': Social Instability and the Problem of Fashion in the *Livre du Chevalier de la Tour Landry*, the *Ménagier de Paris*, and Christine de Pizan's *Livre des trois vertus*," in *Medieval Conduct*, ed. Kathleen Ashley and Robert L. A. Clark (Minneapolis: University of Minnesota Press, 2001), 49–85.

114. Joan Kelly, "Did Women Have a Renaissance?" in *Becoming Visible*, ed. Renate Bridenthal, Claudia Koonz, and Susan Stuard, 2nd ed. (Boston: Houghton Mifflin, 1987), 190.

115. Ruggiero, *The Boundaries of Eros*, 110.

116. Rocke, *Forbidden Friendships*, 38, 109. Rocke sees homosexual liaisons as normal for Florentine men in their transition years to adulthood and that homosexual relationships were replaced by heterosexual ones when a man reached thirty or so and married. He does not find that sodomy was treated as particularly reprehensible to society, as Ruggiero does for Venice.

117. San Bernardino, quoted in Rocke, *Forbidden Friendships*, 38.

118. Jacqueline Murray, "Twice Marginal and Twice Invisible: Lesbians in the Middle Ages," in *Handbook of Medieval Sexuality*, ed. Vern Bullough and James A. Brundage (New York: Garland, 1996), 191–22, and Patricia Simons, "Lesbian (In)Visibility in Italian Renaissance Culture: Diana and Other Cases of '*donna con donna*,'" *Journal of Homosexuality* 12 (1994): 81–122.

119. Ruggiero, *The Boundaries of Eros*, 189n. 21.

120. Rare allegations of lesbianism were acts committed in private that were spied upon by others. See Judith C. Brown, "Lesbian Sexuality in Medieval and Early Modern Europe," in *Hidden from History: Reclaiming the Gay and Lesbian Past*, ed. Martin Duberman, Martha Vicinus, and George Chauncey (New York: New American Library, 1989), 73–74. However, as Brown notes, the term lesbian was not used until the nineteenth century. See also E. Ann Matter, "My Sister, My Spouse," *Journal of Feminist Studies in Religion* 2 (1986): 81–93.

121. Authorities attribute lace-making to Italian seamstresses and lace emerged by the fifteenth century. Picked threads in veils, or mesh-work covering gowns may figure in the origins of lace-making, which was a household craft before it became a trade commodity. See Annarosa Garzelli, *Il ricamo nella attività artistica di Pollaiolo, Botticelli, Bartolomeo di Giovanni* (Florence: Editrice Edam, 1973), 43.

122. "Et predicta vel aliquod predictorum non vendicent sibi locum contra publicas meretrices corpus suum ad libidenem pro pecunia concedentes." Archivio de Stato, Firenze, *Capitoli del Comune di Firenze*, 12, fols. 48–54v, cited in full in Rainey, "Sumptuary Legislation in Renaissance Florence," "Pragmatica of 1356," appendix 3, pp. 680–81.

123. On servants in Florence, see Christiane Klapisch-Zuber, "Women Servants in Florence during the Fourteenth and Fifteenth Centuries," in *Women and Work in Pre-industrial Europe*, ed. Barbara Hanawalt (Bloomington: Indiana University Press, 1986), 56–80. On servants in Venice, see Dennis Romano, *Housecraft and Statecraft:*

Domestic Service in Renaissance Venice, 1400–1600 (Baltimore: Johns Hopkins University Press, 1996).

124. The origin of lace in Europe is obscure but it may be identified in Italy by such fifteenth-century leading authorities as Annarosa Garzelli to claim the innovation for Italy. See her *Il ricamo nella attività artistica di Pollaiolo, Botticelli, Bartolomeo di Giovanni,* 43. On early lace-making, see also Marie Schuette, "Lace," *CIBA Review* 7:73 (April 1949): 2685–98. Schuette notes that the first printed illustration of lace may be found in a Venetian pattern book of 1542 by Matio Pagano, "Giardinetto novo di ponti tagliati." Schuette notes that Renaissance women "probably made their lace at home" before it became an established industry (2686). Mesh is constructed like embroidery. See Labarge, "Stitches in Time." Men as well as women embroidered; see discussion of male embroiderers in Chapter 7.

125. Bonds, "Genoese Noblewomen and Gold Thread Manufacturing."

126. Iris Origo, "The Domestic Enemy: The Eastern Slaves in Tuscany in the Fourteenth and Fifteenth Centuries," *Speculum* 30 (1955): 330–31, citing *Archivio Datini,* Prato, file 1142.

127. David Herlihy, *Opera Muliebria* (New York: McGraw-Hill, 1990), 83.

128. Ibid., 83–94.

129. Brucker, *The Society of Renaissance Florence,* 223, citing *Archivio di Stato, Firenze, Conventi Soppressi,* 78 (Badia), vol. 315, no. 348.

130. Susan Mosher Stuard, "Urban Domestic Slavery in Medieval Ragusa," *Journal of Medieval History* 9 (1983): 155–71.

131. Susan Mosher Stuard, "Ancillary Evidence on the Decline of Medieval Slavery," *Past and Present* 149 (1995): 1–28, and Charles Verlinden, "Le recrutement des esclaves à Venice aux XIV et XV siècles," *Bulletin de l'Institut Historique Belge de Rome* 34 (1968): 83–202.

132. Brucker, *The Society of Renaissance Florence,* 223–24, citing *Archivio di Stato, Firenze, Atti dei Capitano,* 2107, n.p., September 12, 1399.

133. Romano, *Housecraft and Statecraft,* 90, and Frederic C. Lane, "Andrea Barbarigo, Merchant of Venice," *Johns Hopkins University Studies in Historical and Political Science* 62 (1944): 29.

134. On women's alleged slight impact on economic output through their labor in households, see David Herlihy, "Deaths, Marriage, Births, and the Tuscan Economy," in *Population Patterns in the Past,* ed. Ronald Demos Lee (New York: Academic Press, 1977), 163. See also Judith Brown, "A Woman's Place Was in the Home," in *Rewriting the Renaissance: The Discourse of Sexual Difference in Early Modern Europe,* ed. Margaret W. Ferguson, Maureen Quilligan, and Nancy J. Vickers (Chicago: University of Chicago Press, 1986), 191–205. This study suggests that women's production and innovation in fashion may have been considerable, if difficult to document, in the fourteenth century. See also Herlihy's comments and responses from Anne-Marie Pruz, Margret Wensky, and Angela Groppi in *La donna nell'economia secc. XIII–XVIII,* ed. Simonetta Cavaciocchi (Florence: Le Monnier, 1993), 103–55, on the decline of women's roles in the late medieval economy.

135. Chojnacki, "Dowries and Kinsmen in Early Renaissance Venice," 173–88.

136. Niccolini di Camugliano, *Chronicles of a Florentine Family,* 66–68.

137. "ex quo domine Veneciarum, tam nobiles quam populares, passe sunt magnum incommodum et sinistrum, quia nunquam ibunt in Rivoaltum." Venetian State Archives, *Maggior Consiglio, Deliberationes, Leona,* reg. 21, fols. 74v–75r for April 14, 1394. See Romano, "Gender and the Urban Geography of Renaissance Venice," 341. See

also Newett, "Sumptuary Laws of Venice," 270–71, although she cites reg. 27, fol. 71, for this law.

138. This is an American term used in the early nineteenth century. Italian equivalents would be *chincaglieri, minuterie,* or *merce di poco valore.*

139. On hiring jewels, see Newett, "Sumptuary Laws of Venice," 251. By the fifteenth century what a woman spent to hire jewelry was limited by law at Venice. Throughout the medieval period men's fashions appear to have been more expensive than women's. See also Piponnier and Mane, *Dress in the Middle Ages,* 77–78.

140. *Parentado* was a generic term for an entire group of in-laws acquired at marriage.

141. For the Strozzi correspondence, see Phillips, *The Memoir of Marco Parenti,* 43.

142. Chojnacki, "From Trousseau to Groomgift," 150–58.

143. Klapisch-Zuber, "The Griselda Complex," 240–45.

144. Frick, "Dressing a Renaissance City," 16–67.

145. Jane Fair Bestor, "Marriage Transactions in Renaissance Italy and Mauss's Essay on the Gift," *Past and Present* 164 (August, 1999): 6–46.

146. On the Petrarch and Boccaccio versions of the Griselda story, see Vittore Branca, "Per il testo del Decamerone," *Studi di filologia italiana* 11 (1953): 389–405, and "Sulla diffusione della griselda petrarchesca," *Studi petrarcheschi* 6 (1956): 221–24, for a list of manuscripts of this popular story.

147. "et totam me optuli ei . . . pormisi . . . non offendere eum cum aliquo membrorum, accusando singillatim omnia membra singulariter." Elizabeth Petroff's translation from her *Body and Soul: Essays on Medieval Women and Mysticism* (New York: Oxford University Press, 1994), 212.

148. Cohn, *Women in the Streets,* 55, 57–76. For St. Catherine of Siena's correspondence, see Catherine of Siena, *Le lettere* (Turin: Paolini, 1987), and Catherine of Siena, *I, Catherine: Selected Writings of Catherine of Siena,* ed. and trans. Kenelm Foster and Mary J. Ronayne (London: Collins, 1980).

149. Michael Goodich, "'*Ancilla dei*': The Servant as Saint in the Middle Ages," in *Women in the Medieval World,* ed. Suzanne Wemple and Julius Kirshner (Oxford: Blackwell, 1985), 119–28.

150. "[A] enigmatice prospexit, quantum apud Deum interioris animae plenitudo jam fuisset deformata: nempe, cum iterum atque iterum lumina studiosius infigeret, teterrimi spiritus imaginem se gestare, non hominis, in ipsis vestibus manifeste deprehendit." Elizabeth Petroff's translation in *Body and Soul,* 175. The Blessed Villana's vita was composed almost a century after her death by a Florentine Dominican, Johannes Carolus: Johannes Carolus, *Vita Villana Bottia Florentiae in Etruria: Acta Sanctorum,* August 26, pp. 865–67.

Chapter 5

1. Braudel, *The Structures of Everyday Life,* 315–25. Braudel placed the turn in 1350 or later, however. Newton, *Fashion in the Age of the Black Prince,* places the turn in 1340, while Levi Pisetzky, *Storia del costume in Italia,* vol. 2, writes of a more gradual turn to fashion in this era. The emphasis on display and use of precious metals for fastenings and decorations grew in the first two decades of the fourteenth century, and

for that reason this study pinpoints the era as a first gilded age for the economy of Europe.

2. Frederic C. Lane, "Consumption and Economic Change," *Journal of Economic History* 15 (1955): 107–9.

3. Robert S. Lopez and Harry A. Miskimin, "The Economic Depression of the Renaissance," *Economic History Review*, 2nd ser., 14 (1962): 408–26; Carlo Cipolla, *Before the Industrial Revolution: European Society and Economy, 1000–1700*, 2nd ed. (New York: Norton, 1976), 214–19; and Richard Roehl, "Patterns and Structure of Demand, 1000–1500," in *Fontana Economic History of Europe*, ed. Carlo M. Cipolla (London: Collins/Fontana, 1972), 107–42.

4. Frangioni, *Chiedere e ottenere*, 9–21. Frangioni would add Cremona, Crema, and Pavia to the list. Foreign centers of production would also figure.

5. Goldthwaite, "The Renaissance Economy."

6. See discussion in Melissa Meriam Bullard, S. R. Epstein, Benjamin G. Kohl, and Susan Mosher Stuard, "Where History and Theory Interact: Frederic C. Lane on the Emergence of Capitalism," *Speculum* 79 (2004): 88–119.

7. Costs of luxury wares here mean costs to consumers.

8. Roncière, *Prix et salaires à Florence*; Goldthwaite, *Building of Renaissance Florence*; Queller, "A Different Approach to the Pre-modern Cost of Living"; Louise Buenger Robbert, "Money and Prices in Thirteenth-Century Venice," *Journal of Medieval History* 20 (1994): 373–90; compare Susan Connell, *The Employment of Sculptors and Stonemasons in Venice in the Fifteenth Century* (New York: Garland, 1988), 80–152, 208–21.

9. Raymond de Roover, *Money, Banking and Credit in Medieval Bruges: Italian Merchant Bankers, Lombards, and Money Changers* (Cambridge, Mass.: Medieval Academy of America, 1948), and *The Rise and Decline of the Medici Bank, 1397–1494* (New York: Norton, 1966). Also see de Roover's numerous articles. Sapori, *La crisi delle compagnie mercantili dei Bardi e dei Peruzzi*. Carlo M. Cipolla, *The Monetary Policy of Fourteenth-Century Florence* (Berkeley: University of California Press, 1982), and *Studi in onore di Armando Sapori* (Milan: Istituto Editoriale Cisalpino, 1957), give some idea of developments in research since Sapori wrote. For a bibliography of the debate on the economic crisis of the Renaissance, see John Day, *The Medieval Market Economy* (Oxford: Blackwell, 1987), 219–24.

10. Lane and Mueller, *Money and Banking in Medieval and Renaissance Venice: Coins and Moneys of Account*, and Reinhold C. Mueller, *The Venetian Money Market: Banks, Panics and the Public Debt, 1200–1500*, vol. 2 of *Money and Banking in Medieval and Renaissance Venice*, ed. Frederic C. Lane and Reinhold C. Mueller (Baltimore: Johns Hopkins University Press, 1997).

11. Spufford, *Money and Its Use*.

12. Stahl, *Zecca*.

13. Beyond the work by John Day cited above, see also John Munro, *Bullion Flows and Monetary Policies in England and the Low Countries, 1350–1500* (Hampshire: Variorum, 1992), 97–158, for the north. See Mueller, *The Venetian Money Market*, 145–61, on the complexities of silver importing into Venice. See also Goldthwaite, *Building of Renaissance Florence*, 417–18, and Goldthwaite, *Wealth and Demand for Art in Italy*, 12–40.

14. Mueller, *The Venetian Money Market*, 589.

15. Jevons, *Money and the Mechanism of Exchange*, 78–80. For example, the differential between, say, the *fiorino di suggello*, of slightly less and then of diminishing value,

and a full weight gold florin was referred to as the *agio*. Rates of exchange were figured in the *fiorino di suggello* from the mid-fourteenth century onward. Mueller, *The Venetian Money Market*, 593.

16. Mueller, *The Venetian Money Market*, 589. *Agio* may be thought of as the premium made on exchange.

17. Beyond the work by Mueller cited above, see Enrico Bensa, *Francesco di Marco da Prato: Notizie e documenti sulla mercatura italiana del secolo XIV* (Milan: Fratelli Treves, 1928); Federigo Melis, *Aspetti della vita economica medievale: Studi nell'Archivio Datini di Prato* (Siena: Monte dei Paschi di Siena, 1962); and Origo, *The Merchant of Prato*.

18. This would continue through the fifteenth century in Italy. See Jane Bridgeman, "'Pagare le pompe': Why Quattrocento Sumptuary Laws Did Not Work," in *Women in Italian Renaissance Culture and Society*, ed. Letizia Panizza (Oxford: European Humanities Research Center, 2000), 209–26, to compare to costs of luxuries for the fifteenth century.

19. For the *estimo* of 1379, see Gino Luzzatto, "Les activités économiques du patriciat vénitien (X^e–XIVe siècles)," in *Studi di storia economica veneziana* (Padua: CEDAM, 1954), 134. See also Romanin, *Storia documentata di Venezia*, 3:1367, for an *estimo* of 1367. An *estimo* must be used with caution. In this instance Venetian officials multiplied nobles' real estate holdings by ten to reach their figures. The estimo included about 40 percent non-noble persons in Venice.

20. Queller, "A Different Approach to the Pre-modern Cost of Living," 444–64.

21. Two grandsons of Marco Zaccaria received 174 ducats a year, which is significantly higher than the allowances left by other noblemen or by commoners at Venice in this era. Queller, "A Different Approach to the Pre-modern Cost of Living," 455.

22. Brian Pullan, *Rich and Poor in Renaissance Venice: The Social Institutions of a Catholic State, to 1620* (Cambridge, Mass.: Harvard University Press, 1971), 63. See also Romano, *Patrician and Popolani*, 56–64.

23. See Pullan, *Rich and Poor in Renaissance Venice*, 81, and 229–31, on poor nobles in Venice.

24. Queller, "A Different Approach to the Pre-modern Cost of Living," 460–61.

25. For the law of 1360, see Romanin, *Storia documentata di Venezia*, 3:280–82 (Avogaria di Comun), for the text. See Newett, "Sumptuary Laws of Venice," 268–69. On sumptuary law, see Bistort, *Il magistrato alle pompe*.

26. Chojnacki, "Dowries and Kinsmen in Early Renaissance Venice," 173.

27. For text of the sumptuary law of 1299, see Foucard, *Lo statuto inedito delle nozze veneziane*.

28. For the text of the sumptuary law of 1334, see *Deliberationes*, ed. Cessi and Brunetti, 2:314 for May 26, 1334, and 2:323–26 for June 20, 1334. In this instance ten *savii* were commissioned to report back recommendations.

29. Chojnacki, in "Dowries and Kinsmen in Early Renaissance Venice," 173–98, argues that whereas Venetian men gave large gifts to direct heirs, Venetian women tended to give numerous gifts to a number of female relatives. A bride might therefore collect her finery from a number of sources.

30. Newett, "Sumptuary Laws of Venice," 269–70, citing Venetian State Archives, *Senato, Delib. Miste*, reg. XLI, fol. 56. This is an old-style reference. See Romanin, *Storia documentata di Venezia*, 3:280–82.

31. Foucard, *Lo statuto inedito delle nozze veneziane*, no. 7, p. 12. See also Newett, "Sumptuary Laws of Venice," 262.

32. Mueller, "The Procurators of San Marco," notes the Procuratori worked in offices filled with sacks of precious goods either left in their care or confiscated.

33. See Romanin, *Storia documentata di Venezia*, 3:280–82, for text. It was significant that dowries were only reviewed and not limited by the law in Venice. According to Roman law a dowry was a daughter's inheritance or Falcidian quarter. Surveillance of dowries would allow officials a talking point in regard to keeping dowries within limits, but it seems clear that Venetian lawmakers were loath to interfere directly with the rights of individuals to control and pass on their estates to heirs, particularly in the era after the first visitation of the Black Plague when large estates funneled into the hands of a few or even a single heir.

34. Dubrovnik State Archives, *Diversa cancellariae*, 10, fol. 27, *die 21 madii* 1333.

35. Zupko, *Italian Weights and Measures*, and Kisch, *Scales and Weights*, provide the differing scales in use in various city-states and give equivalents in metric scale. The Florentine pound was equal to 339.5 grams (Kisch, *Scales and Weights*, 228). Silver and gold were weighed by goldsmiths in carats, an ancient system based on the east Mediterranean locust bean (Spufford, *Money and Its Use*, 7). A Roman system of coin weight based on the *exagia* was also in use. Worked silver was seldom at the standard of the mint in terms of fineness, so its price in florins would be figured by weight and fineness for each object, and it is significant that this law did not specify the more precise standards employed by goldsmiths. It merely indicated a gross weight of two pounds of silver, fineness unspecified. *Tarifa zoè noticia dy pexi èmexure di luogi etere che s'adovre marcandatia per le mondo*, ed. V. Orlandini (Venice: C. Ferrari, 1925), 12, provides two separate scales for silver, gold, and pearl on one hand, and for coinage on the other.

Venetian and Florentine measures differed from each other: the heavy Venetian pound weighed 301.23 grams; the Florentine pound weighed 339.5 grams. See Zupko, *Italian Weights and Measures*, 129–37, and Kisch, *Scales and Weights*, 235. The *braccia* in Venice equaled about 68 cm, but in Florence it was about 58 cm.

36. The Great Council had put curbs on weddings in 1235, but sumptuary legislation is lacking for the subsequent century.

37. Dubrovnik State Archives, *Diversa notariae*, V, fol. 149v.

38. Dubrovnik State Archives, *Diversa cancellariae*, V, fol. 41.

39. The only items I have found that rival great belts in value were crowns, which when jeweled sold for 70, 100, or even 150 florins. See Levi Pisetzky, *Storia del costume in Italia*, 2:127–35. Women in towns wore crowns. The *Ufficiale delle donne* referred to elaborate jeweled garlands and crowns interchangeably. See Florentine State Archives, *Esecutore dei Ordinamenti, dei Giusticie*, 83 (1346), for examples cited in Chapter 4.

40. Robbert, "Money and Prices in Thirteenth-Century Venice," 383.

41. Ibid.

42. An exception would be clothes made from gold cloth or lavishly trimmed with a fur like ermine.

43. Compare as well the jewels and luxury wares in Lopez, "Note sulla composizione dei patrimoni privata," 205–64.

44. Romanin, *Storia documentata di Venezia*, 3:280.

45. Roncière, *Prix et salaires*, 63–68.

46. While in Venice large-scale wars like the War of Chioggia have received attention as major causes for inflation and financial difficulties, at Florence the Revolt of the Ciompi has been treated as politically disruptive but not a major cause of internal economic dislocation. See Gene Brucker, *Florentine Politics and Society, 1343–1378* (Princeton, N.J.: Princeton University Press, 1962), and Alessandro Stella, *La révolte des*

Ciompi: Les hommes, les lieux, le travail (Paris: L'École des Hautes Études en Sciences Sociales, 1993).

47. Cipolla, *The Monetary Policy of Fourteenth-Century Florence*, 49.

48. See Spufford, *Handbook of Medieval Exchange*, 5–11.

49. Roncière, *Prix et salaires*, 292–94.

50. Goldthwaite, *Building of Renaissance Florence*, 333–39.

51. Ibid., 343–47, is more pessimistic about purchasing power compared to the price of food.

52. Cipolla, *The Monetary Policy of Fourteenth-Century Florence*, 21.

53. Ibid., ix–x. Cipolla claims this for the era after the middle years of the twelfth century.

54. Carlo Cipolla, *Money, Prices and Civilization in the Mediterranean World: Fifth to Seventeenth Century* (Princeton, N.J.: Princeton University Press, 1956), 60.

55. Klapisch-Zuber, "Women Servants in Florence," 62.

56. Stella, *La révolte des Ciompi*, 182. See also Roncière, *Prix et salaires*, 292–380; Richard Trexler, "Neighbors and Comrades: The Revolutionaries of Florence, 1378," *Social Analysis* 14 (1983): 53–106; and John Henderson, *Piety and Charity in Late Medieval and Renaissance Florence* (Oxford: Oxford University Press, 1994).

57. Graziano Concioni, Claudio Ferri, and Giuseppe Ghilarducci, *Orafi medioevale: Lucca, secc. VIII–XV* (Lucca: Rugani edizioni arte in Lucca, 1991), 44. The pearl may well have been a false pearl or margarita.

58. Lancia, "Legge suntuaria," 374. Franco Francheschi, "Florence and Silk in the Fifteenth Century," *Italian History and Culture, Villa le Balze, Georgetown University* 1 (1995): 3–22, argues that the silk industry was encouraged at Florence in the latter decades of the fourteenth century. This effort to create an industry might affect specific provisions in sumptuary legislation

59. "forzierino, e le robe sue e le nozze e la gabella, e che lasciai per donor a messer Bindo," in "Frammenti della cronaca di messer Luca di Totto da Panzano da una copia di V. Borghini," ed. P. Berti, *Giornale storico degli archivi toscani* 5 (1861): 61–73. This unusually high countergift to the dowry is discussed in Klapisch-Zuber, "The Griselda Complex," 221.

60. This continued in the fifteenth century. Carole Frick has found that there was little differential in the value of men's and women's wardrobes ("Dressing a Renaissance City," 458).

61. Machetti, "Orafi Senesi," 43.

62. Giovanni Bartolus, *Opera Omnia* (Venice: Juntas, 1590–1602), X, 21v: *consilium* I, 82, cited by Anna Toole Sheedy, *Bartolus on Social Conditions in the Fourteenth Century* (New York: Columbia University Press, 1942), 46.

63. Alan Stahl and Louis Waldman, "The Earliest Known Medalists: The Sesto Brothers of Venice," *American Journal of Numismatics*, 2nd ser., 5–6 (1993–94): 176.

64. Ibid., 181n. 45. Over the century salaries had ranged from 40 to 70 ducats.

65. Machetti, "Orafi Senesi," 47.

66. Renato Piattoli, "Un inventario di oreficeria del trecento," *Rivista d'arte* 13 (1931): 247–52.

67. Eugène Müntz, "L'Antipape Clément VII: Essai sur l'histoire des arts à Avignon vers la fin du XIVᵉ siècle," *Revue Archéologique*, 3rd ser., 11 (1888): 8–18, 168–83. Papal inventories are a rich source of information on luxury consumption.

68. Mazzi, *Argenti degli Acciaiuoli*, 8.

69. See Brucker, *The Society of Renaissance Florence*, 179–80, for this translation. For discussion, see Rainey, "Sumptuary Legislation in Renaissance Florence," 204–6.

70. Rainey, "Sumptuary Legislation in Renaissance Florence," 154. The *Ufficiale delle donne* often referred to fines in lira rather than florins. In 1347 the 2-florin limit for garlands was referred to as a 6-lira limit. The lira, which had been pegged to the florin as 1 lira = 1 florin in the 1250s, had reached over 3 lira to the florin by 1347. See Spufford, *Handbook of Medieval Exchange*, 6.

71. Gino Corti, "Sul commercio dei quadri à Firenze verso la fine del Secolo XIV," *Commentari* 22 (1971): 84–91.

72. Brucker, *The Society of Renaissance Florence*, 224.

73. Mazzi, *Argenti degli Acciaiuoli*, 6–30.

74. Robbert, "Twelfth-Century Italian Prices." Fortunately this descriptive inventory arranged items for sale so prices were assigned to all the articles. This was a rare occurrence.

75. On secondhand markets and goods, see Richard Mackenney, *Tradesmen and Traders: The World of Guilds in Venice and Europe, c. 1250–1650* (Totawa, N.J.: Barnes and Noble, 1987), 12. See also Giovanni Monticolo, *I capitolari delle arti veneziani sottoposto alla Giustizia e poi alla Giustizla Vecchia dalle origini al 1330* (Rome: Istituo Storico Italiano, 1896–1914), 1:135–38, for statutes of traders in secondhand cloth at Venice in 1233, with some later additions. See *Statuti dell'arte dei rigattieri e linaioli di Firenze (1296–1340)*, ed. Ferdinando Sartini (Florence: Le Monnier, 1940), 3–136, for Florentine guild statutes of the *Rigattieri* from 1296 to 1324 for secondhand dealers in cloth.

76. Niccolini di Camugliano, *Chronicles of a Florentine Family*, 66.

77. Dotson, *Merchant Culture in Fourteenth-Century Venice*, 76–81.

78. Origo, *The Merchant of Prato*, 256.

79. "Inventario dell'ereditia spettante a Fabbiano e a Benedetta del fu Dondidio speziale, 1259," in Lopez, *Studi sull'economia Genovese*, 257.

80. Reinhold C. Mueller, "The Jewish Moneylenders of Late Trecento Venice: A Revisitation," *Mediterranean Historical Review* 10 (1995): 202–17. The dilemma for Jews who took pawns in Venice in the late fourteenth century was that they had been directed by government charter to lend to the poor, while only the affluent possessed genuinely valuable pawns like silver and spices.

81. Muzzarelli, *Guardaroba medievale*. See in particular the 1335 inventory of the goods of Jacopo Belvise, doctor of law in Bologna (117–21) and of Colombina of Bologna (59–68).

82. Molmenti, *Venice*, 1:198: "Inventari delle cose lasciate dal Doge Francesco Dandolo (m. *1339*)."

83. Major sumptuary laws were enacted in 1299, 1334, and 1360 in Venice, then again at the turn of the fifteenth century. At Florence legislating on display and consumption occurred in synodal (church) legislation in 1310, civic laws in the 1320s, 1354, 1365, and 1393. See Rainey, "Sumptuary Legislation in Renaissance Florence," appendices 1–7, pp. 647–742, for texts of the laws.

84. Goldthwaite, *Building of Renaissance Florence*, 56.

85. Carole Frick, in "Dressing the Renaissance City," 67, argues that it is a fiction that fifteenth-century Florentines willed their clothes from generation to generation. Instead she found that fine clothes tended to be sold or pawned within a generation.

86. See Milia Davenport, "Personal Adornment," in *The Secular Spirit: Life and Art at the End of the Middle Ages*, ed. Timothy Husband and Jane Hayward, exhibition catalog (New York: E. P. Dutton, 1975), 69–83, on dated styles in clothes and accessories. A different view may be found in Garzelli, *Il ricamo nella attività artistica di Pollaiolo, Botticelli, Bartolomeo di Giovanni*, and Levi Pisetzky, *Storia del costume in Italia*, 2:82–84.

87. Molmenti, *Venice*, 1:196–201.

88. Mueller, "The Procurators of San Marco," 153, 168.

89. See Spufford, *Money and Its Use*, 345–49, for these and other large hoards.

90. Harry Miskimin, *Economy of the Early Renaissance* (Englewood Cliffs, N.J.: Prentice Hall, 1969), 134–38.

91. Spufford, *Money and Its Use*, 347.

92. Two nobles from each *albergo* and two *popolo* from each *conestagia* (ward) were responsible for lists of taxable persons, but estimates of movables relied on estimates of value, and "such taxes were always difficult to set and to collect" (Epstein, *Genoa and the Genoese*, 235). See also Spufford, *Money and Its Use*, 349. The Sardinian mint closed by 1365 at Genoa because no more newly minted silver was available.

93. William Caferro, *Mercenary Companies and the Decline of Siena* (Baltimore: Johns Hopkins University Press, 1998), 103–26.

94. The *estimo* is perhaps the most consulted record of fourteenth-century Venice and there is a vast literature on it. For a review, see Mueller, *The Venetian Money Market*, 418–515.

95. Mueller, *The Venetian Money Market*, 488–515. Assessments follow this pattern from 1280 on: "Personal property was evaluated one to one, that is, 1,000 ducats of real value corresponded to 1,000 *lire d'estimo*. Expressly mentioned were cash, gems, silver, and silverware, which were considered '*boni denari*'; household furnishings that were not gold or silver were exempted" (494). Mueller provides a balanced treatment of the original study of the *estimo*: Gino Luzzatto, *Il debito pubblico della repubblica di Venezia* (Milan: Istituto Editoriale Cisalpino, 1963).

96. Stahl, *Zecca*, 184. See also Roberto Cessi, ed., *Problemi monetari veneziani fino a tutto il sec. XIV* (Padua: PAN, 1937), 157–66. To compare Florentine minting policy, see Mario Bernocchi, *Le monete della repubblica fiorentina*, Arte e archeologia, Studi e documenti 5–7, 11, 24 (Florence: L. S. Olschki, 1974–85), vol. 3 (7) *Documentazioni*.

97. David Herlihy and Christiane Klapisch-Zuber, *Toscans et leurs familles* (Paris: SEVPEN, 1978), 67–71.

98. Giovanni Rucellai, *Zibaldone*, ed. Alessandro Perosa (London: Warburg, 1960), 1:62. Also translated by Baldassarri and Saiber, *Images of Quattrocento Florence*, 75.

99. Rucellai, *Zibaldone*, argues that the terrible war that followed these fat years was all the more devastating because of this earlier prosperity.

100. Since this is the age when both Venice and Florence began to survey private wealth, it is significant that wealth in luxury wares of silver and gold was largely excluded.

Chapter 6

1. Compare Muzzarelli, *Guardaroba medievale*, 148–49.

2. Sartini, *Statuti dell'arte dei rigattieri e linaioli di Firenze*, 2:23, *Statuti dei rigattieri*, 1296.

3. Mackenney, *Tradesmen and Traders*, 3.

4. Ibid., 17.

5. Warnke, *The Court Artist*, 7–14.

6. Mackenney, *Tradesmen and Traders*, 5.

7. Epstein, *Genoa and the Genoese*, 276, and Muzzarelli, *Guardaroba medievale*, 150.

8. Mackenney, *Tradesmen and Traders*, 13.

9. King, "The Trecento," 1: 216–33.

10. On the organization of a dye shop, see Piero Guarducci, "Le materie prime nell'arte tintoria senese del basso medio evo," *Archeologie medievale* 6 (1979): 371–86. On the uses of cloth, see Frances Pritchard, "The Uses of Textiles, c. 1000–1500," in *Cambridge History of Western Textiles*, ed. David Jenkins (Cambridge: Cambridge University Press, 2003), 1:353–77.

11. Mola, *La comunità dei Lucchesi a Venezia*, 21–72; Anna Multhesius, "Silk in the Medieval World," in *Cambridge History of Western Textiles*, ed. David Jenkins (Cambridge: Cambridge University Press, 2003), 1:325–54; F. de Roover, "Andrea Banchi," and "Lucchese Silk Industry"; Muzzarelli, *Guardaroba medievale*, 177–84.

12. Muzzarelli, *Guardaroba medievale*, 184–204.

13. For the statues of goldsmiths at Venice, 1233 with additions, see Monticolo, *I capitolari delle arti veneziani*, 1:113–34, 257–63.

14. Odd Langholm, *The Merchant in the Confessional* (Leiden: Brill, 2002).

15. Benedetto Cotrugli, *Il libro dell'arte di Mercatura*, ed. Ugo Tucci (Venice: Arsenale, 1990), 176–77.

16. On the disastrous conditions faced by Sienese goldsmiths and other prosperous citizens of the fourteenth century, see Caferro, *Mercenary Companies and the Decline of Siena*, 103–20. Maristella Botticini, "A Tale of 'Benevolent' Governments: Private Credit Markets, Public Finance, and the Role of Jewish Lenders in Medieval and Renaissance Italy," *Journal of Economic History* 60 (2000): 172, provides a table of numerous aggregate shocks to the economy of Pistoia (1296–1459) that range from subventions to pay Florence to costs related to famine, war, and pestilence.

17. Machetti, "Orafi senesi," 5–110.

18. Concioni, Ferri, and Ghilarducci, *Orafi medioevale*, 12–13. See in particular goldsmithing tools for stamping out buttons (68–69), and account book of Foriano de Frediano (48–50) for sales of buttons in dozens. For Florence, see Guidotti, *L'oreficeria nella Firenze*.

19. Concioni, Ferri, and Ghilarducci, *Orafi medioevale*, 48–50.

20. Piattoli, "Un inventario di oreficeria del trecento." This inventory, most likely from the 1360s, contains many objects for sacramental use. However, much of the plate listed here was just as likely to serve household needs of the clergy, or laity for that matter. On the three Datini shops in Avignon and the supply of goods to them, see Frangioni, *Chiedere e ottenere*, 23–35.

21. Constantino G. Bulgari, *Argentieri, gemmari e orafi d'Italia* (Rome: L. del Turso, 1958), vol. 1. Of the ninety-six goldsmiths identified as active in Rome from 1403 to the end of the fifteenth century, only four were Sienese, six were non-Italians (one Spanish, one Flemish, and four Germans), while fifty were identified in general terms as Italians or Piedmontese. Fifteen of the Italian goldsmiths were identified as Florentines; sometimes they worked from Florence and at other times their workshops had been relocated to Rome.

22. For general works, see Cennini, *Il libro dell'arte*; Benvenuto Cellini, *The Treatises of Benvenuto Cellini on Goldsmithing and Sculpture*, trans. C. R. Ashbee (London, 1888; reprint, New York: Dover, 1967); Sergi Grandjean, *L'orfevrerie du XIXe siècle en Europe* (Paris: Presses Universitaires de France, 1962); and H. Wilson, *Silverwork and Jewellry: A Text-Book for Students and Workers in Metal* (London: Pitman, 1931).

23. The exception of course is France in the later decades of the fourteenth century when goldsmiths like Jean Duivier and Michel Arrode along with the talented Master Gusmin received major royal commissions for work with gold. See Lightbown, *Secular Goldsmiths' Work in Medieval France,* 85–86.

24. In Venice the Sesto brothers, Marco and Laurencio, filled important offices at the mint, but they participated in the family goldsmith shop as well, fulfilling commissions for consumer goods. See Stahl and Waldman, "The Earliest Known Medalists." On assaying silver and gold, see Stahl, *Zecca,* 147–52, 323–25.

25. See Kisch, *Scales and Weights,* on medieval methods for assessing bullion. See also Zupko, *Weights and Measures,* 81–83, entry "Carato."

26. Cherry, *Goldsmiths,* 69–70. This information is from an inventory of Winchester that is not cited.

27. Stahl, *Zecca,* 139–61.

28. Monticolo, *I capitolari delle arti veneziani,* 1:116–17, chap. 3. Jewelers were regulated under the statutes of goldsmiths at Venice and elsewhere.

29. Spufford, *Money and Its Use,* 20–24.

30. José Valdovinos and Manuel Cruz, "Escuela Italiana," in *El Prado, Colecciones de Pintura* (Barcelona: Lunwerg Editores, 1994), 221–23. These companion works had been variously attributed to Taddeo and Agnolo Gaddi over the years.

31. Andrew Ladis, *Taddeo Gaddi: Critical Reappraisal and Catalogue Raisonné* (Columbia: University of Missouri Press, 1982), does not include this diptych, now in Madrid at the Museo del Prado, among Gaddi's authenticated works, so it was likely an incorrect attribution; however, the Master of the Madonna of Mercy may have been one of Gaddi's followers. In the background of this work the *bottega* contains products for sale, in this instance a line of great belts or *zonas.* This marks the work as a specific reference to a contemporary fourteenth-century goldsmith's shop.

32. Other patron saints of goldsmiths included St. Dunstan of England.

33. Franco Iacometti, "I sigilli della bibliotecca communale di Siena," *Rassegna d'Arte Senesi* 20 (1927): 222.

34. *Medieval and Renaissance Miniatures from the National Gallery of Art,* ed. Gary Vikan (Washington, D.C.: National Gallery of Art, 1975), 54–56.

35. Henry Martin, ed., *Légende de Saint Denis* (Paris: H. Champion, 1908), plates 35, 36, 45, 50, 52, 60, 63.

36. Virginia Egbert, *The Medieval Artist at Work* (Princeton, N.J.: Princeton University Press, 1967), 71, plate XXV. Glazier Collection in the Pierpont Morgan Library, New York, Ms. G 52, fol. 1r, third quarter of the fourteenth century.

37. Egbert, *The Medieval Artist at Work,* 91. Church of St. Simeon, Zadar, 1380.

38. Janet Backhouse, *Luttrell Psalter* (London: British Library, 1967), fol. 52r, for detail in lower margin. British Museum, Add. 4230, fol. 52r, c. 1340.

39. For example, in Venice there were officials to supervise the waterfront and confiscate coin. See Cecchetti, "Le industrie in Venezia," 212–25. See also *Venice and History: The Collected Papers of Frederic C. Lane,* ed. by a committee of colleagues and former students (Baltimore: Johns Hopkins University Press, 1966), 251. *Officiales denariorum Rascie* inspected crews, arms, and loading as well as coin entering and leaving Venice. See Cessi, *Problemi monetari veneziani,* for relevant documents about mint officials. A good review of the development of the Venetian mint is in Stahl, *Zecca,* 148, as well as an illustration of a set of gold marking tools.

40. Lightbown, *Secular Goldsmiths' Work in Medieval France,* 85.

41. Chronicles 2, 1:14–15.

42. Proverbs 3:13–14.

43. Proverbs 10:20.

44. Gianfranco Folena and Gian Lorenzo Mellini, eds., *Bibbia istoriata Padovana della fine del Trecento* (Venice: Neri Pozza, 1962), *esodo* 117, 118, 127, pp. 35–37, and plate 106.

45. Mueller, *The Venetian Money Market*, 146.

46. Laiou, "Venice as a Centre of Trade," 19. Rock crystal was considered a precious stone in the Middle Ages.

47. F. De Roover, "Lucchese Silk Industry," 2920.

48. Dante Alighieri, *The Divine Comedy*, vol. 3, pt. 1, pp. 218–19, *Paradiso*, canto 19, 140–44.

49. Theophilus, *The Various Artists*, ed. and trans. C. R. Dodwell (Oxford: Clarendon, 1986), pp. 67–68.

50. Dubrovnik State Archives, *Diversa notariae*, 3, fol. 121v, *die v Marcii* 1319.

51. Marian Campbell, "Gold, Silver and Precious Stones," in *English Medieval Industries*, ed. John Blair and Nigel Ramsey (London: Hambledon, 1991), 133. See discussion in Chapter 7 for trade in gold thread by the Venetian merchant Andrea Barbarigo.

52. Concioni, Ferri, and Ghilarducci, *Orafi medioevale*, 30–31, for Bonacorso di Vitale Belladi and Ottavanti, *battilori d'ore*.

53. Concioni, Ferri, and Ghilarducci, *Orafi medioevale*, 16. See also Florence Edler de Roover, *L'arte della seta a Firenze nei secoli XIV e XV*, ed. Sergio Tognetti (Florence: Olschki, 1999), 87–98.

54. Pietro Pazzi, *Dizionario biografico degli, orefici, argentieri, gioiellieri* (Treviso: Grafische Crivellari, 1998), 252.

55. Pazzi, *Dizionario biografico*, 640–41.

56. F. de Roover, "Lucchese Silk Industry," 2916. Compare Margret Wensky's female silk guilds in Cologne in the fourteenth century. Wensky, "Comments," in *La donna nell'economia secc. XIII–XVIII*, ed. Cavaciocchi, 137–42. Wensky records women gold spinners as wives of gold beaters.

57. Stella, *La révolte des Ciompi*, 116, claims that at the time of the revolt of the Ciompi the greater part of the Florentine female population were spinners. He relies for comparison on the estimate of Pitti made in the seventeenth century for the number of spinners (traditionally female spinners) to sustain each weaver.

58. For the role of women in the silk industry in sixteenth-century Venice, see Mola, *The Silk Industry of Renaissance Venice*, 15–16, 198–99, 203–4.

59. Women and industry in Italy is a topic that presents major difficulties for researchers, although there is ample evidence of women active in significant industries like textiles. See Judith C. Brown and Jordan Goodman, "Women and Industry in Florence," *Journal of Economic History* 40 (1980): 73–80, and J. Brown, "A Woman's Place Was in the Home." David Herlihy found that medieval women workers' productivity in Florence was very low ("Deaths, Marriage, Births, and the Tuscan Economy," 163), but the problem may be more lack of documentation than women's actual contribution to the economy. See Herlihy's comments and replies from Anne-Marie Pruz, Margret Wensky, and Angela Groppi in *La donna nell'economia secc. XIII–XVIII*, ed. Cavaciocchi, 103–55, on the question of decline in women's participation in the economy of the later Middle Ages. Cohn, *Women in the Streets*, 1–15, addresses the difficulty of finding out about women who were not part of a Renaissance elite. In northern Europe much more is known about women's work and contribution to the economy.

See Natalie Davis, "Women in the *Arts Mécaniques* in Sixteenth-Century Lyon," in *Lyon et L'Europe, Mélanges en hommage de Richard Gascon*, ed. Jean-Pierre Gutton (Lyon: Presses Universitaires, 1980); Merry E. Wiesner, "Spinsters and Seamstresses: Women in Cloth and Clothing Production," in *Rewriting the Renaissance*, ed. Ferguson, Quilligan, and Vickers, 175–90; and Martha Howell, *Women, Production, and Patriarchy in Late Medieval Cities* (Chicago: University of Chicago Press, 1986). On the silk industry in later centuries at Florence, see Jordan Goodman, "The Florentine Silk Industry in Seventeenth-Century Florence" (Ph.D. diss., London School of Economics, 1977). By the fifteenth century in Florence women were established as weavers of taffeta although they earned considerably less than men who wove brocade. F. De Roover, "Andrea Banchi."

60. The silk industry in Lucca has received significant attention from scholars. See in particular, Salvatore Bongi, *Della mercatura dei Lucchesi nei secoli XIII e XIV*, 2nd ed., Atti della R. Accademia Lucchese, vol. 23 (Lucca: Tipografia Giusti, 1884); Eugenio Lazzareschi, ed., *L'arte della seta in Lucca: Seconda "Settimana lucchese," maggio MCMXXX–VIII* (Pescia: Edizioni Benedetti e Niccolai, 1930). On Lucchese merchant companies, see Thomas W. Blomquist, "The Castracani Family of Thirteenth-Century Lucca," *Speculum* 46 (1971): 459–76, and his other articles on the merchant companies of Lucca. On representations of silk in the work of fourteenth-century Italian artists, see Klesse, *Seidenstoffe in der Italienischen Malerei des 14 Jahrhunderts*. Mola, *The Silk Industry in Renaissance Venice*, is a valuable addition to the literature that follows Lucchese silk workers who migrated to Venice. On the diaspora of silk workers from Lucca, see Luca Mola, "L'industria della seta a Lucca nel tardo Medioevo: Emigrazione della manodopera e creazione di una rete produttiva a Bologna e Venezia," in *La seta in Europa, sec. XIII–XX*, ed. Cavaciocchi, 435–45.

61. Machetti, "Orafi senesi," 5–110.

62. Ibid., 10.

63. See Caferro, *Mercenary Companies and the Decline of Siena*, for population shrinkage in response to war and bribes to mercenaries. For a list of goldsmiths, see Machetti, "Orafi senesi," 37–40.

64. Cyril G. E. Bunt, *The Goldsmiths of Italy* (London: Hopkinson, 1926), 13.

65. Machetti, "Orafi senesi," 47.

66. Ristori, "Gilding," 12: 621. See also Campbell, "Gold, Silver, and Precious Stones," 127. Marie Madeleine Gauthier, *Emaux du Moyen Age Occidental*, 2nd. ed. (Fribourg: Office de livre, 1972), is the standard authority on these techniques. On the eclectic nature of fourteenth-century artistic production, see King, "The Trecento," 1:216–33.

67. Giorgio Vasari, *Vasari on Technique*, trans. Louisa S. Maclehose (New York: Dover, 1960), chap. XIX (XXXIII), p. 278.

68. William M. Milliken, "Early Enamels in the Cleveland Museum of Art," *Connoisseur* 74 (October 1926): 68.

69. William Wixom, *Treasures from Medieval France*, exhibition catalog (Cleveland: Cleveland Museum of Art, 1967), 252–53.

70. Lightbown, *Secular Goldsmiths' Work in Medieval France*, 75.

71. Theophilus, *The Various Artists*, 128.

72. Cennini, *Il libro dell'arte*, 60–119.

73. See Ristori, "Gilding," 621.

74. Origo, *The Merchant of Prato*, 261.

75. Cennini, *Il libro dell'arte*, 72–73. On gilding stone, see Connell, *The Employment of Sculptors and Stonemasons*, 148–50.

76. Child, "Mirrors," 21:719.

77. Piattoli, "Un inventario di oreficeria del trecento," 250.

78. "Testamenta di Pietro Vioni, Veneziano, fatto in Tauris (Persie) MCCLXIV, x Dicembre," *Archivio Veneto*, n.s. 26 (1883): 161–65; introduction, pp. 161–62, signed "C."

79. *Deliberationes*, ed. Cessi and Brunetti, 2:40, no. 129.

80. Laiou, "Venice as a Centre of Trade," 19. For the document, see Robert S. Lopez, "Venezia e le grandi linee dell'espansione commerciale nel secolo XIII," in *La civiltà veneziana de secolo di Marco Polo*, ed. Riccardo Barchelli et al. (Florence: Sansoni, 1955), 50–51.

81. "XVIII stampe da stampare bottoni tra picciole et grandi," Inventory of *Marcus condam Raynalduccii, aurifex civis Lucanus, Orafi medioevale (Lucca secc. VII–XV)*, 68, citing Archivio di Stato, Lucca, *Notari parte prima* 281, f. 24–24v.

82. Pazzi, *Dizionario biografico*, 638–39, inventory of Zuanne, *orefice di Udine* (1347–87).

83. Concioni, Ferri, and Ghilarducci, *Orafi medioevale*. See in particular goldsmithing tools for stamping out buttons (68–69), and account book of Foraino de Frediano (43–46), for sales of buttons in dozens. See also *Les fastes du Gothique: Le siècle de Charles V*, exhibition catalog (Paris: Ministère de la Culture, 1981), 242–45.

84. Concioni, Ferri, and Ghilarducci, *Orafi medioevale*, 45.

85. Muzzarelli, *Gli inganni delle apparenze*, 33–39.

86. Frangioni, *Chiedere e ottenere*, 37–38.

87. Alan Stahl, *The Venetian Tornesello: A Medieval Colonial Coinage* (New York: American Numismatic Association, 1985), is valuable on minting practices at Venice. See other work by Stahl.

88. By Regulation of the Small Council in 1327, Ragusa/Dubrovnik. Goldsmiths could charge 22 *grossi* an ounce for working in *argento fino* or *argento de glama*, 16 *grossi* for working in *argento biancho*, and 4 *grossi* for working the lowest grade of silver. *Monumenta Ragusina (Libri Reformationes)*, Monumenta spectantia historiam Slavorum Meridionalium, ed. Fr. Racki (Zagreb, 1879–97), 5:229.

89. Mueller, *The Venetian Money Market*, 28.

90. Cecchetti, "Le industrie in Venezia," 244–45.

91. Pietro Pazzi, *I Punzoni dell'argenteria e oreficeria veneziana* (Venice: Monestero de San Lazzaro degli Armenni, 1990), and Bulgari, *Argentieri*. For a picture of an English touchstone, see Campbell, "Gold, Silver, and Precious Stones," 112, fig. 53. On traditional methods for jewelry making, see Wilson, *Silverwork and Jewellry*, especially for diagrams. See also Theophilus, *The Various Artists*.

92. Warnke, *The Court Artist*, 7–14.

93. Ghiberti, *Commentaries*, bk. 2, pp. 16–22.

94. Concioni, Ferri, and Ghilarducci, *Orafi medioevale*, 22.

95. Bulgari, *Argentieri*, pt. 4, pp. 192, 212.

96. Muzzarelli, *Guardaroba medievale*, 117–46.

97. Bulgari, *Argentieri*, pt. 4, p. 233.

98. Muzzarelli, *Guardaroba medievale*, 276–82.

99. Sally McKee, ed., *Wills from Late Medieval Crete, 1312–1420* (Washington, D.C.: Dumbarton Oaks, 1998), 1:467.

100. Pazzi, *Dizionario biografico*, 253.

101. Bulgari, *Argentieri*, pt. 3, pp. 295, 391.

102. Pazzi, *Dizionario biografico*, 448, 538.

103. Ibid., 586; Reinhold C. Mueller, "Aspects of Venetian Sovereignty in Medieval and Renaissance Dalmatia," in *Quattrocento Adriatico,* Papers from a colloquium held at Villa Spelman, Florence, 1994, intro. Charles Dempsey (Bologna: Villa Spelman Colloquia, 1996) 5:49.

104. Cvito Fisković, "Dubrovački Zlatari od XIII do XVII stoljeća," *Starohrvatska Prosvjeta,* 1st ser. 3 (1949): 143–249. See list on pp. 241–46.

105. Fisković, "Dubrovački Zlatari," 153–55, 241–46. For Guido Baldi in Buda, see "The Diary of Buonaccorso Pitti," in *Two Memoirs of Renaissance Florence,* trans. Julia Martines (Prospect Heights, Ill.: Waveland, 1967), 26.

106. For example, Pribil, goldsmith, identified solely by his first name in 1368, may be the Pribil Brumas or the Pribil Branojević mentioned in the 1370s.

107. Jorjo Tadić, "Le Port de Raguse au Moyen Age," *Le Navire et l'économie maritime du Moyen Age au XVIIIᵉ siècle,* in Travaux du deuxième colloque international d'histoire maritime (Paris: SEVPEN, 1959), 18.

108. Verena Han, *Tri veka dubrovačkog staklarstva, XIV–XVI* (Belgrade: SAN, 1981). The earliest glassblowers in Ragusa apparently arrived from Padua. On arms and armor at Ragusa, see Petrović, *Dubrovačko Oruzje u XIV Veku,* 214–15, which illustrates a rare depiction of a silver knife from the fourteenth century.

109. Josip Lučić, *Obrti i usluge u Dubrovniku od početka do XIV stoljeća* (Zagreb: JAZU, 1979).

110. Dubrovnik State Archives, *Diversa cancellariae,* 5, fol. 74v, *die xi septembris,* 1313. See Verena Han, ed., *Arhivska grada o staklu i staklarstvu u Dubrovniku: xiv–xvi* (Belgrade: SAN, 1979), 31.

111. Wenzel, "Bosnian History and Austro-Hungarian Policy," 29–54.

112. Cherry, *Goldsmiths,* 47, fig. 52. This may be the *Magister Pietro, aurifex, popolo di San Clemente* in Siena, whose son received a grant of dowry in 1324. Machetti, "Orafi senesi," 37.

113. Lightbown, *Secular Goldsmiths' Work in Medieval France,* 91.

114. Bulgari, *Argentieri,* pt. 2, pp. 210–326.

115. Cecchetti, "Le industrie in Venezia," 212–25. See Molmenti, *La storia di Venezia della vita privata,* 210–23. On industrial arts at Venice, see Laiou, "Venice as a Centre of Trade," and Bistort, *Il magistrato alle pompe.* On merchandizing in Venice, see Yves Renouard, "Mercati e mercanti veneziano alla fine del duecento," in *La Civiltà del Secolo di Marco Polo,* ed. Riccardo Barchelli et al. (Florence: Sansoni, 1955), 85–108.

116. See Monticolo, *I capitolari delle arti veneziani,* 1:115–34, 257–63, for statutes governing goldsmiths from 1233 with later additions.

117. F. De Roover, "Lucchese Silk Industry," 2906.

118. See Mola, *La comunità dei lucchesi a Venezia.*

119. Trexler, "The Magi Enter Florence," 163, citing Baldassare Ubriachi's will from 1395.

120. Trexler, "The Magi Enter Florence," 163 n. 137. Trexler suggests the family had interests in the small hospital of San Giovanni Battista on Murano, so it is possible that Benedetto had some training from the glassmakers of Murano as well.

121. Randolph Starn, *Contrary Commonwealth: The Theme of Exile in Medieval and Renaissance Italy* (Berkeley: University of California Press, 1982), is valuable on Italy's political exiles and emphasizes their cultural and political dilemmas.

122. Others included Benetto Pagano (1324), Donado Macalorsa (1372), Piero Fontano (1368–92), and certainly the Sesto brothers (1390). Pazzi, *Punzoni dell'argenteria,* 170–77.

123. Mueller, *The Venetian Money Market*, 90.

124. Ibid., 93.

125. Pazzi, *Punzoni dell'argenteria*, 14.

126. Ibid., 27.

127. Mueller, *The Venetian Money Market*, 28, citing Venetian State Archives, Zecca reg. 6bis, *Capitolare dei massari all'argento*, fols. 27v–28v (1351).

128. Venetian State Archives, *Maggior Consiglii, Deliberationes, Spiritus (copia)* fol. 106v (180v). Frederic C. Lane, "Venetian Bankers, 1469–1533," in *Venice and History*, 77, states that Rialto bankers dealt in pawns but no longer entered the retail trade in gold and silver wares by the Renaissance. He bases his opinion on information from Marino Sanuto's diaries. In the fourteenth century bankers and money changers had done brisk business in retailing gold and silver wares, and bankers successfully fought off forays into this traditional business operation. See also Gino Luzzatto, *Storia economica di Venezia dall'XI al XVI secolo* (Venice: Centro internationale della arti e del costume, 1961), 99–101. Mueller, *The Venetian Money Market*, 28–29, argues that fourteenth-century bankers readily ceded this business to goldsmiths, but research presented in Chapter 7 disputes that opinion.

129. Mueller, "Jewish Moneylenders," 210–11, citing Venetian State Archives, *Signori di notte al criminal*, reg. 12, fol. 27v, May 13, 1392.

130. "quod omni die tenetur super banchis pro vendendo." Cessi, *Problemi monetari veneziani*, doc. 160, p. 149.

131. Mueller, *The Venetian Money Market*, 28n. 79, citing Venetian State Archives, *Avogaria di Commun*, reg. 3643, fol. 18v for 1361.

132. Mueller, *The Venetian Money Market*, 28, citing Venetian State Archives, *Avogaria di Comun*, reg. 3643, fol. 18v.

133. Venetian State Archives, *Maggior Consiglio, Deliberationi Leona*, reg. 21, fols. 74v–75r (April 14, 1394). On the stated reason that women would not frequent the markets at the Rialto, see Romano, "Gender and the Urban Geography of Renaissance Venice," 341.

134. Stahl and Waldman, "The Earliest Known Medalists," 176–77, 185–87.

135. Guidotti, *L'oreficeria nella Firenze*, 414–15; Piattoli, "Un inventario di orificeria del trecento," 97–156.

136. Cennini, *Il libro dell'arte*, 1.

137. Trexler, *Synodal Law in Florence and Fiesole*, Constitution of 1310, p. 230, and introduction, p. 105.

138. Rainey, "Sumptuary Legislation in Renaissance Florence," 49–57, 95–98, nn. 36, 47. Florentine State Archives, Statuti 1322–25, I, p. 229: "Item quod nullus aurifex vel alie persona vendat seu vendi fatiat in civitate vel districtu Florentie aliquod de ornamentis aut rebus supra vetitis ferri vel haveri per mulieres, domines, vel viros nisi forensibus vel civibus seu districtualibus florentie, qui cives vel districtuales ea vel eas deferrant vel deferri facerent extra civitatem et districtum Florentie, sub pena librarum 100 f.p."

139. Guidotti, *L'oreficeria nella Firenze*, 101–17.

140. Louis Ausseil, *L'orfèvrerie en Rousillon: Les orfèvres de la juridiction de Perpignan du XIIIᵉ au XIXᵉ siècle* (Perpignan: Archives Départementales, 1994), 105.

141. Luigi Rizzoli Jun, "Artisti alla Zecca dei Principi da Carrara," *Rivista italiana di numismatica e scienze affini* 13 (1900): 225–38.

142. Guidotti, *L'oreficeria nella Firenze*, 153–55.

143. Bulgari, *Argentieri*, vol. 1, records a major influx of Florentine goldsmiths to Rome after 1403.

144. Pazzi, *Dizionario biografico*, p. 220, 416.

145. Vincentio Makušev, *Monumenta historica Slavorum Meridionalium vicinorumque populorum e tabulariis et bibliothecis italicis deprompta* (Warsaw, 1874), vol. 1, doc. 7, p. 435. *Die 13 Februarii, XV Ind. 1403:* "mercatanti da Ragugia, che sono nella nostra città, anno facto utile e sono stati cari e buoni a tutti la nostra cittadinanca e comi essi anno ripieno tutto il nostro comune d'ariento, che quasi in gran parte abbiamo fatto l'acquisto della città di Pisa col detto ariento, che eglio anno condocto qua." Pisa cost Florence 206,000 florins in 1406.

146. Of course there are exceptions, for example in the Treasury of Colmar and in a few museum collections. See in particular plates 1–80 in Lightbown, *Secular Goldsmiths' Work in Medieval France*. It should also be noted, however, that these superb examples of fourteenth-century craftsmanship were largely objects for domestic use rather than objects for personal adornment and display in public.

147. Bunt, *Goldsmiths of Italy*, 37.

148. Bulgari, *Argentieri*, pt. 4, p. 211.

149. Cherry, *Goldsmiths*, 69.

150. McKee, *Wills from Late Medieval Crete*, 1:240–41.

151. T. F. Reddaway, *The Early History of the Goldsmiths' Company, 1327–1509* (London: Arnold, 1975), 47.

152. Newton, *Fashion in the Age of the Black Prince*, 27.

153. F. De Roover, "Lucchese Silk Industry," 2910.

154. Stuard, "The Adriatic Trade in Silver," 109–22.

155. Goldthwaite, *Building of Renaissance Florence*, 416.

156. Warnke, *The Court Artist*, 13.

157. King, "The Trecento," 1:229, and plates 242 and 246. See also Mario Salmi, "Il Paliotto di Manresa e l'opus florentinus," *Bollettino d'arte* 24 (1930–31): 385–406.

158. See Mazzi, *Argenti degli Acciaiuoli*, for the entire inventory.

159. Lightbown, *Secular Goldsmiths' Work in Medieval France*, 33–41.

160. Egan and Pritchard, *Dress Accessories*, 18–32 and plate 12c.

Chapter 7

1. Laiou, "Venice as a Centre of Trade," 11–26.

2. For badges that originated in Italy and reached the north, see Spencer, *Pilgrim Souvenirs*, 251–54. Mitchiner, *Medieval Pilgrim and Secular Badges*, 341–96, contains Continental badges found in England. On Italian badges, see Alessandra Rodolfo, "Signa super vestes," in *Romei e giubilei: Il pellegrinaggio medievale a San Pietro*, ed. Mario D'Onofrio (Rome: Electa, 1999), 151–56, and illustrations, pp. 334–65.

3. For examples of ex-votos of silver stamped with a facsimile of St. Blaise's leg reliquary (Byzantine style, eleventh century), see the cases flanking the side altars in the Dubrovnik Cathedral. On the Treasury, see *The Dubrovnik Chathedral* [sic], ed. Don Stanko Lǎsić (Dubrovnik: Gradski župni ured Gospe Velike Dubrovnik, n.d.), pamphlet, p. 6.

4. Mueller, *The Venetian Money Market*, 28, citing Venetian State Archives, *Avogaria di Commune*, reg. 3643, fol. 18v. Small luxuries might also be traded for coin although money changers were not licensed as pawnbrokers, see p. 142.

5. Mueller, *The Venetian Money Market*, 29.

6. Mueller, "Jewish Moneylenders," 210–11, citing Venetian State Archives, *Signori di notte al criminal,* reg. 12, fol. 27, for May 13, 1392.

7. Venetian State Archives, *Maggior Consiglio, Deliberationes, Leona,* 28, fols. 70v–71 (74v–75). "Cum ab antiquo fuerit permissum, et consuetum, quod in diebus mercati quod fit in platea Sancti Marci et Sancti Pauli, venditores maspillorum et perlarum, localium, ac mercium auri et argenti, possent libere vendere de dictis mercibus . . . et vendiderint a longo tempore citra, quod fuit et est magnum comodium de nativi de Veneto et foresterii, et pulceritudo mercanti, i honorificentia terre habere. Et nuper per Iusticiarios Veteres mandatum fuerit dictis venditoribus, quod nullo modo vendant de dictis rebus in dictis mercatis, ex quo domine Veneciarum, tam nobiles quam populares, passe sunt magnum incommodum et sinistrum, quia nunquam ibunt in Rivoaltum, ad emendum de talibus mercibus; et propterea supplicaverunt dicti venditores humiliter sibi concedi quod possint vendere in diebus mercati de dictis suis localibus et mercibus; cumque predicti iustitiarii dixerint quod per matriculam aurificum prohibitum est, quod tales venditores non possint vendere in dictis mercatis, sed dominatio ducalis nichilominus providere potest sicut placet: Vadit pars, predictis consideratis, quod concedatur dictis venditoribus quod de dictis localibus, rebus, et mercibus auri et argenti possint vendere in dictis mercatis Sancti Marci and Sancti Pauli, sicut petunt." Newett, "The Sumptuary Laws of Venice," cites this text with some omissions (270–71); Romano, "Gender and the Urban Geography of Venice," 339–53, cites it as well.

8. Robert Brun, "Notes sur le commerce des objets d'art à Avignon à la fin du XIV siècle," *Bibliothèque de l'École de Chartes* 95 (1934): 328.

9. See Ronald Weissman, *Ritual Brotherhood in Renaissance Florence* (New York: Academic Press, 1982), 63.

10. Trexler, "The Magi Enter Florence," 164–71.

11. See Ignacij Voje, "Bencius del Buono," *Istorijski Časopis* 18 (1971): 189–99; Bariša Krekić, "Four Florentine Commercial Companies in Dubrovnik (Ragusa) in the First Half of the Fourteenth Century," in *The Medieval City,* ed. Harry A. Miskimin, David Herlihy, and Abraham L. Udovitch (New Haven, Conn.: Yale University Press, 1977), 25–41, and *Dubrovnik (Raguse) et le Levant au Moyen Age* (Paris: SEVPEN, 1966). For Benci's activity at Venice, see Reinhold C. Mueller, "Mercanti e imprenditori fiorentini a Venezia nel tardo medioevo," *Società e storia* 55 (1992): 29–60, 41n. 24.

12. Susan Mosher Stuard, "*Gravitas* and Consumption," in *Conflicting Identities and Multiple Masculinities,* ed. Jacqueline Murray (New York: Garland, 1999), 215–42.

13. See Speros Vyronis, "The Question of the Byzantine Mines," *Speculum* 37:1 (1962): 1–17.

14. Dubrovnik State Archives, *Diversa cancellariae,* 8, fol. 144v, 145, *die xviii januarii* 1327.

15. Dubrovnik State Archives, *Diversa cancellariae,* 10, fol. 23, *die x madii* 1333; *Diversa cancellariae,* 12, fol. 82v, *die xxii aprilis* 1335.

16. Venetian State Archives, *Grazie* 5, fol. 50 (1334); see also *Grazie,* reg. 7, fol. 37 (1336), *Grazie* 6, fol. 40v (1336), fol. 81v (1344).

17. Stahl, *Zecca,* 42–47.

18. Dubrovnik State Archives, *Diversa cancellariae,* 8, fol. 200, *die xii julii* 1330.

19. Dubrovnik State Archives, *Diversa cancellariae* 7, fol. 12, *die v julii* 1323.

20. Dubrovnik State Archives, *Diversa cancellariae* 7, fol. 35, *die xxvi octobris* 1323.

21. Gregor Čremošnik, ed., *Kancelarijski i notarski spisi, 1278–1301* (Belgrade: Zbornik za Istoriju, Jezik I Književnost, IJK, 1932), III, sec. 3, bk. 1, doc. 68, pp. 44–45 and doc. 307, p. 107.

22. Dubrovnik State Archives, *Diversa cancellariae*, 12, fol. 114, *die xiii junii* 1335, and *Diversa cancellariae*, 16, fol. 60v, *die xviiii marcii* 1349. Special conditions pertained in some contracts if silver of Nova Brdo was found to not contain gold. See, for example, *Diversa cancellariae* fol. 107v, *die iiii junii* 1335.

23. Dubrovnik State Archives, *Diversa cancellariae*, 16, fol. 16v, *die xxvi novembris* 1348, and fol. 102v, *die viii julii* 1349. See Mueller, *The Venetian Money Market*, 29, who notes that Venetian goldsmiths produced fabricated wares at less than the standard of the mint as well.

24. Spufford, *Money and Its Use*, 269–70, 341–42; Frederic C. Lane, *Venice: A Maritime Republic* (Baltimore: Johns Hopkins University Press, 1973), 148–50. See also citations in this chapter to studies by Roberto Cessi, Gino Luzzatto, Alan Stahl, Frederic C. Lane, and Reinhold C. Mueller.

25. Stahl, *The Venetian Tornesello*, and Lane and Mueller, *Money and Banking in Medieval and Renaissance Venice*, 1:336–54.

26. Lane and Mueller, *Money and Banking in Medieval and Renaissance Venice*, 1:16–23, 371–73; Luzzatto, *Storia economica di Venezia*, 93–99; Cessi, *Problemi monetari veneziani*, xxxix–xlv.

27. Dubrovnik State Archives, *Diversa notaria*, 3, fol. 121v; *Diversa cancellariae*, 6, fols. 46, 90, *Diversa cancellariae*, 8, fol. 114.

28. Spufford, *Money and Its Use*, 269.

29. Laiou, "Venice as a Centre of Trade." See also Cecchetti, "Le industrie in Venezia," 212–25, for examples.

30. Venetian State Archives, *Grazie*, reg. 6, fols. 40v and 81v (1344).

31. Lane, "Venetian Bankers," 77. Jewelwork had been regulated by the statutes of the goldsmiths since 1233 at Venice. Monticolo, *I capitolari delle arti veneziani*, 1:116–17.

32. Christine Meek, "La donna, la famiglia e la legge nell'epoca di Ilaria del Carretto," in *Ilaria del Carretto e il suo monumento: Sezione Internazionale di cultura umanistica*, ed. Stéphane Toussaint (Lucca: Atti del Convegno internazionale di studi, 1994), 156.

33. Standards for quality of worked silver dated from 1233 at Venice. Monticolo, *I capitolari delle arti veneziani*, 1:116, chap. 2.

34. Venetian State Archives, *Maggior Consiglii, Deliberationes, Spiritus (copia)* fol. 106v (180v). Lane, "Venetian Bankers," 77, stated that Rialto bankers dealt in pawns but no longer entered the retail trade in gold and silver wares during the Renaissance centuries, basing his opinion on information from Marino Sanuto's *Diarii*. In the fourteenth century bankers and money changers had done brisk business in retailing gold and silver wares and successfully fought off goldsmiths' forays into this traditional basis of operation. See also Luzzatto, *Storia economica di Venezia*, 100–101.

35. Monticolo, *I capitolari delle arti veneziani*, 2:259–60.

36. Mueller, *The Venetian Money Market*, 265.

37. A citizen *de intus* had to have fifteen years' residence at Venice to qualify.

38. Mueller, *The Venetian Money Market*, 265.

39. Sacchetti, *Il Trecentonovelle*, Novella XCVIII, 79.

40. Stahl, *Zecca*, 126–67.

41. Susan Mosher Stuard, *A State of Deference: Ragusa/Dubrovnik in the Medieval Centuries* (Philadelphia: University of Pennsylvania Press, 1992), 175–76.

42. Venetian State Archives, *Grazie*, reg. 6, fol. 81v. Catarino Quintavalle and Marcos Stornado both traded silver belts and were fined for failing to send one-fifth of the silver traded to the mint.

43. Reinhold C. Mueller, "Foreign Investment in Venetian Government Bonds and the Case of Paolo Guinigi, Lord of Lucca, Early 15th Century," in *Cities of Finance*, ed. Herman Diederiks and David A. Reeder (Amsterdam: North-Holland, 1996), 69.

44. The Balkan mines did not lie under the jurisdiction of the republic of Ragusa. Bosnian mines were opened in the fourteenth century and Serbian mines soon followed. All these lay in the West Balkans where Ragusan merchants plied their trade.

45. Makušev, *Monumenta historica*, vol. 1, pt. 2, doc. 7, p. 435.

46. Reinhold C. Mueller, "La crisi economica-monetaria venetiana di metà Quattrocento nel contesto generale," in *Aspetto della vita economica medievale*, Atti del Convegno di studi nel X anniversario della Morte di Federigo Melis, Firenze-Pisa-Prato, March 10–14, 1984 (Florence, 1985), 541–56. On fifteenth-century silver fabrication at Florence, see Guidotti, *L'oreficeria nella Firenze*, and R. Kent Lancaster, "Artists, Suppliers, and Clerks to Henry III: The Human Factors in the Art Patronage of Kings," *Journal of the Warburg and Courtauld Institutes* 35 (1972): 81–91.

Silver for fabricating wares might eat into stores of bullion, but it was unlikely a major cause of bullion shortages. Mint runs were on such a grand scale, especially in the north, and export of silver ingots and coin to the Levant so large, that small shipments of pounds of silver, while significant in themselves for fabricating wares, were unlikely to be a major contribution to the bullion famine. See Day, *The Medieval Market Economy*, 1–55, and Spufford, *Money and Its Use*, 339–62.

47. Spufford, *Money and Its Use*, 352.

48. Mueller, *The Venetian Money Market*, 262.

49. Sacchetti, *Il Trecenonovelle*, Novella XCVIII, "Egli ha fatto una sucida beffa; però che quella cappellina era sucidissima!" (221).

50. Dante Alighieri, *Divine Comedy*, vol. 3, *Paradiso*, canto 15, ll. 97–102, p. 169.

51. Sacchetti, *Il Trecentonovelle*, Novella CLIII: "si può chiamare cacleria e non cavalleria," (360). *Caca* is translated as excrement. Carol Lansing provides valuable analysis of Sacchetti's attitudes toward parvenues in *The Florentine Magnates: Lineage and Faction in a Medieval Commune* (Princeton, N.J.: Princeton University Press, 1991), 239–40.

52. Mueller, *The Venetian Money Market*, 132.

53. Ibid., 140–51.

54. Ibid., 144.

55. Brucker, *Florentine Politics and Society*, 15.

56. John Day, "The Great Bullion Famine of the Fifteenth Century," in *The Medieval Market Economy*, 1–55.

57. Sacchetti, *Il Trecentonovelle*, Novella LXIII, pp. 137–39.

58. Ibid., 139.

59. Both Ignatij Voje and Bariša Krekić warn that Robert Davidsohn's *Storia di Firenze*, trans. G. Miccoli (Florence: Sansoni, 1965), vol. 4, pt. 2, pp. 347–407, 774–78, contains inaccuracies on this family.

60. Gaetano Salvemini, *Magnati e popolani in Firenze dal 1280 al 1295* (Florence: Carnesecchi, 1899), 375–77. Salvemini relied on the chronicle of Neri Strinati. See also Brucker, *The Civic World of Early Renaissance Florence*, 143, 279–82; Lansing, *The Magnates of Florence*, 41, 79, 239–40; and Marvin B. Becker, "A Study of Political Failure: The Florentine Magnates, 1280–1343," *Mediaeval Studies* 27 (1965): 246–308.

61. "Grand'era già la colonna del Vaio, Sacchetti, Giuochi, Fifanti e Barucci e Galli." Dante Alighieri, *Divine Comedy*, vol. 3, pt. 1, *Paradiso*, canto XVI, ll. 103–5, pp. 180–81.

62. On enforcement of the Ordinances of Justice, see *Dino Campagni's Chronicle*

of Florence, ed. and trans. Daniel E. Bornstein (Philadelphia: University of Pennsylvania Press, 1986), bk. 1, chap. 12, pp. 14–16.

63. Sacchetti, *Il Trecentonovelle*, Novella XCVIII. This novella is translated by Steegman in *Tales from Sacchetti*, 79.

64. The following incident is discussed by Mueller, "Foreign Investment in Venetian Government Bonds."

65. Mueller, "Foreign Investment in Venetian Government Bonds," 80.

66. Ibid., 83–84.

67. See Botticini, "A Tale of 'Benevolent' Governments," 176–77; see also Mueller, *The Venetian Money Market*, 26, and Anthony Molho, "A Note on Jewish Moneylenders in Tuscany in the Late Trecento and Early Quattrocento," in *Renaissance Studies in Honor of Hans Baron*, ed. Anthony Molho and John A. Tedeschi (Florence: Sansoni, 1971), 99–117.

68. Corti, "Sul commercio dei quadri a Firenze.

69. Cotrugli, *Il libro dell'arte di Mercatura*, 176–77.

70. Piattoli, "Un inventario di oreficeria del trecento."

71. Armando Sapori, *La compagnia dei Frescobaldi in Inghilterra* (Florence: Olschki, 1947), 58–61. See also Richard W. Kaeuper, "The Frescobaldi of Florence and the English Crown," *Studies in Medieval and Renaissance History* 10 (1973): 89.

72. Bellorini and Hoddle, *Visit to the Holy Places*, 35.

73. Cotrugli, *Il libro dell'arte di Mercatura*, 176–77.

74. Trexler, "The Magi Enter Florence," 133. Trexler cites "Lippo Guida e Donato degli Ibriati da Firenze," *I libri commemoriali della republica di venezia*, Regesti II (Venice, 1878), bk. 3, n. 15. See Davidsohn, *Storia di Firenze*, 6:864. See also Gegnano, "La bottega degli Embriachi a proposito di opere ignoto o poco note," 221–28.

75. Trexler, "The Magi Enter Florence," 135, citing *Archivio di Stato, Prato, fondo Datini*, file number 710.

76. On the confraternity of Notre Dame la Majour at Avignon, see Joelle Rollo-Koster, "Forever After: The Dead in the Avignonese Confraternity of Notre Dame la Majour (1329–1381)," *Journal of Medieval History* 25 (1999): 115–40. The records of members for the 1350s are not extant but the confraternity was known to have enrolled a significant number of Florentine traders, and Datini's other business partners were members. For Datini's *Libro del chiesto di Avignone*, see Frangioni, *Chiedere e ottenere*, 99–166, which contains orders for numerous Florentine wares.

77. Trexler, "The Magi Enter Florence," 136. March 1.

78. Trexler, "The Magi Enter Florence," 137.

79. Gino Scaramella, ed., *Il tumulto dei Ciompi: Cronache e memorie* (Bologna: N. Zanichelli, 1934), 115, cited by Trexler, "The Magi Enter Florence," 143n. 50.

80. Anne of Bohemia was the daughter of Emperor Charles and Empress Elizabeth. On Jean Duc de Berri, see Trexler, "The Magi Enter Florence," 182.

81. "The Diary of Buonoccorso Pitti," in *Two Memoirs of Renaissance Florence*, ed. Brucker, 36.

82. Trexler, "The Magi Enter Florence," 137.

83. Venetian State Archives, *Proccuatori di San Marco*, reg. 135, bundle 1 for 1382–83, cited by Trexler, "The Magi Enter Florence," 162.

84. Brun, "Notes sur le commerce des objets d'art."

85. *Cassone*, attributed to the "Embriachi" workshop of Venice, at the Nelson-Atkins Museum of Art, Kansas City, Missouri, is a chest decorated with wedding motifs thought to be from the late fourteenth or early fifteenth century. However, Venice was

more likely to produce other types of chests, while the identifiable wedding *cassone* of the fourteenth century have been attributed to only one workshop in Florence. See also Gegnano, "La bottega degli Embriachi a proposito di opere ignoto o poco note," 221–28.

86. On the transport of enamels by courier, see also Brun, "Notes sur le commerce des objets d'art."

87. Trexler, "The Magi Enter Florence," 164–65.

88. Reddaway, *Early History of the Goldsmiths' Company*, 37. See Chapter 5 for the pairing of goldsmiths and long-distance merchants and bankers.

89. H. T. Riley, ed., *Memorials of London and London Life in the XIII, XIV and XV Centuries, 1276–1419* (London: Longmans Green, 1868), 203–4.

90. R. Kent Lancaster, "Art Patronage of Henry II," *Journal of the Warburg and Courtauld Institutes* 35 (1972): 81–91.

91. John M. Bowers, "Chaste Marriage: Fashion and Texts at the Court of Richard II," *Pacific Coast Philology* 30 (1995): 15–26.

92. Filippo Lippi, *Francesco di Marco Datini as Donor*, Galleria Comunale, Prato.

93. Frangioni, *Chiedere e ottenere*, argues that successful Italian products traded to foreigners were known by their provenance and a famous Italian locality was an asset in selling. See a list of products from 1363–1411, most by locality of manufacture (13–19). Cesare Guasti, *Lettere di un notaro ad un mercante del secolo XIV* (Florence, 1880), 2:274. See also Datini's will for appreciation of fine wares. Francesco di Marco Datini, *Testamentum*.

94. On Francesco di Marco's business dealings, see Bensa, *Francesco di Marco da Prato*. See Frangioni, *Chiedere e ottenere*, 24, for Boninsegna di Matteo and other associates and agents of Datini. On his private life, see Origo, *The Merchant of Prato*.

95. Piattoli, "Un inventario di oreficeria del trecento." According to Piattoli this inventory was interleaved among Datini's records from 1361 to 1363.

96. For the last mentioned, see Piattoli, "Un inventario di oreficeria del trecento," 251. This item alone seems to have surpassed the notary's ability to estimate a minimum value in florins although the weight estimate was 53 marks, 4 ounces. There were some internal estimates of value in florins given.

97. Both Bensa, *Francesco di Marco da Prato*, and Origo, *The Merchant of Prato*, stress Datini's hardheaded attitudes toward trade and his counsels of caution and diligence to his partners and associates. For the predominance of arms and armor among Datini trade goods, see Frangioni, *Chidere e ottenere*, 99–174. Milan was a major supplier.

98. Brun, "Notes sur le commerce des objets d'art," 327–46. See in particular the printed documents on pp. 330–31, and 331n. 2.

99. Piattoli, "Un inventario di oreficeria del trecento," 238–45, and "Un mercante dei trecento e gli artisti del tempo suo," *Rivista d'arte* 12 (1930): 97–156; Brun, "Notes sur le commerce des objets d'art," 342–43. On contracts for artists, see David Sanderson Chambers, *Patrons and Artists in the Italian Renaissance* (Columbia: University of South Carolina Press, 1971), xxvi–xxvii. The contracts translated here cover the fifteenth century.

100. Brun, "Notes sur le commerce des objets d'art," 342–46.

101. Frangioni, *Chiedere e ottenere*, 37–47.

102. Pegolotti, *La pratica della mercatura*, 293–97.

103. Venetian State Archives, *Procuratori di s. Marco, Misti*, vol. 152, n. 2, *Testamentum*, published in Cecchetti, *La vita dei veneziani*, 123–30. On doubts about Polo's

travels, see Frances Wood, *Did Marco Polo Visit China?* (Boulder, Colo.: Westview, 1996).

104. Mueller, "The Procurators of San Marco," 151–52. Stahl, *Zecca*, 131–32.

105. Lane and Mueller, *Money and Banking in Medieval and Renaissance Venice*, 320, citing Ferruccio Zago, ed., *Consiglio dei Dieci—Deliberazioni Miste—Registri III–IV (1325–1335)*, Fonti per la Storia di Venezia (Venice, 1968), reg. 3, docs. 393, 396.

106. R. de Roover, *The Rise and Decline of the Medici Bank*, 272. A more statistical approach to market conditions is taken in Lopez and Miskimin, "The Economic Depression of the Renaissance," but its generally negative findings cannot be borne out by this study. Herlihy and Klapisch-Zuber, *Toscans et leurs familles*, 67–71, provide a useful example of why luxury production continued. Holdings in movables or *massarizie di casa* came under exemption in the Florentine Catasto provisions of 1427, allowing embellishment and artistic production to flourish. But, according to the authors, this had a pernicious effect on investment in the economy generally. The Catasto law had the added effect of permitting wealth in luxury goods to be passed on through inheritance.

107. This is perhaps most popularly stated in Robert S. Lopez, "Hard Times and Investment in Culture," in *The Renaissance: A Symposium* (New York: Metropolitan Museum of Art, 1953), 19–32. The buoyant consumer market for luxury goods fails to confirm Lopez's pessimistic assessment of a fourteenth-century onset of depression in the economy. Economic dislocations abounded but the market for Italian consumer goods remained vibrant.

108. Lane, "Andrea Barbarigo," 59. Barbarigo belonged to the Cretan branch of the family.

109. Ibid., 57.

110. Ibid., 69.

111. Ibid., 126.

112. Ibid., 66, 68.

113. Ibid., 170.

114. Ibid., 198.

115. At Ragusa, thirteenth- and fourteenth-century dowries were awarded in cash. By the fifteenth century many of the patriciate awarded jewels and other luxury goods as a portion of a dowry. Stuard, "Dowry Increase and Increments in Wealth."

116. Frick, *"Dressing the Renaissance City."* See also Philip Jacks and William Caferro, *The Spinelli of Florence: Fortunes of a Renaissance Merchant Family* (University Park: Pennsylvania State University Press, 2001), 287–350. Inventories of Spinelli estates list rich goods but they tend to be domestic items.

117. Goldthwaite, *Wealth and Demand for Art in Italy*.

118. Spufford, *Money and Its Use*, 346. In 1409 the Paris mint complained that the mint had come to a standstill because money changers would not supply their office as usual. The money changers explained that Monseigneur de Berry needed gold to mount his collection of gems, as did Monseigneur de Guyenne and the king of Sicily. See also Rey, *Le domaine du roi*, 131.

119. Baxandall, *Painting and Experience in Fifteenth-Century Italy*, 15.

120. Spufford, *Money and Its Use*, 346.

121. Ibid., 340. Edward I was able to collect jewels and gold and silver objects over and above this reminting of the realm's silver coin. Inventory of jewels and other objects belonging to Edward I, in roll format, Ms. 8 (Olim Goodhart 38), England, 1301, Special Collections, Bryn Mawr College Library.

122. Stahl, *Zecca*, 147–52, 323–26.

123. Anna Rosa Calderoni Masetti, "Francisco di Grillo e altri orafi a Lucca fra tre e quattrocento," *Bollettino d'arte* 43, Supplemento al N. 43 (1958): 61, and fig. 4 for the Lucchese goldsmith Francesco di Grillo's hallmarks on a cross, Barga (Lucca) Duomo. Religious objects were more likely to be hallmarked than secular objects in the fourteenth century.

124. Mueller, *The Venetian Money Market*, 28.

125. Cotrugli, *Il libro dell'arte di Mercatura*, 176–77.

126. On *prestiti* and the *estimo*, see Mueller, *The Venetian Money Market*, 466–515; Luzzatto, *Il debito pubblico della repubblica di Venezia*, 133–76; and Luzzatto, *Storia economica di Venezia*, 129–30.

127. Rucellai, *Zibaldone*, 60–61. Translated into English in *Images of Quattrocento Florence*, ed. Baldassarri and Saiber, 74.

128. Spufford, *Money and Its Use*, 349; Day, "The Great Bullion Famine of the Fifteenth Century" 1–55; and John Munro, "Bullion Flows and Monetary Contraction in Late-Medieval England and the Low Countries," in *Precious Metals in the Later Medieval and Early Modern Worlds*, ed. J. F. Richards (Durham: Carolina Academic Press, 1983), 97–158. Also available in Munro, *Bullion Flows and Monetary Policies in England and the Low Countries*, 97–158.

129. Cipolla, *The Monetary Policy of Fourteenth-Century Florence*, 28. Bernocchio, *Le monete della repubblica fiorentina*, vol. 1, "Il libro della zecca," p. 82, noted "defectu monete argenti" as early as 1345.

130. The richest 3,000 Florentine families of 1427, 5 percent of the population of Tuscany, held more wealth than all the remaining 57,000 Tuscan households, both in and outside the city. Herlihy and Klapisch-Zuber, *Toscans et leurs familles*, 251. Less exact census material is available for Venice, but the differential in wealth is great as well.

Florentine and Venetian weights were similar but not identical. The light pound in Florence equaled 339.5 grams; the old Venetian light pound equaled 301.23 grams. Kisch, *Scales and Weights*, 228, 235, and Zupko, *Italian Weights and Measures*, 129–36.

131. Stahl, *Zecca*, 371. See Bernocchio, *Le monete della repubblica fiorentina*, 3:252–53. Semesters ran 28/5/1390–27/11/1390; 28/11/1390–27/5/1391; and 28/5/1391–27/11/1391. The figures for the 1350s were obtained by adding together five-month minting periods for 1350–51 and comparing those to the two periods, 1/11/1352–30/4/1353 and 1/5/1353–31/10/1353. In the succeeding minting period no silver coins were produced.

132. Venetian State Archives, *Maggior Consiglii, Deliberationes, Spiritus* (copia) fol. 106v (180v) *die martii*, 1331; Monticolo, *I capitulari dei arti delle veneziani*, 2:259–60. The role of bankers at the Rialto in retailing luxury goods is more problematic. Reinhold C. Mueller argues that Rialto bankers were less interested in retailing fabricated goods even if they stored jewels and took pawns as collateral on loans. He acknowledges that these pawns could amount to astounding sums but believes that worked silver and jewelry were only a sideline with bankers and as this sideline disappears, it "permits a first measure of distinction between those located at the Rialto and those at San Marco" (*The Venetian Money Market*, 28–29). In other words monetary functions and deposit banking became more specialized services of bankers at the Rialto in part at least through disassociation from the services performed by Venetian money changers, including trading worked silver, gilt silver, and jewels. Aided by legislation passed in 1322 and 1356, which added to the concept of distinct banks with their own personnel, specialized banking services at the Rialto became known as "banchi di scritta" by

the end of the fourteenth century. By the fifteenth century the word *campsor* was restricted to money changers, who were businessmen of lesser importance than the great bankers at Rialto, Mueller argues. This is a persuasive argument about the increasing specialization of banking services in Europe's premier "city of finance." Nevertheless, it is difficult to understand why the "banchi di scritta" would relinquish the high end of a market as lucrative as trading precious metals and jewels to their most wealthy customers when they had fought so hard to protect it from encroaching goldsmiths in 1331. While bankers could still tempt large investors to take away some of their earned bank interest in goods rather than interest, a role in retailing to wealthy customers held attractions.

133. Francesco Petrarch, *Four Dialogues for Scholars*, trans. Conrad Rawski (Cleveland: Press of Western Reserve University, 1967), 73.

134. Leon Battista Alberti, *On Painting and On Sculpture: The Latin Texts of De pictura and de statua*, trans. Cecil Grayson (London: Phaidon, 1972).

Chapter 8

1. Day, *The Medieval Market Economy*, 199.

2. See Manuel and Manuel, *Utopian Thought in the Western World*, 33–114, on premodern utopian visions.

3. Rainey, "Sumptuary Legislation in Renaissance Florence," 292–427.

4. See Frank, *Luxury Fever*, for his valuable ideas about the social role of context in luxury spending.

5. Jakob Burckhardt, *The Civilization of the Renaissance in Italy*, trans. S. G. C. Middlemore (Oxford: Phaidon, 1945). First published in 1860, this was widely read in Werner Sombart's day.

6. Sombart, *Luxury and Capitalism*. See other works by Georg Simmel, Norbert Elias, and others cited in Chapter 1.

7. Baldassare Castiglione, *The Book of the Courtier*, trans. Charles S. Singleton (Garden City, N.Y.: Doubleday, 1959).

8. Mola, *The Silk Industry of Renaissance Venice*.

9. Stahl, *Zecca*, 147–52, and 323–26.

10. Lopez and Miskimin, "The Economic Depression of the Renaissance." A more popular version of this thesis appeared in Lopez, "Hard Times and Investment in Culture."

11. Carlo M. Cipolla, Robert S. Lopez, and Harry A. Miskimin, "Economic Depression of the Renaissance: Reply and Rejoinder," *Economic History Review*, 2nd. ser., 16 (1964): 519–26. Goldthwaite echoes Cipolla's opinion in "The Renaissance Economy."

12. Desiderius Erasmus, *De civilitate morum puerilium (1530)*, trans. Brian McGregor, in *Collected Works of Erasmus*, ed. J. K. Sowards (Toronto: University of Toronto Press, 1985).

13. Norbert Elias, *The Civilizing Process*, trans. Edmund Jephcott (Oxford: Blackwell, 1994), 67.

14. Baldassarri and Saiber, *Images of Quattrocento Florence*, 56. For the original text, see Giovanni Morelli, *Ricordi*, ed. Vittore Branca (Florence: Le Monnier, 1956), 90–91.

15. Grant McCracken, *Culture and Consumption* (Bloomington: Indiana University Press, 1988), 68.

16. Rodolfo Pallucchini, *La pittura veneziana del trecento* (Venice: Istituto per la Collaborazione Culturale, 1964), 200–207. Giovanni Mariacher, *Il museo correr di Venezia: Dipinti dal XIV al XVI secolo* (Venice: Neri Pozza, 1957), 1:93–94, doubts the attribution to Jacobello di Bonomo.

Bibliography

Archival Sources

Venetian State Archives

Avogaria di Comun, Deliberationi del Maggior Consiglio, Magnus
    Deliberationi del Maggior Consiglio, Leona
    Deliberationi del Maggior Consiglio, Spiritus (copia)
Consiglio dei Rogati, Deliberationi, Miste, reg. 1
Grazie. Reg. 2–11
Zecca, Capitulare massarii all'argento. Reg. 6

Dubrovnik State Archives

Testamenta Notariae
(1) 1282–83; (2) 1295–1324; (3) 1324–48; (4) 1347–65; (5) 1345–65; (6) 1365–79; (7) 1381–91
    (8) 1391–1402
Diversa Cancellariae
(3) 1295; (4) 1305; (5) 1312–14; (6) 1320–22; (7) 1323; (8) 1325–27; (9) 1328–30; (10) 1333–34;
    (11) 1334–36; (12) 1334–7 and 1350–51; (13) 1341–51; (14) 1328–29 and 1343–45; (15)
    1347–48; (16) 1348–50; (17) 1351–52; (18) 1354–56; (19) 1362–71; (20) 1365–66; (21)
    1367–68; (22) 1369–70
Diversa Notariae
(1) 1310–13; (2) 1314–17; (3) 1318–20; (4) 1324–25; (5) 1324–30; (6) 1339–41; (7) 1352–58;
    (8) 1362–70; (9) 1370–79; (10) 1387–91; (11) 1402–8

Florentine State Archives

Esecutore degli Ordinamenti, 1346–47

Special Collections, Bryn Mawr College Library

Inventory of jewels and other objects belonging to Edward I, in roll format
MS 8 (Olim Goodhart 38), England 1301

Published Sources

Primary Sources

Alberti, Leon Battista. *On Painting and On Sculpture: The Latin Texts of De pictura and de statua.* Trans. Cecil Grayson. London: Phaidon, 1972.

Alcune lettere familiari del secolo XIV. Ed. Pietro Dazzi. Bologna, 1868. Reprint, Commissione per i testi di lingua, 1968.

Anonimo Romano. *Historiae romanae fragmenta ab anno MCCCXXVII usque ad MCCCLIX.* Vol. 3, cols. 307–9. In *Rerum Italicarum Scriptores,* ed. Ludovico Antonio Muratori. Milan: ex typographia Societatis Palatinae 1723–51.

Aristotle. *Aristotle's Politics and Poetics.* Trans. Benjamin Jowett and Thomas Twining. New York: Viking, 1957.

Baldassarri, Stefano Ugo, and Arielle Saiber, eds. and trans. *Images of Quattrocento Florence.* New Haven, Conn.: Yale University Press, 2000.

Barberino, Francesco da. *Del reggimento e costumi di donna, di Messer Francesco Barberini, secondo la lazione dell'antico testo a penna Barberiano.* Ed. Carlo Baudi di Vesme. Bologna: Gaetano Romagnoli, 1875.

———. *Reggimento e costumi di donna.* Ed. Giuseppe E. Sansone. Turin: Loescher-Chiantore, 1957.

Bartolus, Giovanni. *Opera Omnia.* Venice: Juntas, 1615.

Bellorini, Fr. Theophilus, and Fr. Eugene Hoddle, eds. and trans. *Visit to the Holy Places of Egypt, Sinai, Palestine and Syria in 1384 by Frescobaldi, Gucci, and Siglo.* Jerusalem: Franciscan Press, 1948.

Bentham, Jeremy. *Principles of Morals and Legislation.* Oxford: Clarendon, 1789.

Berti, P., ed. "Frammenti della cronaca di messer Luca di Totto da Panzano da una copia V. Borghini." *Giornale storico degli archivi toscani* 5 (1861): 61–78.

Bibbia istoriata padovana della fine del Trecento. Ed. Gianfranco Folena and Gian Lorenzo Mellini. Venice: N. Pozza, 1962.

Bistort, Giulio. *Il magistrato alle pompe della Republica di Venezia: Studio storica.* Bologna: Forni, 1912. Reprint, 1969.

Boccaccio, Giovanni. *Concerning Famous Women.* Ed. and trans. Guido Aldo Guarino. New Brunswick, N.J.: Rutgers University Press, 1963.

———. *The Decameron.* Trans. Frances Winwar. New York: Modern Library, 1955.

Bogišić, Baltazar and Constantin Jireček, eds. *Liber statutorum civitatis Ragusii compositus anno 1272 cum legibus aetate posteriore insertis atque cum summariis, adnotationibus et scholiis a veteribus iuris consultis ragusinis additis.* Monumenta historico-juridica Slavorum meridionalium. Vol. 10. Zagreb: JAZU, 1904.

Boilleau, Etienne. *Livre des métiers.* Ed. René de Lespinasse and Françoise Bonnardet. Paris: Imprimerie nationale, 1879.

Bonaventura, St. *Meditations on the Life of Christ.* Trans. Isa Ragusa. Ed. Isa Ragusa and Rosalie B. Green. Princeton, N.J.: Princeton University Press, 1961.

Borlandi, Antonia, ed. *Il Manuale di Mercatura di Saminiato de Ricci.* Genoa: Di Stefano, 1963.

Bornstein, Daniel E., ed. and trans. *Dino Campagni's Chronicle of Florence.* Philadelphia: University of Pennsylvania Press, 1986.

Branca, Vittore, ed. *Mercanti Scittori.* Milan: Rusconi, 1986.

Brucker, Gene A., ed. *Two Memoirs of Renaissance Florence: The Diaries of Buonacorso*

Piti and Gregorio Dati. Trans. Julia Martines. Prospect Heights, Ill.: Waveland Press, 1967.

Bruckner, Matilda Tomaryn, Laurie Shepard, and Sara Melhado White, eds. and trans. *Songs of the Women Troubadours*. New York: Garland, 1995.

Caggese, Romolo, ed. *Statuti della Repubblica Florentina*. 2 vols. Florence: Tip. Galileiana, 1910.

Castiglione, Baldassare. *The Book of the Courtier*. Trans. Charles S. Singleton. Garden City, N.Y.: Doubleday, 1959.

Catherine of Siena. *I, Catherine: Selected Writings of St. Catherine of Siena*. Ed. and trans. Kenelm Foster and Mary J. Ronayne. London: Collins, 1980.

———. *Le lettere*. Turin: Paolini, 1987.

———. *The Letters of Catherine of Siena*. Ed. Suzanne Noffke. 2 vols. Tempe, Ariz.: Medieval and Renaissance Texts and Studies, 2000.

Cellini, Benvenuto. *The Autobiography of Benvenuto Cellini*. Trans. Addington Symonds. Garden City, N.Y.: Garden City Publishers, 1927.

———. *The Treatises of Benvenuto Cellini on Goldsmithing and Sculpture*. Trans. C. R. Ashbee. London, 1888. Reprint, New York: Dover, 1967.

Cennini, Cennino. *Il libro dell'arte*. 2 vols. Trans. Daniel V. Thompson. New York: Yale University Press, 1933.

Certaldo, Paolo de. *Libro di buoni costumi*. Ed. Afredo Schiaffini. Florence: Le Monnier, 1945.

Cessi, Roberto, ed. *Problemi monetari veneziani*. Rome, Academia dei Lincei Ser IV. Vol. 1, Padua: A. Milani, 1937.

Cessi, Roberto, and Mario Brunetti, eds. *Deliberationes del Consiglio dei Rogati (Senato) serie "mixtorum" Libri XV–XVI*. Vol. 2. Venice: A Spese della Deputazione, 1961.

Chaucer, Geoffrey. *Canterbury Tales*. Ed. and trans. Helen Cooper. Oxford: Clarendon, 1989.

Chiaudano, Mario, ed. *Studi e documenti per la storia del diritto commerciale italiano nel secolo XIII*. Memorie dell'Istituto Giuridico. Turin: Presso Istituto Giuridico della R. Università, 1930.

Christine de Pizan. *Le livre des Trois Vertus*. Ed. and trans. Charity Cannon Willard and Eric Hicks. Paris: Champton, 1989.

Chronica Johannis de Reading et Anonymi Cantuariensis. Ed. James Tait. Manchester: Manchester University Press, 1914.

Cocito, Luciana, ed. *Anonimo Genovese: Poesie*. Rome: Ateneo, 1970.

Compagni, Dino. *Dino Compagni's Chronicle of Florence*. Trans. Daniel E. Bernstein. Philadelphia: University of Pennsylvania Press, 1986.

Cotrugli, Benedetto. *Il libro dell'arte di Mercatura*. Ed. Ugo Tucci. Venice: Arsenale, 1990.

Čremošnik, Gregor, ed. *Kancelarijski I notarski spisi, 1278–1301*. Belgrade: Zbornik za Istoriju, Jezik I Književnost, IJK, 1932. III. Sec. 3. Bk. 1.

Dante Alighieri. *The Divine Comedy*. Trans. Charles Singleton. Princeton, N.J.: Princeton University Press, 1977.

D'Arcq, Louis Douet, ed. *Comptes de l'argenterie des rois de France au XIVᵉ siècle*. Paris: Librarie Renouard, 1851.

———. *Nouveau recueil de comptes de l'argenterie des rois de France*. Paris: Librarie Renouard, 1874.

Datini, Francesco de Marco. *Le lettere di Margherita Datini a Francesco di Marco (1384–1410)*. Ed. Valeria Rosati. Prato: Cassa di Risparmi e Depositi, 1977.

Dazzi, Pietro, ed. *Alcune lettere familiari del secolo XIV.* Bologna: G. Romagnoli, 1868.

Dehaisnes, M. Le Chanoine. *Documents et extraits divers concernant l'histoire de l'art dans la Flandre, l'Artois et le Hainaut avant le XVème siècle.* Lille: L. Daniel, 1886.

Diana's Hunt: Caccia di Diana, Boccaccio's First Fiction. Ed. and trans. Anthony K. Cassell and Victoria Kirkham. Philadelphia: University of Pennsylvania Press, 1991.

Dotson, John E., ed and trans. *Merchant Culture in Fourteenth-Century Venice: The Zibaldone da Canal.* Binghamton, N.Y.: Medieval and Renaissance Texts and Studies, 1994.

Embriachi, Baldassare. *Embriachi, Il trittico di Pavia.* Milan: F. M. Ricci, 1982.

Erasmus, Desiderius. *De civilitate morum puerilium (1530).* Trans. Brian McGregor. In *Collected Works of Erasmus,* ed. J. K. Sowards, 271–89. Toronto: University of Toronto Press, 1985.

Fiamma, Galvano (Gualvanus della Flamma, 1283–1344). *Opusculum de rebus gestis.* Ed. Carlo Castiglioni. *Rerum italicarum Scriptores.* Ed. L. Muratori. New ed. Vol. 12. Pt 4. Bologna: N. Zanichelli, 1938.

Foucard, Cesare, ed. *Lo statute inedito delle nozze veneziane nell'1299, nozze.* Venice: Tipografia del Commercio, 1858.

(Fra) Paolino Minorita. *Trattato de regimine rectoris nell'anno 1314.* Nozze. Ed. Cesare Foucard. Venice: Pietro Naratovich, 1856.

Frescobaldi, Lionardo di. *Viaggio in Terrasanta.* Ed. Cesare Angelini. Florence: Le Monnier, 1944.

Galliccioli, Giambattista. *Storie e memorie venete antiche.* 8 vols. Venice: Domenico Fracasso, 1795.

Gherardi, Alessandro, ed. *Le consulte della repubblica fiorentina dall'anno 1280 all'anno 1298.* 2 vols. Florence: G. C. Sansoni, 1896–98.

Ghiberti, Lorenzo. *I commentari.* Ed. Ottavio Morisani. Naples: Ricciardi, 1947.

———. *Commentaries.* Pamphlet. Trans. by the staff of the Courtauld Institute of Art. Book 2. London: Courtauld Institute of Art, 1962.

Giudice, Giuseppe del. "Una legge suntuaria inedita del 1290." *Atti dell'accademia pontaniana* 16:2 (1886): 1–154.

Gratian, *Decretum.* Ed. Emil Friedberg in *Corpus Juris Canonici.* Vol. 1. Graz: Bernard Tauchnitz, 1911.

Grendler, Marcell, ed. *The "Trattato Political-morale" of Giovanni Cavalcanti, 1381–c. 1451.* Geneva: Librairie Droz, 1973.

Guasti, Cesare, ed. *Testamentum: Lettere di un notaro ad un mercante del secolo XIV. Vol. 2.* Florence, 1880.

Guasti, Cesare, and Alessandro Gherardi, eds. *I capitoli del comune di Firenze.* Vol. 2. Florence: M. Cellini, 1866–93.

Johannes Carolus. *Vita Villana Bottia Florentiae in Etruruia: Acta Sanctorum.* Pp. 865–67. August 26.

Johannes of Hildesheim. *The Three Kings of Cologne: An early English Translation of the "Historia Trium Regum."* Ed. Carl Hortsmann. Early English Text Society, 85. London: N. Trubner, 1886.

Knighton, Henry. *Chronicon Henrici Knighton vel Critthon, Monachi Leycestrensis.* Ed. Joseph Rawson Lumby. Rolls series, 92. 2 vols. London: Eyre and Spottiswoode, 1889–95.

Kohl, Benjamin G., and Ronald G. Witt, eds. *The Earthly Republic: Italian Humanists on Government and Society.* Philadelphia: University of Pennsylvania Press, 1978.

Lancia, Andrea. "Legge suntuaria fatta dal commune di Firenze l'anno 1355 e volgarizzata. nel 1356," *L'Etruria* 1 (1851): 366–443.

Légende de Saint Denis. Ed. Henry Martin. Paris: H. Champion, 1908.

Livy. *Historia*. Trans. Evan T. Sage. Loeb Classical Library. 9 vols. London: W. Heinemann, 1935.

Luttrell Psalter. Ed. Janet Backhouse. London: British Museum, 1967.

Machiavelli, Niccolò. *Istorie fiorentine*. Trans. Laura Banfield and Harvey Mansfield, Jr. Princeton, N.J.: Princeton University Press, 1988.

Makušev, Vincentio. *Monumenta historica Slavorum meridionalium vicinorum que popolorum e tabulariis et bibliothechis italicis de prompta*. 8 vols. Warsaw, 1874.

Martin da Canal. *Les estoires de Venice*. Ed. Alberto Limentani. Civiltà Veneziana fonti e testi, no. 12, 3rd ser., 3. Florence: Olschki, 1972.

Mazzi, Curzio, ed. *Argenti degli Acciaiuoli, nozze, Lungo-Bacci*. Siena, 189?.

McKee, Sally, ed. *Wills from Late Medieval Crete, 1312–1420*. 3 vols. Washington, D.C.: Dumbarton Oaks, 1998.

Ménagier de Paris. Ed. Brereton and Ferrier. Trans. Karin Uelschi. *Lettres Gothiques*. Paris: Livre de Poche, 1994.

Merchant Culture in Fourteenth-Century Venice: The Zibaldone da Canal. Ed. and trans. John E. Dotson. Binghamton, N.Y.: Medieval and Renaissance Texts and Studies, 1994.

Monticolo, Giovanni. *I capitolari delle arti veneziani sottoposto alla Giustizia e poi alla Giustizia Vecchia dalle origini al 1330*. 3 vols. Rome: Istituto Storico Italiano, 1896–1914.

Moranvillé, Henri, ed. *Inventarie de l'orfèverie et des joyaux de Louis I, duc d'Anjou*. Paris: E. Leroux, 1903–6.

Morelli, Giovanni. *Ricordi*. Ed. Vittore Branca. Florence: Le Monnier, 1956.

Muzzarelli, Giuseppina Maria. *La legislazione suntuaria, secoli XIII–XVI, Emilia-Romagna*. Rome: Ministero per i Beni e le Attività Culturali-Direzione Generale per Gli Archivi, 2002.

Niccolini di Camugliano, Ginevra. *The Chronicles of a Florentine Family, 1200–1470*. London: J. Cape, 1933.

Orlandini, V., ed. *Tarifa zoè noticia dy pexi e mexure di luogi etere che s'adovre marcandatia per le mondo*. Venice: C. Ferrari, 1925.

Pegolotti, Francesco de Balduccio. *La pratica de mercatura*. Ed. Allan Evans. Cambridge, Mass.: Harvard University Press, 1936.

Petrarca, Francesco. *Four Dialogues for Scholars*. Trans. Conrad Rawski. Cleveland: Press of Western Reserve University, 1967.

Rački, Fr, ed. *Monumenta Ragusina (Libri Reformationes)*. Monumenta spectantia historiam Slavorum meridionalium, vols. 5, 10, 13, 27, 28, 29. Zagreb, 1879–97.

Ricobaldo da Ferrara (Riccobaldus Ferrariensis). *Historia Imperatorum Romano Germanicorum a Carolo Magno usque ad annum MCCXCVII*. In *Rerum italicarum Scriptores*, ed. L. A. Muratori. Vol. 9. Milan: A. Forni, 1723–51.

Riley, H. T., ed. *Memorials of London and London Life in the XIII, XIV, and XV Centuries. Being a Series of Extracts, Local, Social and Political from the Early Archives of the City of London*, A.D. 1276–1419. London: Longmans Green, 1868.

Romanin, Samuele, ed. *Storia documentata di Venezia*. 3rd. ed. 10 vols. Venice: Filippi, 1972–75.

Rucellai, Giovanni. *Zibaldone*. Ed. Alessandro Perosa. London: Warburg Institute-University of London, 1960.

Sacchetti, Franco. *La battaglia delle belle donne, le lettere, le sposizioni di Vangeli*. Ed. Alberto Chiari. Bari: Laterza, Figli, 1938.

———. *Il libro delle rime*. Ed. Alberto Chiari. Bari: Laterza, Figli, 1936.

———. *Tales from Sacchetti*. Trans. Mary G. Steegman. New York: Dent, 1908.

———. *Il Trecentonovelle*. Ed. Vincenzo Pernicone. Florence: Sansoni, 1946.

Salimbene de Adam. *The Chronicle of Salimbene de Adam*. Ed. and trans. Joseph L. Baird, Giuseppe Baglivi, and John Robert Kane. Binghamton, N.Y.: Medieval and Renaissance Texts and Studies, 1986.

———. *Cronica*. Ed. Giuseppe Scalia. Bari: G. Laterza, 1966.

Sartini, Ferdinando, ed. *Statuti dell'arte dei rigattieri e linaioli di Firenze (1296–1340)*. Florence: Le Monnier, 1940.

"Testamenta di Pietro Vioni, Veneziano, fatto in Tauris (Persie) MCCLXIV, x Dicembre." *Archivio Veneto*, n.s. 26 (1883): 161–65.

Theophilus, Presbyter. *The Various Artists*. Ed. and trans. C. R. Dodwell. Oxford: Clarendon, 1986.

Treatise on the Seven Vices, Genoa, 1350–1400. London: British Library, Add. 7695.

Trexler, Richard, ed. *Synodal Law in Florence and Fiesole, 1306–1518*. Vatican City: Biblioteca Apostolica Vaticana, 1971.

Vasari, Giorgio. *Vasari on Technique*. Trans. Louisa S. Maclehose. New York: Dover, 1960.

Venette, Jean de. *The Chronicle of Jean de Venette*. Ed. and trans. Jean Birdsell. New York: Columbia University Press, 1953.

Verga, Ettore. "Leggi suntuarie Milanesi." *Archivio historico Lombardo* 25 (1898): 5–79.

Villani, Filippo. *De origine civitatis Florentie et de eiusdem famosis civibus*. Ed. Giuliano Tanturli. Padua: Antenore, 1997.

Villani, Giovanni. *Chroniche de Giovanni, Matteo e Filippo Villani*. Ed. A. Racheli. 2 vols. Trieste: Austriaco, 1857.

Willard, Charity Cannon, ed. *The Writings of Christine de Pizan*. New York: Persea Books, 1994.

Secondary Sources

Abbott, Reginald. "What Becomes a Legend Most?: Fur in the Medieval Romance." *Dress* 21 (1994): 5–16.

Ady, Cecilia. *Bologna under the Bentivoglio*. 1937. Reprint, London: Oxford University Press, 1969.

Allerston, Patricia. "Wedding Finery in Sixteenth-Century Venice." In *Marriage in Italy, 1300–1650*," ed. Trevor Dean and K. J. P. Lowe, 25–40. Cambridge: Cambridge University Press, 1998.

Appadurai, Arjun, ed. *The Social Life of Things: Commodities in Cultural Perspective*. Cambridge: Cambridge University Press, 1986.

Appleby, Joyce. "Consumption in Early Modern Social Thought." In *Consumption and the World of Goods*, ed. John Brewer and Roy Porter, 162–77. London: Routledge, 1993.

Art and the Courts: France and England from 1259 to 1328. Exhibition catalog. Ed. Peter Brieger and Philippe Verdier. Ottawa: National Gallery of Canada, 1972.

Ashley, Kathleen, and Robert L. A. Clark, eds. *Medieval Conduct*. Medieval Cultures Series. Vol. 29. Ed. Rita Copeland, Barbara A. Hanawalt, and David Wallace. Minneapolis: University of Minnesota Press, 2001.

Ausseil, Louis. *L'orfèvrerie en Rousillon: Les orfèvres de la juridiction de Perpignan du XIIIᵉ au XIXᵉ siècle.* Perpignan: Archives Départmentales, 1994.

Banner, Lois. "The Fashionable Sex, 1100–1600." *History Today* 42 (1992): 37–44.

Banzato, Davide. *Giotto e la pittura del trecento a Padova.* Venice: Marsilio, 1998.

Baron, Hans. "Franciscan Poverty and Civic Wealth as Factors in the Rise of Humanistic Thought." *Speculum* 13 (1938): 1–37.

Baxandall, Michael. *Giotto and the Orators.* Oxford: Oxford University Press, 1971.

———. *Painting and Experience in Fifteenth-Century Italy: A Primer in the Social History of Pictorial Style.* Oxford: Clarendon, 1972.

———. *Patterns of Intention: On the Historical Explanation of Pictures.* New Haven, Conn.: Yale University Press, 1985.

Beaulieu, Michèle. "Le costume, miroir des mentalités de la France médiévale (1350–1500)." In *Mélanges offerts à Jean Dauvillier,* 65–87. Toulouse: Centre d'Histoire Juridique Méridionale, 1979.

Becker, Marvin B. "A Study of Political Failure: The Florentine Magnates, 1280–1343." *Mediaeval Studies* 27 (1965): 246–308.

Belgrano, Luigi Tommaso. *Vita privata dei Genovesi.* Genoa, 1875. Reprint, Rome: Multigrafica Editrice, 1970.

Bell, Quentin. *On Human Finery.* New York: Schocken Books, 1976.

Bellomo, Manlio. *The Common Legal Past of Europe.* Trans. Lydia G. Cochrane. Washington, D.C.: Catholic University Press, 1995.

———. *La condizione giuridica della donna in Italia: Vicende antiche e moderne.* Turin: Eri, 1970.

Beltrami, Luca. *La certosa di Pavia.* 2nd ed. Milan: U. Hoepli, 1907.

Bensa, Enrico. *Francesco di Marco da Prato: Notizie e documenti sulla mercatura italiana del secolo XIV.* Milan: Fratelli Treves, 1928.

Berenson, Bernard. *Homeless Paintings of the Renaissance.* Ed. Hanna Kiel. Bloomington: Indiana University Press, 1969.

———. *Italian Pictures of the Renaissance: A List of the Principal Artists and Their Works.* 2 vols. New York: Phaidon, 1963.

Bernocchi, Mario. *Le monete della repubblica fiorentina.* Arte e archeologia, Studi e documenti 5–7, 11, 24. 5 vols. Florence: L. S. Olschki, 1974–85.

Berry, Christopher. *The Idea of Luxury.* Cambridge: Cambridge University Press, 1994.

Besta, Enrico. *La famiglia nella storia del diritto italiano.* Milan: A. Giuffre, 1962.

Bestor, Jane Fair. "Marriage Transactions in Renaissance Italy and Mauss's Essay on the Gift." *Past and Present* 164 (August 1999): 6–46.

Birbari, Elizabeth. *Dress in Italian Painting, 1460–1500.* London: J. Murray, 1975.

Bistort, Giulio. *Il magistrato alle pompe nella Repubblica di Venezia.* Bologna: Forni, 1912. Reprint, 1969.

Blanc, Odile. "From Battlefield to Court: The Invention of Fashion in the Fourteenth Century." In *Encountering Medieval Textiles and Dress,* ed. Désirée G. Koslin and Janet E. Snyder, 157–72. New York: Palgrave, 2002.

Blomquist, Thomas W. "The Castracani Family of Thirteenth-Century Lucca." *Speculum* 46 (1971): 459–76.

Blomquist, Thomas W., and Maureen Mazzaoui, eds. *The "Other Tuscany": Essays in the History of Lucca, Pisa, and Siena during the Thirteenth, Fourteenth and Fifteenth Centuries.* Kalamazoo, Mich.: Medieval Institute, 1994.

Blunt, Anthony. *Artistic Theory in Italy, 1450–1600.* Oxford: Clarendon Press, 1940.

Boccia, Lionello. "Ancient Italian Pieces in the Kienbusch Collection." In *Studies in*

European Arms and Armor: The C. Otto von Kienbusch Collection in the Philadel-
    phia Museum of Art, ed. Jane Watkins, 33–65. Philadelphia: Philadelphia Museum
    of Art, 1992.
Boerio, Giuseppi. Dizionario del dialetto venezino. Milan: A. Martello, 1971.
Boholm, Asa. Venetian Worlds: Nobility and Cultural Construction of Society. Goteborg:
    IASSA, 1993.
Bonds, William N. "Genoese Noblewomen and Gold Thread Manufacturing." Medie-
    valia et Humanistica, old ser. 17 (1966): 79–81.
Bongi, Salvatore. Della mercatura dei Lucchesi nei secoli XIII e XIV. 2nd ed. Atti della R.
    Accademia Lucchese. Vol 23. Lucca: Tipografia Giusti, 1884.
Bostrom, Antonia. "Embriachi." In Dictionary of the History of Art, ed. Jane Turner,
    10:178–80. New York: Grove, 1996.
Botticini, Maristella. "A Tale of 'Benevolent' Governments: Private Credit Markets,
    Public Finance, and the Role of Jewish Lenders in Medieval and Renaissance
    Italy." Journal of Economic History 60:1 (2000): 164–89.
Bourdua, Louise. "Altichiero's 'anchona' for Margareta Lupi: A Context for a Lost
    Painting." Burlington Magazine 144 (May 2002): 291–93.
Bowers, John M. "Chaste Marriage: Fashion and Texts at the Court of Richard II."
    Pacific Coast Philology 30 (1995): 15–26.
Branca, Vittore. Boccaccio: The Man and His Works. Trans. Richard Monges. New York:
    New York University Press, 1976.
———. "Per il testo del Decamerone." Studi filologia italiana 11 (1953): 389–405.
———. "Sulla diffusione della griselda petrarchesca." Studi petrarcheschi 6 (1956):
    221–24.
Braudel, Fernand. Capitalism and Material Life, 1400–1800. Trans. Miriam Kochan.
    New York: Harper, 1967.
———. The Structures of Everyday Life. Vol. 1 of Civilization and Capitalism. Trans.
    Sian Reynolds. New York: Harper and Row, 1979.
Brewer, John, and Roy Porter, eds. Consumption and the World of Goods. London:
    Routledge, 1993.
Brewer, John, and Ann Berningham, eds. The Consumption of Culture, 1600–1800:
    Image, Object, Text. London: Routledge, 1995.
Brewer, John, and Susan Staves, eds. Early Modern Conceptions of Property. London:
    Routledge, 1995.
Bridgeman, Jane. "'Pagare le pompe': Why Quattrocento Sumptuary Laws Did Not
    Work." In Women in Italian Renaissance Culture and Society, ed. Letizia Panizza,
    209–26. Oxford: European Humanities Research Center, 2000.
Brod, Harry. "Constructions of Masculinities in the Canonical Texts of Western Politi-
    cal Theory." Paper presented at the Society for Women in Philosophy, Pacific
    Division Meeting, May 21, 1994, California State Polytechnic University, Pomona.
Brown, Judith C. "Lesbian Sexuality in Medieval and Early Modern Europe." In Hid-
    den from History: Reclaiming the Gay and Lesbian Past, ed. Martin Duberman,
    Martha Vicinus, and George Chauncey, 67–75. New York: New American Library,
    1989.
———. "A Woman's Place Was in the Home." In Rewriting the Renaissance: The Dis-
    course of Sexual Difference in Early Modern Europe, ed. Margaret W. Ferguson,
    Maureen Quilligan, and Nancy J. Vickers, 191–205. Chicago: University of Chi-
    cago Press, 1986.
Brown, Judith C. and Jordan Goodman. "Women and Industry in Florence." Journal
    of Economic History 40 (1980): 73–80.

Brown, Katharine R. "Six Gothic Brooches at the Cloisters." In *The Cloisters: Studies in Honor of the Fiftieth Anniversary*, ed. Elizabeth C. Parker, 409–19. New York: Metropolitan Museum of Art, 1992.

Brown, Peter. "The Saint as Exemplar in Late Antiquity." *Representations* 2 (1983): 1–25.

Brucker, Gene A. *The Civic World of Early Renaissance Florence*. Princeton, N.J.: Princeton University Press, 1977.

———. *Florentine Politics and Society, 1343–1378*. Princeton, N.J.: Princeton University Press, 1962.

———, comp. *The Society of Renaissance Florence: A Documentary Study*. New York: Harper, 1971.

Brun, Robert. "Notes sur le commerce des objets d'art à Avignon à la fin du XIV siècle." *Bibliothèque de l'École des Chartes* 95 (1934): 26–46.

Brundage, James A. *Law, Sex and Christian Society in Medieval Europe*. Chicago: University of Chicago Press, 1987.

———. "Prostitution in the Medieval Canon Law." *Signs* 1:4 (1976): 825–45.

———. "Sumptuary Laws and Prostitution in Late Medieval Italy," *Journal of Medieval History* 13 (1987): 343–55.

Bulgari, Constantino G. *Argentieri, gemmari, e orafi d'Italia: Notizie storiche e raccolta dei loro contrassegni con la riproduzione grafica dei punzoni individuali e dei panzoni de stato*. 4 vols. Rome: L. del Turso, 1958–74.

Bullard, Melissa Meriam, S. R. Epstein, Benjamin C. Kohl, and Susan Mosher Stuard. "Where History and Theory Intersect: Frederic C. Lane on the Emergence of Capitalism." *Speculum* 79 (2004): 88–119.

Bunt, Cyril G. E. *The Goldsmiths of Italy*. London: Hopkinson, 1926.

Burckhardt, Jakob. *The Altarpiece in Renaissance Italy*. Trans. Peter Humfrey. Oxford: Phaidon, 1988.

———. *The Civilization of the Renaissance in Italy*. Trans. S. G. C. Middlemore. Oxford: Phaidon, 1945.

Burns, E. Jane. *Courtly Love Undressed*. Philadelphia: University of Pennsylvania Press, 2002.

Caferro, William. *Mercenary Companies and the Decline of Siena*. Baltimore: Johns Hopkins University Press, 1998.

Calderoni Masetti, Anna Rosa. "Francesco di Grillo e altri orafi a Lucca fra tre e quattrocento." *Bollettino d'arte, Supplemento* al N. 43 (1958): 61–74.

Callmann, Ellen. *Appollonio di Giovanni*. Oxford: Clarendon, 1974.

———. "Cassone." in *Dictionary of Art History*, ed. Jane Turner, 6:1–5. New York: Grove, 1996.

Cambridge History of Western Textiles. Ed. David Jenkins. 2 vols. Cambridge: Cambridge University Press, 2003.

Camille, Michael. "Before the Gaze: The Internal Senses and Late Medieval Practices of Seeing." In *Visuality Before and Beyond the Renaissance*, ed. Robert S. Nelson, 197–223. Cambridge: Cambridge University Press, 2000.

———. "Signs of the City: Place, Power and Public Fantasy in Medieval Paris." In *Medieval Practices of Space*, ed. Barbara A. Hanawalt and Michal Kobialka, 1–36. Minneapolis: University of Minnesota Press, 1997.

Campbell, Marian. "Gold, Silver and Precious Stones." In *English Medieval Industries*, ed. John Blair and Nigel Ramsay, 107–660. London: Hambledon, 1991.

Carnesecchi, Carlo. *Donne e lusso a Firenze nel secolo XVI: Cosimo I e la sua legge suntuaria del 1562*. Florence: Cocchi e Chiti, 1902.

Carr, Dawson. *Andrea Mantegna: The Adoration of the Magi.* Los Angeles: J. Paul Getty Museum, 1997.

Cassidy, Brendan. "A Relic, Some Pictures, and the Mothers of Florence in the Late Fourteenth Century." *Gesta* 30:2 (1991): 91–99.

Caswell, James O. *Recalling the Past: A Selection of Early Chinese Art from the Victor Shaw Collection.* Exhibition catalog. Vancouver: University of British Columbia Museum of Anthropology, 1997.

Cavaciocchi, Simonetta, ed. *La donna nell'economia secc. XIII–XVIII.* Florence: Le Monnier, 1993.

———, ed. *La Seta in Europa secc. XIII–XIV.* Settimana di studi dell'Istituto internazionale di storia economic "F. Datini" di Prato. Florence, 1993.

Cecchetti, Bartolomeo. "La donna nel medio evo a Venezia." *Archivio Veneto,* n.s. 31 (1899): pt. 1, 33–69, pt. 2, 305–45.

———. "Le industrie in Venezia." *Archivio Veneto* 4 (1872): 212–57.

———. *La vita dei veneziani nel 1300.* Venice: Emiliana, 1886.

Chabot, Isabel. "Risorse e Diritti Patrimoniali." In *Il lavoro delle donne,* ed. Renata Ago and A. Groppi, 47–70. Rome: Laterza, 1996.

Chambers, David Sanderson, ed. *Patrons and Artists in the Italian Renaissance.* Columbia: University of South Carolina Press, 1971.

Cherry, John F. *Goldsmiths.* Toronto: University of Toronto Press, 1992.

———. "Jewellery." In *Age of Chivalry: Art in Plantagenet England, 1200–1400,* ed. Jonathan Alexander and Paul Binski, 176–78. Exhibition catalog. London: Weidenfeld and Nicolson, 1987.

Child, Graham. "Mirrors." In *Dictionary of Art,* ed. Jane Turner, 21:711–22. New York: Grove, 1996.

Chojnacki, Stanley. "Daughters and Oligarchs: Gender and the Early Renaissance State." In *Gender and Society in Renaissance Italy,* ed. Judith C. Brown and Robert C. Davis, 63–86. New York: Longman, 1998.

———. "Dowries and Kinsmen in Early Renaissance Venice." In *Women in Medieval Society,* ed. Susan Mosher Stuard, 173–98. Philadelphia: University of Pennsylvania Press, 1976.

———. "From Trousseau to Groomgift in Late Medieval Venice." In *Medieval and Renaissance Venice,* ed. Ellen Kittell and Thomas Madden, 141–65. Urbana: University of Illinois Press, 1999.

———. "Patrician Women in Early Renaissance Venice." *Studies in the Renaissance* 21 (1974): 176–203.

Christianson, Gerald, and Thomas M. Izbicki. *Nicolas of Cusa on Christ and the Church.* Leiden: E. J. Brill, 1996.

Cipolla, Carlo M. *Before the Industrial Revolution: European Society and Economy, 1000–1700.* 2nd ed. New York: Norton, 1976.

———, ed. *The Fontana Economic History of Europe.* 4 vols. London: Collins/Fontana, 1972.

———. "The Italian and Iberian Peninsulas." In *The Cambridge Economic History of Europe.* 2nd ed. Ed. Michael M. Postan, E. E. Rich, and Edward Miller 3: 397–410. Cambridge: Cambridge University Press, 1963.

———. *The Monetary Policy of Fourteenth-Century Florence.* Berkeley: University of California Press, 1982.

———. *Money, Prices and Civilization in the Mediterranean World: Fifth to Seventeenth Century.* Princeton, N.J.: Princeton University Press, 1956.

————. *Studi in onore di Armando Sapori*. Milano: Instituto Editoriale Cisalpino, 1957.

Cipolla, Carlo M., Robert S. Lopez, and Harry A. Miskimin. "Economic Depression of the Renaissance: Rejoinder and Reply." *Economic History Review*, 2nd ser., 16 (1964): 519–26.

Ciriacono, Salvatore. "Les manufactures de luxe à Venise." In *Cities and the Transmission of Cultural Values*, 235–51. Brussels: Crédit Commmunal, Collection Histoire 17th International Colloquium, 1996.

Cirković, Sima. "The Production of Gold, Silver and Copper in the Central Parts of the Balkans from the Thirteenth to the Sixteenth Century." In *Beitrage zur Wirtschaftsgeschichte: Precious Metals in the Age of Expansion*, ed. Hermann Kellenbenz, 41–69. Stuttgart: Klett-Cotta, 1981.

Clunas, Craig. "Modernity Global and Local: Consumption and the Rise of the West." *American Historical Review* 104:5 (1999): 1497–1511.

Cohn, Samuel K., Jr. *The Laboring Classes in Renaissance Florence*. New York: Academic Press, 1980.

————. "Women and Work in Renaissance Italy." In *Gender and Society in Renaissance Italy*, ed. Judith C. Brown and Robert C. Davis, 107–26. New York: Longman, 1998.

————. *Women in the Streets: Essays on Sex and Power in Renaissance Italy*. Baltimore: Johns Hopkins University Press, 1996.

Cole, Bruce. *Giotto and Florentine Painting, 1280–1375*. New York: Harper and Row, 1976.

Concioni, Graziano, Claudio Ferri, and Giuseppe Ghilarducci. *Orafi medioevale: Lucca, secc. VIII–XV*. Lucca: Rugani edizioni d'arte in Lucca, 1991.

Congdon, Eleanor A. "Datini and Venice: News from the Mediterranean Trade Network." In *Across the Mediterranean Frontier: Trade Politics and Religion, 650–1450*, ed. Dionisius A. Agius and Ian Richard Netton, 157–71. Amsterdam: Turnhout, Brepols, 1997.

Connell, Susan. *The Employment of Sculptors and Stonemasons in the Fifteenth Century*. New York: Garland, 1988.

Corso, R. "Patti d'amore: I doni nuziali." *Revue d'ethnographie et de socioligie* 2 (1911): 228–54.

Cortelazzo, Manlio. *Dizionario etimologico della lingua italiana*. 3 vols. Bologna: Zanichelli, 1979–88.

Corti, Gino. "Sul commercio dei quadri à Firenze verso la fine del secolo XIV." *Commentari* 22 (1971): 84–91.

Coulton, George Gordon. *From St. Francis to Dante*. 2nd ed. revised. Philadelphia: University of Pennsylvania Press, 1972.

Courajod, Louis Charles Jean. *Leçons professées à l'école du Louvre, 1887–96*. 3 vols. Paris: A. Picard, 1899–1903.

Cozzi, Gaetano. *Gli ebrei e venezia, secoli XIV–XVIII*. Atti del Convegno Internazionale organizzato dalla Fondazione G. Cini, Venezia, Isola di San Giorgio Maggiore, 5–10 giugno 1983. Milan: Edizioni Communitá, 1987.

Craddock, P. T. "Fire Gilding." In *The Dictionary of Art*, ed. Jane Turner, 12:624. New York: Grove, 1996.

Crane, Susan. *The Performance of Self*. Philadelphia: University of Pennsylvania Press, 2002.

Crum, Roger J. "Controlling Women or Women Controlled? Suggestions for Gender Roles and Visual Culture in the Italian Renaissance Palace." In *Beyond Isabella:*

Secular Women Patrons of Art in Renaissance Italy, ed. Sheryl E. Reiss and David G. Wilkins, 37–50. Kirksville, Mo.: Truman State University Press, 2001.

Curtin, Philip D. *Cross-Cultural Trade in World History.* Cambridge: Cambridge University Press, 1984.

Davenport, Milia. "Personal Adornment." In *The Secular Spirit: Life and Art at the End of the Middle Ages,* ed. Timothy Husband and Jane Hayward, 69–95. Exhibition catalog. New York: E. P. Dutton, 1975.

Davidsohn, Robert. *Storia di Firenze.* Trans. G. Miccoli. 5 vol. in 8. Florence: Sansoni, 1965.

Davis, Fred. *Fashion, Culture and Identity.* Chicago: University of Chicago Press, 1992.

Davis, Natalie. "Women in the *Arts Mécaniques* in Sixteenth-Century Lyon." In *Lyon et L'Europe, Melanges en hommage de Richard Gascon,* ed. Jean-Pierre Gutton, 139–67. Lyon: Presses Universitaires, 1980.

Day, John. *The Medieval Market Economy.* Oxford: Blackwell, 1987.

De Roover, Florence Edler. "Andrea Banchi: Florentine Silk Manufacturer and Merchant in the Fifteenth Century." *Studies in Medieval and Renaissance History* 3 (1966): 221–86.

———. *L'arte della seta a Firenze nei secoli XIV e XV.* Ed. Sergio Tognetti. Florence: Olschki, 1999.

———. "The Beginnings and the Commercial Aspects of the Lucchese Silk Industry." *CIBA Review* 80 (June 1950): 2902–30.

De Roover, Raymond Adam. *Money, Banking and Credit in Medieval Bruges: Italian Merchant Bankers, Lombards, and Money Changers.* Cambridge, Mass.: Medieval Academy of America, 1948.

———. *The Rise and Decline of the Medici Bank, 1397–1494.* New York: Norton, 1966.

Donkon, R. A. *Beyond Price, Pearls and Pearl-Fishing: Origins to the Age of Discoveries.* Philadelphia: American Philosophical Society, 1998.

D'Onofrio, Mario, ed. *Romei & Giubilei: Il pellegrinaggio medievale a San Pietro (350–1350).* Milan: Electa, 1999.

Doren, Alfred Jakob. *Itallienische Wirtschaftsgeschichte.* Jena: G. Fischer, 1934.

Dotson, John E. "Perceptions of the East in Italian Merchants' Manuals." In *Across the Mediterranean Frontiers: Trade, Politics and Religion, 650–1450,* ed. Dionisius A. Agius and Ian Richard Netton, 1173–92. Brussels: Turnhout, Brepols, 1997.

Douglas, Mary, and Baron Isherwood. *The World of Goods.* New York: Basic Books, 1979.

Dubois, Henri. "Commerce international, métaux précieux et flux monétaires aux confins orientaux du royaume de France." In *La moneta nell'economica europea secoli XIII–XVIII,* ed. Vera Barbagli Bagnoli, 681–97. Istituto Internazionale di Storia Economica "Datini," Prato, Serie II. Atti delle "Settimane di studio," 11–17 Aprile 1975. Florence: Le Monnier, 1981.

Duby, Georges. *The Early Growth of the European Economy: Warriors and Peasants from the Seventh to the Twelfth Century.* Trans. Howard B. Clarke. Ithaca, N.Y.: Cornell University Press, 1974.

———, ed. *A History of Private Life.* Trans. Arthur Goldhammer Cambridge, Mass.: Belknap, 1987.

Dulac, Liliane. "Mystical Inspiration and Political Knowledge: Advice to Widows from Francesco da Barberino and Christine de Pizan." Trans. Thelma Fenster in *Upon My Husband's Death: Widows in the Literature and Histories of Medieval Europe,* ed. Louise Mirrer, 223–58. Ann Arbor: University of Michigan Press, 1992.

Early, Alice K. *English Dolls, Effigies and Puppets.* London: Batsford, 1955.

Eco, Umberto. *Art and Beauty in the Middle Ages.* Trans. Hugh Bredin. New Haven, Conn.: Yale University Press, 1986.

Egan, Geoff, and Frances Pritchard. *Dress Accessories, c. 1150–1450.* Woodbridge, Suffolk: Boydell Press, 2002.

Egbert, Virginia. *The Medieval Artist at Work.* Princeton, N.J.: Princeton University Press, 1967.

Elias, Norbert. *The Civilizing Process.* Trans. Edmund Jephcott. Oxford: Blackwell, 1994.

———. *The Court Society.* Trans. Edmund Jephcott. New York: Pantheon, 1983.

Elliott, Dyan. "Dress as Mediator between Inner and Outer Self: The Pious Matron in the High and Later Middle Ages." *Mediaeval Studies* 53 (1991): 279–309.

Epstein, Steven A. *Genoa and the Genoese.* Chapel Hill: University of North Carolina Press, 1996.

———. *Speaking of Slavery.* Ithaca, N.Y.: Cornell University Press, 2001.

———. *Wage and Labor Guilds in Medieval Europe.* Chapel Hill: University of North Carolina Press, 1991.

Evans, Joan. *Dress in Mediaeval France.* Oxford: Clarendon, 1952.

———. *A History of Jewellery, 1180–1870.* Boston: Boston Book and Art, 1970.

Farr, James R. *Artisans in Europe, 1300–1914.* Cambridge: Cambridge University Press, 2000.

Les fastes du Gothique: Le siècle de Charles V. Exhibition catalog. Paris: Ministère de la Culture, 1981.

Favier, Jean. *Gold and Spices: The Rise of Commerce in the Middle Ages.* Trans. Caroline Higgitt. New York: Holmes and Meier, 1998.

Ferguson, George. *Signs and Symbols in Christian Art.* New York: Oxford, 1955.

Findlen, Paula. "Possessing the Past: The Material World of the Italian Renaissance." *American Historical Review* 103 (1998): 83–114.

Fingerlin, Ilse. *Gürtel des hohen und späten Mittelalters.* Munich: Deutscher Kunstverlag, 1971.

Fisković, Cvito. "Dubrovački Zlatari od XIII do XVII stoljeća." *Starohrvatska Prosvjeta,* 1st ser. 3 (1949): 143–249.

Flandrin, Jean-Louis. "Repression and Change in the Sexual Life of Young People in Medieval and Early Modern Times." *Journal of Family History* 2 (1977): 196–210.

Francheschi, Franco. "Florence and Silk in the Fifteenth Century." *Italian History and Culture, Villa le Balze, Georgetown University* 1 (1995): 3–22.

Frangioni, Luciana. *Chiedere e ottenere: L'approvvigionamento di prodotti di successo della bottega Datini di Avignone nel XIV secolo.* Florence: Opus Libri, 2002.

Frank, Robert. *Luxury Fever.* New York: Free Press, 1999.

Fraser, Antonia. *Dolls.* New York: G. P. Putman, 1963.

Frati, Lodovico. *La vita privata in Bologna dal secolo XII al XVII.* Bologna: Zanichelli, 1928.

Freudenberger, Herman. "Fashion, Sumptuary Laws, and Business." *Business History Review* 37 (1963): 37–48.

Frick, Carole Collier. *Dressing Renaissance Florence.* Baltimore: Johns Hopkins University Press, 2002.

———. "Dressing the Renaissance City: Society, Economics and Gender in the Clothing of Fifteenth-Century Florence." Ph.D. diss., University of California, Los Angeles, 1995.

Frugoni, Chiara. *Books, Banks, Buttons and Other Inventions from the Middle Ages.* Trans. William McCuaig. New York: Columbia University Press, 2003.

———. *Pietro and Ambrogio Lorenzetti.* Florence: Scala, 1988.

Garnier, François. *Le langage de l'image au Moyen Age.* Vol. 2. *Il Grammaire des gestes.* Paris: Le Léopard d'Or, 1982.

Garzelli, Annarosa. *Il ricamo nella attività artistica di Pollaiolo, Botticelli, Bartolomeo di Giovanni.* Florence: Editrice Edam, 1973.

Gauthier, Marie Madeleine. *Emaux du Moyen Age occidental.* 2nd ed. Fribourg: Office di Livre, 1972.

Gegnano, M. J. "La bottega degli Embriachi a proposito di opere ignoto o poco note." *Arte Lombardo* 5 (1960): 221–28.

Gérard-Marchant, Laurence. "Compter et nommer l'étoffe à Florence au trecento (1343)." *Médiévales* 29 (1995): 87–104.

Gibbons, Rachel C. "The Queen as 'Social Mannequin': Consumerism and Expenditure at the Court of Isabeau of Bavaria, 1393–1422." *Journal of Medieval History* 26:4 (2000): 371–95.

Gladwell, Malcolm. *The Tipping Point.* Boston: Little, Brown, 2000.

Goldthwaite, Richard A. *The Building of Renaissance Florence: An Economic and Social History.* Baltimore: Johns Hopkins University Press, 1980.

———. "The Renaissance Economy: The Preconditions for Luxury Consumption." In *Aspetti della vita economica medievale,* 659–72. Atti del convegno di studi nel X anniversario della morte de Federigo Melis. Firenze-Pisa-Prato, March 10, 1984.

———. *Wealth and the Demand for Art in Italy, 1300–1600.* Baltimore: John Hopkins University Press, 1993.

Goodich, Michael. "'*Ancilla dei*': The Servant as Saint in the Middle Ages." In *Women in the Medieval World,* ed. Suzanne Wemple and Julius Kirshner, 119–28. Oxford: Blackwell, 1985.

Goodman, Jordan. "The Florentine Silk Industry in Seventeenth-Century Florence." Ph.D. diss., London School of Economics, 1977.

Grandjean, Sergi. *L'orfevrerie du XIXᵉ siècle en Europe.* Paris: Presses Universitaires de France, 1962.

Greci, Roberto. "Donne e Corporazioni: La fluidita di un rapporto." In *Il lavoro delle donne,* ed. Angela Groppi, 71–91. Rome: Laterza, 1996.

Gross, Elizabeth. "Philosophy, Subjectivity, and the Body: Kristeva and Iragaray." In *Feminist Challenges: Social and Political History,* ed. Carole Pateman and Elizabeth Gross, 125–43. Boston: Northeastern University Press, 1986.

Guarducci, Piero. "Le materie prime nell'arte tintoria senese del basso medio evo." *Archeologie medievale* 6 (1979): 371–86.

Guidotti, Alessandro, ed. *L'oreficeria nella Firenze del quattrocento.* Exhibition catalog. Florence: Scelte, 1977.

Guimbard, Catherine. "Appunti sulla legislazione suntuaria à Firenze dal 1281–1384." *Archivio Storico Italiano* 150 (1992): 57–81.

———. "Le reggimento e costumi di donna de Francesco da Barberino." *Revue des études italiennes* 36 (1990): 43–58.

Guzzetti, Linda. "Donne e scrittura a Venezia nel tardo Trecento." *Archivio Veneto* 152 (1999): 5–32.

Han, Verena, ed. *Arhivska grada o staklu i staklarstvu u Dubrovniku: XIV–XVI veku.* Belgrade: SAN, 1979.

———. *Tri veka dubrovačkog staklarstva, XIV–XVI.* Belgrade: SAN, 1981.

Hanawalt, Barbara. *Of Good or Ill Repute*. New York: Oxford University Press, 1998.

Henderson, George. *Gothic*. Harmondsworth: Penguin, 1967.

Henderson, John. *Piety and Charity in Late Medieval and Renaissance Florence*. Oxford: Oxford University Press, 1994.

Hentsch, Alice A. *De la litterature didactique du Moyen Age s'addressant specialment aux femmes*. Cohors, 1903. Reprint, Geneva: Slatkine Reprints, 1975.

Herald, Jacqueline. *Renaissance Dress in Italy, 1400–1500*. London: Bell and Hyman, 1981.

Herlihy, David. "Deaths, Marriage, Births and the Tuscan Economy." In *Population Patterns in the Past*, ed. Ronald Demos Lee, 135–64. New York: Academic Press, 1977.

———. *Opera Muliebria*. New York: McGraw-Hill, 1990.

———. *Pisa in the Early Renaissance: A Study of Urban Growth*. New Haven, Conn.: Yale University Press, 1958.

———. "Treasure Hoards in the Italian Economy, 960–1139." *Economic History Review*, 2nd ser., 10 (1957): 1–14.

Herlihy, David, and Christiane Klapisch-Zuber. *Toscans et leurs familles*. Paris: SEV-PEN, 1978.

Hine, Thomas. *I Want That*. New York: Harper Collins, 2002.

Hills, Paul. *Venetian Colour*. New Haven, Conn.: Yale University Press, 1999.

Hirschman, Albert O. "The Changing Tolerance for Income Inequality in the Course of Economic Development." *Quarterly Journal of Economics* 87 (1973): 504–66.

———. *The Passions and the Interests: Political Arguments for Capitalism before Its Triumph*. Princeton, N.J.: Princeton University Press, 1977.

Hoeniger, Cathleen S. "Cloth of Gold and Silver: Simone Martini's Techniques for Representing Luxury Textiles." *Gesta* 30:2 (1991): 154–62.

Hollingsworth, Mary. *Patronage in Renaissance Italy: From 1400 to the Early Sixteenth Century*. London: John Murray, 1994.

Howard, Deborah. *The Architectural History of Venice*. Rev. ed. New Haven, Conn.: Yale University Press, 2002.

Howell, Martha C. *Women, Production, and Patriarchy in Late Medieval Cities*. Chicago: University of Chicago Press, 1986.

Hughes, Diane Owen. "Distinguishing Signs: Ear-rings, Jews and Fransiscan Rhetoric in the Italian Renaissance City." *Past and Present* 112 (1986): 3–59.

———. "From Bridepiece to Dowry in Mediterranean Europe." *Journal of Family History* 8 (1978): 262–96.

———. "Regulating Women's Fashion." In *A History of Women in the West*. Vol. 2. *Silences of the Middle Ages*, ed. Christiane Klapisch-Zuber, 136–58. Cambridge, Mass.: Belknap Press, 1992.

———. "Sumptuary Law and Social Relations in Renaissance Cities." In *Disputes and Settlements*, ed. John Bossy, 69–100. Cambridge: Cambridge University Press, 1984.

———. "Urban Growth and Family Structure in Medieval Genoa." *Past and Present* 66 (1975): 3–28.

Hunt, Alan. *Governance of the Consuming Passions: A History of Sumptuary Law*. New York: St. Martin's Press, 1996.

Hunt, Edwin S., and James M. Murray. *A History of Business in Medieval Europe, 1200–1500*. Cambridge: Cambridge University Press, 1999.

Iacometti, Franco. "I sigilli della biblioteca communale di Siena." *Rassegna d'Arte Senese* 20 (1927): 221–24.

Ilaria del Carretto e il suo monumento. Sezione Internazionale di Cultura Umanistica. Ed. Stéphane Toussaint. Lucca: Atti del convegno internazionale di studi, 1994.

Izbicki, Thomas. "Pyres of Vanities in *De Ore Domini.*" In *Preaching and the Word in the Middle Ages,* ed. Thomas Amos, Eugene A. Green, and Beverly Mayne Kienzle, 211–34. Kalamazoo, Mich.: Medieval Institute, 1989.

Jacks, Philip, and William Caferro. *The Spinelli of Florence: Fortunes of a Renaissance Merchant Family.* University Park: Pennsylvania State University Press, 2001.

Jacobus, Laura. "Piety and Propriety in the Arena Chapel." *Renaissance Studies* 12 (1998): 177–203.

Jardine, Lisa. *Worldly Goods: A New History of the Renaissance.* New York: W. W. Norton, 1996.

Jardine, Lisa, and Jerry Brotton. *Global Interests.* Ithaca, N.Y.: Cornell University Press, 2000.

Jevons, Sir William Stanley. *Money and the Mechanism of Exchange.* New York: D. Appleton, 1875.

Jirousek, Charlotte. "More than Oriental Splendor: European and Ottoman Headgear, 1380–1580." *Dress* 22 (1995): 22–33.

Jolly, Penny. *Made in God's Image.* Berkeley: University of California Press, 1997.

Jones, Ann Rosalind, and Peter Stallybrass. *Renaissance Clothing and the Materials of Memory.* Cambridge: Cambridge University Press, 2000.

Jones, Philip. *The Italian City-State from Commune to Signoria.* Oxford: Clarendon, 1997.

Kaeuper, Richard. *Bankers to the Crown: The Riccardi of Lucca and Edward I.* Princeton, N.J.: Princeton University Press, 1973.

———. "The Frescobaldi of Florence and the English Crown." *Studies in Medieval and Renaissance History* 10 (1973): 45–94.

Kaftal, George. *Iconography of the Saints in Italy.* 4 vols. Florence: Sansoni, 1952–78.

Katzenellenbogen, Adolf. *Allegories of the Virtues and Vices in Mediaeval Art: From Early Christian Times to the Thirteenth Century.* London: Warburg Institute, 1939. Reprint, Toronto: University of Toronto Press, 1989.

Kedar, Benjamin. *Merchants in Crisis.* New Haven, Conn.: Yale University Press, 1976.

Kelly, Francis M., and Randolph Schwabe. *A Short History of Costume and Armour, Chiefly in England, 1066–1800.* London: B. T. Batsford, 1931.

Kelly, Joan. "Did Women Have a Renaissance?" In *Becoming Visible,* ed. Renate Bridenthal, Claudia Koonz, and Susan Stuard. 2nd ed. Boston: Houghton Mifflin, 1987.

Kelso, Ruth. *Doctrine for the Lady of the Renaissance.* Urbana: University of Illinois Press, 1956.

Kent, Francis W., Patricia Simons, and J. E. Eade, eds. *Patronage, Art and Society in Renaissance Italy.* New York: Oxford University Press, 1987.

Killerby, Catherine Kovesi. "'Heralds of a Well-Instructed Mind': Nicolosa Sanuti's Defence of Women and Their Clothes." *Renaissance Studies* 13 (1999): 255–82.

———. "Practical Problems in the Enforcement of Italian Sumptuary Law, 1200–1500." In *Crime, Society and Law in Renaissance Italy,* ed. Trevor Dean and K. J. P. Lowe. 99–120. Cambridge: Cambridge University Press, 1994.

———. *Sumptuary Law in Italy, 1200–1500.* New York: Oxford University Press, 2002.

King, Catherine. "The Arts of Carving and Casting." In *Siena, Florence and Padua: Art, Society, and Religion, 1280–1400,* ed. Diana Norman, 1:97–121. New Haven, Conn.: Yale University Press, 1995.

————. *Renaissance Women Patrons*. Manchester: Manchester University Press, 1998.

————. "The Trecento: New Ideas, New Evidence." In *Siena, Florence and Padua: Art, Society and Religion, 1280–1400*, ed. Diana Norman, 1:216–33. New Haven, Conn.: Yale University Press, 1995.

King, Margaret. *Women of the Renaissance*. Chicago: University of Chicago Press, 1991.

Kirby, Jo, et al. "Gilding." In *Dictionary of Art*, ed. Jane Turner, 12:620–25. New York: Grove, 1996.

Kirshner, Julius. "Materials for a Gilded Cage: Non-dotal Assets in Florence, 1300–1500." In *The Family in Italy from Antiquity to the Present*, ed. David L. Kertzer and Richard P. Saller, 184–207. New Haven, Conn.: Yale University Press, 1991.

————. "Pursuing Honor while Avoiding Sin: The *Monte delle doti* of Florence." *Studi Senesi* 89, 3rd ser., 26 (1977): 177–258.

Kisch, Bruno. *Scales and Weights: A Historical Outline*. New Haven, Conn.: Yale University Press, 1965.

Klapisch-Zuber, Christiane. *Women, Family and Ritual in Renaissance Italy*. Trans. Lydia Cochrane. Chicago: University of Chicago Press, 1985.

————. "Women Servants in Florence during the Fourteenth and Fifteenth Centuries." In *Women and Work in Pre-industrial Europe*, ed. Barbara Hanawalt, 56–80. Bloomington: Indiana University Press, 1986.

Klesse, Brigitte. *Seidenstoffe in der Italienischen Malerei des 14 Jahrhunderts*. Bern: Stampfli, 1967.

Koechlin, Raymond. *Les ivoires gothiques français*. Paris: A. Picard, 1924.

Kohl, Benjamin. "Fina da Carrara, née Buzzacarini: Consort, Mother, and Patron of Art in Trecento Padua." In *Beyond Isabella: Secular Women Patrons of Art in Renaissance Italy*, ed. Sheryl E. Reiss and David G. Wilkins, 19–35. Kirksville, Mo.: Truman State University Press, 2001.

Kosmer, Ellen. "The 'Noyous Humoure of Lecherie.'" *Art Bulletin* 57 (1975): 1–8.

Kovačević, Desanka. "Les mines d'or et d'argent en Servie et Bosnie." *Annales, E.S.C.* 15 (1960): 248–58.

Krekić, Bariša. "Contribution of Foreigners to Dubrovnik's Economic Life." *Viator* 8 (1978): 67–71.

————. *Dubrovnik (Raguse) et le Levant au Moyen Age*. Paris: Mouton, 1961.

————. "Four Florentine Commercial Companies in Dubrovnik (Ragusa) in the First Half of the Fourteenth Century." In *The Medieval City*, ed. Harry A. Miskimin, David Herlihy, and Abraham L. Udovitch, 25–41. New Haven, Conn.: Yale University Press, 1977.

————. "Kurirski saobraćaj." *Zbornik radova*. Vol. 21. Belgrade: Vizantoloskog Instituta, SAN, 1952.

Krueger, Roberta L. "'Nouvelles choses': Social Instability and the Problem of Fashion in the *Livre du Chevalier de la Tour Landry*, the *Ménagier de Paris* and Christine de Pizan's *Livre des trois vertus*." In *Medieval Conduct*, ed. Kathleen Ashley and Robert L. A. Clark, 49–85. Minneapolis: University of Minnesota Press, 2001.

Kuchta, David. "The Semiotics of Masculinity in Renaissance England." In *Sexuality and Gender in Early Modern Europe: Institutions, Texts, Images*, ed. James Turner, 233–46. Cambridge: Cambridge University Press, 1993.

Kuehn, Thomas. "'*Cum consensu mundualdi*': Legal Guardianship of Women in Quattrocentro Florence." *Viator* 13 (1982): 309–22.

————. "Person and Gender in the Laws." In *Gender and Society in Renaissance Italy*, ed. Judith C. Brown and Robert C. Davis, 87–106. New York: Longman, 1998.

Labarge, Margaret. "Stitches in Time: Medieval Embroidery in Its Social Setting." *Florilegium* 16 (1999): 77–96.

Ladis, Andrew. *Taddeo Gaddi: Critical Reappraisal and Catalogue Raisonné*. Columbia: University of Missouri Press, 1982.

Laiou, Angeliki. "Venice as a Centre of Trade and of Artistic Production in the Thirteenth Century." In *Il medio oriente e l'occidente nell'arte del XIII secolo*, ed. Hans Belting, 11–34. Bologna: CLEUB, 1982.

Lancaster, R. Kent. "Artists, Suppliers, and Clerks to Henry III: The Human Factors in the Art Patronage of Kings." *Journal of the Warburg and Courtauld Institutes* 35 (1972): 81–91.

———. "Art Patronage of Henry II." *Journal of the Warburg and Courtauld Institutes* 35 (1972): 81–91.

Lane, Fredrick C. *Andrea Barbarigo, Merchant of Venice*. Johns Hopkins University Studies in Historical and Political Science 62:1 (1944).

———. "Consumption and Economic Change." *Journal of Economic History* 15 (1955): 107–9.

———. "Some Heirs of Gustav von Schmoller." In *Venice and History: The Collected Papers of Frederic C. Lane*, ed. Committee of Colleagues and Former Graduate Students, 462–95. Baltimore: Johns Hopkins University Press, 1966.

———. *Venice: A Maritime Republic*. Baltimore: Johns Hopkins University Press, 1973.

Lane, Frederic C., and Reinhold C. Mueller. *Coins and Moneys of Account*. Vol 1 of *Money and Banking in Medieval and Renaissance Venice*. Baltimore: Johns Hopkins University Press, 1985.

Langholm, Odd. *The Merchant in the Confessional*. Leiden: Brill, 2003.

Lansing, Carol. *The Florentine Magnates: Lineage and Faction in a Medieval Commune*. Princeton, N.J.: Princeton University Press, 1991.

———. "Gender and Civic Authority: Sexual Control in a Medieval Italian Town." *Journal of Social History* 31 (1997): 33–60.

Lazzareschi, Eugenio, ed. *L'arte della seta in Lucca: Seconda "Settimana lucchese," maggio MCMXXX–VIII*. Pescia: Edizioni Benedetti e Niccolai, 1930.

Lehoux, Françoise. *Jean de France, duc de Berri, sa vie, son action politique (1340–1416)*. 4 vols. Paris: J. Picard, 1966–68.

Levi Pisetzky, Rosita. *Storia del costume in Italia*. 4 vols. Milan: Istituto Editoriale Italiano, 1964.

Lightbown, R. W. *Secular Goldsmiths' Work in Medieval France: A History*. London: Society of Antiquaries of London, 1978.

Limentani, Alberto. *Les estoires de Venise: Cronaca veneziani in lingua francese delle origini al 1275*. Civiltà Veneziana fonti e testi. No. 12. 3rd ser., 3. Florence: L. S. Olschki, 1972.

Little, Lester. "Pride Goes before Avarice: Social Changes and the Vices in Latin Christendom." *American Historical Review* 76 (1971): 16–49.

Livre du Chevalier de la Tour Landry pour l'enseignement de ses filles. Ed. Anatole de Montaiglon. Paris: Jannet, 1854. Reprint, Millwood, N.Y.: Kraus Reprint, 1982.

Lloyd, G. E. R. *Polarity and Analogy: Two Types of Argumentation in Early Greek Thought*. Cambridge: Cambridge University Press, 1971.

Lopez, Robert S. *The Commerical Revolution*. Englewood Cliffs, N.J.: Prentice Hall, 1971.

———. "Hard Times and Investment in Culture." In *The Renaissance: A Symposium*, 19–34. New York: Metropolitan Museum of Art, 1953.

————. "The Origin of the Merino Sheep." *The Joshua Starr Memorial Volume: Studies in History and Philology, Jewish Social Studies* 5. New York, 1953. Pp. 161–68.

————. *Studi sull'economia Genovese nel medioveo*. Documentie studi per la storia del commercio e del diritto commerciale Italiano, 7. Turin: S. Lattes, 1936.

————. "The Trade of Medieval Europe: The South." In *Cambridge Economic History*, ed. Michael M. Postan and H. M. Habakkuk, 2:306–401. 2nd ed. Cambridge: Cambridge University Press, 1973.

————. "Venezia e le grandi linee dell'espansione commerciale nel secolo XIII." In *La civiltà veneziana del secolo di Marco Polo*, ed. Riccardo Barchelli et al., 67–84. Florence: Sansoni, 1955.

Lopez, Robert S., and Harry A. Miskimin. "The Economic Depression of the Renaissance." *Economic History Review*, 2nd ser., 14 (1962): 408–26.

Lopez, Robert S., and Irving Raymond. *Medieval Trade in the Mediterranean World: Illustrated Documents Translated with Introduction and Notes*. New York: Columbia University Press, 1955.

Lučić, Josip. *Obrti i usluge u Dubrovniku od početka do XIV stoljeća*. Zagreb: JAZU, 1979.

Luzzatto, Gino. *Il debito pubblico della repubblica di Venezia*. Milan: Istituto Editoriale Cisalpino, 1963.

————. *Storia economica di Venezia dall'XI al XVI secolo*. Venice: Centro internationale della arti e del costume, 1961.

————. *Studi di storia economica veneziana*. Padua: CEDAM, 1954.

Machetti, Ippolito. "Orafi senesi." *La Diana* 5 (1929): 5–110.

Mack, Rosamond E. *Bazaar to Piazza: Islamic Trade and Italian Art, 1300–1600*. Berkeley: University of California Press, 2002.

Mackenny, Richard. *Tradesmen and Traders: The World of the Guilds in Venice and Europe, c. 1250–1650*. Totowa, N.J.: Barnes and Noble, 1987.

MacLean, Ian. *The Renaissance Notion of Women: A Study of the Fortunes of Scholasticsm and Medieval Science and European Intellectual Life*. Cambridge: Cambridge University Press, 1980.

Manuel, Frank Edward, and Fritzie Manuel. *Utopian Thought in the Western World*. Cambridge, Mass.: Belknap, 1979.

Mariacher, Giovanni. *Il museo correr di Venezia: Dipinti dal XIV al XVI secolo*. Venice: Neri Possa, 1957.

Martin, John, and Dennis Romano, eds. *Venice Reconsidered*. Baltimore: Johns Hopkins University Press, 2000.

Matter, E. Ann. "My Sister, My Spouse." *Journal of Feminist Studies in Religion* 2 (1986): 81–93.

Mauss, Marcel. *The Gift*. Trans. Ian Cunnison. New York: Norton, 1967.

Mazzaoui, Maureen. "The Emigration of Veronese Textile Artisans to Bologna in the Thirteenth Century." *Atti e memorie della Accademia di agricoltura, scienze e lettere di Verona*, 6th ser., 19 (1967–68): 275–321.

————. *The Italian Cotton Industry in the Later Middle Ages, 1100–1600*. Cambridge: Cambridge University Press, 1981.

Mazzi, Curzio. "Alcune leggi suntuarie senesi." *Archivio storico italiano*, 4th ser. 5 (1880): 133–44.

McCracken, Grant. *Culture and Consumption*. Bloomington: Indiana University Press, 1988.

McKee, Sally. "Households in Fourteenth-Century Venetian Crete." *Speculum* 70 (1995): 27–67.

————. "Women under Venetian Colonial Rule in the Early Renaissance: Observations on Their Economic Activities." *Renaissance Quarterly* 51 (1998): 34–67.

McKendrick, Neil, John Brewer, and J. H. Plumb, eds. *The Birth of Consumer Society: The Commercialization of Eighteenth-Century England.* Bloomington: Indiana University Press, 1982.

Medieval and Renaissance Miniatures from the National Gallery of Art. Ed. Gary Vikan. Washington, D.C.: Washington National Gallery of Art, 1975.

Meek, Christine. "La donna, la famiglia e la legge nell'epoca di Ilaria del Carretto." In *Ilaria del Carretto e il suo monumento: Sezione Internazionale di cultura umanistica,* ed. Stéphane Toussaint, 137–63. Lucca: Atti del convegno internazionale di studi, 1994.

Melis, Federigo. *Aspetti della vita economica medievale: Studi nell'Archivio Datini di Prato.* Siena: Monte dei Paschi di Siena, 1962.

Miller, Daniel. *Material Culture and Mass Consumption.* Oxford: Blackwell, 1987.

Milliken, William M. "Early Enamels in the Cleveland Museum of Art." *Connoisseur* 76 (1926): 67–72.

Miskimin, Harry A. *The Economy of the Early Renaissance, 1300–1460.* Englewood Cliffs, N.J.: Prentice-Hall, 1969.

Mitchiner, Michael. *Medieval Pilgrim and Secular Badges.* London: Hawkins, 1986.

Mola, Luca. *La comunità dei Lucchesi a Venezia: Immigrazione e industria della seta nel tardo medioevo.* Venice: Istituto Veneto di Scienze, Lettere ed Arti, 1994.

————. "L'industria della seta a Lucca nel tardo Medioevo: Emigrazione della manodopera e creazione di una rete produttiva a Bologna e Venezia." In *La seta in Europe, sec. XIII–XX,* ed. Simonnetta Cavaciocchi, 435–45. Istituto internazionale di storia economica "F. Datini" Prato, Serie II, Atti delle "Settimane di Studi" e altri Convegni, 24. Florence: Le Monnier, 1993.

————. *The Silk Industry in Renaissance Venice.* Baltimore: Johns Hopkins University Press, 2000.

Molho, Anthony. *Florentine Public Finances in the Early Renaissance, 1400–1433.* Cambridge, Mass.: Harvard University Press, 1971.

————. *Marriage Alliances in Late Medieval Florence.* Cambridge, Mass.: Harvard University Press, 1994.

————. "A Note on Jewish Moneylenders in Tuscany in the Late Trecento and Early Quattrocento." In *Renaissance Studies in Honor of Hans Baron,* ed. Anthony Molho and John A. Tedeschi, 99–117. Florence: Sansoni, 1971.

Molmenti, Pompeo. *La storia di Venezia nella vita privata delle origini alla caduta della republica.* Turin: Roux e Favale, 1885.

————. *Venice: Its Individual Growth from the Earliest Beginnings to the Fall of the Republic.* Trans. Horatio Brown. London: John Murray, 1906. 3 vols.

Monnas, Lisa. "Silk Textiles in the Paintings of Bernardo Daddi, Andrea di Cione and Their Followers." *Zeitschrift fur kunstgeschichte* 53 (1990): 39–59.

Montias, John Michael. *Artists and Artisans in Delft: A Socio-Economic Study of the Seventeenth Century.* Princeton, N.J.: Princeton University Press, 1982.

Moschini, Vittori. *I Vivarini.* Milan: A. Pizzi, 1946.

Mueller, Reinhold C. "Aspects of Venetian Sovereignty in Medieval and Renaissance Dalmatia." In *Quattrocento Adriatico,* 5:29-56. Papers from a colloquium held at Villa Spelman, Florence, 1994. Intr. Charles Dempsey. Bologna: Villa Spelman Colloquia, 1996.

————. "La crisi economica-monetaria veneziana di metà Quattrocento nel contesto generale." In *Aspetto del vita economica medievale*, 541–56. Atti del Convegno di studi nel X anniversario della Morte di Federigo Melis, Firenze-Pisa-Prato, March 10–14, 1984. Florence, 1985.

———. "Foreign Investment in Venetian Government Bonds and the Case of Paolo Guinigi, Lord of Lucca, Early 15th Century." In *Cities of Finance*, ed. Herman Diederiks and David A. Reeder, 69–90. Amsterdam: North-Holland, 1996.

———. "The Jewish Moneylenders of Late Trecento Venice: A Revisitation." *Mediterranean Historical Review* 10 (1995): 202–17.

———. "Mercanti e imprenditori fiorentini a Venezia nel tardo medioevo." *Società e storia* 55 (1992): 29–60.

———. "The Procurators of San Marco in the Thirteenth and Fourteenth Centuries." *Studi Veneziani* 13 (1971): 105–220.

———. *The Venetian Money Market: Banks, Panics and the Public Debt, 1200–1500*. Vol. 2 of *Money and Banking in Medieval and Renaissance Venice*, ed. Frederic C. Lane and Reinhold C. Mueller. Baltimore: Johns Hopkins University Press, 1997.

Muir, Edward. *Civic Ritual Life in Renaissance Venice*. Princeton, N.J.: Princeton University Press, 1981.

Munro, John. "Bullion Flows and Monetary Contraction in Late-Medieval England and the Low Countries." In *Precious Metals in the Later Medieval and Early Modern World*, ed. J. F. Richards, 97–158. Durham: Carolina Academic Press, 1983.

———. *Bullion Flows and Monetary Policies in England and the Low Countries, 1350–1500*. Hampshire: Variorum, 1992.

———. "The Medieval Scarlet." In *Cloth and Clothing in Medieval Europe*, ed. N. B. Harte and K. G. Ponting, 13–70. London: Heineman, 1983.

———. *Wool, Cloth and Gold: The Struggle for Bullion in Anglo-Burgundian Trade, 1340–1478*. Toronto: University of Toronto Press, 1972.

Muntz, Eugene. "L'Antipape Clément VII: Essay sur l'histoire des arts à Avignon vers la fin du XIVe siècle." *Revue Archéologique*, 3rd ser., 11 (1888): 8–18, 168–83.

Murray, Jacqueline. "Hiding behind the Universal Man: Male Sexuality in the Middle Ages," and "Twice Marginal and Twice Invisible: Lesbians in the Middle Ages." In *Handbook of Medieval Sexuality*, ed. Vern Bullough and James A. Brundage, 123–46, 191–222. New York: Garland, 1996.

Musacchio, Jacqueline Marie. "Weasels and Pregnancy in Renaissance Italy." *Renaissance Studies* 15:2 (2001): 172–87.

Museo de Prado. *El Prado Colecciones de Pintura*. Barcelona: Lunwerg Editores, 1994.

Museo Stibbert. *Guerre e assoldati in Toscana, 1260–1364*. Exhibition catalog. Florence: Museo Stibbert, 1982.

Muzzarelli, Maria Giuseppina. *Gli inganni delle apparenze*. Turin: Scriptorium, 1996.

———. *Guardaroba medievale: Vesti e società dal XIII al XVI secolo*. Bologna: Il Mulino, 1999.

———. "Seta posseduta e seta consentita: Dalle aspirazioni individuali alle norme suntuarie nel Basso Medioevo." In *La seta in Italia dal Medioevo al Seicento*, ed. Luca Molà, Reinhold C. Mueller, and Claudio Zanier, 211–32. Venice: Marsilio, 2000.

Newett, Margaret. "The Sumptuary Laws of Venice in the Fourteenth and Fifteenth Centuries." In *Historical Essays*, ed. T. F. Tout and James Tait, 245–77. London: Longmans Green, 1902.

Newman, Peter C. *Company of Adventurers*. New York: Viking, 1985.

Newton, Stella Mary. *Fashion in the Age of the Black Prince: A Study of the Years 1340–1365*. Woodbridge: Boydell Press, 1980.

Norman, Diana. *Siena and the Virgin: Art and Politics in a Late Medieval City State.* New Haven, Conn.: Yale University Press, 1999.

———, ed. *Siena, Florence and Padua: Art, Society and Religion, 1280–1400.* 2 vols. New Haven, Conn.: Yale University Press, 1995.

North, Douglas Cecil, and Robert Paul Thomas. *The Rise of the Western World: A New Economic History.* Cambridge: Cambridge University Press, 1973.

Origo, Iris. "The Domestic Enemy: The Eastern Slaves in Tuscany in the Fourteenth and Fifteenth Centuries." *Speculum* 30 (1955): 321–99.

———. *The Merchant of Prato.* New York: Knopf, 1957.

Pallucchini, Rodolfo. *La pittura veneziana del trecento.* Venice: Istituto per la Collaborazione Culturale, 1964.

Palumbo-Fossati, Isabella. "L'interna della casa nella Venezia de Cinquecento." *Studi veneziani*, n.s. 8 (1966): 109–53.

Panizza, Letizia. "A Guide to Recent Bibliography on Italian Renaissance Writings about and by Women." *Bulletin of the Society for Italian Studies* 22 (1989): 3–24.

Papadopoli, Nicolo. *Le monete di Venezia.* Venice: Tip. Libreria Emiliana, 1893.

Patterson, C. C. "Silver Stocks and Losses in Ancient and Medieval Times." *Economic History Review* 25 (1972): 205–35.

Payer, Pierre J. *The Bridling of Desire: Views of Sex in the Later Middle Ages.* Toronto: University of Toronto Press, 1993.

Pazzi, Pietro. *Dizionario biografico deali orefici, argentieri, gioiellieri.* Treviso: Grafische Crivellari, 1998.

———. *I Punzoni dell'argenteria e oreficeria veneziana.* Venice: Monestero de San Lazzaro degli Armenni, 1990.

Perocco, Guido, and Antonio Salvadori. *Civiltà di Venezia.* Vol. 1. Venice: La Stamperia di Venezia Editrice, 1973.

Petroff, Elizabeth. *Body and Soul: Essays on Medieval Women and Mysticism.* New York: Oxford University Press, 1994.

Petrović, Đurđica. *Dubrovačko Oruzje u XIV Veku.* Belgrade: Vojni Muzej Kosmos, 1976.

Phillips, Mark. *The Memoir of Marco Parenti: A Life in Medici Florence.* Princeton, N.J.: Princeton University Press, 1987.

Piattoli, Renato. "Un inventario di oreficeria del trecento." *Rivista d'arte* 13 (1931): 241–59.

———. "Un mercante dei trecento e gli artisti del tempo suo." *Rivista d'arte* 12 (1930): 97–156.

Piccini, Gabriella. "Le donne nella vita economica, sociale e politica dell'Italia medievale." In *Il lavoro delle donne*, ed. Renata Ago and A. Groppi, 5–46. Rome: Laterza, 1996.

Pilosu, Mario. *La donna, la lussuria, e la chiesa nel Medioeva.* Geneva: Edizioni Culturali Internationali, 1989.

Pincus, Debra. "Hard Times and Ducal Radiance." In *Venice Reconsidered*, ed. John Martin and Dennis Romano, 89–136. Baltimore: Johns Hopkins University Press, 2000.

Piponnier, Françoise, and Perrine Mane. *Dress in the Middle Ages.* Trans. Caroline Beamish. New Haven, Conn.: Yale University Press, 1997.

Pleij, Herman. *Colors Demonic and Divine: Shades of Meaning in the Middle Ages and After.* Trans. Diane Webb. New York: Columbia University Press, 2004.

Plumb, J. H. *In the Light of History.* Boston: Houghton Mifflin, 1973.

Pope-Hennessy, John. *Italian Gothic Sculpture.* Oxford: Phaidon, 1956.

Pullan, Brian S. *Rich and Poor in Renaissance Venice: The Social Institutions of a Catholic State, to 1620.* Cambridge, Mass.: Harvard University Press, 1971.

Pyhrr, Stuart W. *Arms and Armor.* Exhibition catalog. New Haven, Conn.: Yale University Press, 2003.

Queller, Donald. "A Different Approach to the Pre-modern Cost of Living: Venice, 1372–1391." *Journal of European Economic History* 25:2 (1996): 441–64.

Rainey, Ronald E. "Sumptuary Legislation in Renaissance Florence." Ph.D. diss., Columbia University, 1985.

Randolph, Adrian W. B. "Performing the Bridal Body in Fifteenth-Century Florence." *Art History* 21 (1998): 182–200.

———. "Regarding Women as Sacred Space." In *Picturing Women in Renaissance and Baroque Italy,* ed. Geraldine A. Johnson and Sara F. Matthews Grieco, 17–33. Cambridge: Cambridge University Press, 1997.

Reddaway, T. F. *The Early History of the Goldsmiths' Company, 1327–1509.* London: Arnold, 1975.

Renouard, Yves. "Mercati e mercanti veneziano alla fine del duecento." In *La Civiltà del Secolo di Marco Polo,* ed. Riccardo Barchelli et al., 85–108. Florence: Sansoni, 1955.

Rey, Maurice. *Le domaine du roi et les finances extraordinaires sous Charles VI, 1388–1413.* Paris: SEVPEN, 1965.

Ricci, Franco Mario. *Embriachi: Il trittico de Pavia.* Milan: Bondoni, 1982.

Riemer, Eleanor S. "Women in the Medieval City: Sources and Uses of Wealth by Sienese Women the Thirteenth Century." Ph.D. diss., New York University, 1975.

Rizzoli Jun, Luigi. "Artisti alla Zecca dei Principi da Carrara." *Rivista italiana di numismatica e scienze affini* 13 (1900): 225–38.

Robbert, Louise Buenger. "Domenico Gradenigo: A Thirteenth-Century Venetian Merchant and His Family." In *Medieval and Renaissance Venice,* ed. Thomas F. Madden and Ellen E. Kittell, 27–48. Urbana: University of Illinois Press, 1997.

———. "Monetary Flows—Venice 1150 to 1400." In *Precious Metals in the Later Medieval and Early Modern Worlds,* ed. John F. Richards, 53–77. Durham: Carolina Academic Press, 1983.

———. "Money and Prices in Thirteenth-Century Venice." *Journal of Medieval History* 20 (1994): 373–90.

———. "Twelfth-Century Italian Prices: Food and Clothing in Pisa and Venice." *Social Science History* 7:4 (1983): 381–404.

Robinson, Dwight E. "The Importance of Fashions in Taste to Business History: An Introductory Essay." *Business History Review* 37 (1963): 5–36.

Roche, Daniel. *Histoire des choses banales: Naissance de la consommation dans les sociétés traditionnelles (XVIIᵉ–XIXᵉ siècle).* Paris: Fayard, 1997.

Rocke, Michael. *Forbidden Friendships: Homosexuality and Male Culture in Renaissance Florence.* New York: Oxford University Press, 1996.

Roehl, Richard. "Patterns and Structure of Demand, 1000–1500." In *Fontana Economic History of Europe,* ed. Carlo M. Cipolla, 1:107–42. London: Collins/Fontana, 1972.

Rollo-Koster, Joelle. "Forever After: The Dead in the Avignonese Confraternity of Notre Dame la Majour (1329–1381)." *Journal of Medieval History* 25 (1999): 114–41.

Romano, Dennis. "Gender and the Urban Geography of Renaissance Venice." *Journal of Social History* 23 (1989): 339–53.

———. "The Gondola as a Marker of Station in Venetian Society." *Renaissance Studies* 8 (1994): 359–74.

———. *Housecraft and Statecraft: Domestic Service in Renaissance Venice, 1400–1600.* Baltimore: Johns Hopkins University Press, 1996.

———. *Patrician and Popolani: The Social Foundations of the Venetian Renaissance State.* Baltimore: Johns Hopkins University Press, 1987.

Roncière, Charles de la. *Prix et salaires à Florence au XIVe siècle (1280–1380).* Rome: École Française de Rome, 1982.

Rosenthal, Elaine. "The Position of Women in Renaissance Florence: Neither Autonomy nor Subjection." In *Florence and Italy: Renaissance Studies in Honour of Nicolai Rubenstein,* ed. Peter Denley, 369–81. London: Committee on Medieval Studies, Westfield College, 1988.

Ruggiero, Guido. *The Boundaries of Eros: Sex, Crime and Sexuality in Renaissance Venice.* New York: Oxford University Press, 1985.

Salmi, Mario. "Il Paliotto di Manresa e l'opus florentinus." *Bollettino d'arte* 24 (1930–31): 385–406.

Salvemini, Gaetano. *Magnati e popolani in Firenze dal 1280 al 1295.* Florence: Carnesecchi, 1899.

Sapori, Armando. *La compagnia dei Frescobaldi in Inghilterra.* Florence: Olschki, 1947.

———. *La crisi delle compagnie mercantili dei Bardi e dei Peruzzi.* Florence: Olschki, 1926.

Scaramella, Gino, ed. *Il tumulto dei Ciompi: Cronache e memorie. Rerum italicarum Scriptores* XVIII, 3. Bologna: N. Zanichelli, 1917.

Scattergood, John. *Reading the Past.* Portland, Ore.: Four Courts Press, 1996.

Schlosser, Julius von. "Die Werkstatt der Embriachi in Venedig." *Jahrbuch der Kunsthistorischen Sammlungen des Altehochsten Kaiserhauses* 20 (1899): 220–82.

Schuette, Marie. "Lace." *CIBA Review* 7:73 (April 1949): 2675–98.

Sebregondi, Ludovica. "Clothes and Teenagers: What Young Men Wore in Fifteenth-Century Florence." In *The Premodern Teenager,* ed. Konrad Eisenbichler, 27–50. Toronto: Center for Reformation and Renaissance Studies, 2002.

Sekora, John. *Luxury: The Concept in Western Thought from Eden to Smollett.* Baltimore: Johns Hopkins University Press, 1977.

Sheedy, Anna Toole. *Bartolus on Social Conditions in the Fourteenth Century.* New York: Columbia University Press, 1942.

Simmel, Georg. "Fashion." *American Journal of Sociology* 62:6 (1957): 541–58.

Simons, Patricia. "Alert and Erect: Masculinity in Some Italian Renaissance Portraits of Fathers and Sons." In *Gender Rhetorics: Postures of Dominance and Submission in History,* ed. Richard C. Trexler, 163–86. Medieval and Renaissance Studies and Texts, 113. Binghamton, N.Y.: Medieval and Renaissance Texts and Studies, 1994.

———. "Lesbian (In)Visibility in Italian Renaissance Culture: Diana and Other Cases of 'donna con donna.'" *Journal of Homosexuality* 12 (1994): 81–122.

Skinner, Patricia. "Possessions of Lombard Women in Italy." *Medieval Life* 2 (1995): 8–11.

Slanicka, Simona. "Male Markings: Uniforms in the Parisian Civil War as a Blurring of the Gender Order, A.D. 1410–1420." *Medieval History Journal* 2 (1999): 209–44.

Smith, Adam. *The Wealth of Nations: An Inquiry into the Nature and Causes.* New York: Modern Library, 1937.

Smith, Allison. "Gender, Ownership and Domestic Space: Inventories and Family Archives in Renaissance Verona." *Renaissance Studies* 12:3 (1998): 375–91.

Sombart, Werner. *Luxury and Capitalism.* Trans. W. R. Dittmar. Ann Arbor: University of Michigan Press, 1967.

Spencer, Brian. *Pilgrim Souvenirs and Secular Badges.* London: The Stationery Office, 1998.

Spufford, Peter. *Handbook of Medieval Exchange.* London: Royal Historical Society, 1986.

———. *Money and Its Use in Medieval Europe.* Cambridge: Cambridge University Press, 1988.

———. *Profits and Power: The Merchant in Medieval Europe.* London: Thames and Hudson, 2002.

Stahl, Alan M. "The Deathbed Oration of Doge Mocenigo and the Mint of Venice." *Medieval Historical Review* 10 (1995): 284–301.

———. *The Venetian Tornesello: A Medieval Colonial Coinage.* New York: American Numismatic Society, 1985.

———. *Zecca: The Mint of Venice in the Middle Ages.* Baltimore: Johns Hopkins University Press. 2000.

Stahl, Alan M., and Louis Waldman. "The Earliest Known Medalists: The Sesto Brothers of Venice." *American Journal of Numismatics,* 2nd ser., 5–6 (1993–94): 167–88.

Starn, Randolph. *Contrary Commonwealth: The Theme of Exile in Medieval and Renaissance Italy.* Berkeley: University of California Press, 1982.

Stein, Barbara, and Stanley Stein. "Financing Empire: The European Diaspora of Silver by War." In *Colonial Legacies,* ed. Jeremy Adelman, 51–68. New York: Routledge, 1999.

Stella, Alessandro. *La révolte des Ciompi: Les hommes, les lieux, le travail.* Paris: L'École des Hautes Études en Sciences Sociales, 1993.

Strickland, Agnes. *Lives of the Queens of England.* Philadelphia: Barrie, 1902–3.

Stuard, Susan Mosher. "The Adriatic Trade in Silver, c. 1300." *Studi veneziani* 17–18 (1975–76): 95–143.

———. "Ancillary Evidence on the Decline of Medieval Slavery." *Past and Present* 149 (1995): 1–28.

———. "Burdens of Matrimony: Husbanding and Gender in Medieval Italy, c. 1140." In *Medieval Masculinities: Regarding Men in the Middle Ages,* ed. Claire Lees, Thelma S. Fenster, and JoAnn McNamara, 61–72. Minneapolis: University of Minnesota Press, 1994.

———. "A Capital Idea Pursuing Demand." *Review* 24:1 (2001): 163–83.

———. "Dowry Increase and Increments in Wealth in Medieval Ragusa (Dubrovnik)." *Journal of Economic History* 41 (1981): 795–811.

———. "From Women to Woman: New Thinking about Gender, c. 1140." *Thought* 64 (1989): 208–19.

———. "*Gravitas* and Consumption." In *Conflicting Identities and Multiple Masculinities,* ed. Jacqueline Murray, 215–42. New York: Garland, 1999.

———. *A State of Deference: Ragusa/Dubrovnik in the Medieval Centuries.* Philadelphia: University of Pennsylvania Press, 1992.

———. "Toward a Theory of Consumption and Exchange." *Journal of Economic History* 44 (1985): 921–25.

———. "Urban Domestic Slavery in Medieval Ragusa." *Journal of Medieval History* 9 (1983): 155–71.

Sugar, Denis. *A History of Hungary.* Bloomington: Indiana University Press, 1990.

Tadić, Jorjo. "Le Port de Raguse au Moyen Age." In *Le Navire et l'économie maritime du Moyen Age au XVIIIᵉ siècle.* Travaux du deuxième colloque international d'histoire maritime. Paris: SEVPEN, 1959.

Tarassuk, Leonid. *Italian Armor for Princely Courts.* Chicago: The Institute, 1986.

Tarassuk, Leonid, and Claude Blair. *The Complete Encyclopaedia of Arms and Weapons.* London: Batsford, 1982.

Thomas, Bruno, and Ortwin Gamber. "L'arte Milanese dell'armatura." In *Storia di Milano.* 11:698–841, pt. 13. Milan: Alfieri, 1958.

Thornton, Dora. *The Scholar in His Study: Ownership and Experience in Renaissance Italy.* New Haven, Conn.: Yale University Press, 1997.

Thornton, Peter. "Cassoni, Forzieri, Goffani and Cassette." *Apollo* 120 (1984): 246–51.

Tramontana, Salvatore. *Vestirsi e Travestirse in Sicilia: Abbigliamento, feste e spettacoli nel medioeveo.* Palermo: Sellerio, 1993.

Tramontin, Silvio. "Una pagina de folklore." In *La religiosità popolare nella valle padana: Atti del II convegno di studi folklore padano, Modena, Marzo 19–20–21, 1965*, 401–17. Modena: ENAL, 1966.

Treccani degli Alfieri, Giovanni. *Storia de Milano.* 16 vols. Milan: Fondazione Treccani degli Alfieri per la storia di Milano, 1953–62.

Trexler, Richard. *The Journey of the Magi.* Princeton, N.J.: Princeton University Press, 1997.

———. "The Magi Enter Florence." *Studies in Medieval and Renaissance History,* n.s. 1 (1978): 129–219.

———. "A Medieval Census: The Liber Divisionis." *Medievalia et Humanistica,* o.s. 17 (1966): 79–81.

———. "Neighbors and Comrades: The Revolutionaries of Florence, 1378." *Social Analysis* 14 (1983): 53–106.

———. "Ritual Behavior in Renaissance Florence: The Setting." *Medievalia et Humanistica: Studies in Medieval and Renaissance Culture,* n.s. 4 (1973): 125–44.

———. *The Workers of Renaissance Florence: Power and Dependence in Renaissance Florence.* Binghamton, N.Y.: Medieval and Renaissance Texts and Studies, 1993.

Valdovino, José, and Manuel Cruz. "Escuela Italiana." In *El Prado, Colecciones de Pintura,* 221–23. Barcelona: Lunwerg Editores, 1994.

Veblen, Thorstein. *The Theory of the Leisure Class.* New York: Dover, 1994.

Venice and History: The Collected Papers of Frederic C. Lane. Ed. by a Committee of Colleagues and Former Students. Baltimore: Johns Hopkins University Press, 1966.

Verlinden, Charles. "Le recruitement des esclaves à Venice aux XIV et XV siècles." *Bulletin de l'Institut Historique Belge de Rome* 34 (1968): 83–202.

Villard, Ugo Monneret de. *Le leggende orientali sui Magi evangelici.* Vatican City: Biblioteca Apostolica Vaticana, 1952.

Virtue and Beauty: Leonardo's Ginevra de Benci and Renaissance Portraits of Women. Ed. David Alan Brown. Washington, D.C.: National Gallery of Art, 2001.

Voje, Ignacij. "Bencius del Buono." *Istorijski Časopis* 18 (1971): 189–99.

Vries, Jan de. "Between Purchasing Power and the World of Goods: Understanding the Household Economy in Early Modern Europe." In *Consumption and the World of Goods,* ed. John Brewer and Roy Porter, 85–132. London: Routledge, 1993.

———. "The Industrial Revolution and the Industrious Revolution." *Journal of Economic History* 54 (1994): 249–70.

Vyronis, Speros. "The Question of the Byzantine Mines." *Speculum* 37:1 (1962) 1–17.

Wallerstein, Immanuel M. *Capitalist Agriculture and the Origins of the European World Economy in the Sixteenth Century.* New York: Academic Press, 1974.

Wardwell, Anne E. "Panni Tartarici: Eastern Islamic Silks Woven with Gold and Silver." *Islamic Art* 3 (1988–89): 95–173.

Warnke, Martin. *The Court Artist: On the Ancestry of the Modern Artist.* Trans. David McClintock. Cambridge: Cambridge University Press, 1993.

Watt, James C. Y., and Anne E. Wardwell, *When Silk Was Gold.* New York: Metropolitan Museum of Art, 1997.

Wenzel, Marian. "Bosnian History and Austro-Hungarian Policy: Some Medieval Belts, the Bogomil Romance, and the King Tvrtko Graves." *Peristil, Povijesno drustvo Hrvatske* 30 (1987):29–54.

Wiesner, Merry E. "Spinsters and Seamstresses: Women in Cloth and Clothing Production." In *Rewriting the Renaissance: The Discourse of Sexual Difference in Early Modern Europe,* ed. Margaret W. Ferguson, Maureen Quilligan, and Nancy J. Vickers, 175–90. Chicago: University of Chicago Press, 1986.

Weissman, Ronald. *Ritual Brotherhood in Renaissance Florence.* New York: Academic Press, 1982.

White, Lynn. "Technology Assessment from the Stance of a Medieval Historian." *American Historical Review* 79:1 (1974): 1–13.

Wilson, H. *Silverwork and Jewellry: A Text-Book for Students and Workers in Metal.* London: Pitman, 1931.

Wixom, William. *Treasures from Medieval France.* Exhibition Catalog. Cleveland: Cleveland Museum of Art, 1967.

Wood, Frances. *Did Marco Polo Visit China?* Boulder, Colo.: Westview, 1996.

Woodruff, Helen. "The Illustrated Manuscripts of Prudentius." *Art Studies* 7 (1929): 33–79.

Yule, Amy Frances, ed. *Travels of Marco Polo, the Venetian.* 2 vols. New York: Scribners, 1926.

Zupko, Ronald. *Italian Weights and Measures from the Middle Ages to the Nineteenth Century.* Philadelphia: American Philosophical Society, 1981.

Index

Acknowledgments

The University of Pennsylvania Press has been of great help to me in completing this work, and the same may be said of the three other volumes I have published in the Middle Ages Series with the press. I am grateful to Steven A. Epstein for reading the manuscript twice, with helpful comments, and to my anonymous reader. My office in Special Collections, Magill Library, Haverford College, has been an excellent place to work, and I have had the talents of the Academic Computing Center and the library staff at my disposal. Margaret Schaus, reference librarian and editor of the online index *Feminae,* kept me informed about the recent literature in the field and was an invaluable colleague, reader of early drafts, and researcher. Joshua Tucker helped with illustrations and proofed the bibliography and text. Del Ramers made slides for me. My work was supported by a Delmas grant for research in Venice and the Veneto and by a Mellon Foundation grant for emeriti faculty. William Caferro obtained microfilm from the archives of Florence for me when I needed it. Reinhold C. Mueller and Benjamin G. Kohl were a great help to me in the Venetian archives. The staff of the Dubrovnik archives was helpful as always.